THE MONUMENTS

THE MONUMENTS

The Grit and the Glory of Cycling's Greatest One-day Races

Revised and Updated 2nd Edition

Peter Cossins

BLOOMSBURY SPORT

LONDON · OXFORD · NEW YORK · NEW DELHI · SYDNEY

To Elaine, Lewis and Eleanor
for their monumental love and support

BLOOMSBURY SPORT
An imprint of Bloomsbury Publishing Plc
50 Bedford Square London WC1B 3DP UK
29 Earlsfort Terrace, Dublin 2, Ireland

www.bloomsbury.com

BLOOMSBURY, BLOOMSBURY SPORT and the Diana logo are trademarks of Bloomsbury
Publishing Plc

First published 2014
This expanded edition first published 2023

© Peter Cossins, 2014, 2023
Maps by ML Design

Peter Cossins has asserted his right under the Copyright, Designs and
Patents Act, 1988, to be identified as Author of this work.

British Library Cataloguing-in-Publication Data
A catalogue record for this book is available from the British Library.

Library of Congress Cataloguing-in-Publication data has been applied for.

ISBN: PB: 978-1-3994-0786-1; ePub: 978-1-3994-0785-4

2 4 6 8 10 9 7 5 3 1

Typeset by Integra Software Services Pvt. Ltd.
Printed and bound in Great Britain by CPI Group (UK) Ltd, Croydon CR0 4YY

To find out more about our authors and books visit www.bloomsbury.com.
Here you will find extracts, author interviews, details of forthcoming events and
the option to sign up for our newsletters.

CONTENTS

CONTENTS

INTRODUCTION
THE MAKING OF THE MONUMENTS

The final decades of the nineteenth century marked a change in the perception of the bicycle and bike racing. Thanks in part to the invention of the freewheel and John Boyd Dunlop's release in 1888 of the first practical pneumatic tyre, the bike's use as a means of transport became widespread, stimulating public enthusiasm for the fledgling racing scene. Initially, that interest was largely sated by events staged on wooden tracks, which sprang up all over the developing world as towns and cities endeavoured to demonstrate their dynamism and provide diversion for their inhabitants. From the 1890s, though, road racing began to gain an increasing following.

In Europe, the stimulus for the discipline came primarily from the establishment of Bordeaux–Paris and Paris–Brest–Paris in 1891. The former extended to 560km, the latter to twice that. In the modern era, such races would be split into stages run over successive days. Yet, these two mammoth events were effectively non-stop, no allowance being made for eating or sleeping. They were unmistakeably epic and attracted huge popular interest in France and beyond.

In the final decade of the nineteenth century and the opening decade of the twentieth, hundreds of races sprang up as cycling fans attempted to emulate the two great French events. Towns and cities endeavoured to raise their profile and newspapers tried to put each other out of business. Most of the races only lasted a year or two, but others gained a foothold and became well established, most notably Paris–Roubaix, which had been founded in 1896.

Just as Bordeaux–Paris and Paris–Brest–Paris had done, the unveiling of the Tour de France in November 1902 changed everyone's perception of what a bike race could be. It was, after all, the first multi-day stage race. However, rather than killing off single-day races such as Roubaix, the Tour prompted another wave of interest and investment in bike racing. Manufacturers prospered, teams were established, and, in the years leading up to the First World War, the racing calendar began to take shape.

The Tour de France dominated it, but one-day races also flourished, particularly in the great heartlands of the sport – France, Italy and, a little later, Belgium. Over subsequent decades, Milan–Sanremo, the Tour of Flanders, Paris–Roubaix, Liège–Bastogne–Liège and the Tour of Lombardy have become cycling's pre-eminent 'Classics', as the leading one-day races have long been known. More recently, they have been described as 'The Monuments' of the sport, because they stand out as the races all professional riders aspire to win, alongside the grand tours and the World Championship.

It's not clear precisely when this collective noun was first employed as a label for these five events, but it was certainly used during negotiations between the UCI, cycling's ruling body, and the AIOCC, which represents race organisers, relating to the introduction of the ProTour in 2005. Brought in to replace the World Cup, a season-long series that grouped together the major one-day races, the ProTour was implemented by the UCI in order to ensure that the leading teams participated in the biggest races, including the grand tours and the major Classics. As part of this, a ProTour council was established to oversee the new structure. However, the teams were not part of this body, leading Patrice Clerc, then director of ASO, which organises the Tour de France, to state that, 'We are not happy to be excluded from the ProTour council ... so at this point in time, regarding international cycling ... the three grand tours, and four of the five monuments of the sport [Milano–Sanremo, Paris–Roubaix, Liège–Bastogne–Liège and the Tour of Lombardy] and 11 other major races don't have a voice anymore.' While the feuding between the UCI and the race organisers took some years to sort out, the concept of the Monuments rapidly became more widely accepted.

Although they might not have the overarching significance of the golf majors or the grand slams in tennis, they do offer a significantly different, more balanced and more immediate test than the Tour de France, Giro d'Italia and Vuelta a España, where endurance counts above all. Those three-week races may feature the fastest sprinters, the strongest time triallists and the best climbers, but you're unlikely to see the likes of Mark Cavendish, Filippo Ganna and Tadej Pogačar all racing eyeballs out for victory on the same day. Fans turn to the Monuments for that rare thrill and it is that quality combined with their glittering history that makes these five races so special.

Each Monument provides a very different test and, like the Tour, each of them has its great exponents, legends and distinctive battlegrounds. Standing on the fearsome cobbled climbs such as the Oude Kwaremont, Paterberg or Koppenberg provides not only a spectacular perspective on the Tour of Flanders, but also a fascinating insight into the Flemish people, whose culture was to a large extent reasserted via this event and bike racing. Roubaix, dubbed 'cycling's last great folly' by its one-time director Jacques Goddet, has its hellish cobbles. Lombardy features the iconic climb to the cyclists' chapel of the Madonna del Ghisallo and what is undoubtedly the most beautiful course of the cycling year.

Over the last hundred years and more, the Monuments have provided many of cycling's greatest stories, from Sanremo's fourth edition, when only four riders completed the 288km course, to Roubaix's long battle against road gangs determined to resurface every cobble in northern France, to the blizzard-hit 1980 edition of Liège that left winner Bernard Hinault with permanent loss of feeling in some of his fingers.

According to one of cycling's pre-eminent historians, Serge Laget, these races 'are not there as padding or preparation, and even less as consolation. Quite the contrary, in fact. They have their own existence, their own richness, a fantastic history and a legitimacy that goes back to the very origins of cycling.' Unlike the Tour's 22-day soap opera, where might always tends to be right, the Monuments are cycling's unpredictable thrillers, where almost any member of the peloton can prevail given the right combination of great form, tactical nous and simple good luck. Every rider starts them thinking, 'This just might be my day ...'

PART I

LIÈGE-BASTOGNE-LIÈGE – 'LA DOYENNE'

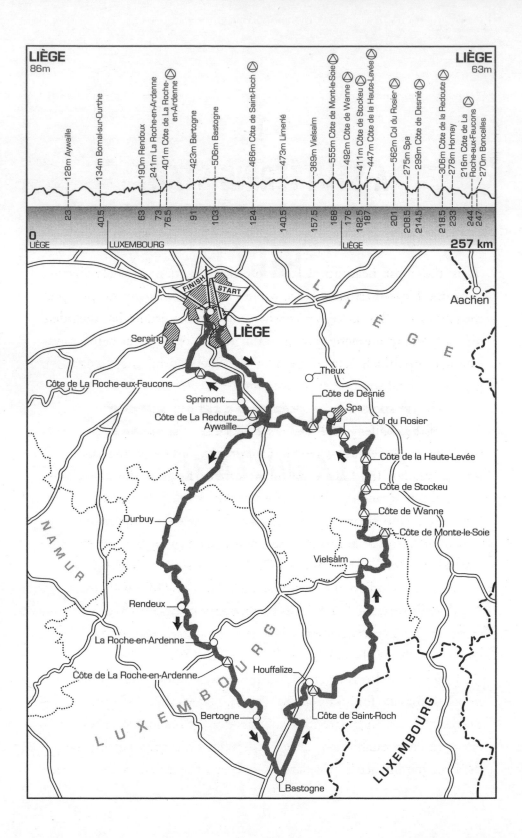

1

A STUTTERING START

'It is the most beautiful Classic on the calendar, Michele Bartoli, two-time Liège–Bastogne–Liège winner, told *Procycling* in his pomp in the late 1990s. 'It's the only race where you can be certain that the riders on the podium are definitely the strongest. In other races being clever can make up for a lack of strength, but not Liège. What matters in Liège is pure physical strength. Tactics count for much less.'

When he spoke of the race's beauty, Bartoli was referring to the purity of the challenge Liège offers, rather than the rolling landscape in the Belgian Ardennes where it takes place, although the terrain is impressive. For the Italian and many others, Liège is the one Classic where the best one-day riders and the best stage race riders meet on terrain that suits them both to an extent, without favouring either.

Founded in 1892, Liège is the longest-standing of the Monuments, which has earned it the name '*La Doyenne*' – The Old Lady. Among the races on the modern international calendar, only Milan–Turin has a lengthier history, the Italian one-day race dating back to 1876, although that first edition was a one-off. The sister race to Sanremo and Lombardy didn't establish itself fully until after the Great War.

Liège also had a rather erratic start. Uniquely among the Monuments, impetus for its founding came directly from the first running of Bordeaux–Paris and, particularly, Paris–Brest–Paris in 1891. Members of the recently established Liège Cyclists' Union – there's no mistaking the British influence in that name – had plans for an epic 845km Liège–

Paris–Liège event. They decided the first step towards that would be a 250km test race from Liège to Bastogne in the south of French-speaking Wallonia and back again. Bastogne was selected as the turning point because the race organisers could get there on the train to make sure the competitors completed the outward leg of the course before they returned north.

In the end, the mooted Liège–Paris–Liège event never materialised, whereas the preparation event for it became relatively well established. The first edition, which was for amateurs only, took place on 29 May 1892. At 5.39 that morning, a few hundred spectators gathered on the Avenue Rogier in central Liège to cheer off 33 intrepid riders and their pacers, whose task was to keep the speed as high as possible for their racer. The course took the riders, all of whom were Belgian, on the main valley roads from north to south, via Angleur, Esneux, Aywaille, Barvaux, Hotton, Marche, Bande, Champlon and on to the checkpoint at a hotel in Bastogne, from where they returned to Liège by the same route.

By Marche, only three of the 33 riders were still in contention: Liège Cyclists' Union member Léon Houa, his clubmate and former Belgian champion Léon Lhoest, and Louis Rasquinet, runner-up in the previous year's Belgian amateur championship. Houa was the most inexperienced of the trio. Small and slim, he was an all-round sportsman from a moneyed Liège family. Adept at boxing and fencing, he had first tried cycling just four months earlier and he was making his competitive debut. Yet it appeared he was a natural. When Rasquinet fell back soon after Marche, Houa only had Lhoest for company. The leading pair continued for some kilometres until Lhoest punctured. Rather than press on alone, Houa asked one of his pacers to lend his bike to Lhoest. Yet it seemed the more experienced rider was fated. The loaned machine also suffered a puncture and, not wanting other riders to catch him, Houa didn't halt a second time.

He was racing on a bike that weighed 11.6kg, half as much again as the state-of-the-art carbon fibre steeds of the modern era. Impressively, though, given his lack of experience and the dire state of the roads, he didn't suffer a single puncture. He reached the turning point in Bastogne in three minutes under five hours. The return trip took him an hour longer, partly as a result of a crash just ten kilometres from home that left him with a pedal damaged beyond use. At the insistence of his pacers, Houa pressed on, pushing the cranks around with one leg. Acclaimed by a large crowd at the finish, he had averaged a little more than 23km/h for the 250km course. Lhoest came in 22 minutes later, with Rasquinet completing the podium when he finished three-quarters of an hour behind Houa.

A second beginning

Deemed a success, the race went ahead again the following season, although Houa came close to being sidelined from it. He had received no monetary reward for winning the inaugural event, but had accepted some financial backing and equipment from a Belgian bike company, effectively making him a professional rather than an amateur. Houa argued the support he had been given was intended to back his bid to win Liège–Paris–Liège, a race that had never taken place. In the end, Houa's argument prevailed and he was allowed to start.

Once again, he led almost from start to finish. He completed the outward leg in less than four hours, one contemporary report saying Houa 'stopped for just 56 seconds, and the commissaire was forced to run alongside him in order to apply the required stamp to his armband'. On the return leg his pace lagged. Based on Houa's reported comments at the finish in Liège's Place du Théâtre, this was largely due to fatigue among his pacers rather than the rider himself running out of gas. Nevertheless, he finished 26 minutes ahead of Michel Borisowski, who claimed to be a Russian prince but was as Belgian as the winner.

That second edition had attracted a field of only 26 riders, which contributed to the decision to open up the third race to professionals.

The route changed, too, starting and finishing in Spa, where the Géronstère velodrome had been opened earlier in 1894. With Bastogne remaining as the turning point, the new course was shorter, at 223km, but considerably hillier than those previously used. Once again, though, Houa came out on top, although his winning margin over his rival Rasquinet was a mere seven minutes. Among the 42 starters was the race's first notable foreign entrant. Frenchman Maurice Garin ended up fourth of the 14 finishers, three years before he earned greater renown with his victory in the second edition of Paris–Roubaix.

After completing a hat-trick of wins in 1894, Houa turned his attention to the flourishing track scene. To an extent, he had little choice as cycle racing on the road disappeared almost completely in the late 1890s right across Belgium. Track racing was king and the members of the Liège Cyclists' Union were ahead of their time. As with many of that bilingual nation's sporting and cultural events, it was the road cycling boom in its far bigger neighbour to the west that re-energised the road scene throughout Belgium. Thanks in part to the desire of French bike manufacturers to establish new markets beyond their borders, the first edition of the Tour of Flanders took place in 1913, by which point Liège had also re-emerged, although rather shakily.

Having amalgamated with the Pesant Club Liégeois, which still runs the race alongside Tour de France organisers ASO, the Liège Cyclists' Union had relaunched Liège–Bastogne–Liège as an amateur event in 1908. Sixty riders lined up on the penultimate day of August to tackle a 235km course. Among them were a small number of French riders. Only one of the French finished, but did so in first place, becoming Liège's first foreign champion. He had a famous name, too, although André Trousselier would never reach the heights of his illustrious older sibling, Louis 'Trou-Trou' Trousselier, who had won Roubaix and the Tour de France in 1905.

Liège continued as an amateur-only event the following season, which produced the first race-deciding sprint. Eugène Charlier won it ahead of Victor Fastre, but their positions were reversed when it became clear Charlier had made an illegal bike change after the forks broke on his machine. More notable in hindsight was the third place finish of Paul Deman, who would go on to win the inaugural Tour of Flanders four years later. Further back still was a 19-year-old from Brussels named Philippe Thys. In the same year Deman claimed that first Flanders title, Thys became the second Belgian to claim the Tour de France, and went on to win it twice more. But for the Great War, Thys would, according to Tour director Henri Desgrange, have won the Tour on five or six occasions.

Once again, though, Liège stalled. By 1910, Roubaix, Milan–Sanremo and the Tour of Lombardy had become very well established and highly prized. Yet racing in Belgium continued to lag, principally because of the strength of the French road scene. For the increasing number of very competitive Belgian riders it made more sense to target the significant financial rewards available in France than to race for little more than prestige at home. It didn't help that Liège's organisers couldn't really decide what format their race should have either.

Open to amateurs in 1908 and 1909, absent from the calendar in 1910 due, apparently, to lack of interest, Liège returned in 1911, when the organisers opened it to independents (professionals who didn't have a team) as well as amateurs. The field was 108-strong, the biggest to date, with all but eight of the starters independents. Joseph Van Daele claimed the title and went on to have a very respectable career, winning stages at the Tour and finishing second in the inaugural edition of Flanders. Behind him were a host of future Belgian stars, including Jean Rossius, Léon Scieur and Louis Mottiat.

Liège was finally attracting a considerable number of high-class racers, but was hampered by being a showcase for these talents. Once they showed they had some class, French teams swooped to sign them in the hope of finding the next Roubaix or Tour champion. Van Daele and Mottiat were snapped up in 1912 by French teams J. B. Louvet and

Thomann, respectively. Scieur went to Armor a year later. Occasionally, the riders who went west did return to ride Liège. However, as it wasn't a priority for the French teams, most didn't.

The sudden glut of talent led to further tinkering with Liège's format in 1912. Previously, the organisers had welcomed amateur riders, but for the first time entry was restricted to professionals and independents, with prizes on offer to racers in both categories. Oddly, the two classes raced separately. The 22 starters in the race for professionals reached the turn at Bastogne half an hour ahead of schedule despite heavy rain. As they slogged northwards again, the conditions took a toll, eventually leaving just two riders to dispute the title at an airfield in Ans, the Liège suburb that hosted the finish between 1992 and 2018.

Fleming Omer Verschoore outsprinted Walloon Jacques Coomans after they had completed a lap of the aerodrome. Coomans protested the verdict, insisting the riders were supposed to do two laps of the installation, but his protest fell on deaf ears. Meanwhile, on the banks of the Meuse just out of the centre of Liège, the independents' race produced a dead heat, Jean Rossius and Dieudonné Gauthy crossing the line arm in arm, just as Bernard Hinault and Greg LeMond would do more than seven decades later on the famous climb of Alpe d'Huez during the 1986 Tour de France.

'Donné' Gauthy would surely have achieved far more if it hadn't been for the outbreak of war. After turning pro, he won the 1913 Tour of Belgium ahead of an impressively strong field that included past and future Tour de France winners François Faber, Lucien Buysse, Firmin Lambot and Léon Scieur. When war broke out, he was posted to the fort of Fléron, close to Liège, where he volunteered to carry out reconnaissance behind German lines on his bike. After several close calls, the Germans captured him. He remained in a POW camp until early 1919, when he went down with the Spanish flu that swept across the world. Unlike millions of others, Gauthy fought off the virus. He returned to racing later that year, finishing an astonishing eleventh at Roubaix soon after his release, and went on to enjoy considerable success on the track with his good friend Rossius before retiring to run a bike shop in Thimister-Clermont, just to the east of Liège.

Preparations for the ninth edition of Liège were well under way in the summer of 1914 when the threat of war led to its cancellation as riders were called up. Belgium had hoped to remain neutral in case of conflict, but, as the world knows, became embroiled when Germany invaded in August of that year. The Belgian army's astonishing resistance against a force ten times its size folded after a month, and many of those who had ridden Liège, Flanders and Roubaix perished during this initial campaign, among them 1909 Liège champion Victor Fastre, who was killed less than two months into the war.

Cycling's most successful village

Unlike the routes of Paris–Roubaix and the Tour of Flanders, which lie much further to the west and were in the middle of some of the Great War's principal battlegrounds, the Liège course avoided most of the devastation. However, the Walloon cycling scene remained stilted. While Roubaix and Flanders both flourished in the inter-war years, partly thanks to the determination of the local population to revitalise these regions, Liège remained a second-tier event. It returned to the race calendar in September 1919, but attracted a disappointingly small field, a mere 27 professionals lining up. Yet there was still quality within the paltry post-war fields, particularly in 1920, when the race featured three of the great names of Walloon cycling: Léon Scieur, Lucien Buysse and Firmin Lambot.

Scieur and Lambot were born and lived in the village of Florennes, south of Charleroi. Both men had to travel a significant distance to work each day, Scieur undertaking a 40km round trip on his bike to the glassworks at Châtelet on the edge of Charleroi, while Lambot covered 50km daily to work as a saddler. But as they trained together, climbing the nearby Côte de Gochenée up to 14 times in a day, their focus turned to bike racing.

Like many other great names in professional cycling's early years, it offered them a way out of their lowly paid drudgery and to riches well beyond what they could otherwise have achieved. Lambot broke through first, appearing in four pre-war Tours and striking up a friendship with Belgium's greatest rider of the era, Philippe Thys. When Thys won the Tour for the second time in 1914, he was also living and training in Florennes with Lambot and Scieur. Between them, the three men went on to claim the Tour title in each of the four years following the war. Lambot started that run in 1919. Thys regained the title in 1920, Scieur succeeded him in 1921 and Lambot took his second yellow jersey in 1922.

Nicknamed 'The Locomotive' – a popular tag in the inter-war years, it was also applied to 1933 Sanremo champion Joseph Demuysere and his successor, Learco 'The Human Locomotive' Guerra – because of the way he could relentlessly turn a big gear, Scieur came out on top at Liège in 1920. He beat another future Tour winner in the sprint, Fleming Lucien Buysse, with his close friend and neighbour Lambot fifth. In 1921, he won the Tour de France, but it was a close-run success. One of his wheels broke on the final stage and he was only able to continue with a spare handed to him by a spectator. In those years, the Tour's rules stated that riders had to present all the equipment they had started with at the finish, so Scieur had to carry his broken wheel on his back, with its axle gouging his flesh all the way to Paris. The incident left him with a large scar that he proudly showed off whenever asked to.

In 1923, Scieur spent eight days in a French hospital after swallowing arsenic in a cup of coffee that had been handed to him during a Tour stage in the Pyrenees by a seemingly benevolent fan, who was apparently peeved by Belgian domination of the Tour and most of the major Classics, including Roubaix and Flanders. Scieur never fully recovered from the effects of the poisoning and retired from racing a year later to run a garage in Florennes, where he continued to ride his bike into his seventies.

Scieur and Lambot's racing exploits may have made them Tour de France legends, but many Walloons insist the rider who succeeded Scieur as Liège champion was their best one of all time, others, that he was at the very least the region's best one-day rider until the arrival of Philippe Gilbert in the twenty-first century. Scieur would have ridden through Louis Mottiat's home village of Bouffioulx when he travelled back and forth to his job in the glassworks. Mottiat never won the Tour, although he did win stages there. But he was one of the great long-distance performers in cycling history.

He came to the fore when he won the 680km Bordeaux–Paris Classic in 1913. In 1920, he won the longest race ever organised, the 1,208km Critérium des As, running from Bordeaux to Paris and back again, which he completed (with just brief stops to sleep) in two days and eight hours, finishing almost two hours ahead of the runner-up. Nicknamed 'The Iron Man', Mottiat could probably have won the Tour if he had prepared for it in the right way and ridden with a degree of caution at key points, but that wasn't his style. He relished being at the front, setting a pace that he knew his rivals would struggle to follow. His relative lack of sprinting speed meant this attritional approach was his best weapon, although he was quick enough to win back-to-back Liège titles, the second of them coming in 1922 on a day of cauldron-like heat, which Mottiat put to his advantage by sapping the strength of his rivals with repeated injections of pace.

In the wake of his first Liège success, Mottiat lined up as favourite at Paris–Brest–Paris, now an amateur-only event but then a major target for the sport's leading professionals. He was convinced he would win. During two nights of racing, he sang to keep his spirits up and to crush those of his rivals. After more than two days in the saddle, he made his winning move with 100km left to Paris. 'The final 50km seemed shorter than the others because an enthusiastic crowd was shouting encouragement and applauding,' he wrote in *Le Miroir des Sports*. 'I wanted to win Paris–Brest. It's the race that definitively establishes the reputation of a cyclist.'

His comments may seem disrespectful to his home Classic, but Liège–Bastogne–Liège was still some way from becoming the great race it is now. It remained no more than a semi-Classic until after the Second World War – a big race, but not at the level of Sanremo, Roubaix and Lombardy. To an extent, it stayed as parochial as the Tour of Flanders, which only had one foreign winner before the Second World War and was regarded by foreign riders as very much a local event. However, Flanders and cycling in general had much greater cultural and sporting significance to the people in the Dutch-speaking half of Belgium than Liège did to its local Walloon population. In Flanders, cycling became engrained in the Flemish identity. It was a means by which the Flemings could assert their identity and language, the use of which had effectively been suppressed among Belgium's professional classes, who stuck to French at all times.

While Flanders grew stronger, at the national level at least, Liège's fortunes continued to fluctuate. Some years, entry was opened to independents in order to guarantee a big field. It returned to professional-only status in 1930, when Germany's Hermann Buse became only the second foreign rider to claim the title. Yet, despite Buse's win, it remained a race that could rarely count on anything other than a strong Walloon presence.

Its status finally began to rise in the approach to the Second World War. In 1937, Eloi Meulenberg claimed the title and went on to win the world crown later that same year, making him the first Walloon to wear the rainbow bands. Indeed, he was the only one until Claude Criquielion emulated him in 1984 and Philippe Gilbert joined them in 2012 – Flanders, on the other hand, has produced 14 world champions. Although Meulenberg's parents were Flemish, by the time he was born, they had moved to Ransart in the northern suburbs of Charleroi. Blessed with fearsome finishing speed, Meulenberg should have won the inaugural edition of Flèche Wallonne in 1936, which finished on the riverside in Liège, but was knocked from his bike by a motorcyclist within sight of the finish.

In 1937, though, good luck and form were with him at Liège, where he got the better of Gustaaf Deloor. Meulenberg went on to win four stages at the Tour de France and then the world crown in Copenhagen. Pino Cerami, who rode with Meulenberg towards the end of his career in the late 1940s, remembered him as 'someone who had a real eye for the ladies, but also a very popular guy with an incredible turn of speed'. After his retirement he ran a café called 'Au Sprinteur' in Ransart, and later in Charleroi.

The Deloor family didn't have to wait long to add their name to Liège's palmarès. That honour went not to Gustaaf, who won the first two editions of the Vuelta a España in the mid-1930s, but to his elder brother Alfons, who finished runner-up to Gustaaf in the 1936 Tour of Spain. The two brothers weren't expecting to make much of an impact at Liège in 1938, and their chances of doing so appeared to have gone when the peloton split and they both ended up in the second group. Alfons was the only rider to bridge across to the leaders.

'There were lots of attacks and Marcel Kint looked like he was going to win. But, with a few other riders, I managed to get across to Kint on the outskirts of Liège,' Alfons Deloor recalled in an interview with *Ciclismo a Fondo*. 'In the sprint, I decided to get on the wheel of "The Black Eagle" [Kint]. It all went my way and I took the best win of my career ahead of Kint and Félicien Vervaecke.'

The outbreak of war brought the racing careers of both brothers to a halt. Gustaaf was mobilised and joined the defence of Eben-Emael fortress that had been built during the 1930s to defend the Meuse from capture in the event of a German invasion. The biggest of its type in the world, the fortification was thought to be impregnable, but was taken in one day in a daring glider raid by German paratroopers. Deloor spent a year as a prisoner of war in Stalag 11B in Germany, his notoriety on two wheels earning him a relatively cushy job in the prison kitchen. After his release, he set up a business manufacturing bike tyres, later moving it to France in order to avoid being sent to Germany as a forced labourer. In the aftermath of the war, he emigrated to the United States and became a mechanic. In the mid-1950s, a friend found him a job working at the Cape Canaveral aerospace centre, where he put his skills to use building and repairing rockets. As for Alfons, he became a crane driver, specialising in the construction of dykes designed to prevent flooding.

Undermined by the Nazis

By the time Albert Ritserveldt won the 1939 edition of Liège, war looked almost certain. Ritserveldt's success led to his selection for the Belgian B team for the Tour de France, where he finished ninth overall, his career clearly on the up. However, less than two months later, the Second World War broke out. Initially, the conflict was largely confined to Poland and Eastern Europe, allowing racing to continue in Western Europe into 1940. That spring, Ritserveldt was leading the Tour of Catalonia when Germany invaded Belgium, whereupon he and the rest of the Belgian team quit the race and returned home to a country that was quickly overrun by the Germans' blitzkrieg tactics.

Unlike Flanders, where the German occupying forces supported bike racing and encouraged the running of the Tour of Flanders and other big events as part of their policy to encourage a division between the Dutch- and French-speaking regions of Belgium, racing in Wallonia was much more piecemeal. The occupying forces persistently scuppered plans for the thirtieth running of *La Doyenne*, which did not take place again until 1943 because the Germans refused to allow the race to finish in the centre of Liège.

Unable to consider the traditional city centre finale, the Pesant Club Liégeois eventually found a new home for the finish on an athletics track surrounding a football pitch in Liège's industrial suburb of Seraing. On 27 June, 63 riders set off from Liège for Bastogne, including defending champion Ritserveldt, many of the leading Flemish riders of the era – notably Alberic 'Briek' Schotte, Stan Ockers and Maurice De Simpelaere – and a young, unknown Walloon, Joseph Didden, who lived close to the new finish.

Late in the race, Richard Depoorter made three attacks. The last of them, on the Côte de Rotheux-Rimière, saw off Schotte and Joseph Somers. Depoorter rode the final 5km to the finish on Seraing's track alone, which was just as well given the mayhem that would almost certainly have ensued if there had been a sprint on a cinder surface more suited to speedway than road racing. The big crowd that cheered him home turned ecstatic when 20-year-old Didden was the next man on to the track a few seconds later.

As the tide of war began to turn against the Germans and an Allied invasion of France looked increasingly likely, plans for the 1944 edition of Liège had to be shelved, largely as a result of Allied bombardment in and around this key industrial centre that was providing steel for German weapons manufacturers. At the end of that year, the heavily wooded hills to the south of Liège became renowned for reasons very different to bike racing. In December 1944, with defeat looking almost certain, the Germans launched a last-ditch counter-offensive in the Ardennes through the thinly spread Allied lines, with the aim of dividing and then encircling the Allied forces, before negotiating a peace settlement. The Battle of the Ardennes, which became better known as the Battle of the Bulge due to the depth of the Germans' incursion into Allied territory, lasted for six weeks into the start of 1945 and became the bloodiest battle the Americans fought in any centre of operations during the war.

Almost 70 years on, there are still plenty of signs of the battle. The route of *La Doyenne* heads past the Battle of the Ardennes Museum in the picturesque town of La Roche-en-Ardenne, which nestles beneath a medieval castle. An American Sherman M4A1 tank and a British Achilles SP17 tank remain as monuments to the small town's liberation. On the road into Bastogne, a tank turret and gun outside the town's barracks mark the point where the return journey to Liège begins. Heading back north again, the route passes over the Côte de Wanne, where a memorial commemorates the men of the 517th Parachute Regimental Combat Team of the US Army. Soon after, at the foot of the fearsome Stockeu climb in Stavelot, a collection of Second World War relics stands next to the strategically important bridge into the town, which the Germans initially took but failed to hold.

The thirty-first edition of *La Doyenne* took place in August 1945, just two months after Germany's final surrender. Among the 43 riders who lined up was 1939 Paris–Roubaix winner Émile Masson Jr, who had spent four years in a German prisoner-of-war camp. Masson, whose father had won Bordeaux–Paris and stages in the Tour de France, had been liberated from the camp by the advancing Red Army in May 1945, and had immediately returned to training. Although he would later admit the war had stolen his best years from him, he did manage to win two Belgian championships and, in 1947, emulated his father's success in Bordeaux–Paris, father and son then conducting a joint lap of honour. Masson went on to become a sports journalist and was president of the Pesant Club Liégeois for 18 years from 1968, playing a key role in the organisation of Liège.

Masson died in 2011 at the age of 95. He put his long life down to a daily tipple or two. 'At breakfast I drink a small whisky mixed with the juice of two oranges and then another whisky in the evening, and I have a glass of red wine, Château Beauval to be precise, at midday. Finally, I smoke my pipe a lot, getting through 50g of tobacco every three days,' he told *La Dernière Heure*.

In 1945, perhaps not too surprisingly given his recent experiences, Masson failed to last the distance, abandoning at Marche on the return leg to Liège. The condition of the roads wouldn't have helped him and his fellow racers either. Many still showed the after-effects of the Battle of the Bulge offensive, while Bastogne stood in ruins. Soon after passing this devastation, three riders broke clear, the main impetus for their attack coming from Jan Engels. Although all were reeled in by the small peloton, Engels continued to ride aggressively, attacking on the climb of the Gros-Chêne, again on the Côte d'Esneux, and yet again on the 4km-long ascent of the Côte de Tilff. A final dig on the Colline de Cointe produced the gap he had been striving for. He went on to finish 47 seconds ahead of a small group led in by Edward Van Dyck.

Few outside Wallonia registered Engels' success. However, having survived two world wars and the indifference of foreign riders, Liège–Bastogne–Liège was on the verge of a golden era that would see it take its place among the great one-day races on the international calendar.

2

THE EMERGENCE OF *LA DOYENNE*

Coming out of the Second World War, Liège–Bastogne–Liège was still a long way from being one of the biggest events on the cycling calendar. It certainly didn't compare with any of the other Monuments, and may not even have been the biggest one-day race in Wallonia given the rapid emergence of Flèche Wallonne immediately before and during the war, when it regularly attracted big fields on a course running between Mons and Charleroi.

Established in 1936 by Walloon sports daily *Les Sports*, Flèche Wallonne initially linked Tournai and Liège, the most distant cities in French-speaking Belgium. Running via Mons, Charleroi, Namur and Huy, it was intended to boost the flagging fortunes of cycling within Wallonia, even at the expense of Liège–Bastogne–Liège, which had persistently failed to attract an international following. *Les Sports'* young editorial and management team had little experience of organising bike races, and none of events at professional level, but they went at the task with such gusto that Flèche was an immediate success. One of that organising team, Alban Collignon, went on to become president of cycling's ruling body, the UCI, a mere three years later, holding the post until 1947.

The new race captured the public imagination in a way that Liège rarely had. Huge crowds turned out to watch it, even on the shortened wartime course where Marcel Kint's reign was almost absolute. Known as 'The Black Eagle' because of his hooked nose and dark jersey, Kint had won the world title in 1938 and still held it as the championships had not subsequently taken place. He might have had a sensational career had it not been for the war, but he still gleaned all he could from those years. 'I was not exuberant, have never been a rider of many words. What did I have to say anyway? I laboured on the bike to have a better life and that's all,' he said of a career that saw him win two world titles, the 1943 edition of Paris–Roubaix and three successive Flèche titles. He also had some success at the Tour de France, and was rumoured to have prepared himself for the parched heat of July by eating large quantities of salted fish.

Such was Kint's almost iconic status in Flanders as one of the region's most typically hard-nosed and rugged riders, that his hat-trick of Flèche wins between 1943 and 1945 undoubtedly raised the race's profile. Yet he was unusual for a Flemish rider in that he loved competing in Wallonia, his connection beginning in 1938 when he had finished runner-up in Liège to Alfons Deloor.

Kint, who spent his entire professional career with French manufacturer Mercier and later sold their bikes at his shop in Kortrijk before establishing a range of bikes under his own name, was adamant his Flèche successes demonstrated he could have won Liège if fortune had gone his way. His biggest regret from that period, though, was a calamitous performance at the 1946 World Championships in Zurich, where he and teammate Rik Van Steenbergen got into the winning break and worked out a deal whereby whichever one of them took the title would pay the other 25,000 Belgian francs, a substantial sum in those days. Yet the agreement failed to take account of two key factors: the presence of Zurich's own Hans Knecht in their three-man break and Van Steenbergen's fatigue, which Kint only became aware of just before his teammate fell back late on, leaving Kint playing cat and mouse with Knecht at the finish, a situation he had not envisaged.

'The organisation left a lot to be desired because there was just a single rope holding the fans back,' Kint later recalled. 'Four Swiss fans ducked under it. The first three were encouraging their compatriot and urging him to sprint. But the fourth one grabbed my saddle and Knecht took advantage of that to start his dash to victory.'

In the post-war years, Flèche gained more of an edge on Liège as it began to attract an increasing number of foreign riders. In 1948, Fermo Camellini took the title, the Italian's success resulting from Flèche's inclusion on the list of races that formed the Desgrange-Colombo Challenge, which was effectively the foundation stone for today's WorldTour comprising the biggest events in the sport. Together with *L'Équipe*, *La Gazzetta dello Sport* and *Het Nieuwsblad-Sportwereld*, *Les Sports* established the first season-long competition for road races, which provided a clear structure for the European calendar. Liège, however, was not part of it.

From 1946, Liège did attract a handful of foreign riders, notably from Luxembourg, which lies just a few kilometres south of Bastogne. There were half a dozen riders from the Grand Duchy on the start line in 1946, including Jean Kirchen, cousin of another Luxembourg pro, Erny Kirchen, whose son Kim wore the Tour de France's yellow jersey for six days in 2008. That 1946 race returned to its pre-war route, starting in Liège's Place St Lambert and taking in several tough climbs including the fabulously named Côte de la Queue de Vache (Cow's Tail Hill), as well as further hill tests at Sinsin, My, Florzée and Hornay. Victory went to Prosper Depredomme, who went on to become a loyal domestique to Fausto Coppi and, later on, to Rik Van Steenbergen. Such was his commitment to the ambitions of others that Depredomme didn't win another major title until he claimed a second Liège success in 1950.

In between Depredomme's two rather unexpected victories, Raymond Impanis started towards an unenviable record for the highest number of second places. Between 1947 and 1955, this Flemish rider of Italian extraction finished runner-up in Liège on four occasions. Known as 'The Baker of Berg', Impanis's first experience with the bike was as a delivery boy for the family bakery. He turned pro in 1947, winning the final time trial at that year's Tour de France, which, at 139km, remains the longest in Tour history, but didn't build on that fast start until the early 1950s, largely due to the long-lasting effects of crashing into an electricity pole during a wartime junior race.

The incident left him with paralysis of the right arm. Although this wasn't total, Impanis only ever regained 20 per cent use of the injured limb and was adamant the injury cost him 'millions'. This wildly overstates the sums riders earned in those days, but you have to wonder what else Impanis might have achieved given that he managed to win Flanders, Roubaix and Paris–Nice in the same year, and was so consistently strong in Liège.

His run started in a race that attracted the biggest field ever, as 168 riders lined up outside the Le Stop café on the banks of the Meuse. Impanis looked the fastest of a group of six riders coming into the finish, but was foiled when 1943 champion Richard Depoorter slipped away in the final kilometre. Impanis was second again in 1948, when Fausto Coppi drew huge crowds to the start in spite of teeming rain. Coppi and brother Serse abandoned soon after the 'Bastogne bend' and well before the winning break went on the Queue de Vache. Just five riders remained coming into the finish, including two Frenchmen, Louis Caput and Camille Danguillaume, who punctured as soon as the sprint got going. Caput led it out, Impanis responded, but Maurice Mollin timed his final acceleration perfectly to deny them both.

Joining the elite

That 1948 race marked a turning point in *La Doyenne*'s long-term future. *Les Sports* joined the Pesant Club Liégeois as part of a more influential organising team, which was able to negotiate the presence of the Coppi brothers and several renowned French riders. In 1949, one of those French riders, the previously unfortunate Danguillaume, became the first foreign winner of Liège since little-remembered Hermann Buse in 1930.

Les Sports' influence became even more apparent when Liège–Bastogne–Liège was added to the Desgrange-Colombo Challenge in 1951. This decision immediately set *La Doyenne* alongside the greatest events on the calendar in terms of significance because of the points that could be won in this season-long competition. Although it still lacked the prestige of the other four Monuments, being part of the Desgrange-Colombo guaranteed a strong field and, finally, a much higher profile for a race that was now almost 60 years old.

As well as bringing what would become cycling's five Monuments under the same umbrella for the first time, Liège's inclusion in the Desgrange-Colombo heralded a golden age for the major Classics. The series comprised just half a dozen other races, including the Tour and Giro, which ensured the sport's biggest names not only lined up in most of them, but also rode to win. In recent decades, the UCI has attempted on several occasions to foster what has effectively been a return to this era, but the ProTour and subsequent WorldTour have had up to 38 events, far too many to guarantee the leading stars facing up to each other regularly. The success of the Desgrange-Colombo would suggest that less is more if a season-long series of races is to thrive.

Les Sports' determination to raise Liège's profile also extended to switching it from the summer to the late spring. In 1951, the organisers went further still, opting to run Flèche and Liège on the same weekend, the former taking place over 220km packed with cobbles and hills on the Saturday, the latter extending to 211 very lumpy kilometres on the Sunday. It was a bold move, and one that resulted in a quite extraordinary performance.

Switzerland's Ferdi Kübler had secured victory in the 1950 Desgrange-Colombo Challenge thanks to his overall success in the Tour de France, where his bizarre antics and riding style had attracted plenty of attention. Unlike his elegant and smooth-pedalling compatriot Hugo Koblet, who carried a comb in his pocket with which to ensure his

Brylcreemed hair was precisely in place as he swept to victory, Kübler was dishevelment personified. Bobbing all over his bike, grunting and wild-eyed, he chuntered away at his rivals, muttering threats in pidgin French: 'Ferdi attack soon, you ready?' Or, most famously, having taken on Mont Ventoux with too much vigour during the 1955 Tour de France, destroying his hopes of victory: 'Stand clear! Ferdi's going to explode!'

With a nose that rivalled Kint's in its beakiness, Kübler was also dubbed 'The Eagle': in his case 'The Eagle of Adiswil', his home town in Switzerland. During the first half of the 1950s, he was one of the sport's outstanding performers, which he demonstrated impressively on that first Ardennes Weekend. At Flèche he led home a lead group of four, who were all Tour de France champions or would go on to take that title – Gino Bartali, Jean Robic and Louison Bobet trailed in behind the Swiss.

Kübler had been built up as the favourite for Liège, but many now doubted he could live up to that status just 24 hours later. That assessment appeared correct when Germain Derycke dropped down the descent into Liège with a clear lead over Frenchman Pierre Barbotin. The first indication the race was not quite done came when drivers of the team, press and official cars and motorbikes tracking Derycke saw a figure fly past them, apparently semi-deranged, given his gesticulations and barely comprehensible bellows, and clearly with little regard for his own safety. Kübler bore down on Derycke as the Belgian crossed the Meuse with the finish almost in sight. After that, the sprint was a formality for Ferdi, who became the first rider to complete the Liège/Flèche double.

Kübler followed that with the double-double. He retained his Flèche title, beating Ockers and Impanis in the sprint, and started *La Doyenne* as favourite, even though the course had been toughened considerably, notably by the addition of the dirt road up and over the Côte de Wanne, 60km from the finish. When Louison Bobet attacked on this hill, the dust billowing as press and officials' motorbikes buzzed around the Frenchman, Kübler shot after him, his twisted features completely belying his fantastic form. Frenchman Jean Robic and Belgian Henri Van Kerckhove bridged across as well. As they bounced over bumps and around potholes on the descent, Bobet punctured. Left with Robic and young Van Kerckhove for company, Kübler rode any sprinting speed they had out of their legs.

Raymond Impanis completed his own double-double three years on from Kübler, adding back-to-back second places to those he had taken in 1947 and 1948. He had no regrets about losing out to Luxembourg's Marcel Ernzer in 1954, who romped away to win by almost three minutes. A year on, however, Impanis felt very differently when he was beaten on the line by teammate Stan Ockers. 'He had won Flèche Wallonne the day before and we had agreed that I could win in Liège. I came towards the finish fairly steadily and then Stan attacked me with 200 metres to go. It was too late to do anything,' he recalled, although his bitterness did not stretch to any bad feeling about *La Doyenne*. 'I consider it the most beautiful, the most testing and the most difficult race to win,' he affirmed.

While Impanis never did take the title, thanks to three wins in four races in the late 1950s, Fred De Bruyne was anointed 'Mr Liège–Bastogne–Liège'. He had had a tough childhood in Berlare, just to the east of Gent, as a result of his father's seven-year imprisonment for collaboration with the occupying forces during the Second World War. An electrician by trade, Dolf De Bruyne became a police constable during the war and was involved in the arrest of Resistance fighters who were subsequently executed. Stigmatised by his father's offences, Fred De Bruyne found the motivation to succeed and win people over with his exploits on the bike.

He turned pro, with his ambition focused on the grand tours, and was for some time hyped as the rider who could finally end Belgium's long drought at the Tour de France, which stretched back to 1939. But he quickly realised he didn't have the ability to compete in the high mountains. Consequently, from 1956 onwards he focused on shorter stage races and the Classics, developing a rivalry with compatriot Rik Van Looy that was always extremely competitive and winning the Desgrange-Colombo Challenge three years running. Close friend Raphaël Geminiani described him as 'a master of the Classics: intelligent, crafty, devious, but very strong and an excellent tactician. He wasn't a sprinter like Van Looy or Van Steenbergen, but he had a good, fast finish, which meant he got results in the biggest Classics.'

He began the 1956 season with victory in Paris–Nice and Milan–Sanremo, this success coming after he dropped Van Looy on the Poggio, the critical climb just a handful of kilometres from the finish. Second at Paris–Roubaix, having set up Mercier-BP teammate Louison Bobet for victory, De Bruyne returned to Belgium for the Ardennes Weekend. A bizarre quirk in the rules then in place regarding team sponsors who came from outside the sport meant he had to sit out Flèche Wallonne because of BP's backing of Mercier. However, a loophole allowed him to line up for Liège the next day as an 'individual' rider. With no team backing, he knew he would be out of the race and perhaps even stranded in the depths of the Ardennes if he suffered any mechanical breakdown.

De Bruyne managed to avoid trouble and saw his chance when, with 20km remaining, Flèche winner Richard Van Genechten skipped away. De Bruyne was quick to join him. The elfin Belgian could climb with the best, but was very limited when it came to sprinting, so De Bruyne wasn't surprised when his compatriot's team manager ordered Van Genechten not to co-operate in order to protect the interests of his Peugeot team leader Stan Ockers. With Sanremo already in his pocket, and having gone close at both Flanders and Roubaix, De Bruyne knew he was in the form of his life and was more than happy to tow Van Genechten all the way to the finish, where he beat him by several lengths.

De Bruyne's subsequent Liège victories in 1958 and 1959 followed a similar pattern – spotting the correct time to move and the right riders to escape with, his finishing speed delivering the final flourish. The only edition to evade him during that four-year period was in 1957, which went down in cycling's annals as one of the most memorable Classics of all time, and not only because it ended up with joint winners.

Appalling but epic

When Louison Bobet returned to the Mercier team hotel in Liège after completing it, his director Antonin Magne addressed his teammates: 'Gentlemen, stand up and applaud. Before you stands a man, a real man!' Bobet had finished ninth, almost a quarter of an hour off the winner's pace, but the Frenchman was among just 27 of the 107 starters to go the whole distance on a day of apocalyptic weather. Most of them no doubt wished they had opted to follow 135 others who had registered but chosen not to take to the start at all.

A clue to the extreme weather that can affect the Ardennes even outside the depths of winter can be found at the top of Côte de Wanne. Opposite the memorial to the men of 517th Parachute Regimental Combat Team, a sign points towards the 'Piste de Ski, Val de Wanne'. A little further on, there are support posts for drag lifts. This 'ski station' stands at a mere 484m, but looking down the slopes into the valley below it's easy to understand why it attracts winter sports enthusiasts. The runs may not rival the Hahnenkamm at Kitzbühel in terms of length or difficulty, but they are steep enough to guarantee plenty of speed. Snow is not hard to come by either.

The hills of the Ardennes start as little more than ripples in the landscape south of the River Meuse, but quickly become more substantial, reaching a peak of 694m at the Signal de Botrange, Belgium's highest point. The roads through the region rollercoaster up and over these hills, cutting through thick forest to reach treeless plateaux, across which the wind can rip viciously. Apart from the occasional swathes that have been cut back by loggers, the forest has a Hansel and Gretel quality to it – it is deep, dark and quite forbidding. It's not the kind of place you'd venture into without a ball of string or a pocketful of pebbles to guide you back. Entering the forest, it is easy to understand how reclusive 1956 Tour de France winner Charly Gaul managed to hide himself away in it for many years without anyone succeeding in tracking him down as he struggled with depression following his split from his second wife.

These hills attract twice as much rain as Belgium's northern flatlands and on the heights there are frosts as often as 130 times a year. It snows more than 30 days a year, too, although rarely beyond the end of March. In 1957, *La Doyenne* took place five days into May and just 24 hours after Raymond Impanis had won Flèche in cold but dry and sunny conditions. When the 107 riders set out from Liège on a course that now stretched to 256km, it was cold and raining steadily, and some older observers were recalling the 1919 race, which halted for two hours at Bastogne so the riders could have a hot meal. Those with even longer memories recollected the 1910 edition of Sanremo, when only four mud-caked riders completed the course.

Thick mist provided an extra complication, particularly on descents, where riders could only see a few metres ahead. This became more of a problem when the temperature dropped steadily and the rain turned to snow. The organisers responded by calling ahead to request hot drinks be provided at the feed station at Houffalize, soon after the turn at Bastogne. As well as steaming cups of coffee and tea, locals turned out with warm clothes for the riders, but that didn't stop 51 from abandoning either at or before Houffalize, with 120km still remaining to the finish.

As the snow grew heavier and the wind picked up, news came through that 5cm were coating the road over the Côte de Rosiers. At Vielsalm and the start of the Côte de Wanne, riders were resorting to urinating on their hands to get some warmth into them. One rider abandoned in tears, while defending champion De Bruyne keeled over, having been unable to free his feet from their straps because his hands were frozen. Teammate Désiré Keteleer tried to revive him, but De Bruyne told him: 'It's no use. Leave me.' Keteleer stayed with him, the pair of them climbing into the broom wagon.

Amid all this there was still a race going on. Approaching the level crossing at Cierreux, four riders begun to chase the early leaders – Bobet, Sante Ranucci, Angelo Miserocchi and Germain Derycke. As they neared it, the barrier came down. The first three jumped it, a manoeuvre that was permitted in France and Italy, but not in Belgium. Derycke hesitated, then followed them. When the group chasing behind reached the barrier, a freight train began to roll through, delaying them for two minutes. On the Côte de Wanne, the remaining riders entered a world of white as the snow and mist formed a freezing curtain. Bobet's quartet closed down the gap on the lead group, who included Britain's Brian Robinson, a Yorkshireman whose home at Mirfield, high on the Pennine moors, sees plenty of weather.

Small groups were still chasing behind the leaders. Raymond Impanis, winner of Flèche the previous day, was in one, but was fading rapidly. He held his hands out towards his team car, pleading: 'Please, take my gloves off for me. I can't manage it any more ...'

On the Haute Levée climb out of Stavelot, Derycke sensed Bobet was wilting and pressed hard, the Italian Ranucci sticking with him. On the Côte de Rosiers, Derycke upped his pace again, dropping Ranucci. He continued to battle the elements on his own, eventually finishing almost three minutes ahead of Frans Schoubben in second and Marcel Buys in third. Fourth place went to Martin Van Geneugden, who rode most of the race wearing the distinctive beret of his team director Antonin Magne, without gloves and in short sleeves. Bobet, who had led the charge over the crossing at Cierreux, lost ten minutes in the final 20km but his personal pride would not allow him to quit. 'It's my job,' Bobet told journalists that evening.

Soon after the frozen Derycke had posed at the finish with podium girl Miss Remington, it was announced that Schoubben had lodged a protest about the incident on the level crossing. Derycke defended his action, insisting he had done no more than follow Bobet. 'I shouted at Bobet not to jump but he didn't hear. There was no official there. I was concerned. The three others had jumped so I followed them,' he explained. However, the officials had to disqualify him and award first place to Schoubben.

Although he had broken the rules as laid down in Belgium, Derycke might have pointed to the 1955 Tour of Flanders as a precedent. On that occasion, eventual winner Louison Bobet and the three other members of the leading group made their way through a closed level crossing, and the race commissaires, or judges, had opted not to disqualify them, such was the extent of their lead over their pursuers. Further back still, 1919 Flanders champion Henri Van Leerberghe had walked through a train that had stopped at a level crossing.

Good sense eventually prevailed, though. A few days later, at the urging of his Peugeot-BP team boss, Léon van der Hulst, Schoubben withdrew his protest, leaving the Belgian Cycling Federation with a considerable headache. Derycke offered them a way out, writing to say the race should be awarded jointly to him and Schoubben. 'Exceptional conditions require exceptional measures,' said federation president Arnold Standaert when he announced they had agreed to Derycke's request.

Tales of incidents and exploits that occurred during the race abounded in the days that followed. Jean Bobet, brother of Louison, admitted the stop at the Cierreux level crossing was far from the only one he had had before abandoning. 'It felt good to get down from the bike, to put your feet back on the ground,' he told journalist Georges Pagnoud. 'My hat froze on my head. Next to me, Gérard Saint imitated a Flandrian. He pissed on his hands to get the circulation back in his fingers … At school they tell you that Belgium is a flat country, a temperate country. I would like to have seen my geography teacher's face that day,' said Bobet, who was eventually picked up by a fan from the roadside and driven back to Liège.

René Van Damme, a Liégeois, revealed he would have quit any other race, but not *La Doyenne*. 'On the Côte de Wanne, I gave my teammate

Schoubben a really good push, so I played a little part in his victory,' he told *Coups de Pédales*. Van Damme's fingers froze so badly he failed to grab his musette at Houffalize and found it next to impossible to dig food out of his back pockets. 'At the famous level crossing at Cierreux, where I stopped like almost everyone else, getting back on the bike was really painful and some of the riders were cursing their stiffened limbs,' he said, adding that a few had climbed into cars for a while to warm up and get a few kilometres further down the course. 'It took me eight days to recover and I earned just 400 Belgian francs for 19th place, a pittance when you consider I had to buy some of my equipment and I didn't have a fixed salary. The expression used at the time was that you were riding "*à la musette*" [without a wage and with only your food as a reward].'

De Bruyne's third win provided a nice postscript to this legendary race. The rider he came to the line with and beat in the two-up sprint was none other than Frans Schoubben. It was to be De Bruyne's last major victory. On the same day in 1961 when his great rival Rik Van Looy won his second world title, De Bruyne crashed and broke his collarbone during a track meeting in Bordeaux. His friend and fellow pro Willy Vannitsen offered to drive him back to Belgium. As they passed through Paris, Vannitsen and another motorist were distracted by the sight of Brigitte Bardot walking down the street and crashed head-on. De Bruyne suffered a dislocated shoulder and a shattered kneecap. Although he did return to racing, he was never the rider he had been. He went on to become a team director, TV commentator and PR man before retiring to Seillans in the South of France in his late fifties. After a long battle with cancer, he died there in 1994, aged 63. The town subsequently renamed a square in his honour.

'Elegant, extremely gentle, he left the world of cycling with ease. These days that doesn't mean much but then attitudes were different: once a Fleming, always a Fleming. We spent ten happy years together,' said fellow Seillans resident Geminiani of his friend, whose love of a drink resulted in some hilarious moments during his years as a TV commentator. 'He used to sound sloshed at the start of a race, and I swear he sometimes had to be held upright by the end of it,' said cycling historian and long-time Belgium resident Les Woodland. 'When they let him loose among the riders, it could be like seeing a drunk stumbling into church.'

Anquetil's final flourish

The demise of the Desgrange-Colombo Challenge in 1958 – the result of disagreements between the organising newspapers – had no effect on the prestige Liège–Bastogne–Liège had achieved during the competition's decade of existence. It did, however, result in a short-lived reversal of the running order for the Ardennes Weekend, Liège switching to the Saturday up to 1964, when Flèche was moved to what is now its well-established position a few days before *La Doyenne*. The Belgians dominated those years, taking four consecutive wins on the back of Dutchman Ab Geldermans' triumph in 1960. The most significant of them was Rik Van Looy's victory in 1961, which made him the first rider in history to win all five Monuments. Once Van Looy had broken clear with Faema teammate Armand Desmet and French climber Marcel Rohrbach, the result was never in doubt. Set up by Desmet, Van Looy won at a canter, not needing to rev himself up to his top sprinting speed to beat Rohrbach.

In 1965, the Ardennes Weekend competition went the same way as the Desgrange-Colombo, as Flèche's race director, Theo Van Griethuysen, decided to take his race on a more independent path. That year also saw the home nation's winning run ended, when Italy claimed victory in *La Doyenne* for the first time. Belgium could, though, claim to have had a significant influence on the career of 1965 champion Carmine Preziosi.

Born in Sant'Angelo all'Esca, deep in rural Campania in southern Italy, Preziosi moved to Belgium at the age of 14 with his parents, who, like tens of thousands of fellow Italians, went north looking for work.

His father found it in the mine at Farciennes, just to the east of Charleroi. Consequently, Preziosi knew the roads of the Ardennes extremely well. As he progressed through the Belgian amateur ranks, he worked as a chauffeur and waiter, before signing with the French Pelforth team in 1963 at the age of just 19.

In 1964, he came home nineteenth behind Willy Bocklant when Liège finished for the first time in the Stade Vélodrome de Rocourt, a 40,000-capacity multi-sports stadium that hosted the World Track Championships on several occasions. The following year, Preziosi was one of a dozen riders who contested the finish on the same rain-wettened track. Vittorio Adorni led on to it, with bespectacled Dutchman Jan Janssen, in the world champion's jersey, on his wheel. As the sprint began, Janssen pushed hard on Adorni's outside – too hard. He slid and hit the track, taking down seven other riders, including Britons Michael Wright and Tom Simpson. Adorni emerged unscathed and looked to have victory in his grasp until Preziosi came up alongside him and shoved him with his left hand. Somehow Adorni stayed upright, but his young compatriot got up to cross the line first.

There seemed little doubt Preziosi would be relegated, but, after Adorni lodged a protest, the finish-line judge said he had not seen the push. The result stood, although Preziosi was subsequently fined for committing a dangerous manoeuvre in a sprint. Although his pro career extended to 1972, Preziosi never achieved these heights again. 'Glory came to me when I was very young. Victory in itself is not difficult to live with, but dealing with it for the rest of your career can cause problems. If you're even a little bit sensitive to public opinion, it can change the course of your career,' he later told *Le Soir*, looking back to that headlining day.

Three days before Preziosi nudged his way on to the top of the Liège podium, Belgium's world amateur champion, Eddy Merckx, turned pro, winning his first race eight days after the Rocourt controversy. Merckx didn't make his Liège debut until 1966, finishing eighth, but a massive 5'24" behind another great name who was a surprising victor.

Five-time Tour de France champion Jacques Anquetil only won three Classics – Gent–Wevelgem in 1964, Bordeaux–Paris in 1965 and Liège in 1966, his only success in a Monument. As early as 1958, this arch-calculator had described the Classics as little more than 'lotteries'. However, the master *rouleur* and time triallist didn't have the weapons required by a Classics contender. He lacked the explosive power of a *puncheur*, who can sprint hard up a climb and maintain that speed for a considerable distance until he gets a gap. That same lack of explosive power compromised him in sprints. Although Anquetil did win a few from small groups, they tended to be the result of him steadily winding the pace up over the final few hundred metres to the point where no one could come past him. One-day races also didn't suit the powers of endurance and recovery that made the smooth-pedalling Frenchman such a stellar performer in grand tours.

Anquetil was approaching the end of his career in 1966. Winner of two Giro titles and the Vuelta, in addition to five Tours, he was looking for new challenges, especially if they provided a chance to needle his long-time rival, Raymond Poulidor. In 1965, he had opted out of riding the Tour in order to take on a ridiculous challenge suggested by his team director, Raphaël Geminiani. 'Gem' proposed Anquetil ride and win the Critérium du Dauphiné and Bordeaux–Paris. The main difficulty, apart from the riding itself, lay in the fact that Bordeaux–Paris started on the same evening the Dauphiné finished, and on the other side of France. Anquetil pulled it off, receiving more praise for this exploit than he had done at any other point in his career.

The following spring, Geminiani's co-director at the Ford-France team, Raymond Louviot, noticed that Anquetil was due to ride two criteriums in the Netherlands on the days in between Flèche and Liège and suggested he include the two Belgian Classics in his programme as well. 'It's an idea, but one I hadn't been considering,' Anquetil responded when it was put to him, adding, 'Will Poulidor be in Belgium?' Told he would be, Anquetil declared: 'Well, I'll go too.'

He may also have been piqued by the sudden arrival on the scene and interest in new Italian sensation Felice Gimondi, who had won the Tour in 1965 and followed up by winning Paris–Roubaix and then Paris–Brussels just eight days later in the early spring of 1966. Comparisons were being made between Gimondi and Fausto Coppi, and also, in a less flattering way, Anquetil, whose record in the Classics, and particularly Roubaix, was poor.

The moody and often prickly Frenchman didn't go into Liège in the best frame of mind. At the finish of Flèche Wallonne, where he was thirteenth and in the same group as Gimondi and Poulidor that came in three minutes down on winner Michele Dancelli, he said he was only intending to ride the first 100km of *La Doyenne*. Maybe it was the sudden and unexpected arrival of the sun, but Anquetil went all the way to the Rocourt track, and in incredible style too.

The route now included 13 climbs, double the number in Liège's early days. Most also had the steep ramps that Anquetil hated more than most because they disrupted his pedalling rhythm. One of them was the Côte de la Bouquette. Approaching it with the main contenders and an escape group a minute up the road, Anquetil accelerated, dropping Merckx, Gimondi and many other big names. On Mont Theux, which starts gently then rears up to 12 per cent as it heads straight up and over the hill towards Remouchamps, Anquetil caught the lead group of three, which included Johny Schleck, father of current pros Andy and Fränk. He drilled by them and rode the final 45km alone in time trial mode, finishing 4′53″ clear of runner-up Vic Van Schil.

The French press was in raptures. *L'Équipe*'s reaction was typical: 'For 12 years we've been waiting for just such an exploit by Jacques Anquetil – to win a classic one-day race. In Liège–Bastogne–Liège, the hardest and most demanding of them all, he finally filled the gap in his palmarès in front of impotent rivals, including Eddy Merckx, who expressed his astonishment at the way in which Jacques had built a lead.'

His success was clouded, though, by his failure to provide a sample at the post-race doping control. 'Too late. If you can collect it from the soapy water there, go ahead. I'm a human being, not a fountain,' he told the official with a flask at the ready. Within minutes Anquetil was off to the Netherlands to fulfil his criterium commitments. Initially disqualified by the Belgian federation, he was subsequently reinstated by the UCI, which ruled the regulations relating to drug testing procedures were not precise enough.

The Liège success was the last major victory of Anquetil's illustrious career. In 1969, he retired to his Normandy estate to devote himself to farming and an extremely bizarre and complicated family life. Having married his doctor's wife, with whom he may or may not have fathered a child, he subsequently had a *ménage à trois* with his wife and stepdaughter, which resulted in the latter having a child. He then had an affair with his stepson's wife that resulted in another child. On this basis alone, Paul Howard's extraordinary biography of the French champion, *Sex, Lies and Handlebar Tape*, is highly recommended.

As Anquetil faded, his position as the sport's dominating figure was about to be usurped by cycling's all-time greatest rider. Liège–Bastogne–Liège was soon to become one of Eddy Merckx's favourite hunting grounds.

3

THE GREATEST CLASSIC EVER?

Eddy Merckx's Classics reputation may have been founded and subsequently cemented at Milan–Sanremo, where he won his first Monument and added no fewer than six more, but *La Doyenne* undoubtedly provided the Belgian with the ideal terrain to show off the full scope of his ability. World amateur champion in 1964, the Belgian Eddy Merckx had turned pro halfway through 1965. With dark good looks, sideburns and his hair Brylcreemed back, Merckx had the features of a leading man. Hailing from Brussels, he was neither Flandrian nor Walloon, giving him an all-encompassing appeal among Belgian fans, which only grew as his tally of wins began to pile up.

Far from the only big name humbled by Jacques Anquetil's final flourish in 1966, Merckx returned in 1967 with two Sanremo victories on his palmarès and his reputation as a Classics all-rounder enhanced by an impressive solo win at Flèche three days before. Some, though, and most notably outgoing Classics strongman Rik Van Looy, believed Walter Godefroot, two years older but still without a Classics victory at that point, would have the edge on Merckx, and events at Liège supported that opinion.

Together with the more seasoned campaigner Willy Monty, the two young wolves of Belgian cycling rode away from the rest of the field on a day of Arctic conditions. Godefroot was particularly active, chasing down Merckx's teammate Ferdinand Bracke, then responding to all Merckx's attacks over the closing kilometres. When Monty tailed off before the finishing dash, Godefroot and Merckx went head to head, and it was the older man who prevailed, his superior finishing speed giving him an edge that Van Looy and many others insisted would prove significant in the long term.

They viewed Merckx's complaint that his wheels had slipped in the puddles standing on the Rocourt cement track as nothing more than whinging. As they saw it, Godefroot had beaten Merckx fair and square. The press, however, called it differently, putting Merckx's defeat down to his lack of experience of the Rocourt track. As for Merckx, he described the defeat as 'a terrible humiliation'. Any loss affected the rider who would soon be dubbed 'The Cannibal', such was his insatiable appetite for victories. Defeats in the biggest races he felt most acutely.

The question of which of them would have the edge remained unresolved in 1968. Godefroot, whose aggression and chops earned him the nickname 'The Flemish Bulldog' – a tag previously given to Gaston Rebry, a Flemish hard man of the pre-war era – won Flanders with his rival in the pack just behind him. Days later, Merckx won Roubaix as Godefroot finished a rather more distant third. Liège provided no answers as Merckx sat it out to prepare for a second tilt at the Giro d'Italia, while Godefroot was undone in a messy sprint won by new pro Valère Van Sweevelt.

Godefroot's second place was largely overlooked by a heated debate about whether Jacques Anquetil had been intending to lead out his traditional foe, Raymond Poulidor. Anquetil led his compatriot on to the track, then accelerated in the back straight with Poulidor on his wheel, catching Godefroot napping when he did so. The young Belgian Van Sweevelt was more alert, and managed to get past the French duo. He never won another race of note.

Merckx and Godefroot went into the 1969 edition of Liège with another spring Classics win apiece, having swapped the Flanders and Roubaix titles. The key moment at Liège came on the Côte de Stockeu, a ramp that launches riders up from the bridge where the American forces valiantly held off the German attempt to take Stavelot in 1944. The approach to it from the Côte de Wanne is extremely fast until the very final moment, when the riders have to negotiate a ridiculously tight 180-degree 'dead' turn, from which the climb starts immediately and steeply. As all but the very front runners lose every bit of momentum they had on the descent, positioning is vital. If you're any more than a handful of riders back from the front, the pitches of up to 24 per cent that lie ahead can be torturous.

Merckx and Faema teammate Vic Van Schil led into the corner and accelerated hard as they climbed the Stockeu. Although one of the shorter climbs on the Liège route, the descent off it back into Stavelot comes just as suddenly and is almost as steep. As the Faema pair plummeted down it, their lead was already 100m. Having swept over the bridge and juddered along the cobbled streets weaving through the centre of picturesque Stavelot, Merckx and Van Schil were quickly on to the much longer Haute Levée, a broad boulevard of a climb. Working in tandem, their advantage stretched hugely.

In the group chasing behind, Britain's Barry Hoban was with Felice Gimondi and Belgians Jos Huysmans and Herman Van Springel. The Briton could sense the Belgian pair were reluctant to help, even though neither was in Faema colours. The fact they would be the following season may have explained their reticence. Nevertheless, Hoban couldn't help but be impressed. 'Basically, Merckx was doing exactly what he wanted.' And what Merckx wanted that day was to put on a demon-stration, to underline that he could pull off feats even his strongest rivals wouldn't contemplate. After working in tandem over the 100km between the Stockeu and the finish, Merckx and Van Schil rode on to the Rocourt eight minutes ahead, the masterful Merckx leading the pair over the line. Hoban won the sprint for third, becoming the first British rider to finish on the Liège podium.

Although Merckx admitted he was never as strong following a terrible crash on the velodrome in Blois in late 1969, when his motor-pacer died and he himself was left unconscious, the incident didn't appear to reduce his potency during the subsequent spring Classics campaign. His five-minute win at Roubaix left everyone but Roger De Vlaeminck astounded. Hailed as the new Van Looy and sharing that star rider's elevated assessment of his own ability and refusal to bend before Merckx, De Vlaeminck insisted he would not have been dropped at Roubaix if he hadn't punctured. Indeed, the incident had encouraged Merckx to attack. De Vlaeminck said he would back up that claim by sticking with Merckx at Liège, and duly delivered on that promise. Better still, he was first over the line at the Rocourt, although controversy still surrounds what exactly went on in the tunnel leading under the grandstands and out on to the track.

All that can be said for certain is that half a dozen riders went into the tunnel together and De Vlaeminck emerged from it at high speed and on his own. De Vlaeminck continues to insist he accelerated into the right-hand bend out of the tunnel as his brother Eric moved left, unintentionally blocking Merckx and in doing so preventing him from responding to that acceleration. After his enforced hesitation, Merckx couldn't do any better than third as Frans Verbeeck led in the quintet left stranded a dozen seconds behind De Vlaeminck.

This defeat rankled with Merckx, even more so when the Belgian press started questioning his comparative lack of success the following spring. For them, a fourth Sanremo win wasn't enough. 'If I win too often, they get tired of it, but if I go three races without winning, they talk about decline,' Merckx complained, having missed out on Flanders and Roubaix and been forced to skip Flèche Wallonne due to a stomach problem. Although this had weakened him and Liège started in conditions so cold 'The Cannibal' was wearing two jerseys and thick woollen gloves, he instructed his Molteni teammates to make the going hard almost from the off with the evident goal of avoiding a repeat of the mugging he had suffered 12 months earlier.

In essence, his strategy mirrored his approach in 1969. He ordered his Molteni lieutenant Jos Bruyère to ride to his limit from the foot of the Stockeu. In *Carnets de Route*, Merckx detailed how the race unfolded from the Stockeu. 'Joseph went *à bloc* [riding as hard as he could, often described as 'full gas' in the modern era] and after 50 metres I pressed on the pedal and went past him. When I turned around a few moments later I was very surprised to see that behind me it was already complete chaos. No one could follow, not even Roger De Vlaeminck. I was alone. Ninety kilometres from Rocourt! But it was too late to rethink. Allowing my rivals to rejoin me would only boost their confidence. On the contrary, I had to deliver a knock-out immediately.'

Although he admitted he had committed his 'first major mistake' of the race, Merckx persisted with his effort, bridging across a six-minute gap to leaders Yves Hézard and his Molteni teammate Jos Spruyt in the space of 20km. After riding with this duo for ten kilometres, Merckx pushed ahead on his own with 60km still to run. 'That was my second big mistake of the day. It was a real moment of madness. Spruyt wasn't "dead" in spite of his long escape. He was still capable of helping me for a very long time. If I had stayed with him I would have finished ten minutes ahead in the Rocourt. But I wanted to do better than that and come in alone. It almost resulted in disaster.'

On the Côte des Forges and, much more severely, on Mont Theux, Merckx began to succumb to the after-effects of his illness. His legs turned to wood and the pain in his lungs was agonising. His five-minute lead began to evaporate. Hearing that Georges Pintens, who thrived in the longest races and on the toughest days but had attacked only with the aim of securing second place, was gaining ground rapidly, Merckx realised he had to get over the cobbled climb of the Côte de Thiers on his own. Once on the flat run-in to the Rocourt, he might have a chance of outwitting Pintens. Cresting the Thiers, his lead was a mere 30 seconds. Merckx coasted down on to the flat, munching his way through two sandwiches. He guessed Pintens would attack as soon as he joined him and prepared himself to counter. 'I knew that if I managed to stay with him the race was as good as won.'

Coming up to the fading leader, Pintens accelerated, but found Merckx on his wheel. Pintens gestured for him to come through, but Merckx refused. 'Even taking into account my fatigue, I could have ridden behind Pintens for hours. Even after barely three kilometres on his wheel, before we reached the velodrome, I felt a lot better. Pintens knew perfectly well what was about to happen. He knew he would not win. He led out the sprint and I passed him without any problem going into the penultimate bend.'

Both men finished happy, Pintens because he had closed down a gap of five minutes in 45km on the world's best rider and almost beaten him, Merckx because Pintens had failed to do so, although he confessed he didn't have the strength to raise a smile. 'I have never suffered so much. It goes without saying that it was the most difficult race of my whole career, and that it is also perhaps one of my most beautiful victories,' he said. He admitted to being presumptuous in his estimation of his strength, but explained, 'It didn't matter. I had won. If Pintens had won I would have crumbled and gone over my mistakes a thousand times. But I had won and so all that was forgotten – the mistakes and the suffering.'

As was the case on other occasions, Merckx's victory against the odds, when it was clear he was suffering, brought him far more praise than his greatest solo exploits. The press acclaimed Merckx for his victory, insisting his determination not to yield, having made such obvious errors, only elevated the status of his success.

Defending the title in 1972, 'The Cannibal' once again attacked on the Stockeu. On this occasion, with the finish located just 45km away in Verviers, his move was reasonable rather than rash, or at least it was for a rider of Merckx's unparalleled quality. He finished 2′40″ up on second-placed Wim Schepers, with his principal rivals scattered in his wake. *La Doyenne* returned to the Rocourt for a final time in 1973,

Merckx wrapping up a third win in a row, although only the photo finish confirmed he had beaten Frans Verbeeck by millimetres.

Toughening up *La Doyenne*

Viral pneumonia prevented Merckx defending his title in 1974 and left him without a spring Classics victory for the first time in his career. It also resulted in him missing two innovations on the Liège route. After a decade-long link with the Rocourt, the finale was moved from the crumbling stadium that has since been demolished to the Boulevard de la Sauvenière in central Liège. Before that, though, the riders would have to tackle a new climb, the Côte de la Redoute, located on the northern edge of Remouchamps and running parallel to the recently opened E25 autoroute linking Liège to Luxembourg.

The approach to the climb provides no clue to the difficulty of the test that lies ahead. After a high-speed descent from Mont Theux down into Remouchamps, the route runs along the east bank of the Amblève and weaves through the town's backstreets to a tight T-junction, where a sharp right leads on to the initial pitches of the climb. Only when the road turns right again after passing beneath the autoroute that runs between Hoek van Holland and the Sicilian city of Palermo do the riders encounter the toughest sections. La Redoute averages 9.5 per cent over 1.7km, with the final 700m averaging 12 per cent as the road climbs past a war memorial marking the scene of the Battle of Sprimont, where the French army defeated the Austrians on 18 September 1794, leading to the end of Austrian rule on the western side of the Rhine.

Without Merckx to provide a focus, his rivals ended up marking each other out of contention, leaving second-string performers to enjoy the limelight. Georges Pintens featured, but once again his lack of finishing speed thwarted him as Flandria's Ronald De Witte took the title. However, it was soon revealed that De Witte had tested positive along with two other top ten finishers, handing Pintens the crown his efforts deserved.

Merckx returned in 1975 as the world champion and on the back of victories at Sanremo and Flanders. Despite these latest additions to his stellar roll of honour, there were signs he was becoming less Cannibal-like in his performances. He depended more on race craft and pure grit than the extraordinary exploits of his earlier years. His by now well telegraphed assault on the Stockeu didn't blow the group containing the likely contenders to smithereens as it would have done even a couple of years before. When he reached the top of the climb, where a monument now stands to mark his achievements – Merckx's power captured perfectly as he is depicted almost blasting out of the bronze cast – he turned to find Godefroot, Roger De Vlaeminck and Bernard Thévenet among the riders on his wheel.

With a group of three still clear, Merckx set about reeling them in, gradually sapping the vim from his rivals' legs. With 15km remaining and Frenchman Jean-Pierre Danguillaume, nephew of 1949 champion Camille, still holding a useful buffer, De Vlaeminck and Frans Verbeeck added more substance to the pace-making. Thanks to them, Danguillaume's hopes ended eight kilometres from home. 'The descents were too long, the straights never-ending,' he complained, but they still offered Merckx a possibility of escaping the faster finishers. He made several attacks, each of them countered by De Vlaeminck, then charged after Thévenet after the Frenchman clipped away on the finishing 'circuit' that went up one side of the Boulevard de la Sauvinière, then turned 180 degrees to come back down the other. Merckx passed Thévenet with several hundred metres remaining and didn't so much sprint as maintain a pace that no one could better. Roared on by a partisan crowd, he was several lengths clear of Thévenet at the line.

Merckx triumphed in just one more Monument, taking his Sanremo haul to seven the following spring. Yet, even though he failed to finish on the podium at Liège in 1976, he played a key role in an emotional victory for his faithful lieutenant Jos Bruyère. Born in nearby Maastricht, just over the border in the Netherlands, but brought up in Liège, Bruyère was at that point best known as Merckx's long-time room-mate and the only rider to have worn the Tour de France's yellow jersey in England, doing so on the race's short foray to Plymouth in 1974.

Sturdy, strong and fiercely loyal to the point where he had been known to punch riders who attempted to escape from the lockdown Molteni would impose, Bruyère was one of six riders who went away with 100km remaining. On La Redoute he eased away from the last of them, Herman Van Springel, and crested it with two minutes in hand on a ten-strong chase group that included Merckx. On this occasion, the Molteni team leader played the loyal domestique, disrupting attempts to pursue Bruyère, who finished almost five minutes clear and was embraced by tearful race organiser Émile Masson. Walloon victories in *La Doyenne* are infrequent, those by riders from Liège even rarer.

Two years later, in 1978, Bruyère completed a second victory in Liège, this one coming in the absence of Merckx, who had ridden his last race in mid-March but didn't announce his retirement for another two months. Bruyère's second *Doyenne* repeated the pattern of his first. He joined a small break a long way out from the finish and rode away from his final companion, Michel Pollentier, on La Redoute.

'The Badger' succeeds 'The Cannibal'

As Merckx faded and Bruyère made the most of that short period riding for his own glory, French riders were re-emerging as a force in the Classics. Since the retirement of Jacques Anquetil at the end of 1969, Raymond Poulidor had usually been a lone French raider on the roads of *La Doyenne*. From the mid-1970s, though, the evergreen veteran was joined by Thévenet, Merckx's conqueror at the 1975 Tour de France, and promising youngsters such as Jean-Pierre Danguillaume, Michel Laurent and Régis Ovion. Best of the crop was Breton Bernard Hinault, who had turned pro in 1975 and quickly established a reputation for being both talented and bull-headed. Boosted by the arrival of the recently retired rider Cyrille Guimard as team director at Gitane in 1976, Hinault had something of Merckx about him. He was nicknamed 'The Badger' and shared that animal's fierceness when cornered, although the tag derived from general use of the word to mean 'mate' or 'buddy' among young Bretons in the 1970s. Although happy to let others take the limelight at lesser events, Hinault tended to feature strongly in those that were particular targets.

Like Merckx, he relished the challenge Liège provided and right from his debut in the race in 1977 it became his Classic of choice. He went into it with a rising reputation elevated further by a solo victory at Gent–Wevelgem five days before, and stayed up towards the front of the bunch as a fierce wind barrelled across the open plains beyond the turn at Bastogne. Just past Houffalize, the peloton split into five sections. The front group of 40-odd riders featured most of the big names. The race was over for everyone behind this group.

World champion Freddy Maertens had just won Flèche Wallonne thanks to a Merckx-like display on the Stockeu and repeated this treatment on that key climb in Liège, reducing the front group to just 11 members, including Merckx, Bruyère, De Vlaeminck, Verbeeck, Germany's Didi Thurau, and Hinault. Maertens, pumping thighs the size of Serrano hams, turned the screw again on the final and steepest ramps of Mont Theux, shedding another half-dozen. On the Côte des Forges, on the outskirts of Liège, Thurau escaped from the world champion's grip. Merckx and De Vlaeminck reeled him in three kilometres later, only for André Dierickx to counter.

Hinault shot after the Belgian, then sat on his wheel as the gap between them and Belgium's three superstars plus Thurau remained at around five seconds. 'Cyrille Guimard drove alongside to ask if I was all right, and I told him that I was really flying, I could hardly feel the pedals. Guimard then told me that if things continued as they were going, and it came to the sprint, for me to go first, then ease, and then kick through again,' Hinault told *International Cycle Sport*.

'For several kilometres, until we came into the Liège limits, I didn't relay the Belgian, whom I considered to be much stronger than I, having already two wins in Flèche Wallonne under his belt. However, when I finally realised that we were really out on our own for good, then I did my part to the full.

'My top gear was just smaller than Dierickx's – I would have to push a 53x14 whilst the Belgian could drop on to a 13 sprocket. However, in the time it took for Dierickx to change up, I was off and away. I couldn't see any finish banner, just that the passage narrowed down and I could see all the photographers at the far end … then I knew that I'd got it. Thanks to Guimard!'

By opting to ride the Vuelta a España in the spring of 1978, claiming his first grand tour win in the process, Hinault passed on the defence of his title. He returned as the Tour de France champion in 1979, finishing second behind solo winner Thurau. A year later, on 20 April 1980, he lined up with 174 others for what would become the most renowned edition of *La Doyenne*, and is perhaps the single most discussed and written about Classic in racing history.

It was cold and snowy when the 174 starters left Liège. As they climbed up to the ridge on the southern edge of the city, riders were already starting to abandon. Belgian climber Lucien Van Impe pulled over to the side of the road and pleaded with the driver of a car heading north to give him a lift back to Liège. Others sought sanctuary in cafés. As the peloton descended from the ridge down towards Aywaille, the snow got thicker, encouraging large groups of riders to pull over and quit. Renault-Gitane team boss Guimard reckoned this was one of the key points of the race, as the snowstorm blew past in a few minutes, but by the time it did there were only 60-odd riders still heading south towards Bastogne.

The snow steadily eased, although it remained bitterly cold. Riding with teammate Maurice Le Guilloux, Hinault talked about quitting at Bastogne, but Le Guilloux urged him to continue. The sun made a brief appearance when the remains of the peloton rode towards and through Bastogne. Seeing it, Hinault decided the worst of the day had passed and pressed on. Yet he began to have second thoughts when the snow returned crossing the open ground above the St-Roch climb at Houffalize.

'If it's still snowing at the feed station, I'm stopping,' Hinault told Le Guilloux, as his teammate used one hand to steer his bike and the other to keep the snow out of his eyes. The feed station was at Vielsalm, right before the climb of the Côte de Wanne, where the serious racing really began. 'I think that if I hadn't been there, "The Badger" would have abandoned,' Le Guilloux told *L'Équipe*'s Philippe Bouvet some years later. 'I think he wanted to be the last one on the team in the race, the final one to abandon the sinking ship.'

Just as it had done at Bastogne, the sun made another brief appearance at Vielsalm. Guimard drove up alongside his team leader. 'Take off your rain-jacket,' he told him. 'The race is starting now.' Hinault initially refused, but Guimard insisted and the jacket came off. 'Until then I hadn't really paid any attention to the race, but now my teeth were chattering and I had no protection. I decided the only thing I could do was to ride as hard as I could to keep myself warm,' he said later.

Hinault headed on to the Côte de Wanne, where snow was lying 20cm deep at the roadside. Thanks to the passage of the first vehicles in the race convoy, the road surface was covered with slush that was more of a discomfort than a danger. Heading off that hill and down towards the foot of the Stockeu, Hinault was a little more than two minutes down on Belgian Rudy Pevenage, with a handful of other riders in the gap between them. This is where Hinault's epic performance really began.

He surged up the Stockeu, going clear of the group chasing Pevenage. On the Haute Levée, which rises steadily out of Stavelot, he collected Ludo Peeters, Henk Lubberding and Silvano Contini, leading them across to Pevenage. Hinault stayed at the front, accelerating slightly, wanting to drag the group away from any other riders who might be chasing behind. After a few hundred metres, he looked back to see if any of his breakaway companions were ready to assist with the pace-making, only to find he was on his own. He was 80km from the finish. The snow had finally relented, but the icy cold hadn't.

Over the Rosiers, La Redoute and the Côte des Forges, Hinault went further and further clear. Asked later about being alone in the cold, he admitted it was hard: 'I didn't look at anything. I didn't see anything. I only thought about myself.' Then he corrected himself, pointing out the one thing he had noticed were the fans who had been waiting all day in the same conditions for the riders to pass. 'It must have been extremely tough for them,' he said.

Hinault rode on to the Boulevard de la Sauvenière, receiving acclaim from dozens of the riders who had abandoned earlier in the day and hundreds of fans, but he barely responded to their cheers. Some suggested he was angered by the ordeal the riders had been put through. Hinault, however, had another explanation for the absence of a finish-line celebration. 'I didn't raise my arms, partly because everyone knew I had won, but also because I was completely done. If I had raised my arms, I would have fallen flat on my face,' he said.

More than nine minutes passed before Hennie Kuiper and Ronny Claes came through to take second and third, respectively. Twenty-seven minutes after Hinault had finished, Norway's Jostein Wilmann, the twenty-first and final finisher, rolled across the line.

Hinault returned to his hotel, where his teammates had a hot bath waiting for him. Instead of climbing in, he emptied it and filled it with cold water, stepped in and began the process of thawing himself out. It took three weeks for the feeling to return fully in his hands, but even now, more than 30 years later, he still feels the after-effects of that race. 'My fingers are still very sensitive to the cold. I always have to wear gloves if it gets down to three or four degrees,' he told *La Dernière Heure* on the thirtieth anniversary of a race that no French rider has subsequently won.

'I still have very good memories of that day, even though I didn't realise how the cold was going to affect my fingers. I suffered, but not physically. My legs were in good shape. I was there to win a race that I enjoyed, unlike the Tour of Flanders and Paris–Roubaix. I used to ride Liège and Flèche just about every year,' he said. Asked about his thought of quitting, he replied: 'When you're in that scenario, when you are at the front, you forget the cold, the snow and the freezing rain. You don't abandon. When you are in form, you can deal with anything. The heat and the cold are tough, but you can deal with them mentally. On the sporting side, it was actually quite an easy win because of the conditions.'

Speaking on his fiftieth birthday to French magazine *Vélo*, whose readers had voted his second win in *La Doyenne* the greatest of his career, Hinault typically played down its significance. 'It was a nice moment in my career. But, the snow apart, I was on a great day, so the victory was logical, although perhaps not easy. I wasn't so much fighting against my rivals as against the cold …'

A new force emerges

During the early 1980s, English-speaking riders began to feature regularly among the contenders at Liège and the other Monuments for the first time. Up to that point, the only English-speaker to win one of the big Classics had been Britain's Tom Simpson, who had bagged the Flanders, Sanremo and Lombardy titles in the early 1960s. Two decades on, a wave of highly talented and competitive English-speakers arrived on the scene, led by Irishmen Stephen Roche and Sean Kelly, both of whom finished in the top ten at Liège in 1982. A year later, Australia's Phil Anderson was fourth. Consequently, it was not a huge surprise when an English-speaker finally took the title in 1984, that honour going to Kelly, who outsprinted Anderson and American Greg LeMond on the Boulevard de la Sauvenière.

Approaching La Redoute, the last big climb of the race, Anderson was on the attack with Tour de France champion Laurent Fignon, who was reluctant to commit himself fully until much closer to the finish. Although Anderson managed to drop Fignon on La Redoute, the Frenchman caught the Australian once they were on the flat section that followed. Encouraged by Panasonic's martinet team director, Peter Post, who came up regularly to bellow instructions at him, Anderson kept attacking, frustrated by Fignon's lack of co-operation. Ultimately, though, the pair's start-stop antics enabled Walloon favourite Claude Criquielion to bridge across at the front of a small group that included Kelly, LeMond and defending champion Steven Rooks.

For 'Criq', whose dark, bushy eyebrows always made him easy to pick out in the years before helmets and sunglasses became *de rigueur*, Liège was the biggest day on the racing calendar. Although born just a handful of kilometres from Geraardsbergen, one of iconic points of the Tour of Flanders, his home in Lessines was on the other side of the border between Wallonia and Flanders. Fourth in 1982, Criquielion had the endurance and explosive climbing ability required to win Liège, but consistently found himself matched against riders who simply had too much finishing speed. In 1984, that man was world number one Kelly. After the sprightly Walloon had tried and failed to go clear, and similar efforts by Renault's Marc Madiot and Fignon had been snuffed out, the latter just 100m from the line, Kelly flashed down the right-hand barriers with Anderson and LeMond vainly trying to get on terms. But the result was never in doubt. Kelly threw his right arm straight up in traditional fashion.

'King' Kelly had a strong attachment to Liège throughout his career. Unlike Roubaix and Flanders, which he viewed as complicated races where crashes were likely and bad luck never too far away, he regarded *La Doyenne* as a more simple affair, but no less tough than the cobbled Classics. 'It's the most beautiful of the Classics. Like the Tour of Lombardy, if you are riding well you are going to be at the front. You're not sure of winning, but in races like that when you are strong it's much easier,' he explained during his post-racing career as a commentator for Eurosport. 'Compared to the Tour of Flanders or Milan–Sanremo, there are also a lot fewer risks. In those races, when you're 80km from the finish, you look around you and see there are still lots of big names. At Liège, when riders are dropped they can't work their way back up to the front.'

Kelly claimed a second victory in Liège five years later, by which time Criquielion had started to realise there would always be at least one man better than him in *La Doyenne*. More often than not, that man was Moreno Argentin, who established himself as the best Ardennes campaigner since Eddy Merckx, although controversy was never too far away from an Italian perhaps not unfairly given the Mafia-like nickname, 'Il Capo'.

4

TOUGHER THAN THE REST

When Claude Criquielion retired at the end of 1991, his reflections on his 13 seasons as a pro centred less on the races he had won – of which there were plenty, including the World Championship in 1984 and the Tour of Flanders three years later – and more on those he hadn't. The one specific race Criq still gets asked about is the 1988 World Championship in Ronse, just eight kilometres from his home in Deux Acren. Coming into the final kilometre with Maurizio Fondriest, Criquielion looked to have the speed and certainly had the experience to beat the young Italian. Yet, with 700m remaining, the duo became a trio, as Canadian Steve Bauer took advantage of the cat-and-mouse between the leading two to bridge up to them.

The three men weaved back and forth on the uphill run to the line until, with 250m remaining, Bauer accelerated from the left- to the right-hand side of the road. Criquielion moved easily on to his wheel and spotted a gap on the Canadian's right alongside the barriers. As the Belgian dived into it, the partisan crowd roaring him on, Bauer reached for the gear lever on his downtube, glanced down for a moment, lurching to the right as he did so, sending Criquielion cartwheeling into the barriers and leaving the rest of the road open to Fondriest, who cruised to the easiest of victories. Bauer was stripped of silver for his manoeuvre and was then hit with a lawsuit by Criquielion, who demanded one million pounds in damages. The case dragged on for three years. Having lost on the road, however, the Belgian then lost again in the courts.

The other question Criquielion faced was how he never managed to win Liège, the race he coveted more than any other. 'I undoubtedly wanted to win it too much and I perhaps committed some errors, such as never really giving myself a chance in the final sprint in the way that I did in 1991,' he confessed to *La Dernière Heure* after retiring. 'But I was part of Argentin's generation and the Italian will go down as one of the great specialists in the Walloon race.'

Sean Kelly described Argentin as a rider who was not a natural climber, which counted against the Italian in grand tours. Yet, what Argentin did have, as Kelly acknowledged, was brute strength. A team pursuit specialist on the track as a youngster, Argentin was blessed with what is generally described now as 'a big engine'. The harder the race, the better Argentin performed, which meant *La Doyenne* suited him perfectly. Yet, it was Criquielion who went into the 1985 race as the clear favourite, partly due to his status as world champion, but largely thanks to a crushing victory in Flèche Wallonne four days before, when Argentin had been almost two minutes down in second place.

By that point, however, Flèche finished atop the one-in-six ramps of the Mur de Huy. Although longer and harder, Liège did not yet feature a tough climb within a few kilometres of its city-centre finish. Consequently, although Criquielion made his form count on the climbs, particularly on La Redoute, he could not shake all of his rivals. Coming into the finish, he still had Argentin and Irishman Stephen Roche for company. Sweeping around the 180-degree turn a few hundred metres from the finish on the Boulevard de la Sauvenière, Criquielion was in the ideal position at the rear of the trio, but threw away this advantage far too far from the line with an attack that did little more than set up Argentin to deliver a winning flourish that kept him just ahead of Roche.

Twelve months later, Criquielion, in dismally wet weather, relived those events almost to the letter. He went clear on La Redoute, was reeled in by Argentin, Adri Van der Poel and Dag-Erik Pedersen on the flat roads that followed, made a last-kilometre dash for glory and ended up last in the sprint as Argentin held on to his crown. In order to take the title, Criquielion ideally needed to come into the finish alone. Failing that, he had to do all he could to shake Argentin. In 1987, he finally managed this, but came away with more regrets than ever.

Oddly, Criquielion went into that edition of *La Doyenne* insisting his chances of winning the title had been compromised by an enforced change to the route that would result in the absence of the Haute Levée climb for several years. Generally, vehicles of more than seven tonnes were prohibited from using the long descent into Stavelot, but the previous August the ban had been temporarily lifted because the alternative route into the town was part of the circuit being used for the Francorchamps 24-hour touring car race. Coming towards the steeper sections at the bottom of the descent, a coach driver lost control of his vehicle when the brakes failed. The coach hurtled through the busy junction at the foot of the Haute Levée and ploughed into a bank on the other side of the highway. Eight people died and 42 were injured in the tragedy, which led to emergency slip roads being built on the Haute Levée.

Unfortunately, a dozen years later, the inefficacy of these emergency escape routes was revealed when a similar incident occurred. A truck driver ignored the signs indicating the ban on heavy vehicles, lost his brakes and crashed into the façade of a hotel at the bottom of the Haute Levée. The truck, which was carrying toluene, a highly flammable substance used in road marking, exploded on impact, killing two people and injuring many others. The resulting fire also destroyed a dozen buildings in Stavelot's old quarter. This incident led to the introduction of additional safety features on the climb, including the construction of a concrete barrier in the middle of the road on the lower section of the Haute Levée that is designed to divert out-of-control vehicles away from the centre of Stavelot.

As it turned out, the absence of the Haute Levée in 1987 worked in Criquielion's favour as, instead of making his usual lone, long-distance bid for glory, he held back, allowing Liège's attritional course to take its toll. He went on to the final climb, the Côte des Forges, with only Argentin and Roche for company. There, the Belgian's acceleration proved too much for the Italian, who steadily lost ground and fell back to Scot Robert Millar and Frenchman Yvon Madiot a minute behind the leading pair as they rode on to the Boulevard de la Sauvenière to decide the race between them.

Yet, Criquielion and Roche had both come into Liège with a monkey on their back. Even though the Belgian had recently won Flanders, he was still concerned about his regular failures at Liège and how best to rectify them. The Irishman Roche, meanwhile, was on the verge of the greatest run of form of his career, which would see him win the Triple Crown of the Giro d'Italia, the Tour de France and the World Championship in the same season, a feat only achieved by Eddy Merckx. However, during the early season, Roche had ridden very well but hadn't claimed the victories he should have. After finishing fourth at Flèche Wallonne, his Carrera team director Davide Boifava told him: 'Stephen, you're riding so, so well but you haven't won any big ones yet this year. You're knocking on the door, you're riding aggressively, you're in all the good moves, but you're just not quite pulling it off. You've got to be prepared to lose to win.'

Four days later, when he rode into Liège with Criquielion, Boifava's words were still in Roche's mind. Writing in his autobiography, *Born to Ride*, Roche recalled: 'I thought that if I led Criquielion out in the sprint there was a good chance he'd beat me, but if he led me out there was a good chance I'd beat him. However, for some totally unfathomable reason, we both forgot that there were still other guys in the race, that the rest of the field hadn't all just climbed off.

'I was so focused on what Boifava had told me that all I could do was think about Criquielion. Coming down the final section on the Boulevard de la Sauvenière, we went around a roundabout and back up the other side of the road we'd just come down. You would imagine that any rider in that position would have glanced across to check what was happening behind. Even now I still think: "Why didn't I look back and see if the other guys were closing?" I can understand why some people don't believe that I didn't see Moreno Argentin coming before we started to sprint.

'With 200 metres remaining, I started to come off Criquielion's wheel and "Whoosh!" Argentin came flying past me and beat me to the line by about half a bike-length, with Criquielion third. Even 25 years on, the hairs still stand out on my arms when I think about that.' On the long drive back to his home in Paris, Roche kept turning over events at the finish. 'I was asking myself: "Did I almost win Liège–Bastogne–Liège? Was I so stupid that I didn't see Argentin coming from behind? Why didn't I look across? Why was I being so stupid focusing completely on Criquielion? How has this happened? Is this a nightmare? Will I wake up and find it didn't happen?" But when I woke the next morning, of course, I was still second and even to this day it haunts me. I think it was the only time after a race that I cried.'

Criquielion was equally disappointed, especially having achieved what had previously proved impossible and dropped Argentin. 'I don't know if you can understand what it is like for a rider who has just done 260km as tough as those, who thinks that he is finally going to win, and then realises at the last moment he has a sprinter on his wheel,' he told *L'Équipe*'s Philippe Bouvet.

The following year, Argentin did end up second behind a lone winner, but it was the Germans who celebrated as Rolf Gölz became their first victor of *La Doyenne*. His triumph was overshadowed, though, by an horrific crash as the bunch descended at high speed into Houffalize, location of the race's first significant climb, the Côte de Saint Roch. Coming unexpectedly upon roadworks on the left-hand side of the course, dozens of riders switched suddenly to the right, unwittingly creating a domino effect that left 50 riders on the deck. Worse still, as the cars in the race convoy immediately behind the riders screeched to a stop, American rider Davis Phinney ploughed into the rear window of the Isoglass team car, sustaining deep cuts to his face that required 150 stitches.

In the wake of that horrific incident, the Pesant Club Liégeois that had organised the race almost since its foundation approached the Société du Tour de France, which also organises Paris–Roubaix, to discuss the possibility of sharing organisational responsibility for Liège. In December 1989, the talks led to a formal agreement between the two sides and some radical alterations to the route. Forced to look for another finish location in 1990 due to substantial redevelopment in the heart of Liège, the new organising team moved it to the Quai Mativa, on the far bank of the Meuse from the city centre. More controversial was the dropping of the Côte de Stockeu, initially made famous by the exploits of Eddy Merckx, but now infamous as the result of an incident in 1985 when the excessive number of cars and motorbikes in the race convoy brought the riders to a halt. Few disputed the need for change and even less so when the 1990 edition produced a home winner.

Finally, a swarthy Belgian with startling eyebrows did finish alone in Liège to end a drought that stretched back to Jos Bruyère's second success in 1978, but that man was Fleming Eric Van Lancker and not Walloon favourite Claude Criquielion. His victory in 1990 came as a surprise to everyone apart from the Belgian, who had won the Dutch Classic, the Amstel Gold Race, the year before. Part of the powerful Panasonic team still tightly marshalled by Peter Post, Van Lancker wasn't in the group of big names that included Argentin, Criquielion and Panasonic duo Steven Rooks and Gert-Jan Theunisse who went clear on La Redoute. However, with two teammates up ahead, Van Lancker didn't have to collaborate in the pursuit undertaken by the second group on the road, which left him relatively fresh when the two groups joined approaching the Côte de Hornay, 20km from the finish.

'When I realised Argentin was in the group, I knew that once again he was the man to beat. We absolutely had to try something to prevent him winning, so I attacked as everyone looked at each other,' Van Lancker explained post-race. Returning to the site of his winning attack two decades later with *Procycling*, Van Lancker pointed out a Q8 petrol station with particular significance for him. 'By the time I reached the petrol station I was committed. The road is still a special one for me. I'll never forget it. It sounds silly but whenever I see a Q8 – even in the centre of Brussels – it reminds me of that day.'

Doping casts a shadow

For the next decade, one man regularly proved he held the key to winning *La Doyenne*. A former domestique to Felice Gimondi in the 1960s who didn't win a race of note as a pro, Giancarlo Ferretti moved into team management with Bianchi in 1973 and over the following three decades established himself as one of the most successful directors in racing history. Nicknamed 'The Iron Sergeant' for the discipline he imposed on his riders or, more commonly, 'Ferron', the Italian and his teams had a particular affinity with the Ardennes Classics.

Ferretti's run of success began in 1982 when Silvano Contini outsprinted Belgian Fons De Wolf and Swiss Stefan Mutter to capture the title for Bianchi. However, Ferretti cemented his reputation when he was brought in to manage the Ariostea team in 1986. With Ferron calling the shots, Ariostea soon began to scoop the prestigious wins the previous directors had been unable to deliver. In 1990, Argentin joined the squad, providing an iron presence on the road to go with Ferretti's in the team car. The new partnership was particularly potent in the Ardennes, Argentin winning a first Flèche Wallonne title that spring, then completing the Ardennes double the year after, relegating Criquielion to second place at Liège once again.

Argentin brought a key ally with him when he joined Ariostea. After an injury- and illness-affected 1988 season, he began to work with Italian sports scientist and training consultant Dr Michele Ferrari.

Widely hailed as the best cycling coach in the business, Ferrari would go on to work with many of the sport's leading riders and would later gain a far less savoury reputation for providing prescriptions for and advice on doping products, including the blood-boosting hormone EPO. However, in the late 1980s at least, there is no evidence that Ferrari was doing anything other than offering riders under his charge the most expert training advice then available.

A race report in *Le Soir* on the 1991 edition of Liège describes Argentin as a 'fully fulfilled' rider as a result of working with Ferrari. He was certainly happy to come out on top in a four-man group that went clear on La Redoute under the impetus of Argentin's Ariostea teammate Rolf Sørensen. Cresting the top of the climb, the Dane was joined by Argentin, Criquielion and Spaniard Miguel Indurain, who would go on to win the first of five consecutive Tour de France titles later that year. Up against two Ariostea riders, the Belgian and the Spaniard never looked likely to win. Although Criquielion pushed Argentin close in the sprint, there was still a bike length between them at the line, where Sørensen, coming through to take third, was already punching the air with delight at his teammate's win.

The success led to the Italian media anointing Ferrari as 'The Sorceror of Liège–Bastogne–Liège'. He played down the nickname, pointing out, 'I've lost more *Doyennes* than I've won. So I am not a magician.' Yet suspicion began to grow that there were some conjurers working with leading members of the professional peloton. This became more evident in the spring of 1994, when Argentin led home Gewiss teammates Giorgio Furlan and Evgeni Berzin at Flèche Wallonne after the trio had gone clear on the second of three ascents of the Mur de Huy with 70km remaining to the finish. Coming on the back of a shock *La Doyenne* win for the hitherto little-known Russian Berzin, who had finished almost two minutes clear of a small group led in by world champion Lance Armstrong, it was an eyebrow-raising result.

In an interview with *L'Équipe* that appeared the day after Flèche, Gewiss team doctor Ferrari, who had followed Argentin to the squad, did little to quell speculation of doping. Although he denied supplying Gewiss riders with EPO, Ferrari declared: 'But one can buy EPO in Switzerland, for example, without a prescription, and if a rider does, that doesn't scandalise me. EPO doesn't fundamentally change the performance of a racer.'

When *L'Équipe*'s Jean-Michel Rouet replied: 'But it is dangerous! Ten Dutch riders have died in the last few years,' Ferrari answered: 'EPO is not dangerous, it's the abuse that is. It's also dangerous to drink ten litres of orange juice.' The furore provoked by this comment resulted in Ferrari being sacked by Gewiss. However, rather than damaging Ferrari's reputation, it appeared to enhance it.

In 1995, he started working with Armstrong, who would become his most famous and ultimately most notorious client when he was stripped of his seven Tour de France titles having admitted to using EPO from that year up to his first retirement from racing in 2005. Among the many who worked with Ferrari were several riders who won Monuments, including Alexandre Vinokourov, Gianluca Bortolami, Mario Cipollini, Claudio Chiappucci, Tony Rominger and Tyler Hamilton. In July 2012, the US Anti-Doping Agency charged Ferrari with administration and trafficking of prohibited substances. When Ferrari failed to contest the indictment, USADA issued him with a lifetime ban from working in professional sport. In an interview with Al-Jazeera in December 2012, Ferrari maintained Armstrong had ridden clean throughout his career, a claim the American shot down himself when he confessed to doping to Oprah Winfrey a month later.

In March 2013, 1993 Liège champion Rolf Sørensen, who had been one of the stalwarts at Ariostea and later the Dutch Rabobank team, admitted he had used EPO 'periodically in the nineties'. The Dane refused to be drawn on specific dates and said the doping he had undertaken was entirely his responsibility. 'There is no other excuse than that I did what I felt compelled to do to be an equal among peers,' he also stated.

More and tougher climbs

When Flèche Wallonne joined the Société du Tour de France stable of races in 1993, Tour director Jean-Marie Leblanc reintroduced the Ardennes Weekend, which had last been contested in 1964. The STDF, which would later be rebranded as the cycling department with the ASO media and events group, had also continued to tinker with the route of *La Doyenne*, switching the finish from the Quai Mativa to Liège's very unremarkable north-western suburb of Ans.

Initially, this made very little difference to the race's finale, apart from making it much less impressive as it now finished on the edge of a supermarket car park, which has at least proved convenient from a logistical point of view. Climbs new and old have also come and gone. Happily for most fans of the race, the so-called 'trilogy of climbs' comprising the Côte de Wanne, the Stockeu and the Haute Levée has featured more often than not. However, many fans and riders insist one new climb changed the complexion of the race entirely, and not for the better.

In 1998, in an attempt to spice up what was a rather grim finale, Leblanc and his organising team added the Côte de Saint Nicolas to the route. Located on the western edge of Liège, it's a brute of a climb – not quite as tough as the Stockeu or Redoute in terms of gradient, but very much on a par with them because it was to come just five kilometres from the finish. The approach to it took the race through Liège's industrial quarter between the city and Seraing, once the generator of much of Belgium's wealth. During the late twentieth and early twenty-first centuries, the giant steel and coking plants and associated factories around them closed, resulting in industrial decay that has impacted heavily on the region's economy. Once Belgium's powerhouse, Liège and the rest of French-speaking Wallonia now lag a good way behind technologically advanced Flanders.

Once over the Meuse, the route wound around the industrial looking red grandstands of Standard Liège football club's stadium, through an industrial estate and some fairly mean streets to the rue du Bordelais, which climbs between terraced houses to two steep switchbacks overlooked by grimy tower blocks. Here, there would be plenty of Italian flags in evidence, the result of an initiative entitled 'Des Hommes contre le Charbon' (Men against Coal), established between Belgium and Italy in the wake of the Second World War. This saw thousands of Italians emigrate to Wallonia and take up residence in what is a 'Little Italy' on the western ridge above Liège.

The issue many had with this climb was that it was so tough it forced the contenders to hold back until the very end of the race, effectively neutralising previous ascents, including those in the trilogy and La Redoute. To back this up, they pointed to the recent lack of Merckxian exploits, those long-range attacks on the Stockeu, Haute Levée and La Redoute that benefited from a relatively straightforward run-in to the centre of Liège. Add in the final testing drag up to the finish in Ans, and you had a very different finish from those used before the 1990s.

'It falls so close to the finish that the favourites wait for it,' said Laurent Jalabert, runner-up to Italy's Michele Bartoli in 1997 and 1998. 'It's not long, but it's long enough to make the difference. At the same time, La Redoute is less decisive than it was. The tendency is for riders to delay their moment to attack until the last instant. They prefer to maintain a position among the leading 20 than to go for a long-range attack.'

To be fair to the race's organisers, Bartoli, who won both the last race before the Saint Nicolas and the first race with it, maintained La Redoute was still almost as significant as it had been before the introduction of the new climb, which was backed up by his success in 1998. With Evgeni Berzin away, Bartoli took up the chase on La Redoute and pulled a strong group across to the Russian on the penultimate climb of the

Côte du Sart-Tilman, where the Italian pressed the accelerator again and rode away to win on his own.

The 1999 race, though, gave a much better indication of the way the Saint Nicolas had changed the nature of the race, and also highlighted the talent of Belgium's newest star and most controversial rider. It came to life on La Redoute, when a group of almost 50 riders ended up shredded by an attack outrageous both in its strength and degree of showboating. The display was put on by Frank Vandenbroucke, a 24-year-old sporting bleached blond hair and goatee, who was already on his third team during what would be an erratic and ultimately tragic career.

It came after Bartoli had tried to impose himself on the climb of La Redoute for the third year in a row. Vandenbroucke eased up to the Italian and half-wheeled him, riding to the side but a little ahead of Bartoli, brazenly suggesting the Italian's attack hadn't troubled him too much while at the same time enquiring what he had left. Piqued by the upstart Belgian, Bartoli rode eyeballs out for a few more seconds, then had nothing left when 'VDB' shot off past him. Although Bartoli managed to stay with the lead group and was still in contention at the foot of the Saint Nicolas, neither he nor anyone else had any answer when Vandenbroucke chased up to Michael Boogerd, before leaving the Dutchman and the rest of the pack for dead.

Vandenbroucke's was the first Belgian triumph since Dirk De Wolf had become the first Liège winner in Ans in 1992. Unlike De Wolf, though, Vandenbroucke was still a rider with most of his career ahead of him, and few suggested it would be anything but glittering. However, after a storming performance later that same year at the Vuelta a España, VDB never won a notable title again. Nevertheless, he created headlines throughout the next decade and more as he lurched from crisis to comeback and back again.

The son of a good amateur rider who had been a mechanic on the Lotto team, and nephew of Jean-Luc Vandenbroucke, who won more than 70 races as a pro and went on to become the team director at Lotto, Frank was exposed to cycling from his early childhood. At the age of four, he used to race on a circuit around the church in his home town of Ploegstraat, near Mouscron. When he was five, VDB was knocked down by a rally car doing reconnaissance, sustaining a broken leg. His mother, Chantal, loved to tell journalists the story of how he didn't cry at all until the doctor took a pair of scissors to his cycling shorts.

Although the incident left him with one leg slightly shorter than the other, which resulted in persistent injury problems when he turned pro, Vandenbroucke was hot property from the off, and not always for the right reasons. He turned pro with uncle Jean-Luc's Lotto team in 1994, riding well enough to gain selection for Belgium's World Championships team that year. Boosted by his success and no lack of self-confidence, he also started to angle for a switch to Mapei, which boasted the sport's biggest budget and best roster of riders. Despite his uncle's determination to block the move, which led to a huge family blow-up, Vandenbroucke joined cycling's super-team in mid-1995.

His march towards the top of the sport was steady. Victory at Paris–Nice in 1998, when he was still only 23, marked him out as a possible grand tour contender. It also persuaded the French Cofidis team to offer him £500,000 a year to lead their talented but misfiring line-up. Victory at Liège–Bastogne–Liège indicated consumer credit company Cofidis had made a wise investment. However, the anything goes atmosphere that pervaded the French squad ultimately proved more seductive to the Belgian. Described by Belgian journalist Philippe Van Holle as 'a man who lives life at 200 kilometres per hour, and who parties to the max after a big win', VDB went on a legendary bender. Just weeks later, Cofidis suspended him for his links with French homeopath Bernard Sainz, dubbed 'Doctor Mabuse' and convicted to a year in prison in 2010 for encouraging riders to use doping products in the 1990s. Following an appeal, Sainz's sentence was reduced from prison time to a fine. However, he was later sentenced to prison in two further cases in 2020, for abetting doping practices and for practising as a doctor and a pharmacist when he had no licence for either profession. That verdict was confirmed in January 2022, when he was sentenced to a year's house arrest.

After two years in the wilderness, VDB rejoined former Mapei director Patrick Lefevere at Domo-Farm Frites in 2002. 'You have to accept him with his few faults and his many good qualities,' Lefevere had previously said of his new signing. 'He's not easy to manage. You have to bear in mind his psychology, overlook his whims.' Yet VDB's whims were getting the upper hand. Within months, police raided his house and seized EPO, Clenbuterol and morphine. Vandenbroucke said some of the products weren't his, insisting they were for his dog. The incident eventually led to a court case and, in December 2004, an admission by the rider that he had used these and other banned products.

What was perhaps his oddest moment came in the summer of 2006 when he turned up at an amateur race in Italy with a licence bearing the name Francesco Del Ponte – a rough translation of his name into Italian – and a photo of world champion Tom Boonen. In August 2009, just weeks after announcing all his problems were behind him and he was enjoying life again, Vandenbroucke died as the result of a pulmonary embolism during a holiday in Senegal. He was 34.

In the wake of Vandenbroucke's 1999 triumph, *La Doyenne* enjoyed mixed fortunes. Paolo Bettini's victorious performances in 2000 and 2002 received huge acclamation within the Italian community on the Côte de Saint Nicolas. Asked some years later where he would want a memorial erected if such an event were ever to take place, Bettini said the top of that climb would be the perfect setting thanks to the support he had received there and because of what his successes meant to Italians living in Belgium.

However, most of *La Doyenne*'s champions during the first decade of the twenty-first century ended up tainted by doping scandals, even though none occurred at the race itself. Liège champions Oscar Camenzind (2001), Tyler Hamilton (2003), Davide Rebellin (2004), Alexandre

Vinokourov (2005), Alejandro Valverde (2006 and 2008) and Danilo Di Luca (2007) all subsequently served bans for doping offences. Apart from Bettini, that decade's only Liège champion with an unblemished record is Luxembourg's Andy Schleck, whose success in 2009 was just the second for the Grand Duchy after Marcel Ernzer's win in 1954.

Another sting in the tail

The willowy Schleck's race-winning attack began on the newest addition to the list of climbs. Located 19km from the finish, La Roche-aux-Faucons was introduced in 2008. Explaining the replacement of the Sart–Tilman climb with the new and much tougher ascent, race director Christian Prudhomme said: 'We want to change little things each year in order to try to perfect the route. We will see if the Côte de la Roche-aux-Faucons will introduce new scenarios to the race, either due to its difficulty or because it breaks with established habits. Seeing a man finish alone would not displease me.'

Although generally listed as being 1.3km in length and averaging 10 per cent with ramps of up to 15 per cent, the climb actually extends to twice that length if the long drag up beyond 'the falcons' rock' is included. Riders generally agree it's this second section that makes the difference, as the strongest racers can extend any advantage they have eked out on those initial ramps, as Schleck demonstrated when he neutralised local hero Philippe Gilbert's bid for glory and rode away to finish more than a minute clear in Ans.

Very different from the much longer drag of the Sart–Tilman, the Roche-aux-Faucons is a close cousin of the Côte de Stockeu. It begins on the road out of Méry that runs alongside the River Ourthe. After a tight turn over a rough level crossing, the riders encounter a 'wall', kicking up immediately and hard. The road rises through a plush residential district – which provides quite a contrast to the setting for the race's final climb – then drops briefly into a saddle, before stepping up again to the Roche-aux-Faucons itself, a promontory offering a huge, vertigo-inducing vista over a sweeping 180-degree bend in the Ourthe, which sits 130m almost directly below. From there, it climbs more steadily but still for some distance to the main road.

Initially, Gilbert was among those who were less than impressed with the new climb, complaining, 'I don't know why they've toughened up the course. It's too much. The race is going to be very different ... The guys that get away there will be able to go all the way to the finish, even if there are only two or three of them.' Two years later, Gilbert's analysis proved spot on, although he was the one to benefit as the Walloon finally won the race he coveted more than any other after following an attack by the Schleck brothers on the Roche-aux-Faucons and outsprinting the pair in Ans.

Born in Verviers and brought up in Remouchamps, the town that sits at the foot of La Redoute, Gilbert looked set for the top even as an amateur, when he regularly got the better of Tom Boonen, Nick Nuyens and other budding Classics stars. His decision to turn pro with the French FDJ team in 2003 raised plenty of eyebrows in Belgium, but was a wise move as it removed him from the pressured environment in his home country, where the press are always on the lookout for the next Merckx, Van Looy or De Vlaeminck. In 2009, he finally returned home, signing for Silence-Lotto, the country's longest-standing team that was then co-sponsored by a company manufacturing a nasal spray to prevent snoring.

Team director Dirk De Wolf, winner of *La Doyenne* in 1992 and previously Gilbert's director when he rode for the Under-23 ABX-Go Pass team, had no doubt Gilbert would start winning major titles regularly. Speaking about his new leader's work ethic, De Wolf declared: 'You would only need ten riders on your team if they were all like Philippe Gilbert.' De Wolf went further, suggesting the Walloon could win any of the five Monuments and could one day put his name alongside those of Merckx, De Vlaeminck and Van Looy, who remain the only men to claim all five. 'Philippe is fast. He can win sprints in a small group and even uphill. He's tough and he's able to explode on small hills. He's an all-rounder. The only question mark I'd have is against Liège–Bastogne–Liège.'

De Wolf felt the changes to Liège's route had dented Gilbert's hopes of winning his favourite race, an assessment with which Gilbert agreed. However, in late 2010 and early 2011, Gilbert's form reached a level rarely seen since Merckx's era. Having retained the Tour of Lombardy crown at the end of 2010, he proved almost invincible in one-day races the following spring, winning the Strade Bianche, Brabantse Pijl, Amstel Gold, Flèche Wallonne and, finally, *La Doyenne*.

Looking back later at his Liège success, and many of those that had preceded it over the decade before, Gilbert pointed out that the bad publicity cycling had endured and that had eventually led to concerted action to tackle doping by the UCI and other bodies had benefited him and many other riders who had previously been illegitimately overshadowed: 'My breakthrough sort of coincided with the advent of the biological passport. I think my generation is very lucky to be tested as often as we are,' he told *Procycling*. 'Sometimes it's a pain – today, for example, we were supposed to be taking a rest from training, yet we got woken up at 7 a.m. to go for a dope test – but I say to myself that it's necessary.'

In 2013, as Gilbert strived for a second Liège success, he was upstaged by another rider who's been clear in his commitment to riding clean. Birmingham-born Irishman Dan Martin is the son of an English ex-pro, Neil Martin, and Tour de France winner Stephen Roche's sister, Maria. Small and frighteningly fragile looking, Martin is in his element on the climbs. Having opted to ride for Ireland rather than Britain, he turned pro in 2008 with the Garmin team, which has a well-established commitment to ensuring its riders and staff adhere strictly to anti-doping guidelines.

Writing in his *Procycling* column in 2009 after his second Liège appearance, the Irishman explained how testing the race was for inexperienced riders, highlighting the foot of the Côte de Wanne as a critical point, 'rarely ever seen on TV. If you are not up front it's pretty much race over as you hit the Wanne, Stockeu and Haute Levée in rapid succession.' He went on to highlight the difficulty of the Roche-aux-Faucons, describing it as 'the place to be', but admitting his only goal when he reached it was to survive to the finish. He reached it in ninety-ninth place.

By 2012, Martin had progressed to the point where he was among the dark horses for victory. Although he barely featured in the main action, he finished fifth behind surprise Kazakh winner Maxim Iglinskiy, demonstrating how *La Doyenne's* route rewarded riders who saved all they could for the tough finale in Ans rather than going all out on La Redoute. In 2013, Martin's strategy resulted in him going one better than his uncle Stephen, becoming the first Irishman since Sean Kelly in 1989 to bag the title.

With the Roche-aux-Faucons out of action because of roadworks, the race came to life on the Côte de Colonster climb that replaced it. On the long and unattractive dual-carriageway drag, Martin's Garmin team-mate Ryder Hesjedal attacked from a small group that had broken away on the climb and led over the top. The Canadian dropped like a stone through Seraing and was still on his own when he reached the Saint Nicolas. Half a dozen riders bridged across to him there, but Hesjedal kept pushing hard, determined to keep the break clear and give his Irish teammate a shot at the title. When featherweight Spanish climber Joaquim Rodríguez fizzed away with a kilometre left, Garmin's hopes appeared to have gone. But on the sapping pull up to the left-hand corner into the finishing straight Martin closed down the Spaniard's lead, urged on by a fan in a panda suit sprinting behind them, and then sprang away.

'I woke up this morning and called my father and said this is one of eight more chances I've got to win this race,' said 26-year-old Martin, who paid tribute to his team — 'the guys have been telling me all week that I've got a good chance of winning today and that extra belief I have from them helps give me an extra edge' – and his director, Eric Van Lancker, who ended a long barren run for Belgium at Liège in 1990. 'He knows Liège so well, his experience really helped me a lot, and because he loves this race so much, having him there really helps my own motivation,' said Martin.

He had praise, too, for his team's strong anti-doping stance, saying: 'This is a sign of how things are changing for the better. The strong anti-doping philosophy is one very important reason why I'm in this team. It's a very open team that race with their hearts on their sleeves.'

He was less fortunate in his defence of the title in the race's 100th edition. The return of Roche-aux-Faucons should have favoured punchy climbers like the Irishman, but a large group came together on the long drag up to the finish in Ans, where Italians Damiano Caruso and Domenico Pozzovivo had a narrow advantage. Knowing he didn't have the finishing kick to prevail in a group finish, Martin attacked nearing the final left-hand corner and got across to Caruso. But as he leaned left and prepared to fire past the Italian, his wheels slid from under him on a patch of oil. He was still getting to his feet as Simon Gerrans flew by to become the first Australian to claim the oldest Classic.

By that point, Liège's finale was dividing opinion. On one side were those, including prominent members of the race organisation, who increasingly regarded it as a six-hour wait for the action to unfold. On the other were the riders who had pretensions of winning, and viewed it as one of the most physically and tactically demanding days of the racing calendar. For them it was a 250km, nerve-shredder where one strategic misstep would be fatal.

La Doyenne had become a waiting game that involved all manner of complications, traps and ambushes that needed to be avoided and negotiated before the final kilometre in Ans. Challenging for victory required the pretenders to be well-positioned at a series of key points: on the sharp rise of the Côte de Saint Roch soon after the turn at Bastogne where the riders towards the rear of the peloton could be slowed to walking pace and even reduced to walking; going into the Côte de Wanne, not because it's an especially hard climb, but because the descent off it leads very quickly into a series of tougher tests, starting with the Stockeu and followed by the Haute Lévée; on the extremely fast descent into Remouchamps and, exiting the town, La Redoute, a climb where critical splits could occur and the favourites needed to be close to the front to ensure they were on the right side of them; on Roche-aux-Faucons, where a winning break was likely to form; and on the Saint Nicolas, where there was an even greater chance of this happening. Like a decisive mountain stage on a grand tour, winning was a matter of a rider making their all-out effort when it had the best chance of paying off – in Ans, for those who were brave and confident enough not to chase their rivals beforehand.

Alejandro Valverde's third success in the race, in 2015, typified the approach required for success. Movistar controlled the race perfectly, keeping their Spanish leader up towards the front, but protected from the wind as much as they could. On Roche-aux-Faucons, Roman Kreuziger and Giampaolo Caruso went clear, and were quickly joined by Jakob Fuglsang. The chasers were always within range, though, and the three escapees were reeled in before Saint Nicolas, where Vincenzo Nibali attacked, eliciting roars of support from the roadside in this Italian district of Liège.

His offensive thinned out the group, but wasn't decisive enough to drop the favourites. Coming on to the Côte d'Ans, Caruso set the pace as a prelude to an attack by his Katusha teammate Dani Moreno, who got what seemed like a winning gap as his rivals all looked to Valverde to chase. Initially, the Spaniard sat tight, confident that he still had the resources and nous to win. He waited for someone else to move, then, when no one did, produced an acceleration that took him up to Moreno on the final left-hand bend and then past his compatriot on the sprint to the line, where young Frenchman Julian Alaphilippe was second, ahead of Joaquim Rodríguez.

The snow-hit 2016 edition followed the same pattern, the incessant pruning of the peloton resulting in four riders contesting the cat-and-mouse on the Côte d'Ans, Wout Poels surprising his opponents with a decisive turn of speed coming out of the final left-hander to leave Michael Albasini and Rui Costa in his wake. The Dutchman's victory was the first for Team Sky in a Monument in their seventh season of racing. A year later, Valverde triumphed for the fourth time with his by now very well-rehearsed strategy, his team keeping him out of the wind and danger until the long drag up towards the Carrefour supermarket in Ans. On this occasion, Dan Martin was the rabbit he chased down going into and around the last bend.

By the time the 2018 edition took place, rumours were already circulating that the old race's finale would be getting a significant overhaul and it would prove to be a case of going back to the future, with the finish returning to the centre of Liège. Before that, though, Ans had one last fling and it didn't run to the time-worn pattern. On Roche-aux-Faucons, former winner Philippe Gilbert forged clear. Four riders bridged up to the Belgian: Sergio Henao, Michael Woods, Jakob Fuglsang and Bob Jungels.

The latter, a prodigious time triallist, attacked on the false flat towards the top of the climb, quickly opening up a good gap as his rivals looked to each other to chase. When Jungels' QuickStep teammate Julian Alaphilippe led another group up to the dallying foursome, the pursuit of the Luxembourg rider lost even more momentum as no one wanted to ferry the fast-finishing Frenchman into Ans. Wonderfully stylish on the bike, Jungels cruised to a lead of a minute as he rode up Saint Nicolas and maintained most of that advantage to the line, where Woods and Romain Bardet clinched podium places with a late attack and Alaphilippe then led in the rest, pointing at his jersey in celebration.

The switch to the new finish on Boulevard d'Avroy in central Liège led to the demise of the Côte de Saint Nicolas, as well as the Côte d'Ans, leaving Roche-aux-Faucons as the last climbing test. Like the year before, it proved decisive and in much the same way as it had for Jungels. On this occasion, a three-man break was clear on the 'easier' false flat on the upper part of this ascent, until Jakob Fuglsang eased away from Michael Woods and Davide Formolo to hare down the fast descent into Liège, his only moment of concern coming when his bike briefly lost traction on a wet corner five kilometres from the line. It made him only the second Dane to win *La Doyenne,* after Rolf Sørensen in 1993.

The Covid-19 pandemic, inevitably, had a significant impact on Liège. Shifted from its spring date to the first weekend of October, it clashed with the Giro d'Italia and took place a week after the World Road Race Championship, won by Julian Alaphilippe, and two weeks on from the Tour de France, which had been captured in sensational fashion by debutant Tadej Pogačar, who swept Slovenian compatriot Primož Roglič aside in the time trial on the penultimate day. Enthrallingly, all three of these riders, plus another Tour relevation, young Swiss Marc Hirschi, went clear on Roche-aux-Faucons. As the quartet raced alongside the River Meuse inside the final kilometre, Matej Mohorič, drawing on his daredevil descending skills, first bridged up and then breezed past them. Alaphilippe reacted quickly, jumping on the wheel of this third Slovenian in the lead group, before accelerating past Mohorič and opening the sprint.

At this point, though, with 150m to the line, the new world champion's sang-froid deserted him. He first lurched to the left, blocking Hirschi's path, then straightened, seemed to have the race won, threw his arms aloft, only for Roglič to dive by on his right to thwart the Frenchman. After a quick review by the race jury, Alaphilippe was relegated to fifth, which promoted Hirschi and Pogačar to second and third, respectively. 'I think that's the first time that's happened to me in my career and I think it'll be the last,' said Alaphilippe, who confessed to making a schoolboy error.

Seven months later, when the race returned to its traditional April slot, Alaphilippe and Pogačar were again involved in a similar climax.

Together with Alejandro Valverde, who was seeking a fifth win to tie Eddy Merckx's record, Mike Woods, who instigated the move, and David Gaudu, they went clear on Roche-aux-Faucons. The Spaniard led out the sprint and Alaphilippe shot by on his right, only to see Pogačar flash by on *his* right in the final few metres, the Tour champion claiming his first success in a Monument.

It could be argued that these two thrilling editions, featuring several of the peloton's most garlanded performers, vindicated the decision made by ASO and the Pesant Club Liégeois to adopt a more traditional finish in Liège. However, in truth, they highlighted a complete change of dynamic within racing, triggered by the emergence of riders like Alaphilippe, Pogačar, Wout van Aert and Mathieu van der Poel who were prepared to take risks, and were also prodigiously talented enough to make their aggressive approach pay off. What's more, the 2022 edition confirmed the arrival of another young rider in this mould.

Twenty-two-year-old Remco Evenepoel had already shown on plenty of occasions that it was unwise for his rivals to allow him too much leeway if he broke clear on his own. Now, on his debut in *La Doyenne*, he demonstrated that against a field comprising most of the pre-eminent climbers and stage racers in the sport. Approaching the top of La Redoute, he accelerated hard, powering away from the other favourites. Over the next few kilometres he caught the survivors from the day's breakaway, breezing past each of them in turn, catching Bruno Armirail, the last of them, just before Roche-aux-Faucons. Most riders would have collaborated with the hard-riding Frenchman, even if only briefly in order to recuperate a little, but Evenepoel thundered on, Armirail soon left in his wake. He eventually crossed the line 48 seconds clear of Quinten Hermans and Wout van Aert as Belgian riders filled the podium for the first time since 1976.

Like its fellow Monuments, *La Doyenne*'s standing, which, for fans at least, was tarnished by the predictability of the finishes in Ans, has been revived. While these great one-day races will never rival the Tour de France for impact and broad audience appeal, their revitalisation as a consequence of being targeted by so many of the sport's biggest stars and, above all, by the aggressive, high-risk-but-what-the-hell approach that these riders have adopted have elevated their status, making them even more significant milestones within the cycling calendar. Liège has, arguably, benefited more than its four peers, because it attracts so many of the racers who are so prominent at the Tour, pitching them into a contest that features more than 4,000m of vertical gain and all manner of traps, and tests every aspect of their competitive armoury. Long regarded as the toughest Classic of the season, but with a finale that was as workmanlike as its former setting in the rusting industrial landscape leading into Ans, it has, like the city of Liège itself, become more vibrant and vital; an old race reborn.

PART II

PARIS-ROUBAIX -
THE HELL OF THE NORTH

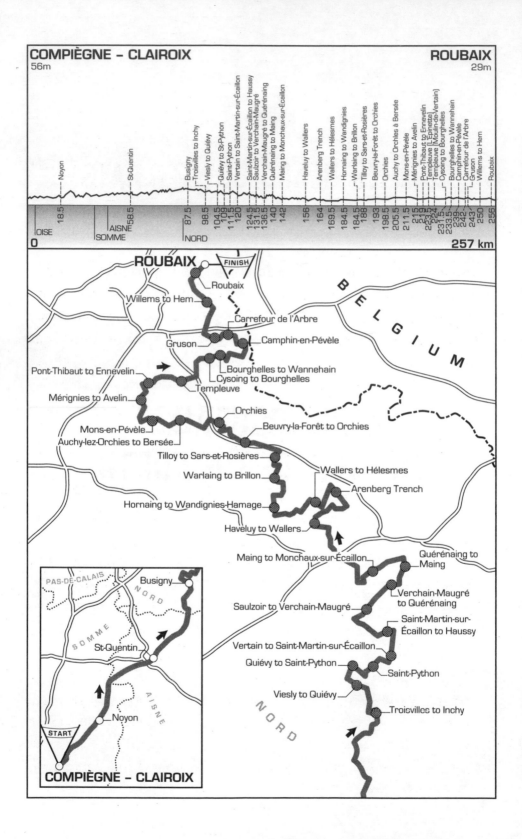

COMPIÈGNE – CLAIROIX
56m

ROUBAIX
29m

Noyon
St-Quentin
Busigny
Troisvilles to Inchy
Viesly to Quiévy
Quiévy to St-Python
Saint-Python
Vertain to Saint-Martin-sur-Écaillon
Saint-Martin-sur-Écaillon to Haussy
Saulzoir to Verchain-Maugré
Verchain-Maugré to Quérénaing
Quérénaing to Maing
Maing to Monchaux-sur-Écaillon
Haveluy to Wallers
Arenberg Trench
Wallers to Hélesmes
Hornaing to Wandignies
Warlaing to Brillon
Tilloy to Sars-et-Rosières
Beuvry-la-Forêt to Orchies
Orchies
Auchy to Orchies à Bersée
Mons-en-Pévèle
Mérignies to Avelin
Pont-Thibaut to Ennevelin
Templeuve (L'Epinette)
Templeuve (Moulin-de-Vertain)
Cysoing to Bourghelles
Bourghelles to Wannehain
Camphin-en-Pévèle
Carrefour de l'Arbre
Gruson
Willems to Hem
Roubaix

0
18.5
58.5
87.5
98.5
104.5
109
111.5
120
124.5
131.5
136.5
140
142
156
164
169.5
184.5
188
193
198.5
205.5
211.5
215
219
223
231.5
233.5
239
242
243
250
256

OISE
AISNE
SOMME
NORD

257 km

ROUBAIX
FINISH
Roubaix
Willems to Hem
Carrefour de l'Arbre
Camphin-en-Pévèle
Gruson
Bourghelles to Wannehain
Pont-Thibaut to Ennevelin
Cysoing to Bourghelles
Templeuve
Mérignies to Avelin
Orchies
Mons-en-Pévèle
Beuvry-la-Forêt to Orchies
Auchy-lez-Orchies to Bersée
Tilloy to Sars-et-Rosières
Warlaing to Brillon
Wallers to Hélesmes
Hornaing to Wandignies-Hamage
Arenberg Trench
Haveluy to Wallers
Maing to Monchaux-sur-Écaillon
Quérénaing to Maing
Verchain-Maugré to Quérénaing
Saulzoir to Verchain-Maugré
Saint-Martin-sur-Écaillon to Haussy
Vertain to Saint-Martin-sur-Écaillon
Quiévy to Saint-Python
Saint-Python
Viesly to Quiévy
Troisvilles to Inchy

BELGIUM

PAS-DE-CALAIS
NORD
SOMME
St-Quentin
Busigny
AISNE
Noyon
START
COMPIÈGNE – CLAIROIX

5

BABIES' HEADS, BOWLER HATS AND BARNUMS

The best-known one-day event in cycling, and arguably the sport's biggest race after the Tour de France, Paris–Roubaix is one of the greatest anachronisms in modern sport. Like racing a Formula 1 car around the tight streets of Monaco, Paris–Roubaix is a throwback to organised sport's early days, an event that provides its competitors with a spectacularly unique challenge. According to its former race director Jacques Goddet, 'Paris–Roubaix is the last test of folly that cycle sport puts before its participants'.

Sitting hard next to France's border with Belgium, a handful of kilometres south-east of Lille, Roubaix had become well established as the country's textile centre in the late nineteenth century, earning it the nickname 'the Manchester of France'. The mills and their associated industries employed tens of thousands of workers, whose one escape from the dirt, noise and drudgery of the factories came on Sundays, when many would make for Roubaix's Barbieux Park to play boules, watch cock-fighting and promenade.

By the early 1890s, cycling events were increasingly common in the Barbieux, partly thanks to the invention of the removable tyre by the Michelin brothers, who ran a rubber factory in Clermont-Ferrand, and also to the success of long-distance races, particularly Paris–Brest–Paris and Paris–Bordeaux, which both emerged in 1891. However, such races were very rare because of the dismal state of French roads, and competition was generally limited to velodromes, which started to spring up all over France in the final decade of the nineteenth century.

Roubaix's track emerged thanks to the impetus and finance provided by two of the city's textiles magnates, Théodore Vienne and Maurice Perez, who bought a parcel of land for the velodrome on the edge of Barbieux Park with a view to raising the city's cultural and sporting profile. It opened in June 1895, when 8,000 spectators provided hugely enthusiastic support for many of France's top racers, including the future winner of the inaugural Tour de France, Maurice Garin. Over the following years, most of the best track riders of the age competed at the Vélodrome Roubaisien, including another future Tour champion, Octave Lapize, and the ground-breaking African American racer Marshall 'Major' Taylor, who was only the second black athlete in any sport to hold a world title (behind Canadian bantamweight boxer George Dixon).

Having made a success of their velodrome, Vienne and Perez came up with a new idea for a road race starting in Paris that would finish on the track and would raise Roubaix's profile a little more. They approached Louis Minart, the editor of sporting daily *Paris-Vélo*, who suggested they contact his boss, Paul Rousseau. The two men wrote to Rousseau, proposing their idea for 'a training race preceding Bordeaux–Paris by four weeks' and describing the distance of 280km as 'child's play' compared to the 560km event that followed. They requested the patronage of Rousseau's paper and its help organising the start.

Rousseau dispatched his main cycling correspondent, Victor Breyer, to survey the route between the capital and Roubaix. Breyer roped in a colleague with a car who took him and his bike as far as Amiens on the first day of his reconnaissance. The next day dawned sunny, but Breyer was soon riding in a deluge. He laboured on for hours, eventually reaching the Vélodrome Roubaisien bedraggled, exhausted and in a foul mood. He considered sending a telegraph to Minart advising him to drop the diabolical project, but decided to wait until he had had dinner with Vienne and Perez. By the next morning, thanks to the hospitality and generosity of his hosts, Breyer viewed the project in a very different light.

Paris-Vélo announced that the first edition of Paris–Roubaix would take place on 19 April 1896. Race legend has it that the Church objected to it happening on Easter Day because the riders would not be able to attend mass. Vienne, it was said, eased ecclesiastical concerns by declaring he would make arrangements for an early morning mass to take place at a chapel close to the start by the Café Gillet on the Boulevard Maillot, at the top edge of the Bois de Boulogne. According to some reports, including one from Breyer, the mass never took place because it was planned for too early in the morning. However, it is more likely it didn't take place because Easter Day had occurred a fortnight before. Nevertheless, in subsequent years, the race was often run on Easter Day, as a result of which it was dubbed '*La Pascale*' – the Easter Race.

Entry was divided into two categories: 'Internationals' and 'Riders from the Lille Area'. A substantial first prize of 1,000 French francs, at a time when the average wage was just four francs a day, drew 118 registrations for the race, which was billed as perfect preparation for Bordeaux–Paris a month later. However, on the morning of 19 April, fewer than half that number signed in at the Café Gillet. Among those absent was Henri Desgrange, who would go on to take charge of Paris–Roubaix in 1901 and to found the Tour de France two years later.

At 5.30 a.m., *Paris-Vélo*'s Paul Rousseau dropped the start flag and 51 riders set off for Roubaix, 280km away. As was the case in most other road events of that period, the riders sat in behind their own pacers, often riding tandems and even triples. The first of them to show was Welshman Arthur Linton, who was being paced by his younger brother, Tom. Although born in the Somerset village of Seavington St Michael, Linton's family moved to the Welsh pit village of Aberaman when he was three. He went to work at the Treaman colliery in the Aberdare

Valley when he was 12, but started to make a name for himself as a racing cyclist during his teenage years. Spotted by athletics and cycling coach James 'Choppy' Warburton, Linton and brother Tom began to race frequently on the Continent. Like most of the other big names riding that first Roubaix, Linton's primary target was Bordeaux–Paris a few weeks later.

By the checkpoint at Amiens, Linton had been joined by Germany's Josef Fischer, with Frenchman Garin five minutes back in third, saving himself for the tougher half of the course that lay before them. As the leaders headed out of Amiens, a dog ran out into the road and under Linton's wheels, sending the Welshman crashing to the ground and damaging his bike beyond repair. Although he continued on another bike after a few minutes, Fischer had flown and Linton's chances had gone with him. The German had his own encounters with animals on the route, but managed to avoid a bolting horse and circumnavigate a herd of cows that had escaped on to the road.

At 2.47 p.m., Josef Fischer completed the last of six laps of the Vélodrome Roubaisien, signed the arrival sheet and knocked back a glass of champagne. Twenty-three minutes passed before Denmark's Charles Meyer took second place, a minute and a half ahead of the bloodied Garin, who had been knocked unconscious and run over by two bikes when the triple pacing him collided with a rival's bike late in the race. The unfortunate Arthur Linton finished fourth.

Fischer's average speed of more than 31km/h was the fastest that had hitherto been recorded for a race of that distance and this no doubt encouraged Vienne and Perez to continue with their venture. At a banquet that evening, they announced that the race would become an annual event and the second edition would take place on Easter Day 1897.

Sadly, Arthur Linton wasn't around to see it. Although the Welshman's health was not good in the wake of Roubaix, he lined up at Bordeaux–Paris four weeks later and ended the race victorious, or at least jointly so alongside Frenchman Gaston Rivière. Yet the event, or perhaps what he took during it, had fatal consequences. The victim of mechanical failure, crashes, a late deviation off the route and exhaustion, which was relieved by the unknown contents of a bottle 'Choppy' Warburton encouraged him to drink, Linton was initially declared the winner, but then disqualified when it became apparent he had not followed the official course. Following an appeal, the Welshman was declared the joint winner with Rivière.

Riders and spectators at the finish described Linton as being in a terrible state. Rather than fulfil other racing engagements, he returned to Aberaman to recuperate, but his condition only worsened. He died on 23 July. His death was put down to complications resulting from typhoid. However, in 1997 an International Olympic Committee report suggested Linton was the first athlete to die as the result of doping during competition, with strychnine cited as the substance he had been given by Warburton, who had subsequently been banned from coaching and died following a heart attack in 1897.

Word of the difficulty of the route resulted in a reduced field for the second edition of Paris–Roubaix. Riders in the inaugural race had been particularly shocked by the state of the pavé used for the entirety of the final 60km of the course. The cobbles were so large they were dubbed 'babies' heads', 'bowler hats' or 'barnums', the latter a reference to the acrobat-like performances needed to deal with them. The racers had to tackle them at speed to reduce the chances of their wheels getting caught in the ruts between them.

The weather undoubtedly played a part, too, in persuading many professional riders to stay away from the race. In his report, Victor Breyer describes the competitors taking shelter beneath the trees around the Café Gillet and says the roads were 'covered with yellowish mud, which was lamentably liquid'. Dutchman Mathieu Cordang was regarded as the man to beat, although most were hoping that Garin, born in Italy's Aosta Valley but now based in Roubaix where he ran a bike shop with his two brothers, would prevail. Small and slight, Garin had previously made a living as a chimney sweep, for which he had the ideal physique. However, he didn't appear to have the build to cope with heavy roads or the cobbles, over which lighter riders tend to bounce rather than glide. Yet he had incredible endurance and desire, and drew on both qualities, allowing Cordang to set the pace before steadily closing in on the Dutchman on the toughest part of the course.

When the two riders came into the velodrome for six laps of the track, they swapped a few words. As they turned on to the track, Cordang slipped and fell. By the time he was back on his bike and under way, Garin was more than half of one 333.33m lap ahead. 'And so began a splendid battle. It was like a marvellous handicap race,' wrote Paul Rousseau. 'The public holds its breath. There's no noise. For the first two laps Garin maintains his advantage, but then Cordang begins to gain ground on him and show he is the strongest. One lap remains! The bell sounds! There are only 30 metres between them! Cordang stands on his pedals; Garin, riding very energetically, zigzags due to the force of his ferocious effort and finishes first at the line, beating Cordang by two metres.'

Rousseau described the unfortunate Dutchman as the moral victor, but lauded Garin for a marvellous and rather surprising performance. Garin agreed with Rousseau and most other observers, acknowledging: 'I won but Cordang was the strongest today. Next time I will win with a more substantial gap ...'

A chance for the worse

Just two editions in, Paris–Roubaix had already started to emerge from the shadow of Bordeaux–Paris. Unlike Liège–Bastogne–Liège, which had disappeared in 1894 after just three editions and did not run again until 1908, Roubaix had quickly become a title that riders wanted to win in its own right. Yet, inexplicably, Messieurs Perez and Vienne decided the format needed spicing up. They announced a race for motor vehicles would take place over the same route on the same day. In addition, they brought in a new rule allowing riders to be paced by motor vehicles or motorcycles. The Union Vélocipédique de France was reluctant to sanction the race; it eventually said it would 'tolerate' the innovation, but wouldn't recognise the finishing times as records. Paris's police weren't so accommodating. They refused to allow the event to start in the capital, forcing the organisers to move it to Chatou on the city's north-west edge.

As many expected, the race was a mess. There were numerous crashes, although the worst incident occurred at Roubaix where the roof of a small building collapsed under the weight of expectant fans perched upon it. Paced by two petrol-driven tandems, defending champion Garin emerged from the dust clouds and melee of vehicles to retain the title in fine fashion, beating Auguste Stéphane by almost half an hour. His time would have been good enough to place him third in the motorcycle race.

The principal weakness of the format was emphasised over the following two years when riders previously known for their exploits on the track won the race. These riders were well used to being paced by motorcycles, giving them an almost unassailable advantage on even the most experienced road racers. The first of the track specialists is the most renowned, although not for his Roubaix success, nor for the many other successes he achieved in the velodromes of Europe and North America.

Albert Champion already had a proven reputation as a 'stayer', as riders who rode huge distances over many hours on the track were known. Although well accustomed to being paced by bikes on the track, he knew two-time victor Garin was the favourite. However, Garin fell victim to the most obvious flaw in the motorised pacing format. When his vehicle broke down, he was stranded. As Garin slowed, Champion urged the driver of the vehicle ahead of him to raise his speed. It was a daring move, and surely too premature. But Champion hung on to take the title, helped by an accident to his closest pursuer, Émile 'The Blond

Adonis' Bouhours, who crashed out when his vehicle swerved to avoid a spectator in the road.

Champion's other love was racing and maintaining motorbikes, for which he made his own extremely reliable spark plugs. After heading across the Atlantic to fulfil a motor-racing contract in 1900, he set up a factory in Boston making spark plugs for cars. The Champion Spark Plug Company thrived as the American car industry boomed. In 1908, after falling out with his backers, he moved to Flint, Michigan, which had become the centre of the American motor industry, to establish a new enterprise, the Champion Ignition Company.

Champion died after suffering a heart attack in 1927. One report suggested his collapse may have been due to an earlier altercation in a Paris nightclub with a prizefighter, who was said to be having an affair with Champion's wife. It is claimed the fighter gave Champion such a pummelling that he never recovered. Although General Motors bought up all the shares in his flourishing company, his name lives on in the two brands of spark plug he developed – AC Spark Plug and Champion Spark Plugs.

Thwarted by ill fortune when he lost out to Champion in 1899, track specialist Bouhours left past winners Fischer and Garin trailing in 1900. His performance in completing the 269km course in little more than seven hours at an average of more than 37km/h was astounding, but race backers Perez and Vienne barely took note. They were already wondering if their event would survive as Bouhours was one of just 19 starters, and surely also took note of the irate Garin, who sat sulking in the centre of their track after refusing to ride the final six laps because, he said, he couldn't see the point. News of a collision between two motorcycles that resulted in 20 people being injured only underlined the impression that a change was needed.

In 1901, Vienne and Perez announced the race would return to its original format, which only allowed riders to be paced by human-powered bikes. More unexpectedly, they also confirmed that technical direction of the race would switch from *Le Vélo* (previously *Paris-Vélo*) to a new sporting daily, *L'Auto-Vélo*. The title had been founded in 1900 under the editorship of former racer Henri Desgrange, who had registered for but not started the inaugural edition of Roubaix.

Financial backing for the paper came from a number of notable industrial impresarios, including tyre manufacturers Adolphe Clément and Édouard Michelin. Their aim was not so much to promote the sport as to drive a former collaborator out of business. They had previously placed much of their advertising in the market-leading title *Le Vélo,* but had become disenchanted with the left-wing stance taken by its editor, Pierre Giffard. The final straw for them was the anti-establishment slant Giffard took during the Dreyfus Affair, a political scandal that split France when a Jewish army officer, Captain Alfred Dreyfus, was unjustly charged and convicted of treason. Giffard supported the pro-Dreyfus stance of intellectuals such as novelist Émile Zola, which led to some of his anti-Dreyfusard advertisers to withdraw their support for *Le Vélo*. Their instruction to Desgrange was to force Giffard's title out of business.

Desgrange's *L'Auto-Vélo,* which would be renamed *L'Auto* after Giffard successfully challenged its previous title in the courts, wouldn't finish off *Le Vélo* until 1904, following the first edition of his Tour de France, but he demonstrated his talent for race organisation by attracting 60 riders to the start of Paris–Roubaix, which returned to the Café Gillet. His lieutenant, Alphonse Steinès, later almost to lose his life scouting out the high mountains of the Pyrenees for Desgrange's Tour, had done reconnaissance of the route a few days beforehand and noted the road conditions were not good. 'We need sun between now and Sunday,' he wrote in *L'Auto-Vélo*. Instead, it sluiced down.

The race became a duel between Cannes-born Swiss rider Jean Gougoltz and Lucien Lesna, who had discovered cycle racing late in life – he was 37 by then – and stood out on even the muddiest of days thanks to his handlebar moustache. He had responded to a question about the conditions with a shrug: 'The mud? Pff, that doesn't frighten me. I've seen it plenty of times before.' Lesna had an ace up his sleeve in the shape of pacemaker Alphonse Baugé, a talented rider who would go on to become one of the Tour de France's great team directors and was already blessed with a canny understanding of tactics and rider psychology.

As Gougoltz and Lesna approached Amiens, the Swiss tried to escape his rival repeatedly, but only succeeded in expending his own resources. Watching this duel from a car following close behind, Baugé felt Gougoltz was flagging. Judging this was the moment when his speed as a pacer would most benefit Lesna, Baugé hopped out of the support car and sprinted up to the front to take over the pace-setting. Gougoltz began to wilt almost immediately. He shouted across to Lesna for some food, but the Frenchman pressed on without speaking, ignoring the yells as Gougoltz fell behind – 'Bandits! I am going to kill you all tomorrow!' Although it never came to that, the Swiss never recovered from his hunger 'knock' and Lesna flew on to win at a canter after a solo break of 140km.

The Frenchman repeated his success in 1902, as the prestige of the race continued to grow under Desgrange's very capable management. By the early 1900s, teams and riders regarded Paris–Roubaix not so much as a preparation race for Bordeaux–Paris, but more as the prestigious opening event of the season. Manufacturers, too, relished the challenge it offered because of the rewards that came with victory and high placings in terms of bike sales. Track specialists also benefited as demand for the very best pacers went up, raising their earnings beyond anything they could demand in most track events. This was one of the first signs that road events were assuming more significance than those on the track.

The balance of power tipped further towards road cycling when in January 1903 *L'Auto* announced the creation of 'a Tour de France'. Roubaix's own Maurice Garin was one of the first to commit to the new race, forsaking Paris–Roubaix as he trained with this new objective in mind. But Garin's absence didn't impact on Roubaix greatly as a new generation of riders produced the most thrilling finish thus far.

Six riders forced the pace for the second half of the race. Coming towards the finish, there was still little between four of them, although Hippolyte Aucouturier appeared to have the race in his pocket. Sporting a handlebar moustache with its ends waxed up in devilish fashion and wearing a red- and blue-hooped jersey, Aucouturier looked like nothing less than the pantomime villain from a Buster Keaton comedy. His nickname, 'The Terrible', appears to back this up, although it stemmed as much from his ability to make the going hard for his rivals with repeated and sustained accelerations as from any underhand tactics he employed when racing.

Approaching Roubaix, Aucouturier found to his surprise that compatriot Claude Chapperon had chased back on to his wheel. Coming into the velodrome, the pair rushed towards the brakeless track bikes on which riders tended to complete the final six laps of the race. In his haste, Chapperon came away with his rival's, which Aucouturier tugged away from him. Chapperon quickly realised his mistake, but he had lost 100m and all chance of glory.

Chapperon may have been unlucky, but Aucouturier was no mug as a rider. He went on to win two stages of the inaugural Tour de France before being kicked off the race for drafting behind a car. In 1904, he demonstrated he didn't need to rely on such shelter from a car, pacer or otherwise, as he retained his Roubaix crown when the race was run without pacers for the first time. As in the year before, Aucouturier found himself pitched against one other rider, on this occasion local favourite and youngest of the three racing Garin brothers, César. Aucouturier finished two lengths clear in a sprint witnessed by a crowd that was no more than a few dozen strong. Pushed along by a persistent tailwind, the two leaders came home 90 minutes ahead of schedule when spectators were still making their way to the velodrome.

Dirty deeds

Later that year, Aucouturier's 'terrible' reputation took on a new aspect. The 1904 Tour de France was a showcase of underhand tactics. Four months after the race had been completed, the French federation disqualified the top four finishers, including Aucouturier, who had been fourth and won four of the six stages. Although the federation never lifted the lid on the precise nature of their misdemeanours, there was talk of illegal pacing by motor vehicles – and even of riders travelling in vehicles – and tacks being scattered by fans and riders on the course.

Such episodes were by no means unique to the Tour. Tacks on the road were a perennial problem at Paris–Roubaix, while Italian fans at the Tour of Lombardy quickly gained a reputation for hindering and even assaulting their favourites' rivals. The number of pacers around riders also enabled all kinds of shenanigans to pass unpunished because race judges were not mobile or numerous enough to follow every bit of the action. This makes the decision to reintroduce pacemakers in 1905 quite unfathomable, but the move appears to have been driven by the riders, who had ridden with them on the track all winter and would do so once again at Bordeaux–Paris.

The race commissaires, or judges, were quick to pick up on infractions of the rules when they did see them, though. In 1905, Henri Cornet, who had inherited the Tour title after the disqualification of the top four, was fined for lining up at the start without socks, an infringement of one of the many rules laid down by the officious Desgrange for all of his races. But that was the least of Cornet's concerns that day. He started as one of the favourites, but destroyed his own hopes by attacking repeatedly throughout the first half of the race, paying the penalty late on when he was unable to follow Louis 'Trou-Trou' Trousselier, who would go on to become the popular winner of the 1905 Tour de France.

Trousselier, another rider who sported a well-groomed handlebar moustache with the ends waxed rakishly upwards, had a deserved reputation as a playboy. He lost all his winnings from his Tour success playing dice one evening at the Buffalo velodrome in Paris, and was later revealed as one of the riders involved in a scam enacted on several restaurateurs around Fontainebleau, to the south of the capital. Trousselier and two or three of his training partners would sit down to dinner at an upmarket establishment. When the meal was finished, they would begin what would soon escalate into a very heated discussion, during which the *patron* would be called to intervene. They would explain they were arguing about which of them was the fastest and ask their host to act as judge by indicating a point down the street they had to race to and back. The patron would set them off with a wave of his napkin, and the riders would speed off, never to return.

Having been outlasted by Trousselier in 1905, Cornet insisted he would learn his lesson and returned the following year in triumph, although his success was overshadowed by the Courrières mining disaster, which cost the lives of 1,099 miners and remains the worst in European history. A month on from that tragedy of 10 March, and just a day before the race, Desgrange made radical changes to the route in order to avoid the villages on the southern edge of Lens most affected by the loss of life as rumours (never really substantiated) spread of vehicles from Roubaix being attacked by irate mobs. The riders appreciated the diversion, not because they feared being assaulted, but because the worst sections of cobbled road were located in the towns and villages in the mining region between Arras and Roubaix. As well as being scarred by constant use by heavy vehicles, these roads were pitted and liable to subsidence caused by the workings beneath them.

Britain opts for isolation

Following Josef Fischer's success in the inaugural Roubaix, French riders had dominated the event, underlining the speed with which road racing was becoming established within *l'Héxagone*. The depth of French talent ensured that new names quickly emerged to replace pioneers such as Maurice Garin and Hippolyte Aucouturier. Yet, a glance at the British names decorating the palmarès of long-distance road events in the later decades of the nineteenth century would have suggested British riders should have been contending as well. However, none emerged in the wake of the ill-starred Arthur Linton.

This stemmed from the total ban on road racing imposed by Britain's National Cyclists' Union in 1890. The NCU insisted all racing take place on velodromes and, later on, on closed circuits. The obvious assumption is that the ban, which remained in place into the 1950s, was implemented because of safety concerns that arose due to the large numbers of people attracted to cycle racing in the late nineteenth century. In fact, the reason for it was much more sinister.

Just as the bike came to be regarded as the means of transport for the working classes, cycle racing followed the same path. The freedom the bicycle offered British working men and women jarred with the upper classes, who objected to bikes – and, more precisely, the people riding them – venturing into the countryside. British Cycling's website maintains the decision to ban cycle racing from the open road 'actually had a kernel of good sense to it', but doesn't make clear how this cycling apartheid benefited anyone beyond the wealthy classes.

More than 70 years would pass before Barry Hoban became the first British rider to finish on the podium at Roubaix, although Britain could claim to have a half-share in 1907 victor Georges Passerieu. Born in the then down-at-heel north London district of Islington in October 1885 to a French father and English mother, Passerieu was not held back by the NCU's ban as he was brought up in France. He turned pro in 1906 and created an instant impact when he finished second in the Tour de France, a performance that quickly led to a contract with the powerful Peugeot team.

Passerieu's arrival at Peugeot coincided with the implementation of a new training strategy by team boss Norbert Peugeot. Previously, teams had focused on one star rider who looked after his own training. However, Peugeot had seen how the rival Alcyon team had benefited from having several big hitters within their ranks who trained together for specific events. Peugeot took this a step further by having his riders, including Passerieu, Cornet and the fast-emerging Gustave Garrigou, train on the Paris–Roubaix route. Like Alcyon, he also hired the best pacemakers – plenty of other riders realised they could make more by hiring themselves out as pace-making mercenaries than they would by depending on their own prospects.

Peugeot's preparations paid off as his riders went on to dominate *La Pascale*, Passerieu breaking clear with 50km remaining and finishing alone. His only moment of concern came just before he entered the velodrome when an officious gendarme waved him to a halt and demanded to see proof that he had paid the tax for owning a bicycle. Knowing riders were closing in behind, Passerieu eventually edged the policeman aside and rode on to complete an emotional victory. 'I would like to point out I am wearing the jersey of the unfortunate René Pottier. He was my mentor and friend,' the victor said of the 1906 Tour de France champion, who had hanged himself two months before, after discovering his wife had been having an affair while he was away winning the Tour. 'If Pottier had been here, his jersey would have been the first one into the velodrome. As it is, it is the first one anyway ...'

While Passerieu provided the emotion, sensation came in the shape of runner-up Cyril Van Hauwaert, a hulking Belgian farm worker who was making his debut for the La Française team. Hailing from Moorslede in West Flanders, he had been spotted by La Française's Belgian agent, who had sent him to the manufacturer's HQ in Paris with a letter of recommendation. La Française *directeur sportif*, Pierre Pierrard, later recalled Van Hauwaert's arrival in his office: 'He was a strapping fellow in peasant's garb with enormous hobnailed boots, carrying a box of clothes and a letter from our agent in Ypres. Naturally, this colossus, who had come to ride Paris–Roubaix, didn't speak a word of French. What was I going to do with him I wondered?'

Pierrard asked his mechanics to set up Van Hauwaert with a bike, while the 'timid and humble' Belgian remained 'as a quiet as a carp' in a corner. That evening Pierrard took him to a hotel for dinner. 'It was evidently the first time he had eaten in a restaurant, and his ingenuity was touching to witness. Incapable of expressing his desires, he contented himself with watching what other diners were eating and pointing his finger and mumbling: "Cook that, cook that!"' Van Hauwaert ate everything put before him, washing it down with milk and then red wine. The legend of 'Ventr'ouvert' ('Open Stomach') had begun.

Figuring the Belgian was a no-hoper and not having any pacers left to offer him anyway, Pierrard gave him the bike and instructed him to follow other riders as best he could. Van Hauwaert did exactly that, but was good enough to stay with the main contenders. Late in the race, as his leaders began to flag, Pierrard ordered some of his remaining pacers to work for the tireless Belgian, who responded by shooting through the field and coming within a minute of catching Passerieu.

The many Belgian fans who had come over the border to see the finish were ecstatic when one of their own finished on the podium for the first time. So used to their compatriots being tail-enders, they now had a standard-bearer, and an unmistakable one at that. His success marked a turning point in the fortunes of Belgian cycling. France's neighbour had not been as quick to adopt the bike as a mode of transport, which meant its racing scene was slower to develop. Yet, the topography and roads in Dutch-speaking Flanders were very similar to those of northern France, making it more than likely that Flemish riders would become a force to be reckoned with in Roubaix.

Certainly, Van Hauwaert was unstoppable in the months that followed, going on to win Bordeaux–Paris and, after signing with Alcyon, the second edition of Milan–Sanremo before returning to Paris–Roubaix. Once again, Henri Desgrange had tinkered with the rules, banning the use of pacemakers and any outside assistance to riders beyond Beauvais, and setting up secret control points to prevent cheating. The removal of pacemakers suited Van Hauwaert perfectly. A year on from finishing second, he rode into Roubaix victorious. His success owed a good deal to luck as Luxembourg's François Faber, a Parisian docker dubbed 'the Giant of Colombes', collided with a child not far from the velodrome when leading the race.

Van Hauwaert's success and Faber's startling performance led many to believe Roubaix would become the domain of cycling's big men, but all would be upstaged during the next three editions by a Frenchman standing at just 1.65m. Octave Lapize turned pro at the start of 1909 having won a bronze medal in the 100km race at the London Olympics the previous summer. For *L'Auto* editor-in-chief and Roubaix race director Desgrange he was the perfect cycling specimen. 'He has an energetic aspect, a solid chin, a focused look, a pointed moustache, all of which give him the look of a racer,' Desgrange wrote, adding: 'He has a solid chest, well-set legs, powerful thighs and the hands of a rider who could destroy any handlebar in the world when he pulls hard on them on the hills.' He could also have added that Lapize was partially deaf, which meant his concentration rarely wavered when racing, and was nicknamed 'Curly' because of his locks.

Although best known for his victory in the 1910 Tour, when he famously yelled 'You're all assassins!' at the race directors as he crossed the summit of the Col du Tourmalet when the high mountains made their first appearance in the race, his Roubaix exploits were equally impressive, particularly as he was regarded primarily as a climber. On his *La Pascale* debut in 1909, he decided against using pacers, believing the risks they took increased the chance of crashing, and followed the main contenders until they were left to their own devices at Beauvais.

Lapize stayed with the leaders all the way, the demands of the race finally reducing the lead group to just three members – 'Curly', 'Trou-Trou' and Belgian Jules Masselis – as they rode into the velodrome where a 10,000-strong crowd had paid record receipts to witness the finale. Trousselier led out the sprint, perhaps believing his young compatriot would struggle to match his speed at the end of such a sapping race. But he had misjudged the little man. Coming into the final straight, Lapize zipped by to win, to the bewilderment of most of those looking on, who had no idea who he was.

When he returned to defend his title, Lapize had become a national hero thanks to his Tour victory. Although Desgrange had modified the rules once again, banning pacemakers completely, the change suited the little man who hadn't depended on them 12 months earlier. The other notable change had occurred in Roubaix, where a new wooden track had been laid and the open stands had been covered. Up to 12,000 people packed the revamped stadium, with thousands more lining the road approaching it. Many of them had come over from Belgium, which still lacked an iconic race of its own despite the relaunch of Liège, but could now boast plenty of riding talent, led by Van Hauwaert.

They cheered and waved their straw boaters when four dust-coated racers rode on to the track. Van Hauwaert led the way for the first five laps, but was unable to respond to Lapize's finishing burst off the final corner. Having claimed the title on successive occasions thanks to his sprinting speed, Lapize confessed he would like to complete a triple with a solo victory. He not only managed this, but finished so far ahead in 1911, his victory was nothing less than an annihilation. He moved first on the hill at Doullens and managed to avoid the tacks that had been scattered on the route soon after. Approaching Roubaix, only Van Hauwaert remained with him at the front, and his hopes went when he punctured on the outskirts of the city.

Even as the political situation deteriorated in Europe, Paris–Roubaix continued its ascent. In the immediate pre-war years, thousands would turn out at the early morning start in Chatou, and tens of thousands more thronged the roadsides. In 1912, as many as 100,000 spectators watched the closing kilometres, most of them first stunned and then euphoric at seeing Roubaix's own Charles Crupelandt and Maurice Leturgie among the leading trio. Gustave Garrigou looked to have the beating of both of them, and perhaps would have triumphed if 'Curly' Lapize hadn't intervened. The defending champion entered the track only seconds behind the leaders, but allowed himself to be caught by them. He already knew his chance of a fourth win had gone, but he ensured his La Française team held the crown by leading out Crupelandt in the sprint.

Crupelandt would probably have retained his title but for a crash that left him with a serious wound in a knee. He wasn't too disappointed, though, to lose out to his good friend François Faber in the sprint, Belgium's Charles Deruyter splitting them. Crupelandt regained the title in 1914, only ten weeks before the assassination of Archduke Franz Ferdinand of Austria led to the outbreak of hostilities in Europe.

6

THE BIRTH OF A LEGEND

The description 'The Hell of the North' stems not from the appalling condition of the roads on which Paris–Roubaix has always been contested, as many have assumed, but from the devastated condition of northern France in the aftermath of the Great War. Set-piece battles at Verdun, the Somme, Arras, Cambrai and many other locations left Picardy and the Pas-de-Calais in ruins. As cycling historian Les Woodland pointed out: 'Nine million had died and more from France than any other nation. Further south, news from the war zone was scant. Communications were down. Sure, there could be another race. But who knew if there was still a road to Roubaix? More than that, was Roubaix still there?'

When Eugène Christophe decided to do some reconnaissance of the Paris–Roubaix in early 1919, race director Henri Desgrange sent *L'Auto* correspondent Victor Breyer with him to assess the viability of running a twentieth edition of *La Pascale*. Initially, the small exploratory party were surprised by the relative normality of the towns and countryside they passed through. However, approaching Amiens, they encountered a very different world. Writing in *L'Auto*, Breyer reported: 'We enter into the centre of the battlefield. There's not a tree. Everything is flattened! There's not a square metre that has not been hurled upside down. There's one shell hole after another. The only things standing out in the churned earth are the crosses with their ribbons in blue, white and red. It is hell!'

The roads had disappeared into the mud, from which only the blackened stumps of trees stood out. The air reeked of decay and death, the stink of raw sewage combining with the odour of rotting livestock. It was hellish, but it would not remain so. Nevertheless, Breyer's description of what he had seen stuck. Paris–Roubaix became 'The Hell of the North', much to the dismay of the region's inhabitants, who didn't appreciate what this label said about them and their homeland.

As well as the devastation in the north, cycling had also suffered many significant losses. Roubaix winners Octave Lapize and François Faber were just two of dozens of prominent pre-war riders killed during the conflict. Many more sustained injuries that prevented them from returning to competitive action, while others were simply too old to consider racing as a profession, especially as the post-war financial returns were hardly substantial. The conflict had also taken a toll on Roubaix's velodrome, which had been stripped of its wooden boards by German troops desperate for firewood.

During the war, many of the major bike manufacturing companies had had to adapt their machinery to produce barrels for guns and rifles rather than the tubing required for bike frames. Switching back was not easy, particularly because of a lack of materials and skilled labour. To circumvent this difficulty until the as yet unspecified point when thousands of working men would be released from military service, the main manufacturers formed a consortium, La Sportive, comprising Alcyon, Peugeot, La Française, Automoto and Gladiator. They pooled their resources, both materially and in terms of personnel. The leading riders, including Christophe and compatriot Henri Pélissier, received a monthly wage of up to 300 francs from the consortium, which was about twice the average wage. It didn't match the income many had received before the war, but it was a good income in a period where many had none at all.

Desgrange stuck with tradition by announcing Paris–Roubaix would take place on Easter Day 1919. He laid out a route that avoided the principal battlegrounds, but still left the 130 riders who lined up at the start with a fearsome challenge. Before they set off, the riders paused for a minute's silence to remember their fallen comrades.

Most of the competitors had barely had any chance to restart their training, so it was little surprise that the peloton stayed pretty much intact for the first 200 of the 280km. The Pélissier brothers, Henri and Francis, instigated the winning move, although Francis, the younger of the brothers, paid the price of both failing to eat enough and three punctures in quick succession. He fell away after Belgium's Philippe Thys had bridged across to the pair and upped the pace. When the two leaders had to halt at a level crossing across which a train had stopped, Honoré Barthélémy joined them.

Never the most patient of men, and realising more riders would soon arrive at the crossing, Henri Pélissier followed the example set by Tour of Flanders winner Henri Van Leerberghe in the exactly the same situation just four weeks before. He shouldered his bike, jumped the barrier, climbed into the nearest carriage, crossed to the door on the other side, jumped down again, and was off. Thys and Barthélémy didn't hesitate in doing the same, and these three pushed on to Roubaix.

With the velodrome still requiring renovation, the finish had been moved to the Avenue des Villas in the centre of the city. The sharp-eyed Pélissier spotted the finish banner first and accelerated before his rivals could respond. Mobbed by fans and the press, his first thoughts were for his brother. He declared himself happy with the win but described it as 'not complete' because Francis had not been with him at the finish. That scenario would have to wait.

Pélissier's average speed was a mere 23km/h, seven less than Charles Crupelandt's average in 1914 and a huge 12 less than François Faber had managed in 1913, emphasising both the very poor state of the roads and the lack of condition of the riders even taking into account poor weather. A year on, the riders were fitter, but many of the roads were still treacherous. As a temporary measure, tiny pieces of gravel had been scattered on many of the muddy arteries in France's north-east, and these produced mechanical mayhem. Heavy rain made the mud cloying, and the gravel within it caused countless chains to snap. Paul Deman, the Flemish winner of the inaugural Tour of Flanders in 1913, survived the chaos to savour a lone victory.

If that race was unremarkable, the following year's was anything but. Most of the top riders were still competing under the umbrella of La Sportive, but the Pélissiers, and particularly the cantankerous and argumentative Henri, didn't want to sign a two-year extension to their deal. La Sportive manager Alphonse Baugé, the canny tactician who during his racing days had helped Lucien Lesna win the 1901 edition of Roubaix, told them they had to sign or they would never win a race again. For Henri Pélissier, who already believed the riders were being fleeced by the manufacturers, this demand was the final straw. He approached former rider Jean-Baptiste Louvet, who was searching for riders to form a team competing on his J. B. Louvet bikes. 'We are going to win Paris–Roubaix for you,' Pélissier told him. Louvet doubted that given that Baugé, whose authoritarian manner had led to him being dubbed 'The Marshal', had instructed his riders to prevent the brothers winning any race 'and especially not Paris–Roubaix'. Louvet believed the Pélissiers had no chance of winning anything, but realised the publicity they would deliver. After reflection, he signed them up.

At the start, a journalist reported hearing Henri tell Francis: 'We will attack at Doullens. I will accelerate, you get on my wheel and don't worry about anyone else. At Arras, we will see who we still have with us …' It seems unlikely they would have discussed tactics in so open a manner, but when the leading group reached the hill out of Doullens this was their strategy. Cresting it, they had only three riders for company, although another two soon bridged across. Punctures saw off three of them, fatigue another, leaving them with former Brussels butcher's assistant René Vermandel for company. For some kilometres they vainly tried to shake him. When Henri attacked on the final hill at Hem, the Belgian was unable to follow.

Francis waited until his brother had a decent advantage then launched his own attack, but was slowed by a puncture. Vermandel passed him, only to suffer the same fate. With no time to change their tyres, the two men sprinted for second place on their wooden rims. Francis took it, giving the Pélissiers and J. B. Louvet an astounding one-two. As in 1919, Henri regretted the fact he hadn't been able to cross the line arm in arm with his brother. Hearing this, a commissaire told him: 'You should be grateful for that puncture. If you had crossed the line with your arms around each other's shoulders, I would have disqualified both of you for providing illegal assistance during the race.' Oddly, no such action had been taken against Jean Rossius and Dieudonné Gauthy when they had done exactly the same thing as joint winners of the independents' Liège–Bastogne–Liège in 1912. As with conduct at closed railway crossings, it appears the rules varied from country to country.

Although *L'Auto* lauded Henri Pélissier's success, its headline trumpeting, 'The thoroughbred triumphs, the best man won', Henri Desgrange could not have been more unhappy with the result. According to Pascal Sergent's detailed account of the race in *Chronique d'une Légende: Paris–Roubaix*, Desgrange had told some of his closest associates just days before: 'I'm starting to get exasperated by these Pélissiers. I never want to see their names printed in the headline of my paper again.'

To be fair to Desgrange, he was far from being the only one who had no time for them, and particularly for Henri, who was very much their main agitator and fell out with the press and his sponsors as well as race organisers such as Desgrange. Although Henri Pélissier campaigned for better wages and working conditions for his peers, he belittled many of them with his arrogant comments.

His relationship with Desgrange reached its nadir during the 1924 Tour when, during an interview given to journalist Albert Londres, he complained riders were nothing less than 'prisoners of the road'. He had taken umbrage after a commissaire had checked to see he was wearing at least the two jerseys laid down in the race regulations. 'I can wear 15. What I can't do is start with two and finish with only one,' he told Londres, before going on to describe and produce the various medications riders used to get through the three-week race, ranging from horse liniment to any number of pills. 'We run on dynamite,' Francis chipped in.

Yet Henri Pélissier had two things on his side: huge class on the bike and the undying support of French fans. He was box office, perhaps even to an extent the Muhammad Ali of his day – great to watch and never dull. Certainly, Desgrange was soon wishing there were a few more French riders around with his ability, confidence and determination. However, the Belgians were coming and were set to take an almost unshakeable grip on *La Pascale*.

A Flemish takeover

From 1922 through to the start of the Second World War, Belgium celebrated no fewer than 14 Paris–Roubaix victories, this astounding run beginning with Albert Dejonghe. Too ill to take part in the Tour of Flanders in March, Dejonghe didn't feel he had fully recovered in time for Roubaix. But despotic La Sportive boss Alphonse Baugé decided otherwise. He wasn't about to let one of his best prospects miss both of northern Europe's Classics.

Henri Pélissier and his J. B. Louvet team led the charge almost from the off. By the top of the hill at Doullens, just nine riders remained at the front. As they approached Arras for the toughest sections of the course, Pélissier slipped back, a victim of hunger 'knock'. He was left begging for food from spectators at the roadside.

As Pélissier folded, Dejonghe accelerated and no one could follow. Soon, he was so far ahead of his rivals and the projected speed that he was riding on roads almost devoid of fans. Concerned by the lack of spectators, he slowed to ask one if he was still on the race route. He finished six minutes clear of runner-up Jean Rossius as Belgians filled the top four places.

Just a handful of riders prevented complete Belgian domination of Roubaix, which they ruled with almost the same unbreakable grip as the Tour of Flanders. The two events had very similar characteristics: the rough roads, the elements and their distance being the principal difficulties. It was only much later that Flanders began to feature lots of short and steep climbs, while Roubaix lost its few hills. One of those who did thwart the Belgians was a figure with whom they were very familiar.

In March 1923, Switzerland's Henry 'Heiri' Suter became the first foreigner to win the Tour of Flanders, a considerable feat considering the next one didn't come along until 1949. Two weeks on from that success, the Swiss started as one of the favourites for Roubaix in a huge field comprising more than 200 professional riders and almost as many 'independents' and amateurs. In all, 389 racers set out with Roubaix's Avenue des Villas as their goal.

As per tradition, the Pélissier brothers, boosted by the presence of younger sibling Charles, blew the field apart at Doullens. Their accelerations reduced the lead group to eight riders, but the in-form Suter led a sustained pursuit, taking 14 others with him. The odds of one Swiss beating a dozen Belgians and as many Frenchmen were not good, but not anywhere near as slim as they had been when Suter had outpaced a peloton comprised almost entirely of hard-bitten Flemings a fortnight before.

With the crowd chanting its support for the Pélissiers, Suter came off Marcel Huot's wheel to become the first rider to complete the Flanders/Roubaix double. 'It wasn't too hard. I was confident and more or less sure of winning,' he said as the band at the finish, unfamiliar with the Swiss national anthem, played the 'Marseillaise'. Suter was in the large group that contested the sprint the following year, but the Belgians weren't about to let him deny them twice. Jules Van Hevel, winner of Flanders four years previously, led them home.

The increasing depth of talent meant biggish bunch sprints increasingly became the norm. From the mid-1920s Italian stars such as

Costante Girardengo, Ottavio Bottecchia, Pietro Linari and Alfredo Binda made regular appearances at Roubaix and were always talked up as favourites. However, the lack of climbs compared to Classics such as Milan–Sanremo and the Tour of Lombardy, where they were all regular contenders, counted against them. The hill on the road out of Doullens provided the major obstacle, but by the mid-1920s it did nothing more than stretch the lead group, which would re-form on the Arras plateau.

Belgians continued to dominate, although the French thought they had found a successor to Henri Pélissier in 1927 when Marseille's Joseph Curtel appeared to overhaul Antwerp's Georges Ronsse on the Avenue des Villas. An overexcited French fan told the band leader he should strike up with the 'Marseillaise', but even as it rang out, finish-line judge André Trialoux was insisting: 'I never uttered Curtel's name. Ronsse won by a just a little bit, that's true, but he did win and very properly so.'

Winner of Liège–Bastogne–Liège in 1925 when still a teenager, Ronsse had made his Roubaix debut the following season, finishing well behind winner Julien Delbecque. On the morning of the next edition, the 21-year-old Belgian got into conversation with budding French star André Leducq, who later said of their encounter: 'I always observed with curiosity the new contingent of young Belgian riders who were showing off their ability in France for the first time. Before the start I happened to exchange a few words with one of these 'debutants': he seemed very gentlemanly, honest and expressed himself very quietly but very correctly, carefully rearranging the folds in his purple jersey as he did so. I certainly didn't think he was going to win the race and become one of the greatest champions cycling has known.'

Leducq's own victory hopes disappeared when he punctured five kilometres from the finish. Although the lead group wasn't moving fast and he quickly unwound a spare tube from around his shoulders and put it on the rim, he was thwarted by an overeager fan who picked up his pump and turned the adjuster, releasing all the air needed for fast inflation. His hopes disappeared with it. Yet the Frenchman knew he had had the legs to win and was in equally good shape when he faced up to Ronsse and the rest of the Belgian contingent a year later.

In Pierre Chany's *La Fabuleuse Histoire des Grandes Classiques*, Leducq provides a fascinating insight into his preparations for the race, describing how he spent the week before the race training with Paul Ruinart, his mentor at the famous Vélo-Club Levallois. Of the day itself, he says: 'On the start line, I pumped up my own tyres, wanting to get the pressure right and I carefully undertook an inventory of my pockets to make sure I hadn't forgotten anything: in one a little spanner, in another a pair of safety goggles in case it was muddy towards the end of the race, a small roll of tape, and a bit of cotton for my ears if the wind was too cold.'

Leducq describes being troubled by a broken piece of metal on his toe-clip and riding along looking for someone in the crowd who might have a knife with which he could remove it. Having dealt with that nagging concern, the Frenchman recalls his chase back up to the leaders after a late puncture, getting back on terms with them with the assistance of his Alcyon teammate Gaston Rebry, 'who had finally decided to wait for me'.

One of just five riders in the lead group coming on to the Avenue des Villas, Leducq goes on to describe the finish. 'My poor André, I said to myself, you are done for because Ronsse has got a turn of speed that condemns his rivals. But, at the same time, it would be annoying to be beaten by [Charles] Meunier ... With the authority of someone who is certain of victory, Ronsse accelerated from a long way out, with 400 metres to the line, and immediately gained four or five lengths. He went hard, the devil! Meunier reacted instantly but, as I said, I had no intention of being beaten by him ... Gritting my teeth, my heart pounding, I went off in pursuit of my personal 'enemy'. I got back up to him centimetre by centimetre, nibbling away at his lead until I finally passed him. And it seemed I was getting close to Ronsse ... There was no doubt, the gap between us was clearly diminishing. No more than a metre, 50 centimetres.

Then I was up to him, passing him – I had passed him! … It was over. I was the winner of Paris–Roubaix!' The success earned him a bonus of 5,000 francs from his Alcyon team, a substantial sum in those days.

Known to one and all as 'Dédé', Leducq's handsome features, joyful manner and undisputed reputation as a ladies' man cloaked his mental and physical strength on the bike. Although initially regarded as a Classics specialist with a strong sprint, he would go on to win the Tour de France twice, establishing a record of 25 stage victories, a mark that stood until Eddy Merckx beat it in 1972. In his memoirs, he revealed that the night before his Roubaix victory he and his girlfriend of the time 'yielded to "tender relations".'

Leducq's success was the last by any non-Belgian until the middle of the next decade. Having been outsprinted by the Frenchman in 1928, Georges Ronsse returned to Paris–Roubaix as the world champion. Victory had evaded him at the Tour of Flanders a fortnight before due to a crash late on. He had been the strongest that day and his form was just as good for *La Pascale*. Unfortunately, cycling's fates were still lined up against him.

All went to plan for the world champion as far as Arras, where he pushed up the pace in the lead group, taking three Belgians with him: Leducq's 'enemy' Meunier, young Aimé Déolet and Alfred Hamerlinck. The first two were Ronsse's teammates at La Française, Hamerlinck the odd man out who dropped out of contention when he punctured going through one of the worst passages of the course at Hénin-Liétard. Ronsse kept pressing, knowing the black coal dust thrown up by the leaders and especially by the vehicles following them would hamper the efforts of those chasing behind. Even a puncture 16km from the new finish at the Stade Amédée-Prouvost in Wattrelos failed to disturb his serene progress towards a second title.

He led on to the stadium's cinders, which provided an ideal surface for athletics but not, as would soon be demonstrated, for the finish of a Classic. The three Belgian teammates eased their way slowly around the track until they approached the last corner, where the sprint began to unfold. As he passed Meunier on the outside, Ronsse slipped sideways, crashing to the track and taking Déolet with him. Meunier cruised on to become an honourable, if somewhat fortunate, victor.

Ronsse got to his feet, lifted his bike on to his shoulder and crossed the line on foot. Once over it, he threw his bike to the ground and started to sob. Sections of the crowd showed their displeasure by invading the track, preventing any more riders finishing on the cinders. The next day's papers were highly critical of the finish, declaring it unworthy of the race and wondering what might have happened if there had been a bunch sprint. Many also questioned the ability and commitment of the French riders after Belgians filled the first five places. Why did they bother turning up, they asked.

Twenty-year-old Frenchman Jean Maréchal left the 1930 race asking himself the same question. His prodigious talent had become evident in 1928 when, at the age of 18, he won the national amateur title, partly thanks to the backing he received from former world hour record holder, Oscar Egg. The Swiss ex-pro ran a bike shop in Paris and signed the young tyro to ride for his team, but soon after Maréchal claimed he had been coerced into the deal and in 1929 he agreed a new one with French manufacturer Dilecta. Egg protested to the French federation, which stripped Maréchal of his national title, banned him from racing for three months and fined him for professional infractions. Branded a trouble-maker, Maréchal struggled to find a new backer. In 1930, he was competing as an *individuel* supported by a bike shop owner in Paris's 15th arrondissement, where Maréchal lived.

Regarded as a no-hoper when he lined up at the start of Paris–Roubaix, Maréchal proved a sensation. Always up with the leaders, he attacked with 65km remaining. Just a single rider stuck with him. Julien Vervaecke, riding in the colours of the powerful Alcyon team managed by Ludovic Feuillet, initially co-operated with his young rival, until Feuillet ordered him to 'sit on' and not do any more work. The experienced Belgian stuck to his orders for a while, whistling as he rode, trying to unnerve Maréchal.

Finally, Vervaecke jumped past, surprising the young Frenchman, but not finishing him off. 'I got back up to him five or six kilometres out of Roubaix, then we got very close to each other and he ended up in the ditch,' Maréchal recalled. 'I finished alone in Roubaix, where I had a bad feeling as soon as I crossed the line.'

Feuillet lodged a protest, demanding Maréchal's disqualification. Minutes later, the commissaires relegated the Frenchman to second place. But this was an odd punishment that did not fit the alleged crime. If Maréchal had been guilty of pushing Vervaecke into the ditch, even unintentionally, he should have been disqualified. The Frenchman insisted any contact with his rival had been accidental and hadn't amounted to much more than a brushing of elbows. Even Feuillet agreed Maréchal had not acted deliberately. So what was going on?

Some have suggested the commissaires had been swayed by Belgian fans angered by Vervaecke's fate. However, a much more likely reason for the commissaires' compromise was real or perceived pressure from Alcyon, whose advertising spend within *L'Auto* was considerable. Maréchal insisted he had been robbed, but his relegation stood. Although he went on to win Paris–Tours later that year, his career steadily fizzled out and he turned to a new career as a driving instructor. Vervaecke's eventual fate was much more tragic. In May 1940, Polish soldiers with the British Army demanded he give up his house to them. When Vervaecke refused, they shot him dead.

'The Bulldog' takes charge

During the inter-war years, Belgium produced a new contender for the Roubaix title almost every season. Undoubtedly the pick of them was a squat man with a never-say-die approach. The son of a West Flanders linen merchant who went on to open a shop selling wool and other knitting paraphernalia, Gaston Rebry turned pro in 1926. Nicknamed 'Breier' ('The Knitter') by his Griffon-Dunlop teammates, he quickly gained a new tag after setting such a fierce pace in a team time trial during the 1927 Tour de France that his teammates struggled to keep up and complained about his excessive physical prowess to Alcyon team manager Ludovic Feuillet. From then on Rebry was 'The Bulldog'. With his creased forehead and protruding ears, the name also suited the Belgian's countenance.

Rebry had a lot of muscle packed into his small frame, most of it seemingly comprising slow- rather than fast-twitch fibres, which meant that although he was relentless in his pace-making, he had none of the acceleration the best sprinters boasted. His victory hopes depended on finishing alone. Consequently, the worse the weather got, the better his prospects became. In 1931, heavy rain and strong winds ensured he was in his element. At the start he told reporters: 'These are like holiday conditions for me ...'

The race started at the Luna Park fairground in Argenteuil, where no fewer than 48 Belgians lined up among the 102 starters. The race came alive before Doullens when the lead group split into echelons in a strong crosswind. These diagonal lines of riders have an odd beauty, but riding in them is hellish if you're not close to the front, not in good form and not a powerhouse like Gaston Rebry. Even in the current era, the word 'echelon' is guaranteed to bring a smile to the face of Flemish riders who have spent their cycling lives battling the gusts and gales that blow in off the North Sea.

Sensing that a change in the direction of the road would make the wind more of a factor, Rebry went to the front of the line, determined to make everyone behind him suffer. His pace barely eased on the climb out of Doullens. Topping it, he had just four riders for company, including Ronsse and Charles Pélissier. As the intensity of the rain increased, Rebry kept pressing until he was finally alone. At the line his advantage had extended to almost two minutes.

Denied by Romain Gijssels in 1932, Rebry's Alcyon team returned to winning ways a year later, although the duel between teammates Julien Vervaecke and Sylvère Maes was a bitter one. The two Belgians had seen off all challengers but looked very well matched. Team director Feuillet went up alongside them and gave instructions to Vervaecke, who, unlike Maes, spoke French.

'What did he say?' Maes asked his teammate.

'Monsieur Ludo came up to tell that you must let me win. Your turn will come next year,' Vervaecke informed him.

First-year pro Maes may have been naïve, but he wasn't an idiot. He whipped Vervaecke in the sprint, claiming the first win in an illustrious career that also included two Tour de France victories.

Alcyon's run continued in 1934, although once again there was controversy at the finish. For the first time since 1928, the French celebrated victory as Roger Lapébie romped away from Rebry and another Belgian, Jean Wauters, on the Avenue des Villas. Within minutes, however, Lapébie had been disqualified for not completing the race with the bike he had started on, as the rules stipulated.

The crucial incident occurred just ten kilometres from the finish. France looked to have the race sewn up as sprinters Lapébie and René Le Grevès both had the beating of Rebry and Wauters, who were noted *rouleurs*, or 'rollers', a term used to describe riders who can turn a big gear for hour after hour, usually on flat terrain. But Roubaix's cobbles still had a final word to say. First, Le Grevès halted, his bars broken. Almost immediately, Lapébie punctured. He slowed and spied a machine at the side of the road. It was only once he was on it that he realised it was a woman's bike, but he continued on until he saw another more suited to racing. Once aboard it, he bore down on the two Belgians and roasted them in the sprint. There was uproar. Lapébie, wearing the colours of the French champion, had triumphed. But the 'Marseillaise' had barely finished before the news of Lapébie's disqualification spread. The title went to Rebry.

That incident undoubtedly played a part in the introduction the following year of new rules allowing riders to exchange wheels with teammates or get new ones from their team car. Bikes were changing, too, thanks to the widespread introduction of the alloy Duralumin, which was used in the manufacture of stronger and lighter wheels, bars, brakes and other components. The product revolutionised bike technology, reducing their weight from more than ten kilograms in 1932 to less than eight kilograms three years later. Some riders were using derailleurs as well, giving them more than a single gear to work with.

There were some complaints that the improvement of bikes and their componentry, the physical preparation of riders and the condition of the roads was making Paris–Roubaix a different kind of race, and nothing like the brutal test it had once been. This point was backed up when the 1935 winner recorded a new average speed of 39.230km/h, although the peloton had been driven along by a tailwind for most of the day. But was that the case?

L'Auto's Jacques Goddet certainly didn't think so, pointing out that the wind may have made the race faster but it didn't make it easier. The pace was red-hot almost from the start, which meant any mechanical mishap was fatal to a rider's chances. Rebry was one of the few who managed to chase back into the leading group after puncturing, although it took him 18km to complete his pursuit. The race was still incredibly hard, just in a different way.

After chasing back up to the lead group, Rebry barely paused to recover before going up to the front of the pack to beat out a murderous rhythm. With 30km remaining, he had just two riders left on his wheel – his own teammate Jean Aerts, and Dédé Leducq. With 20km left, Aerts, his face a picture of distress, fell away, producing a head-to-head between two of the sport's aces.

Rebry showed all his class and ability, jumping off the cobbles and on to the beaten-earth track at the roadsides when he had the chance, hopping back on to the pavé when spectators blocked the way ahead. Leducq tracked his every move, knowing he would win the sprint if he could stay with the Belgian into the new finish at Hippodrome des Flandres racecourse at Marcq-en-Baroeul, where 40,000 fans were waiting. But, with 15km remaining, the Frenchman realised his rear tyre was deflating. He slowed to give it a quick blast of air, but as he did so, Rebry was gone in a cloud of dust. At the racecourse, the 40,000 fans hailed 'Mr Paris–Roubaix', the first rider since Octave Lapize in the pre-war period to win three editions of *La Pascale*.

The Belgian champion, who always prepared for Roubaix by riding 180km of the route five days before the race, almost added a fourth success the following season, but lost out in a three-up sprint to Romain Maes and Georges Speicher. Frenchman Speicher seemed to have the race won, but Tour de France champion Maes – no relation to his compatriot Sylvère – got up to win by half a length. Or at least that is what most of those crammed into the Hippodrome thought. Somehow, though, the commissaires on the line saw it differently. With no photo-finish technology available to correct the apparent mistake, the Duralumin Trophy for the Roubaix champion went to Speicher, much to the consternation of even the partisan French press. It may have seemed as if justice had been done to the French after the misfortunes that had befallen Curtel, Maréchal and Lapébie in previous seasons, but those controversies had nothing to do with Maes, who, it is worth noting, had moved to Labor from Alcyon, where Speicher was one of the leaders.

While that finish was contentious, the following year's was remarkable as Jules Rossi outsprinted no fewer than four Belgians to become Italy's first Roubaix champion. In truth, a good part of his victory belonged to France, where Rossi had moved as a six-year-old with some of his family after being orphaned. He had come up through the ranks with the renowned Vélo Club de Levallois, which had previously brought through Roubaix and Tour de France champions Louis Trousselier and Dédé Leducq.

Lucien Storme's victory in 1938 was just as astonishing as Rossi's because Roubaix was only his fourth race of that season after he'd spent the previous year completing his military service. Mentored by Rebry, the 21-year-old raced in the colours of André Leducq's team. Winner of a stage in the Tour de France the following season, he led a new wave of Belgian talent whose hopes were soon blunted by the outbreak of war. Storme continued to race in Belgium during the war years, but took to smuggling to boost his income. He was arrested in 1942 and faced the prospect of a prison sentence in Belgium, but made a bid to escape, striking a German officer during his attempt. In March 1943, the Germans transported to him to the labour camp at Siegburg, near Cologne. Illness very nearly cost him his life, but he survived to see the Americans liberate the camp in April 1945. Tragically, in the confusion that ensued, Storme sustained a fatal bullet wound in his neck.

The final post-Great War edition fell to another young Belgian, Liège's Émile Masson Jr, whose father had finished third in 1922. Émile Sr regularly told his son: 'I want to see you win Paris–Roubaix and die two hours later. If it ends like that, I will go in peace, telling myself: "I have made a champion of my son. Now, he no longer needs to rely on me …" '

As it turned out, Émile Sr lived until 1973, giving him plenty of time to reflect on his son's towering performance. Having broken away on his own with 25km remaining, Masson punctured and saw the two riders he had just dropped pass him, followed soon after by a 14-strong chase group. He quickly got on the back of this group, caught his breath, then went past them, with only Georges Speicher managing to follow his acceleration. Masson dragged the Frenchman across to Roger Lapébie and Luxembourger Jean Majerus, then pressed hard again and this time no one stayed with him.

By now, another war was almost guaranteed, and it would be four years before Masson's successor was revealed.

7

UNDER ATTACK FROM TARMAC

Despite the outbreak of war in September 1939 and the general mobilisation that was already taking place, Paris–Roubaix's organisers at *L'Auto* continued to plan for the forty-first edition of *La Pascale*. With a German invasion becoming ever more likely and Roubaix at the centre of a key militarised zone, the French high command made it clear to *L'Auto*'s editor-in-chief and Roubaix race director Jacques Goddet that there was absolutely no chance of him running an event into the city in April 1940. Denied this option, Goddet and his team contemplated reversing the route, but the progress of the war soon ended these discussions.

In January 1940, plans for the invasion of France and the Low Countries, codenamed *Fall Gelb* (Case Yellow), were found in the wreckage of a German military plane that crashed in Belgium. They revealed the Germans were planning to delay their offensive until the spring, when better weather was more likely. Although the French army mobilised along its north-eastern border, the Germans stuck to their plan. On 10 May, the invasion began. Exactly two weeks later, German forces occupied Roubaix – a vital gain because of its textile industries. By 1941, three-quarters of the output of Roubaix's mills and factories was being sent to Germany.

As the Germans readied their invasion, *L'Auto* did organise a race for the Duralumin Trophy, which had been presented to Roubaix's winners since 1937. Sixty-three riders – only one of them Belgian – lined up in

Le Mans beneath a banner announcing 'Paris–Roubaix, départ' for a race that finished in Paris at the Parc des Princes stadium, where Frenchman Joseph Soffietti took the trophy. Similar events took place between Paris and Reims the following two years, and were dubbed 'the ersatz Paris–Roubaix' by one journalist. The authentic event returned in 1943 in extremely controversial circumstances.

As the head of a very prominent publication, Goddet's wartime position was delicate and rather complicated. He never hid the fact he was sympathetic to the collaborationist Vichy government of Maréchal Pétain. However, he insisted this stemmed primarily from his respect for First World War hero Pétain and his initially conservative principles, which took on a much more fascistic and sinister aspect in the wake of the complete occupation of France by the Axis powers in November 1942. Goddet was also compromised by the clear German bias of *L'Auto*'s general news pages, which stemmed from his brother, Maurice, selling his share of the business they had inherited from their father, Victor Goddet, to a consortium of German businessmen.

In his 1991 autobiography, *L'Équipée Belle*, Goddet defended his wartime actions, revealing that he allowed *L'Auto*'s presses to be used by fellow publisher and Resistance member Émilien Amaury for the printing of material supporting the campaign against France's occupiers. However, he skirted around his involvement in one of the blackest days in France's wartime history. In July 1942, French police rounded up 13,000 Parisian Jews. The Nazis detained them in the Vel' d'Hiv' arena, which had been built by Henri Desgrange and Jacques Goddet in 1902. The Germans had been handed the keys to the building by Jacques Goddet. Held in cramped, hot and unsanitary conditions due to a complete lack of toilets, the 13,000 men, women and children remained in the arena famed for track racing, roller skating, animal hunts and other spectacles for five days before being transported to Auschwitz. Only 400 of them survived.

The ambiguity of Goddet's wartime position is further complicated by his stance on the Tour de France. He refused to organise it during the wartime years, later suggesting he had prevented the tainting of the event. Yet, due to the Vichy government's prompting, he did organise the Grand Prix du Tour de France, a season-long competition based around a series of one-day races, including Paris–Tours and Paris–Roubaix.

On 25 April 1943, 120 riders lined up in St-Denis for the forty-first edition of Paris–Roubaix, including more than 30 Belgians. The clear favourite was world champion Marcel Kint. Like most Flemings, Kint had been able to continue racing during the war, giving them a distinct advantage over their French rivals, whose racing calendar had been more seriously affected. Although the French contingent did all they could to prevent the Belgians imposing a stranglehold, coming into the finish in Roubaix's velodrome the five-strong lead group contained four riders from across the border, including Kint and teammate Jules Lowie. The odd man out was Frenchman Louis Thiétard, about whom Kint knew very little. His main concern was the finishing speed of Achiel Buysse and Albert Sercu. To neuter the threat they posed, Lowie attacked soon after the quintet arrived on the cement bowl. Buysse and Sercu had to respond. Just as they were getting up to Lowie's wheel, Kint accelerated past them and the title was his.

That evening Kint covered the 25km back to his home in Zwevegem on his bike with his kit in his backpack, as he was generally forced to do given the restrictions imposed on car use due to petrol rationing. 'Not far from home, I bumped into one of my supporters who asked me what I'd been doing. I told him that I'd just won Paris–Roubaix. But he didn't believe me and burst out laughing. In fact no one believed me until they saw the proof of it in the papers the next morning,' Kint told journalist Pascal Sergent many years later. 'I've got so many memories of Paris–Roubaix. More than anything, you had to be an acrobat to jump from the pavement on one side of the road to the other using a gear of 49x17.'

Despite the threat of an Allied invasion, Paris–Roubaix went ahead in 1944, when the start moved to Compiègne for the first time. The title went back across the border with Maurice De Simpelaere, who finished half a length up on Jules Rossi. De Simpelaere was one of just 14 Belgians who were able to return in 1945 as the Allies swept across northern Europe. Although he was one of seven riders who contested the sprint, six French riders outmanoeuvred the defending champion. Paul Maye proved the quickest of them as home riders filled the podium for the first time since 1912.

The Belgians returned in force in 1946, led by De Simpelaere and their latest Classics sensation, Rik Van Steenbergen. Yet both would be upstaged by a compatriot who had spent much of the previous year in Ireland, having been conscripted into the Belgian army in 1945. The image of pedalling perfection, Georges Claes may well be the least renowned of Roubaix winners, and is certainly so of those who won the race twice. Talented and strong enough to finish second in the Tour of Flanders in 1942 and fifth in Roubaix two years later, Claes joined the early break that went away after just 17km. More than 200km later, after the peloton had reeled the escape in, the elegant 26-year-old was still at the front and felt strong enough to attack approaching the '*virage de Wattignies*' (the Wattignies bend), an infamous section of cobbles 22km from the finish that had become one of Roubaix's key points.

Frenchman Louis Gauthier was the only one of the 30-strong group who opted to counter across to Claes, and the pair steadily forged a winning advantage. Known as 'The Chainbreaker', Gauthier managed to avoid that fate. Crucially, though, one of his toe-clips was damaged, which undoubtedly affected his sprint as he was unable to pull on his upstroke with his usual massive force. Yet, even if his bike had been completely intact, it is doubtful Gauthier could have beaten Claes, such was the Belgian's form that day.

Claes' successful defence of his title couldn't have been any more different in its construction. He held back from the early breakaway, which went after 20km and comprised seven riders. By halfway, four had fallen back. Beyond Amiens, with half the race completed, Italian

Olimpio Bizzi had dropped his two other companions and was leading the race on his own. As the rain poured down and the roads became more glutinous, Bizzi ploughed on until, with 17km left, he misjudged his jump off the cobbles and up on to the dirt path alongside them. A heavy landing cost him a broken wheel and most of his two-minute lead. Bizzi pressed on, only to be caught by three riders a mere two kilometres from the finish.

Claes, compatriot Adolf Verschueren and Frenchman Louis Thiétard blasted past the Italian, leaving Bizzi to reflect on his ill fortune. When the trio reached the saturated Roubaix track, Claes positioned himself at the back of the line and tracked his rivals skilfully before shooting through to victory. His secret? 'I only ate 300g of sugar lumps and seven bananas, and I also had a bit of good luck.'

The Belgian's double could easily have become a treble in 1948 if that good fortune had stayed with him. As it turned out, he finished third in what was arguably the strongest field Roubaix had ever seen. The introduction of the Desgrange-Colombo Challenge, comprising three races in each of France, Italy and Belgium, guaranteed the presence of most of the sport's biggest names, including Fiorenzo Magni, Briek Schotte, Ferdi Kübler, Hugo Koblet and Louison Bobet. Yet, most pre-race attention focused on Rik Van Steenbergen.

He had burst on to the scene by winning Flanders as a 20-year-old in 1944 and had won it again two years later. During that period, he always started Roubaix as one of the big favourites, but had been thwarted by mechanical setbacks. As canny as he was classy, Van Steenbergen stayed in the depths of the peloton as a blustery tailwind blew a seven-man break along for more than 200km. Italy's Magni was the biggest name in it, regularly complaining of illness and problems with his derailleur, according to another of the seven, Robert Chapatte, who would go on to become the voice of cycling on French radio and TV, as well as putting forward Chapatte's Law, which has it that it takes a group ten kilometres to chase down a lone rider with a one-minute lead. The 'law' is still mentioned frequently in the current era, although Chapatte's name is not often attached to it.

Magni and compatriot Gildo Monari were the last of the escapees to hold out. More than a dozen riders bridged across to the Italian pair before the *virage de Wattignies*. Passing through this section and over the rough pavé at Ascq, more than half the front group was waylaid by punctures, leaving just six men at the front: the dogged Magni and Monari, Claes, Van Steenbergen, Adolf Verschueren and France's Émile Idée, who was sure he would have no chance in a straight-up sprint against the Belgians.

On the outskirts of Roubaix, Idée attacked. For a few seconds, no one responded. Sitting on Claes' wheel, Van Steenbergen finally committed himself and, partly thanks to the shelter briefly offered by a car, managed to jump across the gap to Idée. The pair entered the velodrome together, where the result was never in doubt, as Idée himself admitted later. The gap between them was ten metres at the line, where the Belgian recorded an average speed of 43.612km/h, the best ever recorded in a major Classic up to that point. Van Steenbergen, who had spent a lot of time racing on the track, said, 'This will be my best and my worst memory. It's the best because my return to road racing has enabled me to win one of the greatest races. It was my worst because I've never suffered as much.'

The race with two winners

Paris–Roubaix had produced plenty of finish-line controversy during its first half-century, but nothing to compare with events at the end of the 1949 race, which culminated in two riders topping the podium. Pitched as a contest between Van Steenbergen and Roubaix debutant Fausto Coppi, it ended up being a contest between a number of the peloton's support players, who took advantage of the favourites' close surveillance of each other.

Jesús Moujica, Spanish-born but a naturalised Frenchman since the previous year, instigated the winning attack at Séclin, 25km from the finish. Belgians Florent Mathieu and Frans Leenen joined Moujica. Late on, Frenchman André Mahé bridged across, just before Mathieu crashed out of contention. As the leading trio approached the velodrome in the wake of a pack of press and official cars, Mahé struck out on his own, determined to reach the track first. Waved on by a gendarme, the Breton followed the cars and Moujica and Leenen followed him. Only when they found themselves behind the grandstand rather than in front of it did the three riders realise they had been directed along the detour for race vehicles and not straight on to the track. In the confusion that followed, Moujica fell and broke a pedal.

Belgian journalist Albert De Wetter, who had just leapt off his press motorbike, grasped what was happening before the riders. He waved Mahé and Leenen up the stairs to the press gallery, from where they were able to clamber down through the crowd and on to the track, where they battled it out for the title. Mahé won the race for the line and was completing a lap of honour when Coppi's younger brother Serse led in the bunch to finish third. After that, there was pandemonium.

Having been told by journalists of Mahé's diversion, Fausto Coppi persuaded Serse to lodge a protest on the basis that Mahé hadn't completed the official route or race distance. Minutes later, the Frenchman emerged from the showers to find the commissaires had ruled Serse Coppi the winner. Five days later, the French federation overturned the result again, declaring Mahé the champion and Leenen the runner-up. On receiving this news, the Italian federation appealed to the UCI. In August, four months on from the event, the sport's ruling body annulled the result pending their Zurich congress in late November.

Just prior to it, Fausto Coppi spoke up about the controversy, telling journalists: 'I want nothing more than to ride Paris–Roubaix again, especially as that magnificent race is missing from my palmarès, but, more than anything, I would like to see them return Serse's victory. If not, it is more than likely that you won't see me at the start next year.' To an extent, he got what he wanted. Ultimately, the UCI tried to please everyone by declaring Mahé and Serse Coppi joint victors.

It was the only major victory of Serse's career, which ended tragically two years later when his wheel got stuck in a tram track in the sprint at the end of Milan–Turin, sending him crashing head-first to the road. Although he rode back to his hotel, he fell ill that night. Rushed to hospital, he died in Fausto's arms having suffered a brain haemorrhage. Moujica, who was eventually classified joint third with Leenen and Georges Martin, also met a sad and premature end. In November 1950, he died in a car crash at Montélimar along with Jean Rey, who had been French champion the year before.

As for Mahé, he continued to question why he had been penalised for a gendarme's mistake. Speaking to *Procycling* in 2007, three years before his death, Mahé also questioned Fausto Coppi's attitude. 'He was a great champion, Coppi, but to do what he did – to protest like that to get a victory for his brother – wasn't dignified for a champion. That was beneath him.' Even six decades on, the 87-year-old Mahé confessed he was still marked by that day's events. 'I was alone. I would have won alone.'

Mahé also offered an insight into the Roubaix of his racing days, recalling: 'There were cobbles from the moment you left Paris … There'd be stretches of surfaced road and often there would be a cycle path or a pavement and sometimes a thin stretch of something smoother. But you never knew where was best to ride and you were forever switching about. You could jump your bike up on to a pavement, but that got harder the more tired you got. In the end, you would get the front wheel up but not the back and you'd go sprawling. And, come what may, you got covered in coal dust and muck.'

Following the controversy of 1949, there was absolutely no doubt about the winner a year on. After a poor debut outing on the pavé that did at least produce a good result in the end, Fausto Coppi returned to

La Pascale determined to add the title to his already lengthy palmarès. He'd completed the Giro/Tour double the previous season, as well as winning Sanremo and Lombardy. Some, though, still felt Roubaix was beyond him, that the Belgian cobbles specialists would overpower him. However, if ever a victory could be described as a romp, this was it.

Coppi tested his rivals out on the hill at Doullens, scattering them, then allowing them to regather. Approaching Arras, Gino Sciardis and Maurice Diot went away, and Coppi sensed his moment was close. Nearing the final feed station at Arras, Coppi went to the front. He had no intention of grabbing a musette and stocking up before the most difficult sections of cobbled roads. Instead, he accelerated and flew across the gap to the two leaders.

His pace immediately proved too much for Sciardis. Diot clung on, offering the occasional relay until instructed to desist by his Mercier team director, Antonin Magne, who hoped Coppi had gone too hard and too soon, and that Mercier leader Van Steenbergen in the group chasing behind would be able to get back on terms. Coppi responded to Diot's tactic by raising his pace once again, spinning a huge 52x15 gear at a cadence the Frenchman couldn't cope with. Over the remaining 45km, the Italian's lead ballooned to the extent that he was able to ease off and savour the crowd's cheers as he rode into Roubaix and on to the velodrome. Diot finished almost three minutes back in second. As he jumped off his bike, he said: 'I've won Paris–Roubaix. Coppi was in another contest!'

A beaming Coppi declared: 'I didn't really suffer at any moment … I rode the last 40km without forcing things and the applause I received in Roubaix really touched me and allowed me to savour my victory.' Writing in *L'Équipe* the next day, Jacques Goddet said it looked as if he was riding on his home trainer.

Coppi's victory marked the start of a golden age for *La Pascale*. Unlike the current era when most stage race specialists stay well clear of the cobbled Classics, almost all of the sport's biggest names would line up at the start in St-Denis, resulting in a succession of thrillingly unpredictable races. Among the best was the fiftieth edition in 1952, which culminated in a duel between Coppi and Van Steenbergen, who had chased back up to the lead group from a seemingly hopeless position, driven on by the thought of the criticism that had been heaped upon him after a poor showing at Flanders the weekend before.

Over the last 20km, Coppi attacked again and again, knowing he would have no chance of defeating the Belgian in a sprint. Van Steenbergen, drawing on every little bit of strength he had, refused to yield. Once in the velodrome, Coppi had no answer to the Belgian's finishing speed. Van Steenbergen admitted that if the Italian had attacked just one more time he would have capitulated.

Three years on, Coppi came to the race with one goal in mind – preventing world champion Louison Bobet from winning. The two men had been good friends, but Coppi had been irked by the Frenchman's steady rise to the summit of the sport, which Bobet had confirmed with two consecutive Tour de France victories and his World Championship success. After Bobet had become the first Frenchman to win the Tour of Flanders a fortnight before Roubaix, Coppi told a journalist: 'If I don't go, he will win, that's for sure. There's absolutely no question about it.' Friendship, it seemed, only went so far.

The riders set off on a cold and wet Easter Day with a significantly altered course ahead of them. The roads department in north-eastern France had been steadily improving the regional network, laying tarmac over the top of the cobbles. Often these works were done at the express request of local mayors and councils who didn't appreciate being part of 'The Hell of the North' and were determined to modernise the region. As a result, the key section from Hénin-Liétard, through Carvin, Séclin and Wattignies, to Lesquin had been removed from the route, which now turned north-east to take the riders up the cobbled climb at Mons-en-Pévèle, before returning to the traditional course at Ascq.

As the race approached this new section, the rain had become torrential and the riders were hard to distinguish. Bobet, his white jersey with its rainbow bands barely recognisable, drove hard on the front of the group chasing behind three riders just seconds ahead. On the hill at Mons-en-Pévèle, Frenchman Jean Forestier emerged as the strongest of this trio, but a powerful group had formed not far behind him, which included Bobet, Coppi and defending champion Raymond Impanis. Forestier's lead was little more than 200m, but none of the riders behind would commit fully to pursuing him. Coppi knew he wouldn't be able to match Bobet in a sprint in the velodrome, while Bobet feared his compatriot Gilbert Scodeller, who had proved too quick for him at Paris–Tours the previous autumn. This resulted in stalemate.

For the final 20km, Forestier remained no more than 300m ahead of his pursuers, but it was enough of a buffer for him to take the title. The sprint for second was fierce, Coppi jumping first but still not quick enough to better the raging Bobet. 'That traitor! That ingrate!' he spat out almost as soon as he had rolled to a stop. 'If Coppi had agreed to ride at the end we would certainly have caught Forestier. Unfortunately, Fausto decided to play the loser's role and opt instead for second place. If I'd been him, I wouldn't have dared to sprint. I raced to win, but Fausto only raced with the aim of beating me.'

Coppi claimed he hadn't been in the best of form, but did at least achieve his objective of preventing Bobet from winning, which didn't do much for their relationship. As for Forestier, a man of few words who was a great stylist on the bike, this victory raised him to a new level. The following year he won Flanders. He later said of Roubaix: 'It's a race that I used to love, not only because I won it, but also because it's very hard – it's every man for himself.'

Bobet put this disappointment behind him that summer with a third consecutive Tour de France victory. But he ended the race tormented by a huge saddle boil. That winter, a surgeon removed a large mass of rotting flesh from the wound, leaving a scar 20cm long with a raised edge that could reopen if he rode in the wet or on especially rough roads. It was widely suggested that Bobet's career as a top-line rider was over, and no one expected him to appear for Roubaix. He later admitted he came close to retiring such was the pain he endured when he returned to racing, but a win the weekend before Roubaix gave him hope, as did a forecast for a dry race.

Once again, the climb at Mons-en-Pévèle proved significant. A strong group formed on the descent from it. Van Steenbergen was up there, as were three Mercier riders: recent Sanremo winner Fred De Bruyne, Bernard Gauthier and, surprisingly, Bobet. Van Steenbergen looked around for his teammate, world champion Stan Ockers, but he'd been waylaid by a puncture. He realised what was about to come and was soon chasing down attacks by De Bruyne and Gauthier, as Bobet looked on. When they reached the track, Van Steenbergen's sprinting speed had been sucked out of him. De Bruyne flew by with Bobet on his wheel, leading him out perfectly as the crowd roared the Frenchman home.

'Monsieur Fred' De Bruyne, a very popular figure in the pro peloton, took a hammering in the Belgian press for helping a Frenchman win Roubaix at Van Steenbergen's expense. That winter, fed up with a lieutenant's role, he left Mercier to become the leader of the Italian Carpano-Coppi team and redeemed himself with a fine solo win in *La Pascale*, despite a puncture a kilometre from the finish. Fittingly, that 1957 success came on the tenth anniversary of his first pro race.

Roubaix under threat

Even as Roubaix's route continued to change, the 1958 edition seeing another shift to the east near the finish through Templeuve and Cysoing rather than Ascq, Belgium's grip remained as tight as ever. De Bruyne was followed to the top of the podium by Léon Van Daele, Noël Foré and Sicilian-born, naturalised Belgian Pino Cerami. The only surprise about those names was the absence of Rik Van Looy's. By 1959, he had won all of the Classics bar Roubaix and Liège–Bastogne–Liège. The latter was understandable given its long hills that favoured better climbers than 'Rik II', but his failure to win Roubaix was almost unfathomable.

Although bad luck had played a part, Van Looy's principal problem was that ability and reputation ensured he always started the race as one of the big favourites, which meant no one was likely to collaborate with him. In addition, the exceedingly unpredictable nature of Roubaix meant Van Looy's 'Red Guard' (riders signed by Faema to do whatever their team leader asked of them, which meant devoting themselves completely to him in the Classics) couldn't implement their usual strategy of riding as hard as they could for as long as they could, softening up Van Looy's rivals before their leader delivered the final stroke. Although hardly flamboyant, the tactic was highly effective. Van Looy defended himself by saying: 'The tougher a race is, the lower the chances are of the smaller riders winning.'

In 1961, this strategy finally paid off. Faema kept the pace high and Van Looy, wearing the world champion's jersey, was in the right position to track the most dangerous moves without overly committing himself. Coming into the velodrome with five other riders, his biggest concern was fellow Belgian Émile Daems. Sweeping around the final bend, Van Looy had the inside line and made it count, holding off his rivals by a bike length. 'I've won Paris–Roubaix! I've won Paris–Roubaix!' he kept repeating. 'I'm the happiest man in the world.' Asked if he would now make the defence of his world title his objective, he responded: 'The World Championship? But I've just won it!' Having got that monkey off his back, Van Looy completed the full set of Classics in Liège later that month.

After soloing to a second Roubaix victory in 1962, Van Looy should have wrapped up a hat-trick, but made a tactical blunder on the final lap, going high up the track in an effort to use the banking to launch himself at the line, but allowing Daems to dive through on his inside to claim the title. This was Belgium's seventh victory in a row and the third time in succession their riders had filled all three positions on the podium. However, while the French press were once again reflecting on why their riders were unable to compete with the Belgians, as they had done in the pre-war years, the race organisers were contemplating a much more fundamental problem.

As the pace of road improvement continued, Paris–Roubaix featured fewer and fewer sections of pavé. It was reaching the point where it was in danger of becoming a race that was unremarkable in every aspect apart from its length – a spring version of Paris–Tours, almost. This was highlighted when Peter Post became the first Dutch winner in 1964, recording a record average speed of 45.131km/h over 265km where the pavé was little more than a foundation for newly laid tarmac. Over the subsequent 12 months, the pace of resurfacing quickened, despite concern being voiced by the event's organisers and many of its biggest names. When Van Looy completed a hat-trick of wins that year, the course included a mere 22km of pavé. In other words, less than ten per cent of the course was now run on cobbled roads.

Route director Jean Garnault warned that if nothing were done to save the pavé there would be none left at all over the final 45km of the course within four years. He met with representatives from the region's department of bridges and roads to voice his concerns, but they fell on deaf ears. In common with almost all of the region's elected representatives, they wanted to provide local drivers with the best road network they could, which meant continuing to cover the hellish cobbles of a race they viewed with disdain because of the negative image most believed it presented of the north.

Although the race was being neutered in terms of the challenge it offered, its status and list of winners remained as elevated as ever. Van Looy described his 1965 win as 'the most beautiful victory of my career'. The implacable Belgian hadn't won a Classic for three seasons and was being written off at the age of 32. Loyally supported by teammate Edward Sels, who many said was the strongest rider in the field on the day, Van Looy attacked from the lead group ten kilometres from the finish. Noël Foré went with him, but punctured almost immediately, allowing Van Looy to savour a second solo victory on the velodrome.

Had Van Looy shed tears as he finished, some wondered? 'The Emperor of Herentals' (named after the small Belgian town where he lived) denied it, but he was unusually talkative at the finish, underlining the height of his emotions. 'If I had failed with my effort, Ward Sels would have countered immediately. And he would certainly have won Paris–Roubaix then. Let's just say that it was me who had luck on his side,' Van Looy confessed in rather untypical fashion.

When Willy Vannitsen took third place, Belgians filled the podium for the fifth time in nine years. With 65 riders on the start line, their entry was double that of France, which had 32, of whom only Raymond Poulidor, Jacques Anquetil and the unlucky Jean Stablinski were likely contenders. The numbers reflected the grounding Flemish riders in particular got in their own Classics and the dozens of kermesses that took place across the region.

Known as *kermis* in Dutch – 'kermesse' derives from the words for church and mass and relates to the festival held to celebrate the anniversary of a church's foundation – these events had become extremely popular in the post-war years. Held on short and tight circuits, usually between five and ten kilometres in length, they often featured cobbles and were run at very high speed, requiring frequent intense efforts when sprinting out of corners and unwavering handling skills – excellent training for Paris–Roubaix.

But even the Belgians couldn't win every year, as Italy's Felice Gimondi demonstrated in 1966. This was a landmark edition, which saw new sections of pavé introduced close to Roubaix. In order to accommodate these without stretching the race distance overly, the finish was moved to Chantilly. In addition, and far more radically, the whole route shifted eastwards, thereby missing long-standing features, most notably the 2.5km climb of the Côte de Doullens.

The alterations gave the race a look that will be more familiar to spectators in the twenty-first century. Walter Godefroot would later say of it: 'When you lead on to the first section of cobbles, you feel like you have won a stage. After that you've got no time to think about anything.' The route didn't feature any notable difficulty until it reached St-Quentin, almost halfway into the 262.5km. The toughest sections fell within the final 80km, including the now key ascent at Mons-en-Pévèle. There was even a modification of this recent introduction, as the organisers opted to send the riders up it on the rough Pas-Rolland lane.

The alterations were so extensive that most of the favourites opted to view them in the days leading up to the race. Salvarani's Vittorio Adorni and Felice Gimondi were among those to ride the final 80km, Gimondi deciding he would attack hard on the Pas-Rolland in an attempt to shake out some of the many riders blessed with a better sprint finish than him. Leading with compatriot Michele Dancelli and Belgium's Jacques de Boever going on to the Pas-Rolland, Gimondi implemented his plan, charging up the cobbles. Alone at the top, and with 40km to the finish, he didn't wait for any help to come up from behind. As the Dutch and the Belgians waited for each other to take up the pursuit, Italy's Tour de France champion rode away to a win reminiscent of Fausto Coppi in his pomp, finishing more than four minutes clear. 'No, no, I'm not Monsieur Coppi, but I hope one day to be worthy of succeeding him,' said Gimondi after the comparison was put to him.

There was a rider in the field who would soon prove worthy of picking up Coppi's mantle, but it wasn't Gimondi. As the peloton sped along less than 50km in, Jean Stablinski rode up alongside Rik Van Looy to ask who the young Belgian was setting such a furious pace so early in the race. 'Jean, you will soon find out all about him, he's called Eddy Merckx,' Van Looy told him.

Merckx finished fourteenth after a bike change and a couple of punctures, then went closer still the following year, 1967, taking eighth in the bunch sprint behind Dutchman Jan Janssen, who edged out Van Looy by half a wheel. 'It's tough to lose by as little as that, but I prefer doing so to Jan. He's a great champion who knows how to take risks,' said Van Looy, whose rivalry with Merckx had been bitter since they spent a season together at Solo-Superia in 1965.

But Merckx's time was coming, as was a new and fearsome addition to the Roubaix route ...

8

THE NORTH FALLS IN LOVE WITH `HELL`

In the wake of the 1967 edition, when the Pas-Rolland had become little more than a beautifully surfaced pimple that barely extended the main contenders, race director Jacques Goddet instructed his route director, ex-pro Albert Bouvet, to continue the search for new sections of pavé. Bouvet turned to his friend Jean Stablinski for guidance. Born and brought up in Bellaing, a few kilometres to the west of Valenciennes, Stablinski was of Polish stock. His father, Martin Stablewski, had come to northern France in the mid-1920s looking for work in the mines, leaving his wife and four children in Poland. Once established, his family joined him in France, only for his wife to die soon after giving birth to a fifth child. He subsequently met and married his second wife in Poland, and returned with her to France. Jean Stablewski was born in 1932.

Four years after his father died (he was run over by a German army truck in June 1940), Jean left school to become an apprentice plumber in order to prevent the family losing their home. Very much against his mother's wishes, he also began to indulge his passion for bike racing, quickly attracting plenty of good newspaper notices, including one that predicted a very bright future for 'Jean Stablinski'. The name stuck.

At 19, Stablinski went to work in the mine at nearby Wallers-Arenberg, moving wagons full of coal and wooden supports for the tunnels dug into coal seams. As he worked underground, his mother would cycle through the Arenberg Forest hundreds of feet above him to her job in a pottery works at St-Amand-les-Eaux. When Albert Bouvet came to see him in 1967, Stablinski took him to investigate this road through the forest. 'I knew where there were hundreds of terrible cobbled stretches deep in the countryside, including the Tranchée d'Arenberg. I was worried about showing him it,' the 1962 world champion and four-time national champion later admitted to *L'Équipe*. 'Nevertheless, I did so and he was impressed. He brought a photographer with him. When they showed Jacques Goddet the pictures, he said to Bouvet: "I asked you to find pavé, not a rutted track."'

Stablinski described the Arenberg Forest as 'a lung for the miners'. Although overlooked by the huge lift tower of the Compagnies des Mines d'Anzin mine at Wallers-Arenberg, the forest remained untouched, offering the locals hunting, fishing and mushroom picking as distractions.

In April 1968, Stablinski, riding his final season, was one of the 136 riders who tackled the Arenberg for the very first time. 'I could never have imagined that Paris–Roubaix would ever go through there,' said Stablinski, who is now commemorated by a monument just to the left of the entrance to the cobbled section through the forest. 'Not many people know it but an underground roadway runs directly below the Tranchée. I am the only man to have walked under and raced over the cobbles of Arenberg ... I felt such extraordinary emotion when I went into the "trench" for my last Paris–Roubaix. My supporters were waiting for me, all dressed as miners.'

What would become the most mythical and feared section of cobbles on the route is often referred to as 'the Arenberg trench', which was how *L'Équipe's* Pierre Chany described it, seeing the way that it cut through the deep forest and the intensity of the contest between the combatants. The description also offers an insight into the peril that riders face in this dank environment untouched by the sun's warming rays. Extending to 2.4km, the riders approach it via a straight and slightly downhill road past the Arenberg mine, ensuring they are travelling at very high speed when they reach the pavé. Unlike the more uniform granite blocks, or setts, seen in Belgium, these stones are more irregular both in their squareness and top surface. Plenty of edges jut up in puncture-inducing fashion.

The road continues to drop over the first 800m through the trench, passing beneath a rusting railway bridge over which no coal trains have rattled since the mine closed in 1990. Although there are dirt paths to either side of the pavé, where the dry soil that lacks any kind of humus-like quality billows up like Moon dust when touched, crowd barriers ensure the riders in the current era have no chance of finding relief on them. The best line, the riders say, is down the central ridge of the pavé, where the cobbles may stand out more proudly because they aren't as worn by traffic, but offer a more regular and less pitted surface than the sides, which at some points sit 20cm below the central crest. The trick, the riders say, is to ride as fast as possible – more than 40km/h is recommended – thereby 'floating' over the cobbles rather than bouncing from one to the next as most amateurs tend to do when riding at a much more sedate, but consequently more bone-jarring, pace.

As well as the introduction of the Arenberg, 1968 saw plenty of other changes, too. Several more cobbled sections featured as the race headed much more towards Valenciennes than Denain, as it had done previously. The result was a total of 56.5km of pavé, more than 30km up on the low of 1965, including one unbroken section of almost 15km between Templeuve and Bachy.

The treacherous new route demanded a masterful performance and it got one as 92 of the 136 starters failed to finish. Forced to quit Paris–Nice through injury, and unable to add a third consecutive win at Sanremo, Eddy Merckx was not looking at all like 'The Ogre' of the previous year. 'If he is the [peloton's] *patron*, let him prove it,' said Rik Van Looy, happy to needle the rider who had unseated him as king of the Classics. Asked about the difficulty of the new route, he commented: 'So much the better, it will impact on the legs of the younger riders.' Meanwhile, Merckx had told his wife, Claudine, he would win Roubaix because it was expected of every great Belgian rider.

After much build-up, the Arenberg passed without creating a great deal of damage beyond slowing the progress of lone leader Roger Pingeon, who punctured. Once the Frenchman had been swept up, the Belgians took over. Four of them escaped from a lead group of 14, Merckx in his world champion's jersey leading the assault, Edward Sels joining him, followed by Herman Van Springel and Willy Bocklant, who soon fell back to the chasing pack.

When Sels also dropped away after a puncture, Merckx and Van Springel pressed on alone. Van Springel led into the velodrome, but never looked as if he had the beating of Merckx, who went up to the top of the track at the top of the penultimate bend and swept down off the final one to beat his rival easily, crowning a convincing performance.

The outbreak of riots across France a month later provided those who wanted to see the back of the cobbles with more support for their arguments. Student demonstrators in Paris and elsewhere ripped up cobblestones from the streets, using them to build barricades and hurl at the police. The French government responded to the unrest by covering over the cobbles in many major cities and encouraging local authorities to do the same. Although this push may not have been directly responsible for the ongoing resurfacing of roads in the north, it undoubtedly chimed with the attitude of many in the region towards the cobbles. This was perfectly summed up by a poster campaign along the route in 1972 proclaiming, 'They don't deserve this!' overlaid on an image of a cobbled road. 'They' could just as easily have referred to the riders, given the new difficulties Bouvet and his associates sniffed out to test them, but instead described local drivers and residents.

If Merckx's first Roubaix success was impressive, Walter Godefroot's a year later was staggering. In the wake of Merckx's win, some observers had complained about the new route provoking so much fear among the riders that little happened until late on. But Godefroot's performance showed that the riders just needed to get to grips with the challenge it offered in a racing situation before taking advantage of the many options it offered those prepared to take risks.

Godefroot and his young Flandria teammate Roger De Vlaeminck were among six Belgians who broke clear in the Arenberg. Merckx was there, too. Although the lead group re-formed with more than two dozen riders, Godefroot was enjoying a day of grace, when turning the pedals was effortless and everything he tried came off. With 60km left, he attacked again, with Merckx right on his tail, together with both Erik and Roger De Vlaeminck. When Flandria's Eric Leman came across, Godefroot's team comprised half of the eight-man break. After Godefroot attacked for the third time, Merckx and Felice Gimondi tried to counter, only to find one of the De Vlaemincks or Leman coasting along on their wheel.

Godefroot, a former gymnast from Gent with rather chubby cheeks that suggested, quite wrongly, he wasn't fully committed to the strictures his profession demanded of its biggest stars, out-Merckxed his compatriot and long-time rival. Almost three minutes clear in the velodrome, he affirmed: 'Even if I had been caught, I was certain to have won the sprint.'

A race that had generally been decided in a sprint between a large group of riders suddenly became the preserve of solo winners. Following the introduction of the Arenberg and Merckx's overwhelming of Van Springel in 1968, *La Pascale* produced six consecutive solo victories. The second of them was undoubtedly the most extraordinary. Perhaps not too surprisingly, it was Merckx who delivered it, despite going into the race complaining of a cold and asking his team director Lomme Driessens if he could abandon given the freezing temperature and persistently heavy rain.

'Abandon?' Driessens replied. 'We'll see about that later. Take off that jacket and breathe. That'll sort you out.'

Crashes had already taken a toll before the peloton reached the Arenberg, where the wet conditions produced carnage. Merckx was right at the front entering the trench and his speed hardly relented as he flew over the pavé. Like a racing car bulleting along a straight creating tremendous disturbance in the air behind it, Merckx's velocity appeared to generate so much turbulence in his wake that few were able to follow. Riders went down like skittles on the sodden pavé. Coming out of the forest, the front group was only seven-strong. Like the previous year, Mars-Flandria had four representatives – the De Vlaemincks, Leman and André Dierickx. This time, though, Merckx had the beating of them, as he showed when he spent 15km chasing back up to the quartet after puncturing.

The race turned when Roger De Vlaeminck, the strongest of the Flandria quartet, punctured 40km from home. Sensing Leman was weakening, Merckx realised this was his moment and attacked. The 'Merckxedes', as one newspaper described him, breezed away to triumph by more than five minutes, the biggest winning margin since the Second World War.

The reactions to this jaw-dropping performance spoke volumes. Mars-Flandria team director Briek Schotte had no words of recrimination for his riders. 'Since I've been in this profession, I've witnessed plenty of famous exploits ... but honestly, since Fausto Coppi, I've never seen anything like that.' Raymond Poulidor shook his head in bewilderment. 'I've never seen anything like that in the time I've been racing. I've seen plenty of special talents, but him ...' Writing in *L'Équipe* the next day, Pierre Chany posed the question: 'Is Merckx the best rider that history has ever seen?' This, it should be remembered, was when he had won only one of what would eventually be five Tour de France titles and less than half of the Monuments that would eventually fall to him.

'Mr Paris–Roubaix'

One rider's reaction was very different, though. Roger De Vlaeminck was beside himself with rage after taking a very distant second place. 'If

I hadn't punctured, Merckx would never have dropped me,' he insisted. Rather than being awestruck by 'The Cannibal', De Vlaeminck used this defeat as motivation. Five days later, he underlined his point by beating Merckx at Liège–Bastogne–Liège. At the end of that 1970 season, he began to undertake specific training for the cobbled Classics. His method was brutally simple: build up to Roubaix with training rides extending to as much as 400km in a day. It would prove hugely effective.

Nicknamed 'The Gypsy' as the result of a short spell his family spent travelling around Belgium in a caravan selling towels, flannels and other linens, De Vlaeminck didn't appreciate the label. He came to cycling late in his teenage years when he had already established himself as a goal-hungry centre-forward for his local football team, FC Eeklo. His head was turned by elder brother Erik's successes in the pro peloton. Lift-off came when the brothers became world cyclo-cross champions on the same day in 1968, Erik taking the professional title just after Roger had claimed the amateur crown. Courted by Merckx, who wanted him as one of his domestiques at Faema, De Vlaeminck boldly declared he didn't want to ride for Merckx but against him. Instead he joined Erik at Flandria in 1969, winning Het Volk in his first professional outing.

His grounding and continued participation in cyclo-cross provided De Vlaeminck with all the skills he needed to flourish in *La Pascale*. The most adept bike handler of his generation, De Vlaeminck thrived in the worst conditions. Sitting low over the bike, his back ramrod straight, his dark, handsome features camouflaged behind a mask of mud and grit, De Vlaeminck had an uncanny ability to position himself in precisely the right place to attack or counter, accelerating when still in the saddle, his mouth wide open, his eyes fixed on a point many metres ahead.

Briek Schotte admitted he had no idea how De Vlaeminck was able to cope with Roubaix's cobbles with such ease. 'More than his participation in cyclo-cross, I attribute it to his perfect mastery of racing. He was always well placed at strategic points and seemed to be able to evade any pitfalls. To be as adept as he was on a course like that, you not only have to be talented but also need extraordinary intelligence,' said the former Classics contender, who was his first team manager at Flandria. Franco Cribiori, his team director at Dreher and, most memorably, at Brooklyn, revealed how most of the team's wheels would be thrown away after Roubaix, but De Vlaeminck's 'could still be used. They were as good as new.'

De Vlaeminck's first Roubaix success came on a dirty day in 1972. A mass pile-up in the Arenberg saw 40 riders hit the deck, including Merckx, who rode into a tree. De Vlaeminck sailed past this and other perils, eventually accelerating away in pursuit of lone leader Willy Van Malderghem at Bachy with 23km remaining when he could see his rivals were completely spent. He was quickly up to and past Van Malderghem, and went on to finish two minutes ahead of runner-up André Dierickx, with Barry Hoban the first British rider to take a podium place in third.

De Vlaeminck put up a valiant defence of his title the following year despite sustaining a deep wound to his arm at Gent–Wevelgem just days before that had required 25 stitches and had not healed up. Having avoided even greater mayhem than usual in the Arenberg, he found himself alone with Merckx with 55km remaining. He spent most of the next few kilometres sitting on Merckx's wheel, telling his rival he was in too much discomfort to take on much of the pace-making. Merckx later admitted he was fairly sure De Vlaeminck wasn't bluffing, but accelerated away with 44km to the line to complete another resounding win, *L'Équipe*'s headline proclaiming, 'Merckx even better than Merckx' as 'The Cannibal' took his 300th victory.

By 1974, Merckx's descent to almost mere human levels of achievement was becoming apparent. At the same time, De Vlaeminck was still on an upward curve, especially at Roubaix, which had a new look to it as the Office of National Forests had denied entry to the Arenberg, which would not appear on the route again until 1983. Few riders lamented its absence, particularly as the course still featured 26 sections of pavé. Once again, Merckx started as favourite and raced as if determined to ride everyone off his wheel. When Walter Godefroot and highly rated young Italian Francesco Moser clipped off the front of the group with 40km remaining, Merckx started to soft-pedal, indicating to those on his wheel that the race would be lost if they didn't start to chase.

Merckx figured De Vlaeminck would take up the chase, but couldn't respond without several others following when his rival did go off in pursuit of the tandem of leaders, who would both succumb to punctures. Moser's misfortune was particularly ill timed as it came just seven kilometres from the line, leaving him no hope of getting back on terms with De Vlaeminck, who completed what appeared to be a straight-forward victory that had in fact taken him right to his limits.

De Vlaeminck's successful defence of the title was no easier. A bout of bronchitis had scuppered his hopes of contending at Flanders, where Merckx had produced one of his most masterful demonstrations. Yet neither man was able to subdue Briek Schotte's troops at Flandria in a Roubaix mudbath until Flandria sprinter Freddy Maertens dropped off the pace, leaving his team without a rider to deliver the final thrust in the velodrome.

A puncture eight kilometres from home meant most of Merckx's finishing zip was expended chasing back up to the leading group, from which De Vlaeminck emerged victorious, although he admitted it had been the toughest of his successes thanks to the conditions. In places the mud was so thick that race vehicles and motorbikes got stuck. 'I'm the world cyclo-cross champion, but if someone had suggested holding a race in that discipline on this route, I would have refused. At twenty-seven, I'm too young to die' was De Vlaeminck's cutting verdict.

He should have taken a fourth title in 1976. Everyone acknowledged he was the strongest on the day, but he sprinted like a novice and lost out to Maertens' faithful teammate Marc Demeyer. The bitterness he felt at that defeat drove him on as he undertook his 400km-plus training rides for the next year's edition of *La Pascale*, which once again had a much-changed course after the northern road gangs had continued to coat the cobbles with tarmac. Route director Albert Bouvet unearthed six new sections of pavé, including the long and difficult passage of Orchies, which remains one of the race's highlights. To accommodate the new twists and turns, the start moved from Chantilly to Compiègne.

By that point, De Vlaeminck's fierce rivalry with Merckx had been superseded by an equally intense relationship with his former team-mate Freddy Maertens, who was the form rider that spring. Maertens had been by far the stronger of the pair at Flanders, but had lost out to De Vlaeminck because he had received an illegal bike change during the race. This provided their clash at Roubaix with an extra edge.

'Your legs look a bit thin. Will they be able to get you to Roubaix?' Maertens asked De Vlaeminck during the build-up.

'Don't worry about them. They are still solid. On Sunday they are going to make you suffer,' De Vlaeminck responded.

The new sections took a significant toll on the main contenders, but De Vlaeminck was at his regal best. 'Roger was sliding skilfully over the pavé as if he knew the position of every single cobble,' said Merckx after what would be his final Roubaix. As the lead group of two dozen riders approached the end of a cobbled section with 25km to the finish, De Vlaeminck, his nose just above the twin peaks of his brake cables, increased his cadence and eased away without any apparent upping of his effort. There would be no sprint this time. The Belgian rode in alone to seal a record-breaking fourth title. *L'Équipe* hailed him as 'Mr Paris–Roubaix'. His final record in 'The Hell of the North' was astounding: 14 starts, 13 finishes, none of them lower than seventh place.

De Vlaeminck's fourth win was the last of ten consecutive Belgian successes. During that time, only four non-Belgians had finished on the podium – hats off to Marino Basso (third in 1971), Barry Hoban (third in 1972) and Francesco Moser (second in 1974 and 1976). After the deluge, though, Belgium experienced a decade-long drought, initiated by Moser.

The Moser years

Crowned world champion in Venezuela in 1977, the Italian had impressed at Roubaix ever since his first encounter with the cobbles in 1974. Many experts suggested Moser's hopes of winning an event he had come to love would not be helped by De Vlaeminck's arrival at his Sanson team in 1978, but the pair had agreed a pact: if either one attacked, the other would commit himself to defending his teammate's position.

Although the rain relented late on, the conditions for a race *L'Équipe* described as 'the Paris–Roubaix of fear', thanks to the introduction of further sections of pavé, were tough. Mud oozed off the fields on to the pavé, where it combined with animal manure to produce an unpleasant, gloopy soup. Some weren't impressed. New French prospect Bernard Hinault said it was more cyclo-cross than road racing after crashing three times and added he wasn't sure he would return.

As ever, the specialists thrived. When Moser attacked 23km from home, De Vlaeminck, Maertens, Dutchman Jan Raas, and Belgians Herman Van Springel and Guido Van Sweevelt bridged across to him. When the Italian went again five kilometres later, Maertens and Raas chased, with De Vlaeminck sticking to his word and to their wheels. Maertens and Raas became temporary allies, but had the life squeezed out of them. Caught in Sanson's pincer, they steadily lost ground as Moser gave Italy its first success since Gimondi's victory in 1966. As expected, De Vlaeminck skipped past Raas and Maertens to deliver a Sanson one-two. He later confessed to *L'Équipe*'s Philippe Brunel that, although he played the team role he'd agreed, he had offered Raas a lot of money to chase down Moser. 'He tried everything he could but when Moser went there wasn't a great deal he could do,' he admitted.

The race had shown there was only room for one Roubaix aspirant at Sanson. De Vlaeminck quickly moved on to the Gis team, triggering a new and bitter rivalry with his erstwhile teammate. 'Moser is an ingrate. Last year after Paris–Roubaix he completely forgot the sacrifice I made and engineered it so that there were sticks in my wheels every time I rode in Italy,' De Vlaeminck had complained before taking a third victory in Milan–Sanremo at the start of the 1979 Classics campaign.

Nicknamed 'The Sheriff' for the ease with which he controlled and outrode his rivals, Moser was ready for the challenge. The youngest and most talented of the four Moser brothers who became professionals, Moser was one of the ultimate stylists and had all the attributes of a modern-day Roubaix specialist – he was tall, powerfully built and a time trial specialist who could turn a big gear for kilometres on end. He had three basic rules for Roubaix: be strong, ride at the front, and be lucky.

The Italian retained his title in successive years by applying those fundamentals. In 1979, De Vlaeminck, Demeyer and Hennie Kuiper all punctured in the same section of pavé at Gruson when chasing Moser. When the Italian punctured a few kilometres on, he got a new wheel so quickly he barely lost any time. 'This time I don't owe anyone anything,' he said pointedly as De Vlaeminck passed by, having finished second again.

His victory in 1980 was his best. When Germany's Didi Thurau attacked with 90km remaining, Moser, De Vlaeminck and Frenchman Gilbert Duclos-Lassalle were quickly across to him. The race was over for everyone else. De Vlaeminck's chance went with a puncture and then a crash as he tried to chase back with 20km left. Duclos-Lassalle tumbled out of contention as he rode eyeballs out trying to stay with Moser. Soon after, Thurau tailed off and Moser steamed on to emulate Octave Lapize's pre-Great War achievement of three consecutive wins.

Duclos-Lassalle's second place, France's first podium finish for 20 years, was almost as astonishing as Moser's hat-trick. Two places behind him was two-time Tour de France champion Bernard Hinault, who once again dismissed *La Pascale*, insisting: 'This isn't a race, it's cyclo-cross.' For good measure, he added: 'Paris–Roubaix is bullshit.'

Asked about Hinault's remarks, race director Jacques Goddet defended the event, asserting: 'Paris–Roubaix's excesses are necessary so that a champion like Moser can express himself completely.' However, Hinault wasn't in the slightest bit convinced. He returned the following year as one of the big favourites, but still venomous in his attitude towards the race. The prospect of mud-coated cobbles didn't improve his mood, but Hinault was determined to impose himself on Roubaix, proving he could deal with the ridiculous challenge he was adamant it offered, as well as with the event's leading exponents.

Naturally, Roubaix wasn't going to offer itself up to Hinault without a struggle. He found himself caught behind fallen riders, at one point forced to shoulder his bike and run through the crowd before remounting. Late on, as he drove the pace at the front of what was already sure to be the winning break, a small dog ran under his front wheel, forcing him to the ground. But the bull-headed Breton wasn't about to be deterred a dozen kilometres from glory. De Vlaeminck, Moser, Demeyer, Kuiper and interloper Guido Van Calster discovered what riders at the grand tours had known for three years: when Hinault imposed himself fully, he asphyxiated the hopes of his rivals by force of will as much as his talent.

When Kuiper led on to the track, the crowd was chanting, 'Ee-no! Ee-no! Ee-no!' France's world champion moved to the front with more than a lap to go and wound up the pace higher and higher. On the back straight, he held off Demeyer's attempt to seize the inside line. Coming off the bend, he was ready for De Vlaeminck's final surge to deliver his country's first victory in a quarter of a century. More than De Vlaeminck and Moser, he had vanquished 'The Hell of the North', and wasn't about to admit he'd warmed to it. 'You won't get me to deny what I've already said about Paris–Roubaix. It's bullshit.' Ninth behind Jan Raas in defence of his title the following year, he never returned, leaving it to the specialists.

The arrival of 'King Kelly'

Hinault's absence in 1983 meant he never experienced the Arenberg, which returned as Hennie Kuiper added a second Dutch win in succession. But the nations that had traditionally dominated Roubaix were about to be shouldered aside by a new Classics king. Irishman Sean Kelly was regarded as a sprinter who couldn't win stage races when he joined the Sem team in 1982. Its manager was Jean de Gribaldy, who had been Kelly's boss and mentor when he had first turned pro with Flandria in 1977.

Under De Gribaldy's guidance, Kelly became a stage race winner and a contender for almost any title on the calendar. Victory in that year's edition of Paris–Nice was the first of seven in succession. His first success in a Monument came at Lombardy at the end of the following season. Unlike De Vlaeminck, for example, who rode hundreds of kilometres a day in preparation for Roubaix, 'The Viscount', as De Gribaldy was known because his sixteenth-century forebears were among the nobility in the kingdom of Savoy, had a very different and modern approach to training and race preparation.

'In those times, riders did unbelievable miles on the bike. They'd go out and do five- and six-hour marathons every day. But he would make you do shorter rides of quality as well as a long mid-week ride. That was ten years before specialised training programmes,' Kelly said of his new regime, which was monastic in its approach to everything – and, yes, that included sex. 'He was there looking over our shoulders all the time, telling us what to eat, saying, "You can't have that, you shouldn't be having that, this is the way you should be training." I think that was the making of my career.'

In March 1984, when the world rankings were first introduced, Kelly topped them and held that position for six years. Second at

Sanremo and Flanders that spring, he went to Roubaix telling his team-mates he would take the title. His main threat appeared to come from the French Renault and La Redoute teams. The latter was a mail order company based in Roubaix and also *La Pascale*'s primary sponsor, and boasted Kelly's compatriot Stephen Roche, local rider Alain Bondue and Germany's Gregor Braun among a strong line-up.

Bondue and Braun led the charge through the Arenberg. When they returned to the paved road at the end of the 2.4km trench, they turned and found they were completely alone. With 100km to the finish, they wondered whether to wait for reinforcements or press on. After a brief chat, they went for it. With 45km to go, Kelly jumped away from the chasing group with young Belgian Rudy Rogiers. After a 25km pursuit, they bridged up to the leaders. Braun was spent and dropped back almost immediately, but track pursuit specialist Bondue was still looking good and was relishing the finish on the velodrome. Unfortunately, he crashed on the penultimate section of pavé, leaving Kelly to deal with the inexperienced Rogiers. It was no contest.

Bondue recovered from his heavy fall to finish a creditable third. 'I'm only twenty-five. I know that one day I will win Paris–Roubaix,' said the Frenchman. Sadly for Bondue, he never did, although France did discover a new Classics hero. Unlike his former Renault teammate Bernard Hinault, Marc Madiot was a Roubaix specialist and racing obsessive. Winner of the junior edition in 1979, Madiot once said of his passion for cycling: 'For me, this is not a job. This is my life ... What I love more than anything is racing. It doesn't matter what race it is, I'm just addicted to it. I need to be see bikes, watch wheels going around, even if it's a junior race taking place near my home.'

His 1985 Roubaix success encapsulated many of Madiot's qualities: his ability to analyse a race and his rivals, to assess when to stay hidden and when to move. Given these skills, it was always likely he would go on to become a team director. In the current era, he is guiding some of the new wave of French talents at FDJ.

The race came alive when three-time winner Moser attacked 90km from the finish. Even for a rider who had broken the world hour record and won the Giro d'Italia the previous year, partly as a result of blood doping he received under the guidance of Italian sports scientist Francesco Conconi, it was a suicidal move given the strong headwind. He eventually yielded, as Eric Vanderaerden, winner of Flanders the week before, went clear. The Belgian, too, misjudged the wind.

On the penultimate section of pavé, at Carrefour de l'Arbre, Madiot, his tongue poking out of the left-hand corner of his mouth in distinctive fashion, pushed on hard and found himself alone with 14km remaining. 'This can't be true. I'm going to win,' he thought. After dusting himself off and shaking hands with team director Cyrille Guimard approaching the velodrome, he entered the concrete bowl with the 'Marseillaise' ringing out. 'That was a moment of intense joy,' he confessed.

In 1986 Kelly won a second Roubaix. The finale caused a huge amount of debate. Not because of the way in which the Irishman dispatched Rudy Dhaenens, Adri van der Poel and Ferdi Van den Haute in the sprint, but because of where that sprint took place. To great consternation, the finish had been moved to the road in front of La Redoute's headquarters on the Avenue des Nations-Unies in the centre of Roubaix. The organisers were accused of selling out the race's history. Although they and La Redoute defended the decision, pointing out that the sponsors' support ensured *La Pascale*'s long-term future, this widely criticised innovation ended in 1989.

After Kelly's second success, the Belgians reasserted themselves with four consecutive victories, before Madiot added a second of his own in 1991. Once again, he launched his decisive attack at Carrefour de l'Arbre, becoming the first French rider for 70 years to win *La Pascale* on two occasions. Strangely, this success came six years after his first, which in turn came half a dozen years on from his junior Roubaix victory. Six years on from Madiot's second title, unheralded Frenchman Frédéric Guesdon took the crown. His team manager? Madiot, of course.

Saving Paris–Roubaix

By the early 1990s, the complexion of Paris–Roubaix had changed considerably. Hitherto, every type of rider apart from the sport's pure climbers marked an X next to the race when drawing up their programme for the season, including stage race specialists such as Hinault, Greg LeMond, Laurent Fignon and Stephen Roche. Since the 1990s, not a single Tour de France champion has risked their wellbeing on *La Pascale's* pavé. More than ever before, it has become a race for specialists. However, at the same time, its long-term future has been guaranteed as opinion towards it in France's north has switched. Locals no longer regard 'The Hell of the North' as an event they believe paints their homeland in a bad light. It has, instead, taken on iconic status, providing the north and Roubaix with a shop window to the rest of the world.

Roubaix route directors Jean Garnault and Albert Bouvet had long railed against the loss of the pavé. When Jean-Marie Leblanc, a very proud northerner and future Roubaix race director, retired from racing and became a journalist with *La Voix du Nord* and later *L'Équipe*, he picked up on their concerns, writing regularly about the threat to the race's future. In 1982, urged on by Roubaix enthusiast Jean-Claude Vallaeys, Leblanc wrote a book entitled *Les Pavés du Nord*, which stirred up the debate, bringing out many who supported the preservation of the pavé, as well as those who wanted roads as smooth as billiard tables. According to Leblanc, 'People began to realise that if there wasn't any pavé, there couldn't be a Paris–Roubaix.'

The year after the publication of Leblanc's book, Vallaeys brought together a handful of supporters and enthusiasts in a new organisation, Les Amis de Paris–Roubaix. They adopted a two-pronged approach. Most obviously, they went out in search of new sections of pavé that could be added to Roubaix's route and, thanks to donations and volunteers, they carried out repairs to existing sections of cobbles. At the same time, the most influential members of Les Amis, notably

Vallaeys and organisation president Alain Bernard, started to lobby mayors and local councils, discovering a huge majority of them were keen to see the race use their roads because of the attention and status it provided.

As plans for new autoroutes and TGV lines got the go-ahead in the late 1980s, the campaign to safeguard the pavé gained further momentum thanks partly to Leblanc's elevation in 1989 to director of ASO's portfolio of races, including Paris–Roubaix and the Tour de France. However, the media's interest in the race, and particularly that of television, played a much more significant role. Broadcast coverage was expanded and the race's popularity around the world increased rapidly. Even though *La Pascale* harked back to a lost past, TV viewers responded to it because it was a sporting anomaly.

Subsequently, although some sections have disappeared or become redundant because they've been cut off by the construction of new communications links, the threat to the pavé has been averted. The crisis of the 1960s and 1970s, highlighted by French writer René Fallet's warning that 'The De Vlaemincks of this world are facing the same threat as baby seals' has become a success story in the modern era.

According to ASO's recently retired route director, Jean-François Pescheux, 'We are no longer losing pavé. On the contrary, we are actually rediscovering them.' Les Amis now estimate there are around 165km of pavé in the north, of which 75km are or could be used in *La Pascale*. The objective each year is to ensure that one kilometre in every three in the final 150km of the course are cobbled. In 2013, there were 52.6km of cobbles, the longest between Quiévy and St-Python extending to 3.7km, the shortest in Roubaix itself just 300m in length.

In truth, since Roubaix has taken off as an international spectator and televisual event, the absence of most of cycling's biggest names hasn't impacted on the race at all. Rather than depending on reflected glory provided by the appearance of Tour de France or Giro d'Italia champions, *La Pascale* has continued to produce its own legends.

The pick of them for French fans was Gilbert Duclos-Lassalle, who had looked like a potential winner since finishing runner-up to Francesco Moser in 1980. His chance appeared to have gone as he went into his fourteenth Roubaix in 1992 with his thirty-eighth birthday not too far away. A hunting enthusiast whose cycling career was threatened when he shot a hole through his left hand in 1983, Duclos had always relished the toughest races on the calendar, particularly Roubaix. Lifted by 36-year-old Sean Kelly's victory in Sanremo the previous month and his own good form going into *La Pascale*, 'Gibus' came out of the Arenberg with just two riders on his wheel – Jean-Paul van Poppel and Rik Van Slycke – and this trio soon picked up a fourth rider from the early break, Swiss Thomas Wegmuller.

On the pavé at Ennevelin, with 45km left, Duclos pushed hard to shake off sprint ace van Poppel. His only moment of concern came at Carrefour de l'Arbre, where German sprinter Olaf Ludwig ate into his advantage, but the Frenchman hung on to win. The most surprising aspect of his victory was not his age, but his use of RockShox suspension forks. Although omnipresent in mountain biking, most road riders regarded them as overly heavy and, although of some benefit on the cobbles, too spongy on the tarmacked roads. However, traditionalist Duclos loved and certainly popularised them.

'This victory gives me the desire to win another,' the Frenchman said in the wake of that success. Twelve months later he managed exactly that in very different circumstances. Coming on to the pavé at Carrefour de l'Arbre, he was with Italian Franco Ballerini, who was urged by his team director, Patrick Lefevere, to drop the Frenchman before the velodrome. The Italian went full gas, but Duclos hung on. Heading into the velodrome for a lap and a half of the track, Duclos drew on his experience of six-day racing, using the banking to get up to speed and unnerve the younger man. Coming off the final bend, he shot by Ballerini, then gave all he had as the Italian came through fast on his right. They both 'threw' their bikes at the line and Ballerini raised his arm to celebrate. Yet the photo-finish showed Duclos was eight centimetres ahead of Ballerini when they hit the line.

The Frenchman had become the race's oldest champion. Ballerini, meanwhile, was inconsolable. 'I will never come back to Roubaix,' he told a journalist. 'My mistake was becoming a bike racer.' In a neat turn of events, Duclos-Lassalle retired two years later after Ballerini had won the first of two Roubaix. Subsequently, the organisers named a section of pavé near Wallers the Pont Gibus in a tribute to the Frenchman.

Ballerini's first victory instigated an almost unprecedented run of success for the well-backed Mapei team and their director Lefevere, who had an unparalleled array of racing talent to draw on. Lefevere's team leader was three-time Flanders winner Johan Museeuw, who restored Belgium to the top of the Roubaix podium with a trio of victories. The first was outstanding in terms of team performance as all three riders who broke clear on the eleventh section of pavé at Tilloy-lez-Marchiennes wore Mapei's colours. Museeuw, Gianluca Bortolami and Andrea Tafi opened up such a gap that the only question that remained in the final 15km was how they would decide which of them would win. A phone call to Giorgio Squinzi, head of adhesives manufacturer Mapei, provided the answer. 'Can they all cross the line at the same time?' he asked Lefevere. Informed they couldn't, he picked Museeuw.

The Italian press was scandalised, mostly by the decision of the Italian owner of an Italian company to hand the race on a plate to a Belgian. Race director Leblanc, who had been hoping for a memorable finish to the race's centenary edition, decried 'The three Mapei riders [who] acted shamelessly and without restraint in front of millions of TV viewers.' Mapei repeated their podium-filling performance two years later, solo victor Ballerini giving the team their third win in four years as he finished more than four minutes up on teammates Tafi and Wilfried Peeters.

As they celebrated, Museeuw was in hospital having surgery on a shattered kneecap after crashing heavily in the Arenberg. During the delicate operation, the surgeons failed to remove some of the mud in the wound, resulting in an infection and the onset of gangrene. Thankfully, the infection was caught quickly and Museeuw returned to Roubaix the following year to claim a top ten finish as teammates Tafi, Peeters and Tom Steels filled the podium.

The most memorable victory of Museeuw's career came in 2000 when he rode into the velodrome alone. As he approached the line, he unclipped his left foot and raised his leg in the air, pointing at his knee as he rolled over the line. 'This is a dream because two years ago I almost lost my leg. After all I've gone through there's nothing more beautiful than winning Paris–Roubaix,' said the tearful Belgian. Victories for Servais Knaven and Museeuw again extended Lefevere's astounding Roubaix run to seven wins in eight seasons.

Two places behind Museeuw in 2002 was new pro Tom Boonen, a 21-year-old Belgian standing 1.92m who had won the under-23 version of the race the previous year. Son of an ex-pro – although André Boonen's name does not feature on the roll of honour of any significant race, his seven-year career ending in 1984 with the intriguingly named Eurosoap-Crack team – Boonen's job that day had been to work for US Postal Classics leader George Hincapie. But when the American crashed into a ditch 18km from home as the pair chased Museeuw, Boonen continued on to take third.

Boonen's arrival signalled the emergence of a new generation of cobbled Classics contenders. 'I am only Tom Boonen and it will take a great deal of time to try to equal what Johan has achieved in his career,' the strapping Belgian declared when asked to compare himself with the race winner, Museeuw. Lefevere was quick to respond to Boonen's show of strength, extricating him from his contract with US Postal and signing him to his QuickStep team to ride with and learn from Museeuw. Having taken over as QuickStep's leader in 2005 following Museeuw's retirement, Boonen revealed himself as Belgium's greatest cobbled Classics talent since Roger De Vlaeminck as he completed a Flanders/Roubaix double.

One vital Roubaix component had been missing during Boonen's dominating display, which culminated in him outsprinting George Hincapie and Juan Antonio Flecha in the velodrome – the Arenberg. Concern about the state of the cobbles in the trench had been raised in the wake of Museeuw's knee-mangling crash, resulting in the riders tackling it in the opposite, uphill, direction the following year. Although that experiment didn't last, subsidence caused by the long-disused mineworks beneath the Arenberg resulted in the trench being dropped from the 2005 race. The local council spent €250,000 carrying out repairs, making improvements and cutting back the foliage on either side of the infamous stones, enabling the sun to penetrate the dank environment and prevent the pavé becoming moss-covered.

The Arenberg returned in 2006, when 'Tornado Tom' Boonen was blown away by Fabian Cancellara, victory going to the Swiss rider otherwise known as 'Spartacus'. The records show he had a winning margin of 1′49″ over Boonen, suggesting a clear win, but three riders finished in between the pair. Leif Hoste, Peter Van Petegem and Vladimir Gusev were disqualified having ducked under the barrier at a level crossing 15km from the finish as they pursued Cancellara. The time they lost because of that hold-up didn't affect the final result as the Swiss was already well clear, but their disqualification would no doubt have amused Henri Pélissier, who, it will be recalled, not only climbed over a barrier but walked through the train on the crossing on the way to one of his two Roubaix victories.

In the years that followed, Boonen and Cancellara continued to dominate Roubaix. The Belgian took a further three wins to join De Vlaeminck at the top of the all-time winners' list, while Cancellara's 2013 success was his third. As was the case when the pair faced each other at Flanders, they were very well matched and a level above their contemporaries. Yet, on occasions they marked each other so tightly that other riders glimpsed an opportunity. In 2014, Dutchman Niki Terpstra, one of the cohort of QuickStep's formidable Classics specialists who were primarily focused on supporting Boonen, was the beneficiary. At Carrefour de l'Arbre, 11 riders were in the lead group, three of them from the Belgian team. When Terpstra struck out on his own 6km from home, coming out of the penultimate section of pavé at Hem, no one committed to chasing right away, all of them aware that doing so would likely give Boonen an armchair ride to a fifth title. As they dallied, Terpstra was fully committed and was soon raising the cobbled trophy aloft.

Boonen and Cancellara were sidelined by injury for the 2015 edition, in which a seven-rider group contested the sprint on the Roubaix velodrome. Once again, QuickStep had the numerical advantage, but 2014 runner-up John Degenkolb outdid them with pure finishing speed to become only the second German victor, after Josef Fischer, winner of the inaugural race. Over subsequent seasons, Degenkolb's love affair with the cobbles broadened. In 2018, he won a Tour de France stage into Roubaix that featured several sections of cobbles. He also contributed financially to their maintenance by Les Amis de Paris–Roubaix and donated money on two occasions in order to keep the junior edition of Roubaix afloat. To recognise his achievements and philanthropy, the cobbled sector between Hornaing and Wandignies-Hamage has been named after him.

With Cancellara and Boonen set to take what were planned to be their final bows in 'The Hell of the North', the 2016 race was guaranteed to be special and it did indeed prove a most memorable edition. Second at Flanders to Peter Sagan the previous Sunday, the Swiss had form on his side. The Belgian, meanwhile, was still working his way back to his best after suffering a fractured skull the previous autumn at the Tour of Abu Dhabi. The illustrious pair were upstaged, though, by another veteran, Australian Mat Hayman, who almost had to miss his fifteenth Roubaix appearance when he suffered a broken arm at Het Nieuwsblad. He spent most of the six weeks leading up to Roubaix riding on his home trainer, his cast-encased right arm propped up on a stepladder in front of him.

With no expectations from his team or anyone else, Hayman endeavoured to join the break of the day, which took significant time to form, eventually going clear after 67km. Crashes and splits in the peloton behind enabled the escapees to stay clear until the Orchies section of pavé. With 60km to go to the finish, a group featuring Boonen bridged up, while Cancellara and Peter Sagan led the pursuit less than a minute behind. Their hopes of reaching the frontrunners disappeared, though, when the Swiss lost control in the mud and went down. Sagan somehow managed to bunny-hop the falling Cancellara, but the Slovak's day was effectively done.

Up at the front, a group of ten steadily slimmed to leave just five riders in contention: Boonen, Hayman, Edvald Boasson Hagen, Ian Stannard and Sep Vanmarcke. The latter was the first to move, attacking at Carrefour de l'Arbre, only to be reeled in on the next cobbled section at Gruson. Stannard tried, then Boonen went several times, Hayman countering after the Belgian's last attempt, but no one could hold a lead. Boonen, a renowned bunch sprinter, appeared to be the favourite as the five went into the final lap on the velodrome. He moved on to Hayman's wheel as the Australian led around the final bend. Coming off it, the Belgian closed and closed, but the line arrived sooner. Mat Hayman had won Paris-Roubaix.

'He played it very well. In the end, I think a guy like him really deserves a victory like this after a career of helping people out and being in the final of Classics a lot, but not really getting the big wins,' Boonen sportingly said of Hayman, who'd just denied him a record-breaking fifth Roubaix victory. The Australian admitted he wouldn't have been disappointed to see Boonen claim that fifth victory. 'For me it was pretty surreal even riding into the velodrome with Tom. He is a guy I have had a lot of respect for,' he said. 'I would have been happy with second. I've never been on the podium in Paris–Roubaix. But today everything just fell into place.'

A year on, a similar scenario played out on the velodrome. Greg Van Avermaet, Zdeněk Štybar and Sebastian Langeveld rode on to it together.

As they slowed and tried to jockey each other to the front, Jasper Stuyven and Gianni Moscon joined them just before the final bend, the Italian attacking immediately. Štybar was quick to respond and opened up a gap going into the final straight, but Olympic champion Van Avermaet had too much finishing speed for the Czech, whose QuickStep teammate Boonen crossed the line in thirteenth place a dozen seconds later, in the final race of his career, which he ended tied with arch-rival Cancellara on seven Monuments each.

In the race's next edition, having been dogged by punctures and other setbacks in previous years, Peter Sagan became the first world champion to win Roubaix since Bernard Hinault in 1981, thanks to an immensely impressive display of power and handling skill. The Slovak attacked from the group of favourites with 55km remaining and quickly bridged up to the three surviving members of the early breakaway. Sven Erik Byström soon fell back as Sagan drove almost relentlessly at the front of the group. Jelle Wallays yielded on the cobbles at Cysoing with 25km left, leaving Sagan with Silvan Dillier for company. Despite the world champion's attempts to drop him, the Swiss clung on tenaciously, like a wagon hitched to a runaway train. Dillier led on to the velodrome and into the final bend, where, inevitably, Sagan unleashed the final burst of power that swept him to victory.

The race was overshadowed, though, by the death of Michael Goolaerts. Making his Roubaix debut for the Verandas Willems-Crelan team, the 23-year-old Belgian suffered a cardiac arrest on the second section of pavé between Viesly and Briastre. Although he received medical help very quickly and was transferred by helicopter to a hospital in Lille, he died that evening. Two months later, that cobbled sector was named in his memory.

QuickStep's five-year Roubaix drought ended in 2019 when 36-year-old Philippe Gilbert became the fourth-oldest winner and in doing so joined the select group of riders who have won four of the five Monuments, alongside Sean Kelly, Fred De Bruyne, Louison Bobet, Germain Derycke and Hennie Kuiper. Gilbert was one of six riders who went clear with 48km to the finish – defending champion Sagan there once again, as were Wout van Aert, Sep Vanmarcke, Nils Politt and, crucially for the eventual winner, his teammate Yves Lampaert. When Politt attacked with 14km left, Gilbert was the only rider to respond as van Aert and Sagan eyed each other, their hesitation ending their hopes. The finale reprised that of the year before with Gilbert in the Sagan role, starting his sprint off his opponent's wheel on the final bend, and Politt, like Dillier, the distant runner-up.

In 2020, the Covid pandemic meant that Paris–Roubaix failed to take place for the first time since the Second World War, the cancellation also affecting the first edition of the women's race. Both races were initially postponed to a late October date, only to be cancelled again as coronavirus cases rose. They did go ahead in 2021, although the ongoing effects of Covid meant that they were postponed until the first weekend of October. The switch from spring to autumn brought with it the first dose of very inclement weather for years, much to the delight of almost everyone apart from those racing, and meant that the Roubaix weekend was suitably hellish. Lizzie Deignan became the first Briton to claim the cobbled trophy after attacking on the first section of pavé and maintaining both her balance in the treacherous conditions and her advantage into the finish.

The men didn't have it any easier the next day. There were crashes throughout and for a long while it looked like the break might go all the way to the finish without being caught. Gianni Moscon was the strongest rider in it, the Italian going solo from 53km out. Behind, a small group featuring Dutchman-of-all-terrains Mathieu van der Poel and another Italian, Sonny Colbrelli, began to close in, hoovering up the other riders from the early break, but the race was still Moscon's to win or lose. He looked serene until a crash and then a puncture reduced his lead and sapped his confidence. He began to slither in the slippery gloop coating the cobbles, and was reeled in and almost instantly dropped by van der Poel, Colbrelli and young Belgian Florian Vermeersch at Carrefour de l'Arbre. The Dutchman was the driving force in this trio and paid for his efforts in the velodrome, where the punchy Colbrelli powered away from his rivals, celebrating victory with a primal scream of delight on the grass in the middle of the track.

The race returned to its traditional mid-April date in 2022 and to what have become typically dry and warm conditions at that time of year. The day after Elisa Longo Borghini had soloed to victory, emulating the achievement of her Trek teammate Deignan, Dutchman Dylan van Baarle finally provided the British Ineos (previously Sky) team with victory in *La Pascale*. Like Longo Borghini, van Baarle rode in alone after accelerating away from Yves Lampaert, Matej Mohorič and Tom Devriendt at Carrefour de l'Arbre. Thanks to a strong tailwind that had pushed the riders along all day, the Dutch rider, who had finished second at Flanders a fortnight earlier, recorded the fastest average speed in Roubaix history, 45.792km/h, half a kilometre per hour faster than Greg Avermaet in 2017.

After his victory, van Baarle, who had finished outside the time limit the previous year, explained his love-hate relationship with the race, saying, 'Once I said that I really hate to ride on the cobbles. Everyone would prefer tarmac over cobbles. I just go quicker over them than others and that makes it fun. It's not so much fun to ride over it, but it's just fun that you can hurt the other guys.' His words give a strong sense of what makes *La Pascale* so unique. Since the Second World War, its organisers have had to face up to the challenge of modernisation, while staying true to its northern roots. They have achieved that admirably, bringing the race back from the brink of ordinariness in the mid-1960s to become one of the great sporting events of the year. Although luck plays a much bigger role in Roubaix than any other Monument, the great champions still tend to come out on top. When Jacques Goddet claimed, 'Paris–Roubaix is the last test of folly that cycle sport puts before its participants,' he went on to add, 'It's a savage race, but not one for brutes,' which encapsulates the challenge of 'The Hell of the North' rather nicely.

PART III

THE TOUR OF LOMBARDY – THE RACE OF THE FALLING LEAVES

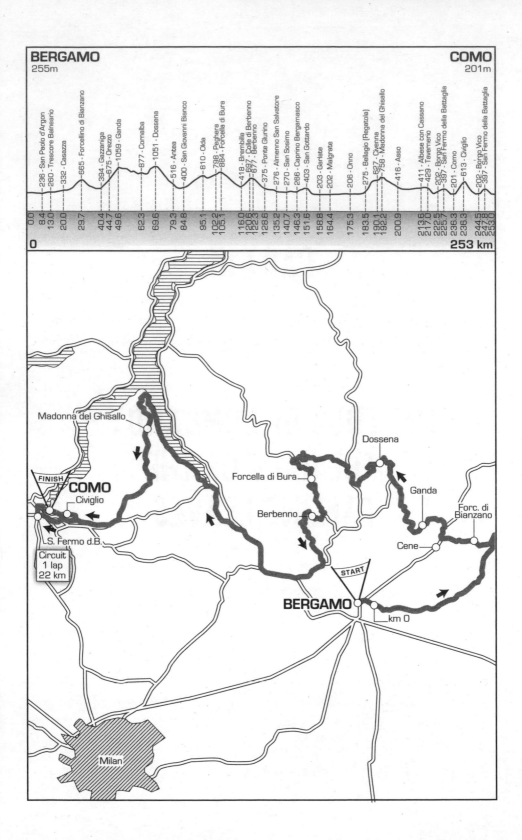

BERGAMO
255m

COMO
201m

Distance (km)	Altitude (m) - Location
0.0	
8.4	236 - San Paolo d'Argon
13.0	260 - Trescore Balneario
20.0	332 - Casazza
29.7	665 - Forcellino di Bianzano
40.4	394 - Gazzaniga
44.7	675 - Orezzo
49.6	1059 - Ganda
62.3	877 - Cornalba
69.6	1051 - Dossena
79.3	516 - Antea
84.8	400 - San Giovanni Bianco
95.1	810 - Olda
102.2	798 - Paghera
105.1	884 - Forcella di Bura
116.0	418 - Brembilla
120.6	697 - Colle di Berbenno
123.3	677 - Berbenno
128.6	375 - Ponte Giurino
135.2	276 - Almenno San Salvatore
140.7	270 - San Sosimo
146.3	266 - Caprino Bergamasco
151.6	403 - San Gottardo
158.8	203 - Garlate
164.4	202 - Malgrate
175.3	206 - Onno
183.5	275 - Bellagio (Regatola)
190.1	627 - Civenna
192.2	758 - Madonna del Ghisallo
200.9	416 - Asso
213.6	411 - Albese con Cassano
217.0	429 - Tavernerio
222.5	202 - Borgo Vico
225.7	397 - San Fermo della Battaglia
236.3	201 - Como
236.3	613 - Civiglio
244.5	202 - Borgo Vico
247.8	397 - San Fermo della Battaglia
253.0	

0

253 km

Madonna del Ghisallo

Dossena

Forcella di Bura

Ganda

Berbenno

Forc. di Bianzano

FINISH

COMO

Civiglio

Cene

S. Fermo d.B.

Circuit
1 lap
22 km

START

BERGAMO

km 0

Milan

9

THE BIRTH OF
'THE AUTUMN CRITERIUM'

'God created the bicycle for men to use as an instrument of effort and exaltation on the hard road of life.' This inscription, beneath a bust of *Il Campionissimo*, Fausto Coppi, captures the attraction of bike racing for working-class men in the early days of the sport, speaking both for those who committed themselves to cycling as a way of escaping from poverty and the many more who turned out to watch them performing, and in doing so enjoyed temporary respite from the drudgery of daily life. Nowadays, the pertinence lies not so much in the words themselves, although they remain relevant, but in the location of the bust outside the Madonna del Ghisallo chapel that overlooks Lakes Como and Lecco, a few dozen kilometres north of Milan.

By pure definition this is the most iconic place in cycle sport. In October 1948, Pope Pius XII lit 'the permanent flame of the Ghisallo'. The lamp containing the flame was transported by car to Milan from the Pope's residence at Castel Gandolfo, near Rome. From there, a relay of cyclists including Coppi and Gino Bartali carried the flame up to the small chapel in the village of Magreglio at the top of the Ghisallo Pass. In October 1949, the Pope declared the chapel would become the site of the patroness of Italian cyclists.

Over subsequent decades the chapel that is little bigger than a large front room has become both a place of pilgrimage and a shrine for riders of all abilities. Its walls are crammed with cycling memorabilia, including Coppi's 1949 Tour de France-winning bike, looking as fragile now as

Coppi did when he rode it; the bike 1992 Olympic champion Fabio Casartelli was riding when he crashed and died during the 1995 Tour, and the machine Francesco Moser used to break the hour record in Mexico City in 1984. There are jerseys donated by the winners of some of the most memorable races in history, as well as many hundreds of tiny photographs of cyclists who have died on Italy's roads.

By the end of the twentieth century, the chapel's collection of cycling artefacts had become so large that plans were drawn up for the construction of a museum to house the greater part of the collection. Opened in 2006 and sited adjacent to the chapel on a bluff that provides a spectacular view down on to Lake Lecco, it is home to the biggest collection of professional cycling-related memorabilia in the world, including everything from a mock-up of Leonardo da Vinci's designs for a wooden 'bike' and Coppi's 1942 hour-record-breaking bike, with fraying fibres spilling from its rotting tyres, to the biggest collection of pink jerseys in the world, comprising more than 50 *maglie rose* donated by winners of the Giro d'Italia.

Many would argue that as well as being the most hallowed place in professional cycling, this spot is the most beautiful. It is certainly easy to be swayed by Percy Bysshe Shelley's belief that, "*This lake exceeds anything I ever beheld in beauty,*" with the views stretching up the blue waters of the lake to snow-covered peaks on Italy's northern border and beyond in Switzerland. It also has great significance from the racing perspective, as the Ghisallo is the most famous point in the final great Classic of the season, the Tour of Lombardy. Just as its sister race, Milan–Sanremo, opens the Classics season, 'the race of the falling leaves' brings the curtain down on it, providing riders with a final chance to relish or redeem their season.

Like the Tour de France and the Giro, Lombardy's birth stemmed from the desire of a newspaper to assert itself over its rivals. In this case the newspaper under threat was the fledgling *La Gazzetta dello Sport*, then published on a Monday and a Friday and, in the early twentieth century, facing a threat to its circulation from newly launched weekly *Gli Sports*. *La Gazzetta*'s cycling editor, Armando Cougnet, later said of the rivalry: 'There was no time to waste, we needed ideas and passion in abundance, we needed to go on the attack first before our rival took that position.'

Since 1903, Cougnet and his team had been tossing around an idea for a race around Lombardy with the directors of the Touring Club Ciclistico Italiano, which had been established in 1894 to promote tourism and cycling within Italy and went on to produce the country's best-known series of maps. However, the roads away from Milan and the other major centres were so poor that the race was deemed unfeasible. *Gli Sports*' launch focused minds in *La Gazzetta*'s editorial department. 'In order to make an impression, the race had to have special characteristics. That was why a date was chosen for it that seemed rather forbidding: the 12th of November, right at the very end limit of the season for a race that would be the sport's Autumn Criterium,' said Cougnet.

La Gazzetta's 9 October 1905 edition announced what the paper described as 'this Autumn Criterium that we have entitled the Tour of Lombardy'. The intention, explained the paper, was to establish a race that tested riders in winter conditions, explaining it was part of their plan to ensure 'cycling is a true propagator of physical education'. On 10 November, *La Gazzetta* issued a final rallying call for an event it depicted as 'rather unusual and even mad' given the advent of winter. It hailed the 74 riders who had registered to take part. Two days later, 53 of those 74 signed in at the Trattoria del Boschetto in Rogoredo, just to the south-east of Milan's centre, for the first edition of the Giro di Lombardia.

At six o'clock on what was still a dark morning, the riders gathered under acetylene lamps for the start. Oddly, the man holding the red start flag was more renowned than any of those lining up. A Milanese track star of the 1890s, Romolo Buni had become famous after taking on William 'Buffalo Bill' Cody in three bike-versus-horse challenges on the trotting course in Milan. Over three hours, Buni covered 99km and Cody 102km, although the American cowboy did go through no fewer than ten horses during that period. When Buni waved the flag in Rogoredo, the wonderfully named Gilberto Marley, a three-time Italian champion of the late 1880s, set the clock running and the riders disappeared off into the gloom.

In the weeks leading up to the race, Peugeot's Giovanni Gerbi had looked over the route as many as 20 times and had realised that the rain would make progress difficult. Yet, he had noticed there was a narrow strip of firmer compacted earth in between the tramlines running from Lodi to Crema in the race's opening kilometres. To get on to this strip, Gerbi went to the front of the group and accelerated hard, then pulled aside as if preparing to abandon. In the rush to respond to his injection of pace, riders clattered into the tracks and each other, resulting in a heap of bikes and riders. Meanwhile, Gerbi coolly stepped in between the rails and got under way again, already on his own with just 30 of the 230km covered. At Bergamo, another 30-odd kilometres into the race, 'The Red Devil', so called because he always wore a jersey of that colour and had a win-at-all-costs attitude that stretched the rules of racing to their limit, had extended his advantage to three minutes and it continued to grow. At the finish on the Corso Sempione in Milan, Gerbi was 40 minutes clear of Giovanni Rossignoli and Luigi Ganna.

Roads were few and far between on the route of that first late autumn edition of Lombardy. Although Fiat had started production in Turin in 1899 and the nascent automobile industry had subsequently spread to Milan and Bergamo, Italy was still very much an agricultural nation and would remain so until the economic miracle that followed the Second World War. For the most part, the riders raced on dirt tracks that were less than half a metre wide and were often so muddy that they had to resort to carrying their bikes. 'In that period, an initial advantage of fifty metres was enough to provoke a selection,' explained Gerbi, who trained alone with a view to seeking out points where his reconnaissance could provide him with an advantage.

The first Italian to ride the Tour de France in 1904, Gerbi wasn't as fortunate the following year, suffering mechanical problems that forced him to abandon the race. Victory went to 24-year-old Cesare Brambilla in spite of a protest lodged by runner-up Carlo Galetti, who objected to his rival weaving back and forth between the corridor of fans lining the finishing straight. In trying to get past Brambilla, whose Swiss-born nephew Pierre is remembered as the man who lost the first post-Second World War Tour de France on the final day, Galetti ended up in the gravel with a puncture, although he later admitted his cause hadn't been helped by a friend handing him a glass of Marsala that was intended to pep him up. Instead, it left his head spinning.

Victory at all costs

The controversy of the 1906 race was nothing compared to the protests and counters that were lodged in the wake of the third edition of Lombardy, which attracted the top three finishers from the 1907 Tour de France: Lucien Petit-Breton, Gustave Garrigou and Émile Georget. Perhaps concerned by the quality of the opposition and determined to put the previous year's disappointment behind him, Gerbi prepared as never before. However, it became apparent during the race, which 'The Red Devil' won at a canter, that he had gone well beyond the boundary separating good preparation from cheating.

Although initially confirmed as the winner after he finished 40 minutes up on Garrigou, Gerbi was relegated to last place the next day. His rivals accused him of numerous illicit manoeuvres, including damage to the route that slowed his rivals and caused them to crash, use of pacers and encouraging his supporters to block a level crossing and spread nails along the route. Gerbi insisted he had done nothing wrong, but received a two-year ban that was later reduced to six months after his angry fans carried out a public burning of copies of *La Gazzetta*.

On his return to Paris, Peugeot team manager Leopold Alibert shed more light on Gerbi's nefarious activities. Alibert said he had been approached on the eve of the race by an Italian rider called Luigi Mori, who tipped him off about an ambush being prepared by Gerbi's supporters at a level crossing 35km into the race. Their goal, Mori informed Alibert, was to prevent any foreign riders progressing beyond that point. The Peugeot boss forewarned his riders, but none of them had any inkling of the lengths Gerbi's fans were prepared to go to. As four riders approached the crossing, with Gerbi leading the way, they sped towards a man standing with a bike at the side of the road. When Gerbi passed, the man threw the bike into the road, sending Switzerland's Henri Rheinweld and Peugeot's Georget tumbling to the ground. By the time they remounted, said Alibert, the crossing, which had been open to Gerbi, had now been closed by his supporters.

Alibert described a chaotic scene, where Romolo Buni and Pilade Carozzi, head of the Italian cycling union, pleaded with fans to open the crossing. 'But the unfortunate riders were only beginning on their painful path. Less than a hundred metres after, the nails appeared and Georget punctured twice. Behind him, at the level crossing, Garrigou and Petit-Breton came up against the same difficulties the others had encountered. Petit-Breton was punched. They had to wait eight minutes before they were allowed to pass,' Alibert reported.

It seemed the race was up for Gerbi's rivals, but Georget gradually ate into the Italian's advantage. Crossing the hill at Como, he was only four minutes behind. Suddenly, though, a group of cars shot past. It stopped 500m ahead of the Frenchman, the occupants jumped out and scattered more nails on the road, causing Garrigou to puncture. As he tried to fit a new tube, breaking his pump in the process, an Italian cycling union official chased the troublemakers across nearby fields.

Alibert admitted he thought he had already seen all the ruses riders and fans employed to cheat rivals, but events at Lombardy had revealed hitherto unknown means of subterfuge, including car drivers using whips to pull riders along. He concluded: 'I've returned from Italy disheartened by the methods employed by Gerbi ... for the future of racing in Italy, it is vital that this criminal is removed from the cycling scene.'

Despite Gerbi's antics and the still deplorable state of the roads, Lombardy had quickly captured the interest of the public. French sports daily *L'Auto* reported that more than 30,000 spectators had turned out to watch the finish of that 1907 race, and praised the high level of organisation, noting in particular the placement of policemen on both sides of the road over the closing two kilometres so that order could be maintained. 'There were as many as 60,000 people lining the final kilometres of the route, and this crowd remained calm until the impending arrival of the first riders was announced, when they became extremely animated and the forces of order were completely overwhelmed,' wrote *L'Auto*'s correspondent.

After the shenanigans of 1907, many of the 208 starters were surprised to see Gerbi back in the line-up in 1908, although there are no reports of his previous antics being repeated. Of equal concern were the misty conditions and the large number of entrants. Soon after the start, these two factors combined to produce a mass crash that left fewer than 20 riders in contention, led by Peugeot's François Faber and 'The Red Devil' himself, Gerbi. The pair led late in the race, but were caught by Giovanni Cuniolo. When Faber accelerated, making what would be a race-winning move, Cuniolo tried to follow but collided with Gerbi, crashing to the ground and puncturing as he did so. For the next three decades, Cuniolo insisted his rival had taken him out deliberately, but on this occasion the judges found in Gerbi's favour and let him keep third place behind clear winner Faber and Luigi Ganna, who finished on the podium for the fourth successive time, although he would never reach Lombardy's top step.

As thousands of Italian fans at the finish gave Faber a huge ovation, the nation's manufacturers sulked, having seen a foreign marque and racer ride off with the title for the second year in a row. They responded by boosting the *primes*, or intermediate prizes, on offer in the fifth edition, adding a bonus if an Italian rider managed to prevent a foreigner taking any of them. They got their reward with a home win for Cuniolo, who proved quickest of the three riders who disputed the first sprint to decide the title. Frenchmen Omer Beaugendre and Louis Trousselier filled the podium places.

Ultimately, though, it would require a far more significant intervention to end the run of foreign success in Lombardy. In 1911, the French were back on top of the podium thanks to their precocious new star, Henri Pélissier. Nicknamed 'La Ficelle', which loosely translates as 'string' but is also the name for the thinnest type of baguette, Pélissier had bumped into Henri Petit-Breton as he walked through Paris one August afternoon.

The older man was well aware Pélissier had finished third in the Tour de France des Indépendants in 1910 and had subsequently shown plenty of potential during his first season as a professional. Did Pélissier wish to come on a racing trip to Italy, he enquired? The only catch, Petit-Breton told Pélissier, was that he was planning to leave on a train with a group of fellow riders just six hours later.

The 22-year-old Pélissier didn't hesitate in taking up the offer and, once in Italy, made an instant impact. He won two races before lining up in Lombardy, where he made his sprinting speed count, leading a group of 14 over the line. *La Gazzetta* applauded the young Frenchman's success, but pointed out that he had been the only member of the front group who hadn't had a puncture all day and suggested any one of the riders who finished behind Pélissier would have won given even a little bit more luck. That may have been true, but Pélissier quickly underlined his aptitude for racing in Italy when he won Milan–Sanremo the following spring.

Although the Frenchman didn't defend his Lombardy crown, he returned in 1913 and added a second title in a chaotic finish that saw a car from the race organisation bring most of the lead group to a halt when they were on the back straight of the final lap at the Trotter di Turro horse-racing track. Pélissier was one of a small number of riders who managed to skirt the mayhem and he sped home ahead of two compatriots, Maurice Brocco and Marcel Godivier, while new Italian favourite Costante Girardengo, who would become the dominant force in post-war Italian racing, and particularly at Milan–Sanremo, shouted blue murder back down the finishing straight.

Despite what Girardengo was angrily claiming, Pélissier had done nothing wrong. However, the Frenchman had benefited significantly from a mistake made by officials when the lead group reached Bergamo. At that point, with 190km covered, the organisers neutralised the race in order to pay tribute to a hugely impressive turnout of fans and local cycling clubs. Pélissier had been trailing three minutes behind the lead group, but he and eight other riders rejoined it during the temporary halt. When the race restarted, none of the officials realised the lead group comprised nine extra riders.

Approaching the racecourse, there were a number of interventions, producing what *La Gazzetta* described as a feeling of 'nausea because of the unseemly and wild scenes and the uncivilised behaviour resulting from the overexcitement of a few fanatics'. The first incident occurred when a fan on a bike somehow ended up riding into the 50-rider bunch, splitting it into three groups, with Pélissier left chasing at the front of the second. When the leaders reached the track, a spectator ran in front of them, enabling Pélissier to regain the ground he'd lost. Finally, as the riders began to size each other up for the sprint finish, a vehicle in the race convoy suddenly emerged on to the racetrack in front of them. Ugo Agostoni braked hard to avoid crashing into it, but Girardengo, who was on his wheel, could not respond as quickly and hit the deck. While the home favourites floundered, the French trio shot by to claim the main prizes, although even they were beaten to the line by another bike-riding fan.

The uproar that ensued was quickly exacerbated by a rumour that Pélissier had deliberately taken out Girardengo. The Frenchman started to celebrate his success, but found himself being surrounded by an angry mob. One report said Girardengo, believing Pélissier had been responsible for his crash, took a swing at him. Several described how the Frenchman had to take refuge in the timekeeper's cabin with two policemen and was only able to leave the circuit an hour later in disguise.

Not a single foreign rider appeared a year later, although this was a consequence of hostilities elsewhere in Europe rather than the unfortunate scenes 12 months earlier. Although allied to Germany and Austria-Hungary by a long-standing treaty, Italy did not enter the First World War in 1914, arguing that its allies had instigated the conflict and had not acted in self-defence. Consequently, normal life continued in Italy, and this included the tenth running of Lombardy. Victory went to Bianchi's Lauro Bordin, who stole by Giuseppe Azzini in the final metres. Subsequently courted by the Allies, Italy did enter the war in May 1915. However, the fighting was confined to the far north-east of the country, enabling Lombardy to continue uninterrupted.

In 1917, *La Gazzetta* pulled off a significant coup by arranging for Henri Pélissier and Philippe Thys to compete while they were on leave from their wartime units. The pair had contested a bitter battle at the 1914 Tour de France, which culminated in victory for the Belgian, but only thanks to an untimely puncture Pélissier suffered on the very final day.

Thys, who held the rank of sergeant and worked as a mechanic in the Belgian air force, and would go on to become an archery champion after his retirement from racing in 1927, was well supported by compatriot Charles Jusseret – perhaps too well supported. Coming into the finishing straight, Jusseret led out Thys, who had Pélissier on his wheel. The Frenchman knew he was the fastest finisher and it quickly became apparent the Belgians did, too. As Pélissier made his move, jerseys were grabbed, fists flung out and Thys held on to win. Despite Pélissier's protest, the judges couldn't say who was to blame for the argy-bargy and let the result stand.

The incredible tale of Alfonsina Strada

Ninety-four minutes after Thys had won the race, the final three of 29 finishers rolled across the line. The last of the trio stood out, the name Alfonsina Strada making clear why. Dubbed 'the devil on wheels' by locals in her home town of Castelfranco Emilia, near Modena, Strada was born Alfonsina Morini in 1891, the second or third child in what was a very large peasant family. Reports about her early years are mixed, but most agree at least six of her siblings were boys and that she was very much a tomboy.

Her obituary in Italian broadsheet newspaper *La Stampa* describes how she would often sneak off on the old bike her father had acquired from a local doctor in exchange for a few chickens, telling her mother she was going to mass. As she rode around with the local boys, it became clear she had talent. At the age of 13, she was persuaded by her brothers to give racing a go, taking victory in her debut race and winning her father over as her prize was a pig.

La Stampa describes her mother being extremely upset having found out what Alfonsina was up to. 'If she wants to do these things let's get her married,' she shouted. At 14, she wed an engraver, the perfectly named Luigi Strada, his surname being the Italian word for road. Like her father, he was also happy to indulge her love of bike racing, presenting her with a new bike as a wedding present. The couple moved to Milan, where she raced more often and her reputation began to grow. In 1909 she received an invitation to Russia to take part in the Grand Prix of St Petersburg, where she met Czar Nicholas II and his wife.

Her participation in two wartime editions of the Tour of Lombardy may have been a publicity stunt by the organisers, but the fact that she finished both races in very respectable times underlines her talent. Indeed, in 1918, although she was the penultimate ride home, she was only 23 minutes down on winner Gaetano Belloni.

Her most renowned feat was her participation in the 1924 edition of the Giro d'Italia. She entered as 'Alfonsin Strada', but the papers soon picked up on who she was. She rode well over the opening half of the race, but her luck, and that of many of her fellow racers, ran out when a deluge made the roads nightmarish on the eighth stage between L'Aquila and Perugia. A crash left her with broken handlebars. Legend has it that she was stranded until a peasant farmer snapped the end off his broom and she jammed that into place. She managed to finish the stage, but was outside the time limit.

Although she was excluded from the race, *La Gazzetta* editor-in-chief Ernesto Colombo encouraged her to continue, paying her expenses all the way to Milan. It was a well-intentioned but shrewd move on Colombo's part. He knew Strada's presence would bring the Giro additional publicity, and so it proved. At the finish, she was given a time more than 28 hours behind winner Giuseppe Enrici and seven behind the final registered finisher. As only a third of the 90 starters made it to Milan, this was still some achievement.

In 1950, four years after the death of her husband in the mental asylum to which he had been committed, Strada married former track sprinter Carlo Messori and they opened a bike shop in Milan. When Messori died in 1957, she continued to run their shop and often attended races on a 500cc Moto Guzzi. One evening, she went out to start the bike, jumping on the start pedal again and again. The effort proved too much for her heart and she died sitting on the machine. She was 68. Alfonsina Strada remains the only woman to ride a Classic or a grand tour.

The introduction of the Ghisallo

Up until 1919, the route of the Giro di Lombardia was essentially flat staying to what Shelley described as 'The waveless plain of Lombardy, bounded by the vaporous air, islanded by cities fair.' The first post-war edition saw the introduction of what would quickly become the race's signature feature, the climb up to the Madonna del Ghisallo chapel from the stunning lakeside town of Bellagio. Dating from the sixth century, the chapel had been erected by the Count of Ghisallo after he escaped unharmed from an attempted kidnap by brigands. It is said he saw a vision of the Virgin Mary, who led him away to safety.

In 1919, the road up to the chapel, which sits at a height of 754m in the village of Magreglio, was a relatively good one for the time, although the hard-packed dirt surface became treacly in wet weather. It rises from Bellagio for just over ten kilometres, averaging a little more than five per cent, which belies its difficulty. It begins easily enough as it leaves Bellagio, but averages nearer nine per cent for the four kilometres leading into Guello, the frequent hairpins rarely providing much of an easing in the gradient, as would often be the case on mountain switchbacks.

A three-kilometre saddle, where the road drops and flattens between Guello and Civenna, is responsible for the relatively gentle average gradient and offers the chance of respite prior to the final 'wall' leading up to the chapel that sits flush against the road, its bell tower offering the first clue that the top of the pass is close. On the other side of the chapel, the view extends back down to Bellagio, surrounded by the waters of Lake Como way below, with a ring of high peaks providing a stunning backdrop.

However, it is unlikely the riders in the 1919 race viewed it that way. After a dry and sunny spell, race day dawned cold and wet. Snow was falling on the peaks and starting to appear in the valleys around them. Writing in *La Gazzetta*, journalist and future editor-in-chief Emilio Colombo had a warning for the 44 riders taking part. 'They say that the climb of the Ghisallo is not too difficult, but it will have to be addressed after the riders have passed numerous other climbs. Remember, before they get to the ascent to the chapel, they will have to tackle the climb at Brinzio and the "steps" at Malnate and Binago, which have put more than one rider in trouble in the past.'

The race started chaotically. Soon after the riders were under way, defending champion Belloni's chain unshipped. His sudden loss of speed sent four riders to the ground, including Henri and Francis Pélissier. The quartet got back to their feet and started chasing the group ahead. After 15km, a tram swung into their path, sending them tumbling once again. That was enough for two-time champion Henri Pélissier.

As snow fell on the climb at Brinzio, Girardengo, who had won the first of six Sanremo titles the year before, accelerated away from his rivals. At the top of the ascent he was two minutes up on Belloni and Switzerland's Heiri Suter. Crossing the Ghisallo, his lead was a quarter of an hour, more than enough time for him to stop at the control point at Erba for a change of clothes and a quick snack. It soon became apparent, though, that whatever he had eaten hadn't agreed with him. 'Gira' began to slow. Then he stopped, left his bike with his mechanic and ran off into a field clutching his stomach. He wasn't held up for long and was soon back in the saddle and pedalling more freely again.

He entered the Trotter di Turro racetrack eight minutes clear of Belloni to complete a stellar season, during which he had won most of Italy's top one-day races and overwhelmed his rivals at the Giro, taking seven stage victories on his way to securing the title. Only half a dozen more riders made it to the finish, the last of them, Antonio De Michiel, more than three and a half hours behind Girardengo.

The bitter rivalry between Girardengo and Henri Pélissier, a man who seemed capable of falling out with absolutely anyone he encountered, had to be put on hold in 1920 as the Italian was in the United States earning substantial amounts of money riding six-day races. In his absence, Pélissier's Bianchi team dominated and the Frenchman became the first rider to win Lombardy three times. Although that year's race featured a record low participation of just 34 riders, many were big names, including Pélissier's compatriots Octave Lapize and Jean Alavoine.

Their presence demonstrated the value manufacturers put on success in the season-ending Classic. The gap of five months in between

Lombardy and the next big event gave them a lot of time to trade on a victorious performance, resulting in a sales lift for the winning manufacturer that could barely be matched at any other time of the year given the frequency of races. Awareness of this also ensured the organisers stuck to the November date despite the likelihood of bad weather. Proposals to move the race a few weeks forward into October were discussed, but rejected on the grounds that another race might usurp Lombardy's end-of-season slot.

Girardengo returned the following year and led home a group of 17 riders on the Sempione Velodrome in Milan. A subsequent successful defence of his title put him level with Pélissier on three victories, but he never won another, despite the participation of foreign riders dropping off dramatically from the early 1920s. *L'Équipe*'s Pierre Chany put this down to a string of scandals that hit the race, implying these gave Lombardy a poor reputation among foreign riders. That may have been the case, but these scandals amounted to nothing more than riders being disqualified for dangerous sprint manoeuvres, illegal wheel changes or failing to sign in at control points. Incidents such as these occurred regularly at races across Europe, so events at Lombardy were hardly exceptional.

There appear to be three more likely explanations. Firstly, the racing calendars within each of Europe's principal cycling powers – France, Italy and Belgium – became far more substantial during the 1920s, enabling professionals in each of those countries to win prestigious titles and earn a decent living without travelling abroad. Secondly, sales of bikes took off across Europe in the post-war period, enabling manufacturers to expand and profit without needing to send their publicity-generating stars abroad. In Lombardy, for example, the population of 5.2 million owned a staggering 1,972,000 bikes between them in 1922. With sales rocketing, wages for the top riders followed suit. As a result, apart from Ottavio Bottecchia, who won the Tour de France twice, Italy's biggest names rarely rode outside the *Bel Paese*. Girardengo and Alfredo Binda, for example, each only started the Tour once.

The final possibility is more difficult to confirm. In late 1922, Benito Mussolini's National Fascist Party became the party of government. By 1925, Mussolini had effectively established himself as Italy's dictator, and the country's relations with other nations deteriorated steadily over the next decade and more. This may have impacted on Italy's attraction to foreign teams and riders, particularly given the tight links that Mussolini and his regime fostered with the authorities in all of the leading sports, using them as propaganda tools to promote fascist ideals and principles.

Just as Mussolini dominated the political and social scene, so Italian cycling and the Tour of Lombardy also found itself under near absolute rule as a new star nicknamed 'The Dictator' emerged to impose his law.

10

ITALIAN CYCLING'S GOLDEN AGE

In the modern era, Alfredo Binda is best known as the former holder of the record for Giro d'Italia stage wins, whose total of 41 was eclipsed by sprinter Mario Cipollini in 2003. Although 'SuperMario' did have occasional days of brilliance in one-day races, he never won a Monument. Binda, on the other hand, won half a dozen and much more besides.

The tenth of 14 children born to a builder in the town of Cittiglio, just a few kilometres from the Brinzio climb on the Giro di Lombardia route, young Alfredo had two passions throughout his life: cycling and music. At the age of 12, his father began to push him towards a career in music after Binda had borrowed a bike from a local shop and raced on it, only to crash during the event, banging himself and the bike up. Spend more time playing the cornet, his father instructed him.

When he was 17, Binda and his brother Primo were sent away to live with an uncle in Nice because his father could not earn enough to support all of his children. The two brothers worked as plasterers, but were given three days off each week to do what they wanted. Mostly, they wanted to ride. Binda took up racing again and, in September 1921, took part in a big amateur race in Nice. He won it, although he was subsequently disqualified. His offence is not recorded.

As Binda continued to progress, word of his exploits spread back to Italy, eventually reaching the ears of Costante Girardengo. In early 1923, with Binda now a first-year pro with La Française, the two Italians met for the first time in Nice-Mont Chauve. Coming on to the final climb,

Binda attacked and left the rest of the field for dead. The Italian papers were stunned by the 'Niçois from Cittiglio', but a year later they and everyone else became better acquainted with Binda's talent when he headed back home to race the Tour of Lombardy for the first time, drawn by the prospect of the 500 lire on offer to the first rider to the summit of the Ghisallo.

Reading *La Gazzetta dello Sport* the day before the race, Binda was surprised to find that he was one of the favourites, but that didn't deter him from the objective he had set himself. With Michele Robotti away at the front as the main pack reached the foot of the Ghisallo, Binda went hard from the first steep ramps just two kilometres into the ten-kilometre ascent. All the favourites went with him, knowing little about the young French-schooled rider apart from the fact that he had a very good reputation. One by one, they slipped off Binda's wheel as he surged up the climb, never rising from his saddle as he pushed his gear smoothly round. Girardengo was the last rider to yield. With 300m to the summit, Binda cruised past Robotti. The 500 lire were his. He went on to finish fourth, more than seven minutes down on defending champion Giovanni Brunero, but right on the heels of Girardengo and Pietro Linari, who filled the other two podium places.

Binda's performance produced an immediate reaction from Eberardo Pavesi, the head of the Legnano team. A canny operator known as 'The Lawyer', he offered Binda a salary of 20,000 lire a year and 5,000 more for every Classic he won. Binda mulled over the offer, asked for a bit more and got it. In 1925, he left La Française for the olive-green colours of Legnano. He made his debut in the Giro and beat Girardengo into second by five minutes. As 'Gira' had won Sanremo at the start of the year, Lombardy became the unofficial decider of which of them was the rider of the season.

For once, it was dry and dusty. On the Ghisallo, Binda eased away, quickly opening a gap on his rivals. His style looked effortless, just as it did when he was riding flat out on the plains or pushing hard in a time trial. French climber René Vietto described his technique as 'incomparable. He could have set off with a full cup of milk on his back, and it would still have been full when he arrived. No weakness. No sense that he was tired. He was at one with his bike. Elegance, purity, he was an artist. He was the epitome of beauty in action.'

At the summit of the Ghisallo his lead was two minutes, while Girardengo was more than five back. Rather than press on with half of the 251km course to run, he sat up and allowed himself to be caught. Girardengo responded bullishly, attacking hard. Ominously for the established champion, Binda was quick to bridge across to him. Within minutes the rest were riding for third place.

As they paused briefly at the Grantola control point, fatigue began to take its toll on Girardengo, who forgot to sign his name. At Brinzio, when the road reared up again, Binda attacked hard. According to *La Gazzetta*, Girardengo 'battled with savage intensity', but had to yield. With 55km to the finish, Binda, his hair swept back, sleeves rolled up and goggles hanging around his neck, glided away, opening up a lead of almost seven minutes on Girardengo, who rolled in totally defeated and, within minutes, was disqualified for forgetting that signature.

If Binda's victory was impressive, his defence of the title was staggering. It was a wet, miserable day. Binda rode as if determined to get in out of the cold as soon as possible. Climbing the Ghisallo with Ottavio Bottecchia and Ermanno Vallazza for company, Binda upped his pace, seemingly determined to take the *prime* on offer at the summit. However, rather than sit up as he had done the previous year, he persisted, riding the final 158km alone to finish half an hour ahead of runner-up Antonio Negrini. Watching from *La Gazzetta*'s press car because of injury, Girardengo expressed his astonishment, admitting Binda's performance was one of the most impressive he had ever witnessed.

By the time he wrapped up a hat-trick of Lombardy victories in 1927, Binda had won the second of what would be five Giro titles and the first of his three World Championships. According to John Foot in

Pedalare! Pedalare!, 'Binda was a cycling superstar whose fame surpassed that of Girardengo before him and all his contemporaries'. The canny Italian was well aware of his image and the need to maintain it. 'Binda's hair was always perfectly slicked back, he was good-looking in a classical, matinee idol way and he dressed stylishly ... He presented himself as an arbiter of good taste. Rich, famous and handsome, he always took his holidays in the posh resort of Alassio in Liguria.'

Yet he became so good that fans began to get bored with his success, and *La Gazzetta* saw evidence of this in falling sales. In 1930, the paper reacted by paying Binda 25,000 lire to skip the Giro after he had won it four years out of five, racking up 33 stage wins in the process. This bounty matched the prize on offer to the race's winner.

Although many Italian writers have declared Binda the best rider of all time, two factors generally count against him when he is compared to the likes of Fausto Coppi, Eddy Merckx and Bernard Hinault. Firstly, he didn't have to contend with a rival at his level, because Girardengo's best years were behind him when Binda emerged, while Learco Guerra, the pick of his contemporaries, was never able to extend him consistently. Secondly, he achieved little of note at the Tour de France, where he would certainly have been tested more rigorously. He only rode it once, in 1930, winning back-to-back mountain stages in the Pyrenees, then quitting the next day after a crash left him with a twisted frame, a broken seatpost and a deficit of more than an hour. Yet the fact that Guerra finished second that year suggests the Tour crown was well within Binda's reach.

In 1928, he went close to completing a fourth successive victory in Lombardy on a day so wet the lakes flooded, forcing the racers on to wooden boardwalks and into water that was up to their axles at some points. Binda punctured four times and spent most of the race chasing. Having got up to the leaders approaching the finish, he took second in the sprint behind Legnano teammate Gaetano Belloni, the 36-year-old veteran completing his third success. Binda's ill-starred day was complete when he was disqualified for an illegal wheel change.

Three years later, in 1931, in equally wet conditions, Binda secured his fourth success in Lombardy, coasting home minutes ahead of outgoing champion Michele Mara. The race was billed as a battle between Binda and new world champion Guerra, but Guerra's bushy eyebrows, dark thatch and rainbow bands were hardly in evidence. By the time he quit with half the race remaining, Binda and his Legnano teammates Remo Bertoni and Luigi Marchisio were already minutes clear. As if to prove a point at the end of a comparatively poor season, Binda left his two allies with 96km remaining. He finished 18 minutes clear and had time to pick up his prize and shower before Mara rode in for second place.

How had he managed it, Binda was asked. By eating raw eggs handed up to him along the route. He had consumed 34 of them. 'It was practically impossible to eat. Everything that we put in our jersey pockets dissolved,' he said. 'The rain fell incessantly and it was difficult to let go of the bars, even with one hand. Only eggs still in their shells were consumable. Thankfully, I've got a strong liver.'

The advent of 'Gino the Pious'

As Binda's career went into a slow decline, new stars were emerging on the Italian racing scene. One stood out in Lombardy. Domenico Piemontesi insisted he had been robbed when he was relegated from first place to fourth in 1930, the jury ruling nine days after the race that he had made use of Antonio Negrini's shoulder to sling himself to the front of the sprint. Finishing second two years later to Negrini in a sprint, Piemontesi left nothing to doubt in 1933.

'The Cyclone of Borgomanero', as Piemontesi was known, after his place of birth, was one of four riders who attacked with only 15km covered. Crossing the Ghisallo, Piemontesi had just Aldo Canazza for company. When he punctured on the descent, Piemontesi rode on alone to win after a breakaway of 215km. 'Is this your best victory?' he was asked. 'No, that was the one I took in 1930 when they relegated me,' he responded cuttingly. A year on, Piemontesi was in the mix again, but acted as watchdog and then lead-out man for Guerra, who steamed out of the final corner to take a comfortable win in front of 10,000 fans in the Milan Arena.

When Binda's career was ended by a devastating crash during Milan–Sanremo in the early weeks of the 1936 season, Legnano already had his successor as leader in their ranks. Winner of the Italian championship at 21, Tuscan Gino Bartali had also announced himself in Lombardy, finishing third behind Enrico Mollo in 1935. When Binda's misfortune pushed Bartali to the top of Legnano's pecking order the following spring, he responded brilliantly, winning the Giro d'Italia. Yet a week after celebrating his victory in Milan, Bartali was hit by a family tragedy that almost caused him to quit the sport.

Earlier that year, his younger brother, Giulio, had signed with Legnano with a view to turning professional with them in 1937. On 14 June, he was racing in an event near Florence that was part of the Tuscan Young Fascists' Championship when he collided with a car and sustained injuries to his chest, shoulder and ribs. Taken to hospital in Florence, he underwent emergency surgery but never regained consciousness. He died two days later.

He was only 19 but his elder brother claimed he would have been the Bartali family's biggest talent. 'Giulio could have done better than me. Nobody could beat him on the climbs,' he said. For several days, Bartali contemplated retirement, but was prompted to continue by his future wife, Adriana. Bartali laid his winning *maglia rosa* from the Giro on his brother's coffin and, two years later, would add the Tour's yellow jersey to the mementos on his brother's grave.

His return to racing produced a string of victories, convincing him he'd made the right decision. The pick of them came at Lombardy, to which the organisers had made one or two changes. The least successful was a change to the Ghisallo, which was tackled from its tougher but less impressive side via Barni. This turned out to be a one-off, even though it produced the key attack of the race, Bartali leading over the top with only Diego Marabelli and Luigi Barral still on his wheel, 'stuck to him like stamps,' said *La Gazzetta*. The trio stayed together all the way into the new finish in Milan on the recently opened Vigorelli velodrome.

Barral led on to the track, 20m ahead of his two breakaway rivals. Bartali let him sit out there until the bell rang for the final lap, then began to wind up his sprint, flashing past Barral in the final straight as Marabelli vainly attempted to come off his wheel. Costante Girardengo described it as 'the best race I've ever watched', and, if nothing else, it established the Vigorelli as Lombardy's preferred finishing point.

Up until 1929, the race had finished on the old Sempione track on many occasions. However, *La Gazzetta*'s editor-in-chief, Emilio Colombo, never warmed to the venue, partly because he didn't like to see a great road race finish on a track, but also because the cinder surface became very treacherous when it was wet, which was often the case in November. It seems he wasn't too keen on the Vigorelli either, at least to start with, but the new track quickly became popular with racers and fans. After Giuseppe Olmo set a new mark of 45.090km for the world hour record on the Vigorelli's boards in October 1935, when 9,000 fans packed into its stands to roar him on, the new arena was chosen as the new finishing venue for Lombardy.

Over the next two decades and more, the Vigorelli became one of cycling's iconic locations. Between 1935 and 1959, seven different riders set a new mark for the hour record on the track, including Fausto Coppi, Jacques Anquetil and Ercole Baldini. Frenchman Roger Rivière set two world hour marks there, his 1959 record of 47.347km standing for eight years. It also hosted three successful attempts on the women's hour record. Plenty of other records also fell on its speed-inducing Swedish pine boards, more than 150 of them at every distance between 200m and 100km.

In addition to several world track championships, the Vigorelli also became a popular venue for boxing and, from the 1960s, for concerts.

The Beatles played there in 1965 and Led Zeppelin in 1971, although their performance was cut short when rioting broke out following clashes between sections of the audience and the police, who fired tear gas into the crowd and, at one point, on to the stage.

By that point, the Vigorelli's fortunes were on the wane. Its association with Lombardy lasted until 1960. The race did return in 1985 to celebrate the fiftieth anniversary of the track's opening, but it was never repeated. Its lowest point, at least in cycling terms, came in 1967 when the ageing Jacques Anquetil returned to Milan for a second shot at the hour record. The Frenchman managed to better Rivière's distance by 150m, but the new mark was never ratified as he refused to undergo a drugs test, having previously been led to believe that none would be carried out.

While his team director Raphaël 'Big Gun' Geminiani raged, Anquetil was almost indifferent to the fuss, just as he had been when he found himself in a similar situation after winning Liège the previous season. 'I couldn't care less whether the record is ratified. I beat it, full stop. The rest is just talk,' he said, adding later: 'After all, I can't very well have a pee in front of everybody … As far as I know Coppi, Baldini and Rivière weren't required to submit to such a test. Does my word not suffice?' Unfortunately for Anquetil, it didn't.

There were attempts to revive the Vigorelli, but by the end of the twentieth century, when covered 250m tracks had become the norm, it was outdated and, increasingly, unloved. In the present century, it became home to two American football teams, the Rhinos and the Seamen. In 2013, a competition was held to push forward the design and redevelopment of the stadium. Among the plans submitted was one proposing the Vigorelli's conversion into a 'Park of Wheels', a multi-purpose public space that would feature cycling as part of Milan's push to promote two-wheeled transport. Although the scheme required the removal of the track, it looked innovative, but it lost out to a design for a new American football stadium, underlining just how far cycling's stock has fallen with the Italian public.

Back in the late 1930s, such an eventuality would have been unthinkable. When Bartali completed solo victories on the Vigorelli in 1939 and 1940, fans packed the arena to acclaim him. The first of those races also saw the Lombardy debut of Fausto Coppi, then riding as an independent, but he failed to finish after a series of punctures.

The following year Coppi was not only part of Bartali's Legnano team but came to the race as Giro d'Italia champion. On the lower slopes of the Ghisallo, Bartali had a problem with a wheel that forced him to stop. His rivals sensed an opportunity and pushed on hard, with Coppi leading the way. Piqued by Coppi's attack, Bartali charged up the Ghisallo, passing rider after rider until only Coppi remained ahead. A kilometre from the summit, he reached Coppi, but instead of pausing and working with his teammate to distance the opposition, he fired by and never looked back, finishing four minutes clear as Coppi faded completely out of the picture.

It would be six years before the Bartali/Coppi duel reached full pitch, but this battle added substance to a rivalry that had begun at the Giro, where Bartali started as leader but had to cede that role to his young lieutenant after colliding with a dog early in the race. On the tenth stage to Modena, Coppi attacked on the Abetone Pass, opening a substantial lead. Bartali, his role as leader usurped, instructed their Legnano teammates to chase down Coppi until team manager Pavesi pulled them all into line.

Although Italy did not enter the Second World War until 1940, the initial outbreak of the conflict had an immediate effect on the country. Fuel and other essentials were rationed from 1939, with the result that only one official vehicle was permitted to follow the races that took place up to 1942. That year's race took place in mid-October on a much shortened course that included the Ghisallo and Valbrona climbs, but a lot of flat riding after them, resulting in a sprint on the Vigorelli contested by 30 riders, Aldo Bini denying Bartali a fourth victory on the line.

By 1943, the war was being fought on Italian soil. Initially, the conflict was an internal one, the result of the king's decision to dismiss and arrest Benito Mussolini. Il Duce's German allies responded by invading and taking control of most of the country. By the time they did so, Allied forces had already taken Sicily and were beginning to advance north on the mainland.

While Coppi ended up as one of the many hundreds of thousands of Italian soldiers captured by the Allies in North Africa, Bartali remained in Tuscany. Although he never joined the Fascist Party and he tried to avoid being drawn into its propaganda, which exploited the successes of Italian athletes across many sports, he could not escape the regime's control completely. In 1938, he had ridden the Tour de France at the instigation of the Fascist government, which revelled in his success, dubbing him 'the conqueror of the French'.

His status as one of Italy's most high-profile and successful sporting heroes exempted him from active wartime service, yet it was long rumoured that he had been involved in helping the partisans against Mussolini's fascists, smuggling forged identity papers even before Italy joined the war. More than 50 years after the end of hostilities, it was finally revealed that Bartali had played a significant role in saving the lives of hundreds of Italian Jews by transporting papers to the underground organisations that helped hide them from the Fascist government and the Nazis. In October 2013, during a ceremony at the Yad Vashem Holocaust memorial in Jerusalem, Bartali was inducted into the Garden of the Righteous Among the Nations for the assistance he gave to the Jewish-Christian rescue network around Florence during the German occupation of Italy.

This led to a general reappraisal of Bartali the public figure, as it didn't fit the image of the man who had been painted so clearly as 'Gino the Pious', the sandal-wearing, God-fearing member of Azione Cattolica and close friend of Christian Democrat leader and Italy's first post-war prime minister Alcide de Gasperi. He was, it had appeared, an arch-conservative, an impression supported by Pope Pius XII's citing of him as an example to all Azione Cattolica members. Consequently, in the eyes of Italians, so many of whom were bike fans, Bartali was the traditionalist while Coppi was the more liberal figure, a view confirmed for many by his adulterous affair with Giulia Occhini, the wife of a doctor who was himself a huge fan of Coppi's, after the revelation of which the Pope urged the rider to return to his own wife.

Coppi in his pomp

For Italians, supporting either Bartali or Coppi became easier following the war when the two men rode for different teams: Bartali leading Legnano, while Coppi moved to Bianchi. The fans' allegiances were cemented during the 1946 Giro, when the two men fought a race-long battle that eventually went in Bartali's favour by 47 seconds, with the third rider more than a quarter of an hour back. Coppi, though, prevailed in both of the great Italian Classics. Having started the season with what remains one of the most fabled winning performances at Sanremo, he ended it on the same note with a victory in Lombardy after Bartali had crashed out.

In *La Gazzetta*, Bruno Roghi wrote: 'At the start of the season in Sanremo he won the race when the almond trees flower … at the close of it in Milan [he won] the race of the falling leaves.' Roghi's poetic description of Lombardy stuck.

L'Équipe editor Jacques Goddet was also impressed with the Italian, but less so with the organisation of the race. 'If it had been run according to the rules in place in France relating to support vehicles, he would have won by five minutes. He needed to be a superman to get the better of the cars,' wrote Goddet, who, on the other hand, was full of praise for the Italian fans, saying: 'Their admiration for their heroes is such that they literally want to provide a cortege for them.'

Turning to Coppi, Goddet described him as 'a precious stone for cycle sport', describing both his elegance and his determination to win.

'This man, who rides on tiptoe when he gets out of the saddle to ease his way up a section at 14%, is blessed with much more talent than the usual road racer ... He has the taste for domination. He always looks straight ahead. He never seems to worry about what is going on behind him ... It is as if he has decided to stick to the same philosophy, blindly obeying Herodotus' precept: "Great deeds usually come from great risks."'

Coppi's long-time mechanic, Giuseppe 'Pinella' de Grandi, described the Bianchi leader's simple tactic at Lombardy. 'He would keep his rivals in check until the first ramps of the Ghisallo, and then he would scatter them. The process was always the same. Fausto used to cross the summit with a significant advantage, which he used to almost double on the descent down to Erba, where we would give him his musette.'

In 1947 this tactic yielded a five-minute victory over Bartali. The following year his advantage over runner-up Adolfo Leoni was just a few seconds under the same mark as he completed the climb up the dirt road to the Madonna del Ghisallo chapel in 25′20″, almost two minutes faster than his previous record. 'This wasn't a race, it was a monologue,' Goddet wrote in *L'Équipe*.

However, the monologue didn't need to exclude Bartali. He had opted not to start following the furore over his and Coppi's actions during the World Championship two months earlier. With their rivalry at its peak, the two men focused on each other, each determined not to let the other win and overlooking the fact they were both representing Italy and not their trade teams. Once they were both sure they had achieved this goal, they withdrew from the race, drawing boos from the crowd in the Dutch town of Valkenburg.

Castigated by the Italian fans, press and federation, the pair received a two-month ban from racing, although this was quickly overturned, giving them the chance to ride Lombardy. Asked about Bartali's absence, Coppi responded: 'He's not ridden to avoid being beaten. If I had lost it would have been a double victory for him.'

This episode led to an agreement between the two men prior to the Tour de France the following year, which was undoubtedly the best of Coppi's career. He won Sanremo, the Giro, the Italian title and the Tour, making him the first man to complete the Giro/Tour double. A fourth successive victory in Lombardy followed, once again forged by an attack on the Ghisallo past the recently consecrated shrine to the patroness of cyclists. His margin at the line was a mere three minutes on Switzerland's Ferdi Kübler.

By the late 1940s, foreign participation in 'the race of the falling leaves' had picked up significantly, partly as a result of the introduction of the Desgrange-Colombo Challenge in 1948. That year Switzerland's Fritz Schär finished third, making him the first foreign rider on the podium since Henri Pélissier in 1920. Three years later, Louison Bobet emulated his compatriot by taking the title in rather surprising circumstances.

Bobet had a simple strategy for the race: to follow Fausto Coppi everywhere he went. The pair crossed the Ghisallo side by side and were in the eight-strong group that formed on the run across the often misty plains of Lombardy and running into Milan.

The Frenchman was up against seven Italians and, once on the Vigorelli, ended up boxed in on the inside of the track as Giuseppe Minardi set a fierce pace on the front for defending champion Renzo Soldani. Realising there was no way through to the front of the group, Bobet eased off, dropped to the back of the line and switched to the outside. Fortunately for him, the Italians stepped off the pace as they started to look at each other. When Minardi picked it up again as the riders came into the final straight, Bobet fired down off the 42-degree banking and swept by on the outside, passing Coppi and then Minardi to win by less than half a wheel, making him the first foreign rider to win Sanremo and Lombardy in the same season.

While the press mobbed the riders, the managers of Bobet's Bottecchia team lodged a protest against Ferdi Kübler. Although the

Swiss had finished more than two minutes back in eleventh place, the points he gained had enabled him to defend the Desgrange-Colombo title. However, Bottecchia pointed out that Kübler had swapped bikes with one of his teammates after puncturing, which was not then permitted by the sport's rules, as, for example, Roger Lapébie had already found to his cost at Roubaix in 1934. The Swiss was disqualified and the Desgrange-Colombo title went to Bobet.

It would be another five years before the Italians missed out at Lombardy again, although they could easily have done so in the deluge-induced chaos of 1953. During the latter part of the race, the rain became so heavy that the organisers decided against having the finish on the Vigorelli's sodden boards, opting to move it into the street outside. The 11 riders in the winning break were informed of the change as they approached Milan.

Two kilometres from the finish, Belgium-based Italian Pino Cerami attacked, but was being reeled in as the riders approached the final roundabout, where a left turn took them towards the Vigorelli. Rather than pointing them to the left, the policeman on the roundabout mistakenly spread his arms wide, indicating the riders could pass on either side of it. Assuming the finish was on the road straight across, nine riders went to the right and only first-year pro Bruno Landi followed Cerami to the left. Seeing his rivals go the other way, Cerami hesitated and Landi shot past him. He crossed the line victorious without needing to sprint.

There is little doubt a number of riders in the break would have beaten Landi in a straight sprint, including Cerami, Frenchman Pierre Barbotin, Belgium's Stan Ockers and the inconsolable Fiorenzo Magni, whose protest was in vain. The result stood. Landi was the champion, but failed to capitalise on his good fortune. He never won another notable title.

Although Fausto Coppi's fifth Lombardy success the next season was not as big a shock as Landi's, it was still surprising given the turmoil that had engulfed him. During 1953, he had begun his affair with Giulia Occhini, having first met her at the Tre Valli Varesine race in 1948, when her husband, Enrico Locatelli, had encouraged her to ask Coppi for an autograph. Their secret relationship emerged when Occhini was pictured with Coppi near the podium after he had won the 1953 world title in Lugano. She was described as 'the woman in white' thanks to the coat she was wearing when first seen with Coppi, and later dubbed, 'The White Lady' by the Italian press, which revelled in details of the affair while insisting on the sordid nature of what was an adulterous and, at that time, criminal relationship. In September 1954, Locatelli insisted on the police enforcing the law relating to adultery, which led to Occhini's arrest. She spent three days in prison before being 'exiled' to her aunt's house in Ancona.

A month later, Coppi lined up in Milan with his focus apparently lying across the country on the Adriatic coast. Yet races offered him the sanctuary he couldn't find anywhere else, such was the extent of the interest in him, and particularly during that period. Although Bartali, who was close to completing his final season, was missing because of flu, the field was strong, with Rik Van Steenbergen, Stan Ockers and Ferdi Kübler leading the foreign challenge, and Magni determined to correct the injustice that had befallen him 12 months earlier. Unusually given what was to follow, Coppi didn't lead over the Ghisallo, trailing a few seconds behind Valerio Chiarlone, but he made it safely into the ten-man group that subsequently formed and headed into the Vigorelli.

Coppi attacked almost straight away, spinning a big gear, challenging the rest to come past him if they could. Magni was the only one who came close but even he was two bike lengths down when Coppi crossed the line for his fifth Lombardy title. 'I rode very wisely for 221 kilometres and 700 metres, then like a novice,' Magni confessed.

After Lombardy, Coppi's next challenge was the court case instigated by Dr Locatelli. In March 1955, he and Occhini, who was by now pregnant with her lover's child, had to give full and intimate details of the relationship, which the Italian press gleefully printed. Coppi received a two-month suspended sentence for adultery, Occhini three months suspended. Once their passports had been returned to them, they had to travel to Argentina for the birth of their son, Faustino, who would not have been recognised as Coppi's child under Italian law at that time.

By now 36, Coppi was in evident decline. That fifth Lombardy victory was his last success in a Classic or grand tour. He continued racing, though, seemingly determined to deliver one final flourish. He almost provided it in Lombardy in 1956, but ended up suffering his most painful defeat.

11

'THE MOST DEMANDING RACE ON THE CALENDAR'

Either no one tried or, more likely, no one managed to persuade Fausto Coppi to retire. When he died on 2 January 1960 of malaria caught during a hunting trip to what was then Upper Volta and is now Burkina Faso, he was already planning to race for another season for a team directed by his old foe Gino Bartali. By that point finishing a race was an achievement for the 40-year-old Coppi, who hadn't been a contender for a major title since the 1956 Tour of Lombardy, where he could have bowed out in grand style despite what was a very narrow and tearful defeat.

That fiftieth edition of 'the race of the falling leaves' ran to what had been the familiar format since the Second World War. Coppi emerged from among the race favourites on the Ghisallo and had closed in on lone leader Diego Ronchini by the summit. Ronchini, riding for the Bianchi team Coppi had deserted for Carpano at the start of that season, stopped working with the five-time champion as the pair dropped down towards the plains leading into Milan. Some reports suggest he had a knee injury, others that Coppi's former mechanic and now Bianchi team director, Pinella de Grandi, ordered young Ronchini to ease off, believing French import André Darrigade was a better bet for the title.

However, Coppi might have won even without Ronchini's aid if it hadn't been for an incident that took place a few minutes after he passed over the Ghisallo. Giulia Occhini was travelling in one of the Carpano support cars, which came up alongside Fiorenzo Magni near the top of the climb. Magni insisted she made an offensive gesture. Some more contemporary accounts suggest she also shouted, 'Coppi is the best!' in his direction and leered at him. Whatever did happen, Magni was riled and set about chasing down Coppi, bringing a number of fast finishers with him.

Magni's 15-strong group, which featured Rik Van Looy, Louison Bobet and Darrigade, caught the leading pair 12km from the finish. The group swept on to the pulsating Vigorelli, where a packed crowd was chanting 'Fausto! Fausto!' In a similar situation two years earlier, Coppi had gone straight to the front and hammered out a rhythm that no one could equal. This time, though, he was confident of his chances in a straight sprint. He got on Magni's wheel and when his rival shot away on the back straight he was right on him. Coming off the final bend, he came around Magni and thought he had the race won, only for Darrigade to pull the same manoeuvre on him to win by ten centimetres.

Coppi's first instinct was to congratulate Darrigade, whom he had recommended to Bianchi when they had been looking for a rider who could match up against Italian sprinter Nino Defilippis in the Italian Classics. When the impact of what had happened hit him, he was inconsolable, and had to be lifted off his bike even as the crowd continued to chant his name. As he sobbed, Magni approached to offer a word, although hardly one of consolation. 'If your woman hadn't been so offensive, I'd never have had the incentive to come after you. And then the Frenchman wouldn't have beaten you, would he?' he muttered.

Only an hour later, having returned to his hotel, did Coppi finally speak. 'I give you my word of honour that today I thought I could compete in a sprint with many famous sprinters. If I hadn't felt that way I would not have entered the track in that position,' he said, before admitting that in the euphoria of approaching victory he had committed a fatal mistake. 'I didn't see Darrigade coming on my right. If I had I would have stuck my elbows out to make it harder for him to pass, which is what is expected when you're sprinting on the track.' He paused for a moment, then added with smile: 'You have to understand what victory would have meant to me today at my age.'

His sadness was shared by almost everyone. The crowd gave him an extended ovation. Even the French press, which celebrated Darrigade's success, felt for the Italian. 'Let us be frank with ourselves. We all felt a great sadness when the chasing pack bridged up to Coppi. Every one of us was saying at that time we hoped victory would be his,' Pierre Chany wrote in *L'Équipe*.

As Coppi's career moved towards his tragic end, cycling and the Tour of Lombardy were changing. *Extrasportif* sponsors, which came from outside the sport, became more frequent from the mid-1950s, bringing more money into cycling, but occasionally with farcical consequences. In 1957, newly crowned world champion Rik Van Steenbergen lined up for a Classic that he never liked bearing the logo of an Italian vermouth on his rainbow jersey as well as those of his Peugeot-BP team. The Belgian rode 100m and then pulled out, excusing himself by saying it was cold and wet and he didn't want to fall ill before the lucrative six-day season. He had, he pointed out, fulfilled his commitment to appear in Lombardy. The fuss no doubt delighted the vermouth manufacturers, who got a greater return on their one-off commitment than they could ever have expected.

The challenge offered by Lombardy was also changing. The rough dirt roads that had provided an extra degree of difficulty were gradually being resurfaced as Italy's industrialization gathered pace, particularly in the corridor from Turin to Milan and on to Venice. In 1958, the road gangs worked up and over the Ghisallo. The impact was instant. Later that year, Frenchman Marcel Rohrbach completed the climb in 22'57", more than two minutes faster than the record mark, set the previous year, while more than 60 riders were in the group that contested the finish. In 1959, the bunch led in by Rik Van Looy contained 85 riders. Race director Vincenzo Torriani looked for a solution to the huge bunch finishes that signalled the race had become less of a climbing test and found it in a wood just off the descent from the Ghisallo.

Climbing from 820m to 1,124m in just two kilometres, the Muro di Sormano averages 15 per cent. Back in 1960, it was little more than a mule trail, badly surfaced, almost unused and followed by a fast and very treacherous descent. Torriani visited it with *La Gazzetta* journalist Rino Negri, who recalled: 'More than a road, it was like a goat track. I told him the riders would have to go on foot because there were sections at 25 per cent. Torriani rubbed his hands and said that everyone would be talking about the race.'

Torriani liked the idea of including it to prevent the sprinters dominating Lombardy, but after seeing it he was afraid 'the wall' might turn the race into a circus. He only confirmed its inclusion the day before the 1960 edition, when *La Stampa*'s Vittorio Varale wrote: 'Tomorrow we will all be watching the national pushing festival!'

The peloton came at it after crossing the Ghisallo, taking a right turn in Asso and following the road through Canova and Sormano to the foot of the climb. The bunch split into two groups: riders and walkers. Imerio Massignan was the first rider to the top, taking 10′9″ to climb the spiralling two-kilometre staircase, his average speed 13.004km/h. The seven riders who struggled up immediately behind him came together on the run down into Milan.

With the big-name sprinters all defeated by the Sormano, 1957 champion Ronchini and Belgium's Émile Daems – described by Negri as 'barrel-shaped ... more like a boxer than a cyclist' – were the favourites, and so it proved on the Vigorelli, Daems beating the Italian by half a wheel.

The riders were almost unanimous in their dislike of Torriani's new addition, many pointing out that it made little difference to the result as most riders had either ridden or pushed their bike up it at a similar pace. Others said it effectively neutralised the race until the riders had passed it because they were so uncertain of its effect. Torriani, though, picked up on a comment made by Jacques Anquetil, who was one of the few who had ridden it in the days before the race. 'If the finish was in Como, the race would take shape earlier and regrouping on the flat would be avoided,' said the French star.

Torriani acted on Anquetil's suggestion, moving the finish to Como, where it would remain until 1984. This added greater significance to the action on the Sormano, particularly as it was preceded by the so-called Super Ghisallo. This still took the riders from Bellagio to the chapel at Magreglio. However, rather than dipping into the saddle at Guello, two-thirds of the way up the climb, it tracked right to Cernobbio, climbing to almost a thousand metres before dropping down the Via Piano Rancio to the Ghisallo a few hundred metres below the chapel.

Three-time champion Gino Bartali wasn't impressed with the decision to retain the Sormano, telling *La Gazzetta*: 'Anyone who's not a pure climber has to get to the bottom of the Muro with an advantage of at least ten minutes. That way he can complete it on foot and take fifteen minutes more than those on their bikes. He'll get to the top five or six minutes behind and can still hope.'

The inclusion of the Super Ghisallo made Bartali's suggestion a near impossibility. Heading on to the Sormano, specialist climbers filled the front rank. Massignan was there again, together with six-time Tour de France King of the Mountains Federico Bahamontes and flyweight Vito Taccone, a tiny man with a temper as explosive as his acceleration up a steep climb. In Como's Sinigaglia stadium, Taccone, whose sprinting speed netted him four consecutive stage wins in the 1963 Giro, swept down off the final banking and beat Massignan by a distance.

As Torriani had hoped, his innovations had produced a more unpredictable race and a very different type of winner. However, apart from the climbers, few other riders were happy with the new course. Giro d'Italia champion of 1958, Ercole Baldini spoke for many when he complained: 'I can't fathom the reason why Torriani wanted a novelty like this. I understand that the Ghisallo didn't offer the guarantee of breaking the race up any more, but, frankly, he's gone overboard in the opposite direction. This climb is simply beastly, impossible to get up.'

Ironically, Baldini went on to set a new record speed for the ascent of the Sormano in 1962. His time of 9'24" was a startling 18 seconds faster than first-year pro Enrico Massignan, younger brother of Imerio, with Taccone another second slower. Baldini's secret weapon on the Sormano was his popularity. Years later he confessed to Torriani: 'Having lots of fans meant getting lots of pushes ... and I had lots of fans.' A famous photo from that year's race shows the Italian being pushed up the Sormano by no fewer than three fans as two more hover at the side of the road, preparing to take over and maintain his momentum.

Baldini was far from the only rider to benefit in this way. Fans flocked to the climb, not to watch their heroes, but to help them. It made a mockery of the race and caused uproar. *La Stampa*'s Vittorio Varale called on the Italian federation to intervene and restore the sport's honour, which, he said, had been blackened by the antics of some fans. Torriani had no alternative but to end the experiment, despite the money that had been invested that year in resurfacing both the Sormano and the descent away from it.

Yet Torriani wasn't about to return Lombardy to the sprint-fest it had threatened to become. Although he also ditched the Super Ghisallo, replacing it with the traditional ascent to the Madonna del Ghisallo chapel at Magreglio, four new climbs were added: the Balisio, Valmara, Intelvi and Schignano. The Valmara was presented by the organisers as 'a more domesticated version of the Sormano', but riders still ended up taking to their feet when some of those at the front of the bunch lost traction in the dust and gravel and keeled over into the crowd. Nevertheless, the alterations received widespread praise, and the fact that the same rider won both the 1962 race with the Sormano and the 1963 edition without it suggests Torriani's tinkering worked out as he hoped.

Dutchman Jo De Roo wasn't an obvious pick as a Lombardy winner. A teammate of Jacques Anquetil at St-Raphaël, De Roo was certainly in form in the autumn of 1962, having won Paris–Tours at a record speed a fortnight before Lombardy. But the French race is known as 'the sprinters'

Classic' because its flat route almost guarantees a bunch finish. Lombardy was a different challenge entirely. De Roo, though, was a rider who was very good at many things but a specialist at none. He could climb well, sprint well and, as he had shown by winning the 557km Bordeaux–Paris race in May 1962, he was perfectly happy riding on the flat.

De Roo described his first Lombardy success as 'the most beautiful of my career', but it wasn't without incident. He led on to the Sormano, but his wheel became jammed against his chainstay as he swung his bike from side to side. His team mechanic was quickly up to him to slip a new wheel into place, but the commissaires whistled their dissent when the mechanic began to push De Roo back up to speed. He wobbled on for a few metres, lurched as his momentum took him sideways rather than forwards, and ended up with his bars caught in the straps of a female spectator's handbag.

As he and the woman disentangled themselves, Livio Trapé went shooting by, a couple of fans providing obvious assistance that the commissaires chose to ignore. De Roo's frustration turned to anger. He reached the top of the Sormano 15 seconds behind Trapé, then dispatched him easily when they went head to head in Como. As fans crowded in behind the finish line, De Roo jumped off his bike and hopped around in front of them, his face a mask of agony as his right calf seized completely with cramp.

Controversy then victory for Simpson

The Dutchman repeated his feat the following year, defending his Paris–Tours crown and then going on to retain the Lombardy title, his track experience giving him an edge on eight rivals. Britain's Tom Simpson, a miner's son from the Nottinghamshire village of Harworth whose exuberant character made him a popular favourite with fans and his peers, had also been well fancied that year, but rolled in a disappointed tenth almost a minute down on the winner, blaming the distraction of his duel with Raymond Poulidor for the Super Prestige Pernod International Trophy for his failure to contend for the title.

The Super Prestige Pernod sprang from the Prestige Pernod, a season-long competition established in 1958 to reward the best French rider of the year. Following the demise of the Desgrange-Colombo Challenge at the end of that same year, Pernod had introduced the Super Prestige Pernod competition to assess the best rider of the year based on points won across all of the major races. Going into Lombardy, the final race of the series, Jacques Anquetil topped the standings, but didn't start, offering Simpson in second place and Poulidor in third the opportunity to leapfrog him.

'Circumstances made us rivals, but if Poulidor had proposed that we split the prize between us I would undoubtedly have accepted,' Simpson told *L'Équipe*. 'That would have been the ideal solution and we could have each ridden our own race. But Poulidor didn't say anything and I ended up neutralising his attacks. He lost the Tour of Lombardy, but I lost it too,' he added, bemoaning the loss of prize money that would have helped fund the building of his new house in Gent.

Simpson rode in his more typical aggressive fashion the following year, but paid the price for doing too much work too soon when he couldn't stay with Italy's bright new star, Gianni Motta, on the run-in to the finish. The Englishman returned in 1965 as the world champion, but under a cloud following a string of exposés in the cycling world that had appeared in a British tabloid, the *People*. Written in the first person, the three pieces promised far more than they delivered. Under the headline that yelled 'World champ but they called me a crook', Simpson lifted the lid on race-fixing. Another entitled 'Nobbled by a secret doper' revealed Simpson's belief that he may have been given a bottle that had been tampered with and contained drugs. The third, which appeared two weeks prior to Lombardy, told of a scuffle Simpson had had with Frenchman Henri Anglade, known as 'Napoléon' to his peers and so unpopular with his compatriots that they ganged up on him to prevent him winning the 1959 Tour.

The insights were hardly revelations, but they caused a stink for Simpson as pro cyclists never spoke openly about such issues. The French press was particularly tough in its criticism of the Englishman, to the point where his Peugeot team considered sacking him as their leader. Simpson responded by saying he had been misquoted and would sue, although he didn't follow this up. Ultimately, he answered his critics with his legs, riding away from a high-class field in Lombardy to win by more than three minutes.

His final challenger had been defending champion Motta. When the pair came to the concluding climb in San Fermo della Battaglia, just ten kilometres from the finish, thousands of *tifosi* urged Motta on, but, like Simpson the year before, he had nothing left to give when the British world champion surged on through the frenzied crowd and crossed the line beaming broadly. At the finish Motta seemed unable to understand what had happened. He blamed hunger for his defeat, then fatigue, before deciding he had lost because Simpson was 'irresistible'.

Simpson featured in the winning break a year later, but his form was not at the level it had been. He lost contact on the Schignano, 40km from the finish, leaving young Peugeot teammate Eddy Merckx to do battle with French rivals Jacques Anquetil and Raymond Poulidor and a trio of Italians – Michele Dancelli, and Salvarani's Vittorio Adorni and Felice Gimondi.

Gimondi attacked once, twice, a third, a fourth and then a fifth time on the steep climb up to San Fermo della Battaglia. On each occasion, Anquetil chased him down. Coming on to the track, the Salvarani duo tried to dictate from the front, but Merckx refused to be denied that position. When Gimondi started to come through on his right, the Belgian edged up towards him. But Merckx left a small gap on the inside that Adorni nipped through. As Gimondi wound up his sprint, Merckx made a move to counter, but suddenly realised Adorni was in his line.

With no room to the right, he went left, on to the grass, helped by a bit of a nudge from Adorni's elbow, regained the track again, but too late to prevent Gimondi adding Lombardy to the Roubaix title he had won earlier in the year.

Gimondi's was a hugely popular win. He came from a poor background in Bergamo, east of Milan, and had learned to ride on his mother's bike. 'She was a postwoman, and our first bike was hers – the bike she delivered letters on. Later she bought me one as a present, but it was years before I had a race bike. They cost a lot of money,' Gimondi recalled in an interview with journalist Daniel Friebe in 2012. 'We weren't wealthy – at all! They were the years of economic miracle in Italy, but you could have fooled us! We didn't see it happening.'

Gimondi became one of Merckx's principal rivals during the late 1960s and early 1970s, winning a few of his skirmishes with 'The Cannibal', but not many. 'In 1965, when I won the Tour, I'd already heard of Merckx. I think he turned pro in the April, not the January like me. That year he didn't do that many races. It was in 1966 that he started hurting us. I think that if Eddy hadn't come along I could have won five Giri like he did. If I'd won five Giri and another Tour, I'd have equalled Coppi. But he came along! I have to admit, though, that, with hindsight, he graced my career in a way. Now everyone talks about our rivalry and it almost lends prestige to my career.'

Despite their rivalry, Gimondi had a good relationship with the Belgian, and remains adamant that he is the best there has ever been. 'He never had bad days. Every now and again, people ask me: would you have preferred to be up against Merckx or Lance Armstrong? I always say Armstrong, because you only had to deal with him at the Tour. Eddy was all over you, all the time – he was inescapable from January to December. At first, it was like banging my head against a wall. I did that for two years before I figured it out. Then the penny dropped. I put my ego to bed and started to become realistic. I realised that I needed to adapt. I needed to change the way I rode. The first, golden rule was – try not to take a beating, then maybe attack at the end. But whatever you did, you could never attack first, because if you did he'd come looking for you and drop you and make you look like a fool.'

The toughest Monument for Merckx

Although Lombardy's tough, hilly course appeared to suit Merckx just as well as any of the other Monuments, it was the one he found hardest to win. After losing out to Gimondi thanks to Adorni's canny intervention, Merckx missed out in each of the following four years, twice to Franco 'Crazy Heart' Bitossi. The nickname derived from singer Little Tony's Number One hit in Italy, 'Cuore Matto', and was acquired by Bitossi not for the obvious reasons but as the result of a physiological weakness caused by psychological pressure.

Bitossi put it down to an incident when he was nine years old and his younger brother, Alberto, disappeared. Hearing his mother calling for him but getting no reply, the young Bitossi was convinced his brother had drowned in the River Arno, which ran by their house deep in the Tuscan countryside. 'At that moment I felt a flutter in my chest – the same one I would feel countless times later in my career. We found Alberto but, for me, that was the start of a long and painful saga,' explained Bitossi.

In 1954 and just turned 14, Bitossi left school to work in a local tile factory. To get there each morning he had to take a boat across the Arno, then ride on an old clunker of a bike. He soon realised he had talent when he sneaked into the bunch in a junior road race one day and found he was stronger than most of the other racers, especially on climbs. He turned pro in 1961, but came close to packing in racing altogether over the following months. On several occasions during the 1962 season, he felt his heart-rate quickening and had to pull over to the side of the road until the palpitations eased. Only when they had could he continue racing.

Specialists carried out all kinds of investigations and reassured him that his heart was healthy and there was no risk of him suffering a heart attack as a result of the palpitations or of continuing to race. The fluttering of his heart, they said, was down to Bitossi's nervous disposition, and it would continue to betray him throughout his career. After toying with retirement in early 1964, his approach to his affliction changed at that year's Giro, when he won four stages, the first of them after being forced to pull over and lean on the guardrail until his heart stopped racing and allowed him to continue to do so.

He still had bad days, one of the worst occurring in the 1966 edition of Lombardy, won by his long-term rival Gimondi. It was suggested that Bitossi looked more like a drainage expert than a pro cyclist given the amount of time he spent in the gutter that day.

Although no great shakes as a time triallist, Bitossi could climb with the best and had a rapid turn of speed in a sprint. In 1967, he joined the early break that went away going over the Ghisallo. As the 22 riders in this group headed through Lecco towards the next climbing test, the Balisio, Bitossi peeled off to the roadside as his heart began to race. Grimacing and gasping for air as he hunched forward over his bike, he waited 90 seconds before getting under way again.

The next big test was the pink-cobbled climb up to San Fedele Intelvi sitting tight against the Swiss border above the western finger of Lake Como. Raymond Poulidor led the way, with Bitossi second on the road, 90 seconds behind the Frenchman. Cresting the pass, nine kilometres later, Bitossi had caught and dropped Poulidor and had two minutes in hand on a group containing Gimondi, Merckx and several other favourites. Over the 60km to the finish in Como, Bitossi held off the inevitable surge that came from behind, notably from Gimondi on the final climb up to San Fermo della Battaglia.

'That's the third year in a row that my heart has begun to race on the way into Lecco and I've had to stop. But someone from my team gave me a bit of a chest massage and a few drops of tonic completed the cure,' Bitossi told the press. 'On the last climb, the San Fermo, I had a moment of weakness perhaps because, due to my anxiety, I had not eaten enough. With three kilometres to go, though, I looked back and although my lead was only about fifty metres I said to myself, "It's done, I'm going to win."'

Bitossi's victory was the start of a run that saw him finish on the Lombardy podium five years in a row. The following season he was caught in a Belgian pincer movement. Joined by Merckx, Gimondi, Gianni Motta and Herman Van Springel just before the San Fermo climb, Bitossi managed to respond to Merckx's fierce acceleration on the climb, but neither man responded when Van Springel bridged up to them and clipped away. After Merckx steadfastly refused to chase down his compatriot, 'Crazy Heart' at least had the consolation of beating 'The Cannibal' to second place.

Bitossi's third place in 1969 came as a result of the disqualification of winner Gerben Karstens, who tested positive after providing a sample of his soigneur's urine for the control without realising the soigneur had been doping. It is better remembered as the first major victory in the tragically short career of Jean-Pierre Monséré. The Belgian won the world title the following season in Leicester, but died six months later after being hit by a car that came on to the course of a small race in eastern Belgium. He was 22 and left a wife and two small children. Five years later, another tragedy befell the family when Monséré's seven-year-old son, Giovanni, died after colliding with a car while riding a bike he'd been given by Freddy Maertens as a first communion gift.

Bitossi's second success in Lombardy owed much to the rivalry between Salvarani's Gimondi and Motta, and Molteni's Merckx. Angered by the excessive support he felt Italian manufacturers were providing the Belgian and other foreign stars, in 1970 Motta committed himself to doing all he could to prevent Merckx living up to his status as favourite. He sat on the Belgian's wheel for every one of the 266km, responding to every attempt Merckx made to shake off his shadow.

While Motta acted as bodyguard, Gimondi went on the attack on the Intelvi. On the descent off the climb, Bitossi shot away in pursuit, bridging up to his compatriot. As Merckx was their mutual threat, the pair co-operated until they reached Como's Sinigaglia stadium, where Bitossi beat Gimondi by a bike length. Two minutes later, Motta finally came out of Merckx's slipstream to pip the Belgian for third. Pressed on Motta's tactics, Merckx muttered, 'I've opened an account with him.' Motta's defence? 'I had to help Felice.'

'His only goal,' said Merckx, 'was to make me lose, as we have all clearly seen. Riding like that is not worthy of a champion. Gianni was very unfair to me. During the race I asked him what he was up to and he tried to justify himself by saying he was trying to mark me because Gimondi was on the attack. That's just a story. Bitossi was with Gimondi and Motta knew that in the sprint Felice would not be able to win. If he had helped me we would have rejoined them and he would also have had a chance of success. Instead, he stuck to marking me ruthlessly, he just wanted me to lose. We will meet again next year ...'

With that Merckx stalked off through the crowds towards his team car, refusing to sign autographs. When a fan shouted out an insult, the Belgian turned, clenching his fists, apparently ready to take them all on, before being encouraged into the sanctuary of the car and away to Milan.

Merckx recognised the unique problem presented by 'the race of the falling leaves'. 'It's an admirably designed race that offers terrain that suits aggressive riders and suits my temperament very well. It is, alongside Liège–Bastogne–Liège, the most demanding race on the calendar. The only pity is that it takes place at the end of the season. Consequently, the majority of the riders who line up are fatigued,' he said, summing up a problem that has subsequently become more of an issue for Lombardy in the modern era when riders focus on specific objectives far earlier in the season, making the Italian Classic an afterthought for most.

Although he had already won two Monuments, the Tour and the World Championship, Merckx didn't look fatigued at all when he sprang away on the upper slopes of the Intelvi in 1971 chased by climber Luis Ocaña. The Spaniard led on to the descent but came to grief when he overran a bend because his brakes failed to grip on a rim dented in an earlier impact with a pothole. Merckx flew by, determined to make the most of the gap they had opened up, no doubt with events of the previous year still very much in his mind. He rode home three minutes ahead of Bitossi to emulate former rival Rik Van Looy in winning all five Monuments.

Having been stymied by that misshapen rim, Ocaña had joined the pursuit of the Belgian, only to become frustrated by the lack of commitment shown by Belgians Georges Pintens, Frans Verbeeck and Roger De Vlaeminck, and Dutchman Joop Zoetemelk. Twenty kilometres from Como, Ocaña pulled hard on his brakes, stopped and got into his team car. 'Nobody was helping me chase behind Merckx. I abandoned telling them this was shit!' Ocaña complained. Later that evening he was still fuming, grumbling: 'If you want to ride for second place the fans will get the impression that a superman is crushing the life out of cycling.'

A second Lombardy success for Merckx followed 12 months later, forged with an attack on the Schignano which rises abruptly from the western shore of Lake Como. No one could counter his move, emphasising how well the Belgian had got to grips with this end-of-season challenge. The fact that only 17 of the 158 starters finished in Como also underlined the acuteness of the test presented by Lombardy. It wasn't as if the weather was poor either.

When Merckx wrapped up a third solo win in succession in 1973 he looked set to challenge Fausto Coppi's record of five Lombardy wins. This most crushing success was born out of the acute disappointment of losing at the Worlds in Barcelona, where Gimondi had been the beneficiary when Merckx and Belgian teammate Freddy Maertens rode with their own interests in mind rather than their national team's. Merckx never appreciated being crossed and, in his pomp, responded by dishing out as much pain as he could, apparently determined to erase the slight from his memory. A month later at Lombardy, his Molteni teammates locked down the race for 200km, allowing none of the big names any leeway. When Merckx moved on the Intelvi, 60km from the finish, no one went with him. 'This is the most beautiful of my three victories,' he admitted.

However, the race had a final twist. Two months later, the UCI announced the Belgian had tested positive for the stimulant norephedine. Merckx protested he had taken the product in Mucantil, a cough medicine that had been prescribed by his team doctor, who admitted culpability. But the UCI refused to budge. The title went to world champion Gimondi, just as it had when Merckx had been ejected from the 1969 Giro in the wake of a positive drugs test.

Merckx contemplated quitting but responded with one of his best seasons ever, winning the Giro, Tour and Worlds, making him the first rider to achieve this triple. At Lombardy he attempted to impose himself in the same way he had the year before, but fatigue and, some said, the accumulation of so much competition over the previous decade told. Roger De Vlaeminck stuck stubbornly to his wheel over the final 60km and cruised past him in the final straight on the Sinigaglia track.

'The Cannibal' was never in contention at Lombardy again. De Vlaeminck's success marked the arrival of a new generation of champions and, increasingly, a plunge in the fortunes of 'the race of the falling leaves'.

12

THE FORGOTTEN MONUMENT

Going all of the way back to the 1920s, when Henri and Francis Pélissier encountered all manner of devilish tricks designed to thwart foreign riders, plenty of *stranieri* had come away from Italian races complaining about underhand tactics. Generally, any bending of the rules was subtle and hard to identify, but this was hardly the case when Francesco Moser took the first of his two Tour of Lombardy victories in 1975.

'The Sheriff' had revealed himself to be an outstanding one-day talent when he finished runner-up at Roubaix in 1974 and won Paris–Tour later that season. Victory in the Italian championship the following year ensured he started a dismal Lombardy day in the *tricolore* jersey. It was, *La Gazzetta* said, 'a Flemish day' of pouring rain and occasional snow on the passes.

The Belgians appeared to relish it. Eddy Merckx set his Molteni team the task of stoking up the pace, shredding the hopes of those riders whose energy reserves and motivation were less than complete at the end of the season. Defending champion Roger De Vlaeminck was eager, too, leading a frantic chase of Moser after the Italian had barrelled away on the descent from the Intelvi.

On the Schignano, Moser went again, followed by compatriots Enrico Paolini and Alfredo Chinetti. As the trio opened a gap, a car from Italian state broadcaster RAI moved in front of the group behind containing Merckx, De Vlaeminck and Freddy Maertens. The blocking manoeuvre was so obvious it was ridiculous, yet the commissaires failed to intervene until the three escapees had a winning lead.

At the finish, Moser was too strong for the nippy Paolini and threw his arms high, his sodden gloves and rolled-down armwarmers giving the impression he was wearing a pair of black Marigold rubber gloves, which wouldn't have been out of place in the atrocious conditions. Asked about Belgian gripes over being blocked, Moser batted back: 'I was in front and rode without looking back and without worrying about such things. It may well be that there was a bit of confusion, but I don't think these complaints come from Merckx and De Vlaeminck, but from their "entourage". The Belgian champions are used to winning, but they also know how to lose without complaining.'

It wasn't the last time Moser appeared to get a helping hand from RAI. In 1984, during a close battle with Laurent Fignon for the Giro d'Italia title, the Frenchman insisted a helicopter covering the race for RAI had flown low over the Italian during the race-deciding time trial on the final day into Verona, using its downdraft to push Moser along the course. Fignon lost the time trial and the leader's *maglia rosa* to the Italian, who had previously benefited from the organisers' decision to cancel a stage over the Stelvio because of bad weather. Later reports suggested conditions were in fact good, although Moser's prospects wouldn't have been if he had had to take on Fignon, a much stronger climber, on that lofty pass.

To their credit, Merckx and De Vlaeminck played down the fuss about the RAI car. De Vlaeminck went on to regain the title a year later, proving too quick for Frenchmen Bernard Thévenet and Raymond Poulidor. However, when Moser took a second Lombardy title in 1978, *La Gazzetta* describing him as coming through like 'a locomotive' to clinch victory in a nine-man sprint, third-placed Bernard Hinault was adamant that his prospects had been dented by the passive attitude of the other riders in the break and the aggression shown towards him by the *tifosi* on the climbs, which resulted in him falling twice. There had been 'conspiracies' against him, the Frenchman claimed.

The situation had been complicated by the Super Prestige Pernod standings. Hinault led going into Lombardy, but Moser could steal the season-long title from him by winning 'the race of the falling leaves'. The night before the race, Hinault revealed his tactical plan to Dutchman Joop Zoetemelk, telling him: 'I am going to stay stuck to Moser's wheel. If he attacks I will follow him, and if he stops to lace up his shoe, I will stop with him!'

This made for a fairly dull race. Although the day was bright and hot, the drop-out rate was huge. By the time the front group reached the summit of the Balisio with barely 100km completed, little more than 30 of the 149 starters were still heading for Como. Climbing the Schignano, Hinault fell off twice when overexcited fans got in his way. His reaction is not recorded, but the spectators involved in those incidents might well have come to regret their exuberance in light of the fact that, some years later, Hinault rode full pelt into a line of striking steelworkers blocking the road at Paris–Nice and threw haymakers in every direction once he had been brought to a halt.

Hinault was not impressed either by the attitude of his fellow breakaways, who included Zoetemelk and defending champion Gianbattista Baronchelli, complaining they had bowed before Moser and dared not go on the attack. In return, though, some of those accused by Hinault pointed out the Frenchman had hardly done much attacking himself.

La Stampa had some sympathy with Hinault's allegations, but focused more on Moser's brilliant season, over the course of which he had netted 38 wins, 'as many as Merckx in his pomp', the paper stated. It painted the statuesque Italian as 'a king without a crown', describing him as the dominant one-day rider of the time. Looking around for rivals, *La Stampa* passed over the more obvious names and picked out a talented but relatively unknown 21-year-old. 'Moser's real rival is called Beppe Saronni. He's got class, but still lacks experience. A boy of 21 should be racing less and much more selectively,' wrote Maurizio Caravella.

Hinault threatened never to race in Italy again, but returned to Lombardy 12 months later with a more uncompromising strategy that paid off with a typically towering performance. He attacked going through the first feed station after just 100km had been covered. Initially, Moser, Saronni and the other favourites thought it was no more than an early show of force. 'I thought he was joking. His tactics weren't right at all,' Saronni later declared. But Hinault was never one for messing around. He had decided he was going to ride as hard as he could for as long as he could, ignoring recent attempts by his Renault team director Cyrille Guimard to encourage him to ride with greater cunning and ruthlessness rather than simply battering his rivals into submission.

By the foot of the Intelvi, Hinault's leading group of seven had opened a gap of four minutes on the other favourites. Hinault had done most of the work on the front of the group and didn't relent on the climb. Cresting the pass, the only rider still on his wheel was 21-year-old Silvano Contini. The Frenchman maintained the pace, Contini going to the front for short periods, but mostly happy to sit in on the Breton's wheel and see where that took him.

The answer was all the way to Como, where the pair faced off on the Lungo Lario Trento. Although the young Italian didn't deserve to win based on the paltry assistance he'd offered Hinault, he had impressed by being the only rider able to stay with the Frenchman. Yet Contini had nothing left for the sprint, which was a non-event. Hinault breezed to victory as his rival's legs tied up with cramp. Crossing the line, Hinault looked cool and unruffled, as if his victory was run-of-the-mill. Several metres behind him, Contini's features were contorted with agony, revealing the true extent of what Hinault had achieved.

'Hinault in the style of Merckx,' *La Stampa*'s headline proclaimed. 'The Breton only obeyed his own feelings, giving full vent to the instincts of a great fighter,' said their report. 'He attacked and attacked again, gradually shedding all rivals and almost humiliating the two Italian cockerels, Moser and Saronni, who fought until the last 25km before surrendering.'

Comparisons were also drawn with Coppi's greatest days at Lombardy. Yet Hinault's success is generally forgotten, perhaps because the media and fans are as guilty as the riders in overlooking the end-of-season Classic. The Italian papers, which had dubbed Hinault 'the bicycling accountant' due to what they saw as the calculated nature of his stage race victories, which were based on superiority in time trials, had to rethink their one-dimensional analysis of the Frenchman.

'Bernard Hinault may never become as great as Fausto Coppi, nor be as strong as Eddy Merckx, but if he ever does merit the label "champion of champions" then the first real step – and a giant step, it must be said – has been taken at this Tour of Lombardy. Riding on instinct, Hinault unleashed all of his power, like a thoroughbred finally given full rein. He won as riders won in the olden days, scattering the competition on the road,' wrote Maurizio Caravella.

Moser and Saronni

Just three years after Francesco Moser had been hailed as 'the king of the Classics', he and Italian cycling were in the doldrums. When Dutchman Hennie Kuiper won the seventy-fifth edition of Lombardy in 1981, Italy ended the season without a single Classics victory for the first time since Eddy Merckx's heyday in 1971. The race ended in mutual recriminations between Moser and arch-rival Saronni as had been the case when Hinault annihilated them both in 1979.

The rivalry is often depicted as the most intense since Coppi and Bartali's in the 1940s and 1950s. In Italy that was undoubtedly the case. However, outside Italy their enmity was far less evident for the simple reason that they were just two of many contenders for the biggest titles. Indeed, the only time the pair regularly squared up outside their homeland was at the World Championships, where the two *azzurri* were committed, if reluctant, teammates.

There was no doubt, though, that Moser and Saronni didn't like each other and, more than on the road, this mutual antipathy was played out in the press, which naturally whipped up the rhetoric between them and forced Italian fans to take the side of one man or the other. In *Pedalare! Pedalare!*, John Foot says: 'In the end, the Moser–Saronni rivalry became rather like a pantomime act and never reached the sporting heights of Coppi versus Bartali, or Binda versus Guerra or Girardengo. Nor did it move beyond the realms of sport. It never touched or cut across political or social divisions. This was a verbal duel which reflected the post-modern spectacle the sport had become.'

Both men have admitted that much of what they said stemmed from a desire to remain in the spotlight. 'Without Moser my career would not have been the same, and I think the same applies to him. Our rivalry stimulated us to perform even better,' Saronni acknowledged in 2008 during the launch of a book on their rivalry written by Beppe Conti.

According to Saronni, the rivalry had its roots in events that took place during the final kilometres of the 1978 World Championship. 'I was on the attack with Raas and Hinault. I knew I could win because I was the fastest in the sprint. However, the Belgians began to lead the chase behind us, with Walter Godefroot setting the pace. We were caught and Moser attacked with Dutchman Gerrie Knetemann, who beat him in the sprint.'

Asked whether Moser had egged the Belgians on, Saronni replied: 'Well, at the end of that year, at the big party he had for his fans, the special guest was Walter Godefroot ...' He then added: 'It must be said, our rivalry cost us too many races.'

When they were interviewed together later that same year in an event organised by *La Gazzetta dello Sport* and cycling magazine *Tuttobici*, Moser denied he had acted maliciously at the 1978 Worlds. He explained the rivalry had begun for him the previous year, his rival's first in the pro ranks, when Saronni outsprinted him to win the Pantalica

Trophy. 'A police motorcycle hindered me in the finale and Beppe won. I never liked to lose, even more so to a stranger.'

The one occasion when the pair went head to head for victory in Lombardy was in 1982, six weeks after Saronni had fired 'the Goodwood rifle-shot' to win the world title in Sussex, his sprint so blisteringly fast that it appeared he'd been shot from a gun. Following Hinault's abandon at Lombardy's first feed station, Saronni was pictured riding alongside Moser and holding up his forefingers in a 'V'. The world champion lived up to his cheeky gesture, keeping his rivals close until the straight, then distancing them with a Goodwood-like flourish that left Frenchman Pascal Jules several lengths back with Moser on his wheel. 'I really wanted this win. I didn't take the sprint having exploited the work of others, which means this win is like a second World Championship,' Saronni said.

As an Italian, Saronni's verdict on Lombardy may have been slanted, but at the same time it did offer an insight into the race's elevated status up to the mid-1980s. Yet over the subsequent two decades 'the race of the falling leaves' lost much of its lustre. Principally, this was the result of the sport's biggest names focusing on fewer objectives during the season, with most favouring the spring Classics, the Giro and the Tour.

Lombardy in decline

Many laid the blame for this on Greg LeMond, winner of the world title in 1983 and only very narrowly beaten by Sean Kelly at Lombardy a few weeks later. The American made no bones about the fact that the Tour was his one overriding objective of the year. At the same time, LeMond's peers benefited from the wide exposure the sport gained as a result of his Tour successes, with salaries rising to the point where a good performance in France during July made a rider's achievements – or even lack of them – over the rest of the season almost irrelevant. In LeMond's defence, it should also be said that he did tend to ride more Classics than he missed, although he never featured at Lombardy again after that near-miss in 1983.

If LeMond instigated the move towards greater specialisation and a reduced focus with regard to objectives, Miguel Indurain, the great Spanish champion of the early 1990s, cemented it. However, a good deal of the responsibility for Lombardy's steady decline can be put down to the event's organisers, who have regularly tinkered with the route, eroding the race's standing. Although there had been many changes before, the tweaking of the route appeared to become an obsession for Candido Cannavò, who took over as *La Gazzetta*'s editorial director in 1983. That year, for example, he and competitions director Vincenzo Torriani decided to move the start to Brescia, largely to compensate for the city missing out on a Giro stage finish the year before as the result of a metalworkers' strike. This new route did not feature the Ghisallo.

Although Lombardy's iconic climb returned in 1984, when Hinault produced another show of strength to take the title, the tinkering continued. On the upside, it resulted in a one-off return to the Vigorelli in 1985 to celebrate the fiftieth anniversary of the Milan track's opening. The race was dedicated to the memory of Fausto Coppi and produced a thrilling finish as Kelly underlined he was the era's 'king of the Classics'. For the next two years, Lombardy finished in the shadow of Milan's wonderful Gothic Duomo.

However, the reintroduction of the Como to Milan route from that 1985 race meant a return to a format that had been abandoned in 1961 because it was considered to be lacking in character and difficulty over the final 60km. From its site next to the Duomo, in 1988 the finish drifted to the less impressive setting of the Corso Venezia for two years. The subsequent decision to move the start and finish to the industrial town of Monza in 1990 only exacerbated the race's slide.

While the organisers fiddled with the route, Lombardy also attracted a good deal of controversy thanks to the antics of those taking part. Gianbattista Baronchelli's second success in 1986 resulted partly from his own good sense of timing when he broke clear from the six-man lead group coming into Milan. But it was later suggested the Italian leader of the Del Tongo team had been the beneficiary either of a breakdown of an understanding between defending Sean Kelly and Australia's Phil Anderson, or of a payment agreed between Kelly and Baronchelli's bike supplier, Ernesto Colnago, when they spoke mid-race. Although neither suggestion is totally accurate, both contain a degree of truth, as Kelly revealed in his autobiography, *Hunger*:

'Del Tongo were desperate to win. Baronchelli dropped back alongside his team car to talk to his *directeur sportif* and some discussions began between our team and his ... Then events took a peculiar turn. I was at the back of the line of riders and suddenly the race organiser's car bumped into me and I went down ... I got up, chased back to the group and eye-balled [race director] Torriani. He looked straight ahead as if nothing had happened. Perhaps it had been a mistake,' Kelly recalled.

'I was starting to think we might have a situation on our hands. We suspected Baronchelli, who was 33, needed a good result to get another contract with Del Tongo for the following year. We knew Torriani would prefer an Italian winner – there had been only one home win at the Tour of Lombardy in seven years.'

The result was a deal between Kelly's Kas and Baronchelli's Del Tongo. If the Italian attacked, Kelly and teammate Acacio Da Silva wouldn't chase him. 'In the streets of Milan, with two or three kilometres to go, Baronchelli attacked. I looked at Anderson. He didn't respond and nor did I. We both knew that if he wasn't going to chase, Baronchelli would ride away to the finish and win the race. And that is exactly what happened. A week later, Da Silva collected the cash and we shared it among the team.'

During the 1990s, these antics took on a more sinister aspect. In 1994, Russia's Vladislav Bobrik, riding for the Gewiss team that had been advised by controversial coach Michele Ferrari and had hoovered up the Ardennes Classics that spring, won in Monza. The Russian disappeared from the top ranks as quickly as he had arrived in them, winning one more race, in 1995, before his career ended in mediocrity four years later.

In 1998, Switzerland's Oscar Camenzind emulated Saronni and just a handful of others when he took the title wearing the world champion's rainbow bands. Forced out of the sport when he tested positive for EPO in 2004, he subsequently had to defend himself against claims from 1998 runner-up Michael Boogerd that the two men had come to an agreement that the winner would pay the other man 40,000 Swiss francs. In an interview in *Wielerland Magazine*, Boogerd said it was common knowledge between his Rabobank team and Camenzind's Mapei that the two riders had struck a deal. 'We agreed: whoever wins pays. That happens sometimes in racing, though I was not a fan of it because it relies on the winner paying up.'

Camenzind rubbished the claim. 'In 2000 at the Tour of Valencia he came to me with that story. Why was he suddenly asking me for money two years later? I want to tell you how it is. I was super that day. Just before Bergamo he offered me a sum of money if I would let him win. I told him that I wanted to win. Moreover, the amount was so low that I could not take him seriously ... Why should I have to give a weaker rider money?'

The lowest point for Lombardy came at the turn of the century when the title went to two riders who became mired in high-profile doping scandals. In 2000, Raimondas Rumsas became the first Lithuanian rider to win a Monument, edging out Francesco Casagrande at the finish in Bergamo. Two years later, Rumsas climbed even higher in cycling's hierarchy when he finished third at the Tour de France. On the same day he was receiving the plaudits of the crowd on Paris' Champs-Élysées, the French police stopped his wife, Edita, at the Chamonix border crossing. A search of the family car turned up 37 different medical products, including EPO, testosterone, growth hormone and steroids. The drugs, she said, were for her mother-in-law.

By that point, Rumsas was already in transit to their family home in Italy and once there he refused to return to France, where his wife remained in prison for 75 days. His repeated protestations of innocence took on a new perspective when he tested positive for EPO at the Giro d'Italia the following season. He and his wife subsequently received suspended four-month prison sentences for importing banned products into France.

The following season, Italy's Danilo Di Luca won 'the race of the falling leaves'. Regarded as one of the brightest stars in Italian cycling, his achievements have been tainted by his involvement in a string of doping cases. The most recent occurred in May 2013, when he tested positive for EPO during the Giro d'Italia less than three weeks after signing with the Vini Fantini team.

Amidst the scandal and dodgy deals, Lombardy has witnessed some memorable moments and in recent years has begun to regain much of its former lustre. Among the most heroic of successes was Charly Mottet's tremendous solo victory in 1988. The Frenchman, best known for his three Dauphiné Libéré wins and subsequent role as route director on that race, was not only one of the most talented riders of his generation but also had a spotless reputation.

In his book *Breaking the Chain*, Willy Voet, the soigneur from the Festina team who was arrested in 1998 after industrial quantities of doping products were found in the team car he was driving to the start of the Tour de France, said of the Frenchman's arrival at the RMO team in 1989: 'Charly Mottet helped to clean up the team. He was the team leader, he had more influence than anyone on the way his teammates thought and he never wanted to know about drugs ... It was only as the races went by and we ate with him and spent time with him that we worked out what kind of a fellow we were dealing with. This was one clean cyclist.

'You could honestly say that Mottet was a victim of drug-taking right through his career – of other riders' drug-taking. If he had used some stuff to help him recover, perhaps only now and then, the list of races which he won – already a long one – would have been considerably longer.'

Small, powerfully built and with a thick fuzz of blond hair, Mottet was a strong all-rounder with a particular penchant for long time trials. A three-time winner of the Grand Prix des Nations, which for decades was the unofficial time trial championship of the world, he wasn't among the principal Lombardy favourites in 1988, but looked strong as he bridged up to world champion Maurizio Fondriest on the Valcava climb. With him was Luc Roosen. When the Belgian punctured on the descent and Fondriest fell back, Mottet persisted with his effort. Climbing the Valpiana, which at 1,000m was the perfect height for a rider who struggled on longer passes, Mottet pushed his lead out to more than three minutes.

Commentating on Italian TV, old rivals Saronni and Moser were astounded by what they were witnessing. The latter admitted the only comparison he could make was with the stories that his older brother Aldo used to tell him about watching Fausto Coppi during his best years. Mottet's raid was, declared Moser, comparable to *Il Campionissimo* in his pomp.

Mottet won by almost two minutes and came close to a second victory two years later, finishing third when compatriot Gilles Delion proved quickest of a five-man group that included Scot Robert Millar.

Delion was another rider mentioned by Voet as being among those who steadfastly refused to engage in doping practices. Voet dubbed him 'Mr Clean' and revealed he had been the butt of a lot of jokes among his French peers because of the suitcase he always carried that was packed with homeopathic remedies. Tall, blond and talented enough to win the best young rider jersey at the Tour de France in 1990, Delion's career promised much but delivered comparatively little, thanks to his own health issues and the curse of doping.

After bowing out from the sport at the end of 1996, he insisted the use of EPO was widespread in the pro peloton. 'I can't see the point of winning when you're "lit up", nor can I see what pride you would gain from doing so,' he said. Asked about these comments and similar ones made by Scottish rider Graeme Obree, UCI president Hein Verbruggen's response said everything about why it took the UCI so long to respond to the extent of the doping problem within cycling. 'I'm not at all impressed by statements made by riders like Delion and Obree who are people at the end of their career, who can't even follow the peloton. I find that cowardly and I won't say another word on it,' said Verbruggen.

The year after Delion took the biggest one-day victory of his career, Sean Kelly joined Henri Pélissier, Costante Girardengo and Gino Bartali as a three-time Lombardy winner, behind only Alfredo Binda with four wins and Fausto Coppi with five. The Irishman's victory was significant both because it had been two years since he had last won a major Classic and because it came just two months after his elder brother, Joe, had died after colliding with a car during a bike race in their home town of Carrick-on-Suir.

'I wanted to quit, his death had destroyed me. I went back to the bike because it's my job, just for that reason,' Kelly said before Lombardy. The race turned on the descent off the Super-Ghisallo. A puncture sent pre-event favourite Maurizio Fondriest crashing to the road. As the Italian waited and waited for his team car to reach him through the mess of vehicles on the tight mountain road, Martial Gayant flew down the descent pursued by a small group of riders including Kelly.

They bridged up to Gayant before the final climb of the Lissolo, where Frenchman Bruno Cornillet's attack split the group. Gayant led the chase up to his compatriot, with Kelly right on his wheel. As Gayant pressed, Cornillet ran out of steam, leaving just two in front. The sprint was a formality for the Irishman, who laid his victory bouquet on his brother's grave when he returned to Ireland.

The location of the finish that year gives an indication of Lombardy's dwindling fortunes. The Viale dell'Industria on the edge of Monza was functional and convenient. Compared to those in Milan just a few years beforehand, which were lined with fans for several kilometres running into the finish and still had an epic feel to them, the sense that something important was taking place, this was a sideshow. It was little surprise when the organisers opted for another major overhaul of the route in 1995, shifting the start to Varese and the finish to Bergamo, the home city of Felice Gimondi and then one of Italy's main cycling centres.

That year's race, won by Italian domestique Gianni Faresin, was overshadowed by the death of Italy's Olympic road race champion, Fabio Casartelli, at the Tour de France in July. Hailing from Como, Casartelli had not shone since winning the gold medal in Barcelona in 1992, but had enjoyed a good Tour riding for the American Motorola team. The fifteenth stage to Cauterets took in several of the race's most renowned Pyrenean passes. It was a hot morning, so the 24-year-old Italian decided not to wear the helmet he usually favoured during the opening kilometres, suspecting the pace early on was sure to be easy.

The riders started out over the Portet d'Aspet, which was no more than a stepping stone to four much bigger climbs. Not far into the descent, a touch of wheels in the bunch sent a number of riders crashing. Frenchman Dante Rezze shot between the squat stone pillars on the edge of the road and fell into the ravine below, fracturing a leg. Casartelli hit one of these pillars, sustaining a fatal head injury. He never regained consciousness and died on the way to hospital. He had been married for less than two years and had become a father just two months before.

His wife, Annalisa, subsequently donated his Motorola team bike and his Olympic jersey to the Madonna del Ghisallo chapel. The bike hangs between Gianni Motta's 1966 Giro-winning machine and a bike donated by Eddy Merckx above a wall covered with images of cyclists, a few of them famous but most of them ordinary riders, who lost their lives while racing and riding.

The museum augurs better days

In October 1999, by which time the chapel could only display a small quantity of the many thousands of items that had been donated, the first stone was laid in Madonna del Ghisallo Cycling Museum. Seven years later, Pope Benedict XVI gave his blessing to the museum's final stone, which bears the message 'Omnia Vincit Amor' – love conquers everything – and sits within the museum atop a bared piece of the rock that forms the building's foundations.

Its design is as impressive as the extensive collection it contains. Entering the front door, where former Giro and Lombardy race director Angelo Zomegnan can often be found in his role as the principal curator, a ramp sweeps down into the main hall via two big switchbacks. These not only provide an initial overview of the whole collection, but also offer a reminder of the inspiration for the museum and for each visitor's presence.

The permanent exhibits include many items that were previously housed in the chapel, as well as a large number of bikes, jerseys and other paraphernalia donated by Italian cycling legend Fiorenzo Magni, who was the museum's president until his death in October 2012 and very much the driving force behind its creation, especially when rallying local government and councils to provide financial backing. His death and the concurrent economic crisis in Italy and beyond has impacted significantly on the museum. In late 2013, it was closed until the following spring, and some suggested it might not reopen at all given daily visitor numbers were often in single figures. However, it has managed to survive and thrive.

To an extent, the difficulties the museum faced testified to cycling's decline within Lombardy, which had long been the focal point of the sport in Italy. Marco Pinotti, one of the most insightful pros in the modern peloton, who retired at the end of 2013 after winning six national time trial titles, says of the region: 'I was lucky to be from an area where there's a lot of passion for cycling, which really developed after the war with Felice Gimondi. In the 1980s and 1990s, you got the ripple effect of Gimondi and that generation. There were lots of clubs in the area and in the second half of the 1990s, there were something like 27 professionals living in Bergamo, some born there and some from other regions and countries.'

Those heady days have passed, however. 'Now it's very different and there are only a handful of pros in Bergamo,' said Pinotti just before his retirement. 'I think there are two reasons why it's changed so much. One is that people just don't ride bikes as much any more. The other is that the foreigners aren't coming to Bergamo any more, because it's no longer a good place to train. If a young rider asks me to recommend a place to stay and train in Italy, I'd like to say Bergamo but I tell them to go somewhere else, where there's less traffic.'

After several seasons when the race finished in Bergamo, 'the race of the falling leaves' has moved closer to the historic climbs with which it is best associated. In 2004, the finish moved back to Como, 20 years after Bernard Hinault had won the last race into the lakeside city. The change also enabled the return of the Intelvi, Balisio and San Fermo della Battaglia climbs. The winner that year was Damiano Cunego, 'The Little Prince', who had emerged as Italy's new king of the mountains by winning four stages and the overall crown at the Giro at the age of just 22.

In 2005, Italy's latest Olympic champion, Paolo Bettini, became the first rider in more than 20 years to lead the race over the Ghisallo and go on to take the title. After dispatching Gilberto Simoni and Fränk Schleck in the final sprint, the Italian – nicknamed 'The Cricket' because of his repeated attacks – said of his exploit, 'The Ghisallo is a mythical climb. I've suffered on there many times. But on this occasion I wanted to be the first to the summit and I managed it.'

Bettini's suffering was of a very different kind 12 months later, when Lombardy celebrated its 100th edition. Weeks before, he had finally secured an elusive victory in the World Championship, but, just as Sean Kelly had 15 years earlier, Bettini came to Lombardy in mourning following the death of his elder brother, Sauro, who had been killed in a car accident while on his way to organise a post-World Championships celebration party. Bettini had contemplated missing Lombardy, but opted to defend his title and thereby pay tribute to his brother.

Once again he led over the Ghisallo, his surge near the top forcing the strongest riders clear. Possessed by grief and determination, Bettini drove hard going up and over the tight and technical Civiglio climb, dropping everyone bar Fabian Wegmann, who somehow clung on but eventually yielded on the sharp rise up to San Fermo. Although the chasers were never far behind Bettini, he held them off, crossing the line in tears and pointing both hands to the sky. 'Today I did not pedal alone. I will never forget this day,' he said after embracing his parents, wife and daughter at the finish.

After Cunego added two more victories to join the great names who have won Lombardy three times and Philippe Gilbert announced his arrival as one of the new generation's leading one-day campaigners with a first win in a Monument in 2009, rumours began to spread of a possible return to the Muro di Sormano, which had last featured in 1962. Race director Angelo Zomegnan knocked back these stories, describing a return to infamous Sormano as 'a fascinating idea but, unfortunately, a difficult option for a race route'. Yet he didn't discount the idea completely, telling *Procycling*: 'If the local authorities are interested, we'll be ready to look at potential solutions.'

Thanks to the efforts of a small group of fans who wanted to see the Sormano restored to the Lombardy route, those solutions weren't far off. Their lobbying led to Lombardy's regional government agreeing to invest €150,000 to resurface the climb. Reopened in 2006, the road was as steep as ever, but looked very different thanks to the addition of a unique artwork. Inspired by fans painting their imprecations to riders on mountain passes, local architect Franco Tagliabue Volontè laid out a design that pays tribute to the history of the Sormano, while at the same time tormenting those who are riding up it.

Every metre gained in altitude is marked in precise and, for those riding, agonising detail, starting at an altitude of 824m at the foot of the climb and steepling up to 1,120m at the top. In small letters next to each carefully stencilled number is the Latin name of a type of tree in the surrounding woodland – *Corylus avellana* (hazel), *Betula pendula* (silver birch) and many others. Just in case those struggling up the Sormano aren't fully aware of its significance, Tagliabue Volontè's design also features the quotes made in the early 1960s by the horror-struck Gino Bartali and Ercole Baldini when they encountered the Sormano, as well as the times taken by the fastest ten riders on the Sormano in each of the three years it featured in the race between 1960 and 1962.

Although most riders and expert observers of the cycling scene continued to insist a return to the Sormano was impossible, 'Magician Zom', as the Italian press referred to Zomegnan, pulled something out of his organiser's hat. Just months after saying it couldn't happen, Zomegnan revealed the Sormano would appear, although it was the nearby and rather easier Colma di Sormano rather than the Muro that would feature. From the Sormano, the riders shot down the frighteningly steep and treacherous road into the lakeside village of Nesso, where the houses built on the mountain side of the road tower like skyscrapers over their waterside neighbours so vicious is the angle of the drop. From there the route swept south along the lakeshore towards Como, passing over the San Fermo on the way. 'It's tough and beautiful,' said Zomegnan. 'It's a monumental Classic.'

The weather made it even more monumental, with rain like stair-rods and icy cold. Only 34 of the 195 starters finished in Como, although Gilbert was unfazed, admitting: 'It was a tough race but I always go pretty well in the wet and cold. I'm from Belgium, I'm used to it.'

In 2011, after Zomegnan had been ousted as director of the races in the RCS group's stable, the finish moved from Como to Lecco, allowing the reintroduction of the brutal ramps of the Valcava as well as a new final climb up to the hilltop village of Villa Vergano. The changes appeared to confuse the favourites, which left the door open to Swiss climber Oliver Zaugg, a 30-year-old domestique who had never previously won a pro race.

A year later came a change that even Zomegnan had baulked at. Rebranded as Il Lombardia, the race started in Bergamo to honour Felice Gimondi on his seventieth birthday, took in the Valcava and Colle Brianza, then tackled the Muro di Sormano for the first time in 50 years.

Speaking as dark clouds hung over the start ready to drench what was one of the strongest line-ups the race had seen since the 1980s, newly crowned world champion Gilbert commented, 'It's going to be interesting with the rain today. I think that the race could be won and lost on the descents.' The Belgian's prediction was spot on, at least as far as he was concerned. He slid off twice on the descent from the Sormano, where first-year French pro Romain Bardet had the honour of leading the race over the summit.

After the riders had been softened up on the Valcava, Sormano and Ghisallo, the climb to Villa Vergano saw the strongest riders emerge, led by the season's number one rider, tiny Spaniard Joaquim Rodríguez. His nickname 'Purito' came from the Spanish word for a small cigar and stemmed from a gesture he had made to teammates as he breezed past them on a climb during a training camp, pretending to smoke a cigar to indicate how easy it was. Although the laidback Catalan maintained his reputation for clowning, his ability on steep ascents was almost unparalleled. At Villa Vergano, Rodríguez flew away as if launched from a catapult, his attack giving him just enough of a cushion to hold off the chase group behind. The 106th edition of 'the race of the falling leaves' had delivered its first Spanish winner. Rodríguez retained his title in 2013, attacking next to the same lamppost where he had launched his winning move 12 months earlier.

As the result of a four-year deal struck with Bergamo and Como, which would see Lombardy switch its start and finish points between the two cities each season, the 2014 race returned to a course very similar to those of the late 1990s and into the early part of this century. Starting in Como meant the Ghisallo came a mere 58km into a meaty 256km course. Sadly, the Sormano didn't feature, but there was still plenty to raise the pulses of the peloton's mountain goats. Unfortunately in terms of racing spectacle, they all watched each other until the cobbled ramps up to Bergamo Alta inside the final five kilometres.

Swooping down from the old town, a nine-man sprint featuring Alejandro Valverde, Gilbert and Rodríguez seemed inevitable. However, sitting at the back of the line barrelling into Bergamo, Ireland's Dan Martin knew he had no prospects in a sprint. With 800m left, Martin flew. As his rivals looked at each other, the Irishman avoided his last-corner slide at Liège and cruised up the straight to claim a second Monument. 'Lombardia is a beautiful, beautiful race. I understand the history of the race, it's one of the biggest of the year. To have my name on the race palmarès is incredible,' Martin declared.

Heading in the opposite direction the following year, the finale was considerably more spectacular. Valverde started as favourite, while Italian hopes rested on their national champion, Vincenzo Nibali, who had made Lombardia his primary end-of-season target after being disqualified from the Vuelta a España for getting a tow from his team car. Michał Kwiatkowski and Tim Wellens led the way up the steepling slopes of the Sormano, while Nibali's Astana team policed the group chasing close behind. On the penultimate climb of the Civiglio, the two leaders were reeled in and a flurry of attacks followed, none of them sticking. Nibali was one of those who'd tried and he went to the front again to lead into the tight turns that tumble down the hillside.

What followed was a demonstration of the highest skill and nerve, the Italian's acceleration out of the corners so quick and his handling so adept that he almost raced into the back of a motorbike at one point and went close to going over the crash barrier at another. In little more than four kilometres, he gained 40 seconds. Although he lost half of that on the short final ascent to San Fermo della Battaglia to Dani Moreno, his pre-eminence going downhill ensured he stayed clear of the Spaniard, with Frenchman Thibaut Pinot in third.

For the 110th edition in 2016, organisers RCS plotted out a new route into Bergamo. With 4,400m of vertical gain, 1,000m more than in 2014 when Dan Martin was the victor, it was designed to be more selective, to prevent a large group coming into the finish together, and it did precisely that. Four riders went clear on the penultimate of the race's eight climbs, the Selvino. The move was instigated by Colombian Esteban Chaves, enjoying the best season of his career after podium finishes at the Giro d'Italia and Vuelta a España. With him were his compatriot Rigoberto Urán, Italy's Diego Rosa and Frenchman Romain Bardet. On the final sharp climb into Bergamo's old town, Bardet dropped off the pace, leaving three to dispute the spoils. On paper, the tiny figure of Chaves, a typically pure Colombian climber, appeared the least likely winner, but he finessed the situation perfectly, sitting in as Urán chased down Rosa's late attack, then, as Urán began to wilt, stealing by on the Italian's left in the final metres to become the first Colombian to win a Monument.

Nibali produced a near-repeat performance of his 2015 victory the following season, when the final stages of the race saw all kinds of drama. In the most frightening incidents, first Laurens De Plus, who was in the break with Mikael Chérel, crashed over the guardrail on the steep and technical descent off the Sormano, sustaining a fractured knee. Minutes later, his Belgian compatriot Jan Bakelants went off the road at the same point, breaking several ribs and four vertebrae in his fall.

Chérel was still at the front going on to the Civiglio, but now had two-time winner Philippe Gilbert, Alessandro Di Marchi and Pello Bilbao for company. The chasing pack were soon on them, though, led initially by Gianni Moscon, who had a cluster of climbers on his tail. Thibaut Pinot emerged as the pick of them, sashaying away with Nibali the only one able to follow. Cresting the climb, the Italian went to the front and delivered another demonstration of speed and control. To his credit, Pinot wasn't distanced by much, but it was enough. Nibali increased his advantage climbing to San Fermo della Battaglia, and cruised in well clear of Frenchman Julian Alaphilippe, with Moscon third.

After alternating the finish between Bergamo and Como for four seasons, 'The Race of the Falling Leaves' travelled from the former city to the latter for the next three. This is the more traditional *percorso* for Il Lombardia, anchoring its emblematic climb of the Ghisallo as a key point in the finale rather than being a simple point of passage as it's often been when the raced has concluded in Bergamo. It also brings the Sormano into play much more. This was fully exemplified in 2018, when a very classy quartet emerged as the pretenders to the title on the Muro.

Primož Roglič led the way, with an attack that only defending champion Nibali and Pinot, victorious three days earlier at Milan–Turin, could follow. Colombia's Egan Bernal bridged up to them after the descent. On the Civiglio, Nibali and Pinot dropped their two rivals, yet, remembering what had happened in previous years, the Frenchman was completely determined to avoid reaching the top of the climb with the Italian. Another acceleration took him clear and, despite an occasional frailty on descents, Pinot never faltered to become the first French winner since 1997.

The last Dutch win had been almost twice as far back as that, Hennie Kuiper the victor in 1981, until Bauke Mollema claimed a surprise success in 2019. Like Pinot, he made his winning attack on the Civiglio, distancing an elite group who all waited for the others to chase and left it too long.

There wasn't a falling leaf in sight when Lombardia got under way in the Covid-affected season that followed. Initially pushed right back to the last day of October, then brought forward to mid-August to take place a week after Milan–Sanremo and concurrently with the Critérium du Dauphiné, it was still as captivating as ever. Once more, the winning break formed on the Muro di Sormano. Unfortunately, yet again, there was a frightening crash on the descent away from it. It involved the highly feted, highly rated young Belgian star Remco Evenepoel, who misjudged a sweeping turn on to a viaduct and crashed over the parapet and into the ravine below, fracturing his pelvis.

With defending champion Mollema, Nibali and Giulio Ciccone in the lead group of six, Trek looked well set to take the title, but all three were dropped when Jakob Fuglsang accelerated on the Civiglio, taking his Astana teammate Aleksandr Vlasov and New Zealander George Bennett with him. The Kiwi did all he could to drop his two rivals on the rise up to San Fermo della Battaglia. He did shake off Vlasov, but Fuglsang was simply too strong for him and he soloed away to become Lombardy's first Danish champion.

Another long drought ended in 2021, when Tadej Pogačar became the first reigning Tour de France champion to win Lombardy since Bernard Hinault in 1979. To a degree, this 42-year hiatus underlined how the race's fortunes have fluctuated over that period. In the decade either side of the Millennium, Lombardy went most of the way to regaining the parochial feel of its early editions, when the foreign stars rarely made the trip and an Italian victory was almost guaranteed. Over the past decade or so, though, it has regained the standing and significance it had prior to the 1990s.

There is no single outstanding reason for this resurgence, more an accumulation of factors. The evolving perception of the Monuments as five unique and prestigious races that every racer should strive to add to their palmarès has undoubtedly elevated Lombardy more than its four peers, because its status had lagged so far behind the others. Star names would often miss it because of its position so late in the calendar. They would end their season well before there was a hint of autumn in the air, after the Vuelta a España or even the Tour de France.

In addition, the organisers have settled on a recognised route, or two in fact, each of them with clear allure for riders and fans, especially the Como option in which the linking of the Ghisallo, Muro di Sormano, Civiglio and San Fermo della Battaglia in the finale stands out like the *capi*, Cipressa and Poggio at Sanremo, or the Koppenberg, Oude Kwaremont and Paterberg at Flanders. As a result, Lombardy is almost always guaranteed to provide a spectacle on the road to compare with its stunning setting in the hills and woods overlooking Lakes Como and Lecco. After many years when it was little more than a marker of the season's end, 'the race of the falling leaves' is relevant again, worthy of its status as a Monument.

Pogačar's victory encapsulated Lombardy's new-found vitality. It was a showcase for the young Slovenian's verve and thirst for major titles, highlighted by a dazzling attack on the Passo di Ganda that took him clear of his biggest rivals and culminating with an exuberant victory celebration after dispatching Fausto Masnada in a two-up sprint – a great champion victorious in a magnificent race.

The Slovenian retained the title in a 2022 edition that started in Bergamo and finished in Como. The finale was a little different to usual, with the Sormano omitted reportedly due to concerns about dangerous sections on the descent to Nesso and an additional ascent to San Fermo della Battaglia added in its place. The race was pitched as a reprise of the Tour de France duel between two-time winner Pogačar and Jonas Vingegaard, the Dane who had ultimately triumphed in that competition. Vingegaard's Jumbo-Visma team endeavoured to make the race as hard as possible by riding at a quick pace into the Ghisallo. But Pogačar's UAE Team Emirates teammates weren't ruffled.

They took control on the second half of the Ghisallo and set about scattering the peloton. After Davide Formolo, the last of UAE's henchmen, delivered a final acceleration climbing the Civiglio, Pogačar sped off, Enric Mas and Mikel Landa the only riders able to follow him. Landa was dropped towards the top, regained contact with the stronger pair on the descent, only to be dropped again on the second ascent to San Fermo della Battaglia, where Pogačar and Mas attacked each other. Neither had the decisive edge, though, and it came down to a sprint. Mas led it out, but Pogačar breezed it in front of huge crowds in Como, testament to Lombardy's bourgeoning vitality.

PART IV

MILAN–SANREMO: *'LA CLASSICISSIMA'*

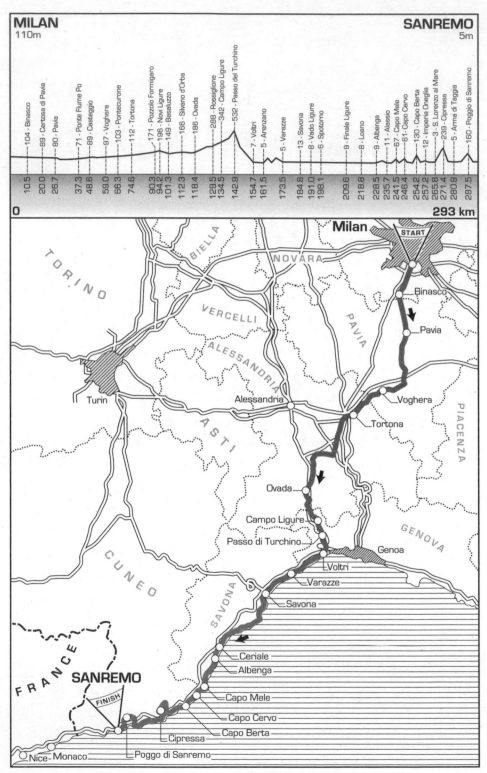

MILAN
110m

SANREMO
5m

104 - Binasco
89 - Certosa di Pavia
80 - Pavia
71 - Ponte Fiume Po
89 - Casteggio
97 - Voghera
103 - Pontecurone
112 - Tortona
171 - Pozzolo Formigaro
196 - Novi Ligure
149 - Basaluzzo
166 - Silvano d'Orba
186 - Ovada
288 - Rossiglione
342 - Campo Ligure
532 - Passo del Turchino
7 - Voltri
5 - Arenzano
5 - Varazze
13 - Savona
8 - Vado Ligure
6 - Spotorno
9 - Finale Ligure
8 - Loano
9 - Albenga
11 - Alassio
67 - Capo Mele
61 - Capo Cervo
130 - Capo Berta
12 - Imperia Oneglia
3 - S. Lorenzo al Mare
239 - Cipressa
5 - Arma di Taggia
160 - Poggio di Sanremo

10.5
20.0
26.7
37.3
48.6
59.0
66.3
74.6
90.3
94.2
101.3
112.3
118.4
129.5
134.5
142.9
154.7
161.5
173.5
184.8
191.0
198.1
209.6
218.8
228.5
235.7
241.5
246.4
254.2
257.2
265.8
271.4
280.9
287.5

0

293 km

TORINO
BIELLA
NOVARA
VERCELLI
PAVIA
PIACENZA
ALESSANDRIA
ASTI
GENOVA
CUNEO
SAVONA
FRANCE

Milan
START
Binasco
Pavia
Voghera
Tortona
Turin
Alessandria
Ovada
Campo Ligure
Passo di Turchino
Genoa
Voltri
Varazze
Savona
Ceriale
Albenga
Capo Mele
Capo Cervo
Cipressa
Capo Berta
Poggio di Sanremo
Nice - Monaco
SANREMO
FINISH

13

PUTTING SANREMO ON THE MAP

Famous for its festival, flowers and casino, Sanremo has long depended on tourism for its wellbeing. From the early eighteenth century, grand hotels were built along the seafront beneath the medieval walled town of La Pigna, which sits on a promontory overlooking the sea. The hotels quickly found favour with wealthy tourists drawn by the temperate climate. In 1872, when the town was connected by railway to the French Riviera to the west and to Genoa to the east, its popularity boomed as new and ever more lavish hotels were constructed, attracting members of the European aristocracy. Tsarina Maria Aleksandrovna and Kaiser Friedrich Wilhelm III were among the notables who sang its praises, raising its profile still further.

However, even as Sanremo grew it was always playing catch-up with the Côte d'Azur and trendy Monte Carlo, 50km to the west. That plush enclave in the tiny principality of Monaco had been connected to the railway in 1868. Ten years later, it boasted one of the grandest casinos in the world. In 1905, Sanremo hit back with the opening of its own Casino Municipio, a magnificent Liberty-style building that still dominates the western end of the town. Yet tourists, and particularly those from Britain, still favoured the French end of the Riviera.

In August 1906, a group of Sanremo notables met in the Caffè Rigolé with the aim of establishing an event that would boost the resort's profile across Europe. Although chastened by the failure of a Milan–Sanremo car rally that had been backed by the town and organised by

La Gazzetta dello Sport, the group hoped to persuade the paper's co-owner, Eugenio Camillo Costamagna, to support a new proposal for a bike race again linking Milan and Sanremo.

Costamagna had spent a good deal of his youth in Oneglia, close to nearby Imperia, and knew his fellow diners well. Marcello Ameglio was a lawyer from a well-established local family, Stefano Sghirla a respected engineer and Giambattista Rubino a banker and first president of the Sanremese Ciclismo cycling club. They fully expected to persuade Costamagna to back their new event, particularly as his newspaper had successfully launched the Giro di Lombardia in the autumn of 1905. However, Costamagna reminded them of the fate of the rally just days before. Only two of the 33 cars that started in Milan had reached the finish in Sanremo after two brutal days on unsurfaced and rutted roads. How could cyclists be expected to cover the same distance in a single day, he asked them.

The state of the roads wasn't the only obstacle. Although Lombardy had been a success and a second edition was due to take place just a few weeks later, that event started and finished in Milan. This new event, however, would finish 300km away from its start point, which was unlikely to make it attractive to riders, who would have to find their own way back to Milan. The route would also require cyclists on bikes equipped with just a single gear to cross the Ligurian Apennines, which form a substantial barrier between the flat agricultural lands of southern Piedmont and the Mediterranean coast.

Costamagna turned the proposal down, but said he would reconsider if it could be shown cyclists could complete the proposed course and the money raised to finance it. He told his three companions he would find the riders to test out the route, but finding the cash to back the event was down to them.

La Gazzetta's director knew Lombardy's first winner, Giovanni Gerbi, trained on the roads between Milan and the Turchino Pass, which was the obvious crossing point from Piemonte into Liguria, the coastal region from the French border in the west to Tuscany in the east and narrowly hemmed by the Apennines on its northern edge. Gerbi's group also featured Luigi Ganna and Carlo Galetti, who had finished third and fourth, respectively, in Lombardy. Costamagna promised them some coverage in his paper if they could cross the pass. Some days later, Gerbi's group managed to do so, making the scheme more realistic if the trio of Sanremo notables could find a way of financing it.

Back in Sanremo, the three businessmen turned to the local press, asking citizens to support the project via a public subscription, which raised 700 lire. The Unione Sportiva Sanremese came forward with an offer to provide logistical backing, assisted by members of cycling clubs along the route. Costamagna and fellow director Armando Cougnet were all but persuaded, but the engineer Sghirla had another card to play. Well aware of the runaway success of the Tour de France, which had just celebrated its fourth edition, he put out feelers to some of France's leading riders, pointing out to them that the race would finish close to their favoured training grounds around Nice and Cannes. The race could, he told them, provide a convenient early season test of their form and a useful opportunity to boost their earnings.

Late in 1906, *La Gazzetta dello Sport* announced: 'On 14 April next the great international race Milan–Sanremo will take place, organised by *La Gazzetta dello Sport* with the support of the Unione Sportiva Sanremese. The event will be open to all professional riders and to amateurs who hold an Italian Cycling Federation licence.' The first prize was set at 300 lire, while the rules reflected the growing trend for riders to race without any outside back-up at all. There would be no feed stations, riders would be responsible for all repairs to their bikes and pacing behind cars and motorbikes, which was allowed in other major one-day races of that era, most notably Paris–Roubaix and Bordeaux–Paris, was expressly forbidden.

The leading Italian riders soon signed up, among them Gerbi, Ganna and Galetti. Meanwhile, Cougnet had handed responsibility for liaising with their French counterparts to *La Gazzetta* reporter A. C. Rossini, who headed to the Côte d'Azur to follow up on Sghirla's initial contact. Rossini described his encounter with some of France's leading lights: 'One morning towards the end of February, when I was certain that the best of the French riders had gone to the Côte d'Azur to train, I headed for Nice and came upon a group of riders led by [Lucien] Petit-Breton and [Louis] Trousselier in a bar close to the station, where they were having a drink before breakfast ... Speaking for his colleagues, Petit-Breton asked me to find them some support from one of the good Italian teams ... Two days later, [Gian Fernando] Tommaselli from Bianchi was in direct contact with him and within a few days they had signed a deal.' Discovering Bianchi had boosted their attack for the new season-opening race, Peugeot's representatives in Italy, the Turin-based Picena brothers, signed up two Frenchmen of their own, Philippe Pautrat and the promising Gustave Garrigou.

The news that four French riders would be on the start line didn't please most of the Italians who had signed up for the new event. They didn't have much regard for Bianchi's Lombardy champion Gerbi. With Petit-Breton and Trousselier on his side, 'The Red Devil' now looked invincible. Consequently, when the riders began to gather at Milan's Porta Ticinese in the early hours of Sunday 14 April, almost half of the 62 competitors who had registered failed to turn up. At 4.30 that morning, just 33 riders set out on the 288km slog to Sanremo.

Early French domination

However, Gerbi's rivals had misjudged him – to an extent, anyway. Although he was well used to spraying the *spumante* produced in his home town of Asti, on this occasion the canny 22-year-old had quickly worked out that he could earn far more by collaborating with his illustrious new teammate, Petit-Breton. Bianchi had promised Gerbi two and a half lire for every kilometre covered if he were to win Sanremo.

Yet Gerbi had heard Bianchi had offered Petit-Breton six times that for the victory. Not long after the small peloton started on its long ride south, Gerbi edged up alongside Petit-Breton and whispered: 'If I help, will you split your winnings in half?'

'*D'accord*,' Petit-Breton murmured back. No sooner had he agreed than Gerbi accelerated away, leaving his new teammate somewhat bewildered as to what the Italian's intentions were. It says much about Gerbi's reputation that some of his rivals claimed after the race that he had not only organised for a path of sorts to be laid for his own use, but had also worsened the condition of the rest of the road. Quite how one man could have done this on his own is not explained, but Gerbi was clearly a rider who many believed capable of anything when it came to winning a race, even major construction/destruction.

The conditions were wet enough for the anxious mother of Italian rider Giovanni Rossignoli to try to hand him an umbrella as the race passed through his home town of Pavia. The rain turned to swirling snow, blown around in a cold wind, as the riders climbed the Turchino Pass, where Gerbi's advantage reached more than four minutes. If his plan was to triple his winnings by working for Petit-Breton, it looked to be going awry, especially as the Frenchman was finding the climb hard going and had fallen behind Garrigou, Galetti and Ganna. Descending off the Turchino and down to the coast road, Garrigou dropped the two Italians and began to pursue 'The Red Devil'. At the grim industrial port of Savona, with more than 100km still left to race, Garrigou caught the Italian.

Gerbi had had some experience of racing in France and was well aware he was unlikely to beat Garrigou in a sprint. He also knew Petit-Breton would have a much better chance of defeating his compatriot, but couldn't have known his one-off teammate was by now six minutes behind the lead duo and feeling the effects of hunger. Petit-Breton would later reveal the only thing he'd eaten all day was a bar of chocolate.

The wily Gerbi decided his best hope lay in refusing to co-operate with Garrigou. Indeed, he went further than simply refusing to share the pace-making. He started to abuse and argue with his French rival, who responded in kind, not realising Gerbi's sole objective was to distract him in the hope that Petit-Breton could close down the gap to the two leaders. The ruse may not feature in any guide to bike-racing tactics, but it was wholly effective. Climbing Capo Berta, with 40km left to the finish in Sanremo, Petit-Breton bridged up to Gerbi and Garrigou.

Peugeot's Garrigou, a small man known for his dapper dress sense and, later, his astonishing ability on the highest of mountains, must have known he had little chance of outsmarting and beating two riders from Bianchi, but Gerbi, who would pocket more than 1,000 lire if Petit-Breton took the title, wasn't about to let him try. As Petit-Breton opened the sprint 500m from the finish line, Gerbi grabbed Garrigou's collar and all but yanked him to a halt.

After a touch more than 11 hours of racing, Petit-Breton crossed the line just ahead of Gerbi, with Garrigou well distanced in third. The race judges were sure that something underhand had taken place in the sprint, but couldn't say exactly what. Gerbi clouded the issue by complaining that Garrigou had grabbed him, which led to a brawl involving the pair and some of their team staff. In the end, five days after the race, the judges relegated Gerbi from second place to third, but confirmed Petit-Breton as the winner. Gerbi protested his innocence, but eventually admitted to his misdemeanour – albeit 30 years later!

On the same day that news of Gerbi's relegation was announced, Petit-Breton, by now in Paris, was writing a letter to the race organisers at *La Gazzetta*, praising the race and encouraging them to run it again the following season. Initially, Costamagna's organising team were not at all convinced Milan–Sanremo had a future given the many logistical difficulties involved in such a lengthy point-to-point race. However, the Frenchman's support and the coverage that the new race received in the French press as a result of his victory almost certainly played a significant role in persuading them to run the event again in 1908, especially as

Petit-Breton went on that summer to win the first of consecutive Tour de France titles, with Garrigou taking second place.

On 5 April 1908, the second edition of Milan–Sanremo took place, although on this occasion without the unscrupulous Gerbi, who was serving a six-month ban for cheating at the Tour of Lombardy. His absence made the likelihood of an Italian victory very remote, especially as many of the biggest foreign names of that era had signed up to ride, including the powerful Alcyon team from France. They prepared for the race by riding to Milan from Paris via the Côte d'Azur. Their team featured a quartet of leaders: Frenchmen Henri Lignon, Louis Trousselier and André Pottier, plus Belgian Cyrille Van Hauwaert, winner of Bordeaux–Paris the previous season.

Such was the quality of the field that *L'Auto*, the newspaper that had established and ran the Tour de France, asked one signore Perrone to provide them with reports. On the eve of the race, Perrone wrote: 'I don't know if *La Gazzetta dello Sport* had foreseen that this race would become hugely important. Let's hope it provides as much passion in the years to come as it does today, and that it continues to be an extremely interesting curtain-raiser to the season.'

Perrone's words were prescient as, like *L'Auto* in France, *La Gazzetta*'s management realised their fledgling race had huge appeal to both riders and fans. The riders appreciated a tough opening test to the season that enabled them to assess their own form and, hopefully, gain a psychological boost thanks to a strong finish in Sanremo. As for cycling's rapidly growing army of fans, who were starting to show more interest in road racing rather than the track scene, which had hitherto dominated, they turned out in their tens of thousands to watch new races such as Sanremo and to buy the newspapers that covered them. Relating to these new heroes of the road was easier for a public that was becoming increasingly dependent on the bicycle as a means of transport and understood very well how difficult it could be to ride on roads that were still largely unpaved and treacherous to negotiate in anything other than fine weather, when billowing dust could still make them a lottery.

Like the previous year, the 48 riders who set out from Milan just after dawn were not blessed with the best of days. Although it wasn't cold enough for persistent rain to turn to snow, the rain was heavy enough to require a 45-minute delay before the start flag was dropped. That made the surface of the roads more glutinous than they would have been in freezing conditions.

The favourites stayed together crossing the Turchino. Heading past huge crowds in Savona, teammates Lignon and Van Hauwaert had begun to distance their rivals. Climbing the bulky Capo Berta headland between Diano Marina and Oneglia, with 40km remaining, Van Hauwaert made his move, accelerating away from Lignon, who promptly abandoned the race. As well as 'Open Stomach', Van Hauwaert had also been anointed 'The Mud Man', such was his ability on the most sapping of courses. Although Italian favourite Luigi Ganna did make inroads into the Belgian's advantage towards the finish, it was too late to prevent Van Hauwaert living up to his alternative nickname. 'The Mud Man' completed the course in 11 hours and 33 minutes, his celeste-blue Alcyon jersey unrecognisable. Ganna finished three minutes later to a huge ovation, with Alcyon's Pottier a similar distance behind in third as only 14 riders completed the race.

When Van Hauwaert went on to win the *L'Auto*-organised Paris–Roubaix a fortnight later, Milan–Sanremo's status rose even further among bike racing's cognoscenti. A further boost came later in 1908 when *La Gazzetta* announced it would be organising the first Giro d'Italia in May 1909. The establishment of the Giro was a calculated gamble on the part of Costamagna and Cougnet, who didn't have the funds to finance a race that would compare in scale with the Tour de France. But the two men had got wind of a plan by rival paper *Corriere della Sera* to launch an Italian national tour assisted by Bianchi. Just as they had when launching Lombardy in order to face down a threat from a rival title, *La Gazzetta*'s directors had to commit or face losing their grip on the top level of the sport in Italy.

Their gamble with the Giro would pay off. Indeed, Cougnet would remain as Giro race director until 1948, while the race is now under the control of the RCS group that owns *La Gazzetta*. The other events in the company's growing portfolio also benefited from the establishment of the Giro, with Lombardy attracting 200 entries in 1908, double the number from the previous year. In April 1909, Sanremo attracted precisely the same number, and 102 of them took to the start line on the first Sunday of the month.

The previously draconian rules that allowed no outside assistance or even a bike change in case of mechanical breakdown were eased a touch to allow riders to swap to a new bike as long as it came from the official vehicle of the team they represented. Underlining the event's growing status, *L'Auto* stepped up its coverage, sending correspondent Charles Ravaud from Paris, who wrote rather pompously: 'One simple fact will demonstrate to what extent the French sportsmen are interested in Milan–Sanremo: *L'Auto* has decided to send one of its contributors to follow the event …'

Sticking with the same tactless approach, Ravaud went on to point out that an Italian hadn't yet finished first in Sanremo and added that the roads were so bad there was no chance of anyone bettering the time Petit-Breton had recorded in winning the inaugural race. Backing up this analysis, Louis Trousselier adjudged the roads so poor that he opted not to start in order to avoid jeopardising his prospects for Paris–Roubaix.

Ravaud's initial reports were sent by telegram to Paris from key points along the route, such as Pavia, Ovada and Voltri. Necessarily brief, they outlined the battle between riders in the colours of France's Peugeot and Alcyon and Italy's Bianchi and Atala. The contest appeared to tip in favour of Alcyon's Émile Georget, but the Frenchman went off course coming into Savona, allowing Atala's Luigi 'Luison' Ganna, a former stonemason, to get on terms. Ravaud suggests that Georget might well have won the duel with the Italian, but suffered three punctures heading along the coast road towards Sanremo, enabling Ganna to open a lead he maintained into the finish on the Corso Cavallotti.

Ravaud describes fans taking up every possible vantage point to see the finish, and absolute delirium when Ganna appeared in the final straight. However, he makes no mention of the fact that the Italian smashed Petit-Breton's record for the course, completing it at 30.42km/h in nine hours and 32 minutes. After being mobbed by exultant Italian fans at the finish, Ganna revealed he had spent the previous two months training for the race, making him the first rider to target Sanremo as a major objective rather than as a guide to form leading into the new season.

He had opted against using a rear wheel with a double sprocket, which enabled riders to flip the wheel over and select a gear that better suited the terrain they were on. He felt they were too heavy for the race's muddy roads. Instead, he took advantage of the change in the rules, riding a bike with 46x16 gear on the flat roads to the foot of the Turchino Pass, then exchanging it for one fitted with 46x18 gear more suited to this climb and the many headlands along the coast. Such was Atala's faith in Ganna's chances of victory that these bikes were just two of 15 they positioned along the route in case of mechanical failure.

In a longer account submitted to *L'Auto* the next day, Ravaud provides far more details on what he says was 'a frighteningly tough course'. As in the previous two years, the weather was poor despite it being early April. 'The descent of the Turchino was indescribable,' he writes. 'I am surprised we didn't have some deaths to announce. On one occasion I thought I'd witnessed a catastrophe. [Georges] Passerieux did a frightening somersault. He tumbled down into the bottom of a ravine. But just as we were preparing to go and look for his remains, we saw him reappear, mad with rage, thinking only of rejoining the peloton.'

The race with four finishers

After the fastest Sanremo came the slowest. A huge field of 256 riders registered, but just 71 took the line. Could it be that most of the rest had a look at the weather forecast before heading to Milan? Certainly, conditions were bad enough that, as there would be more than 100 years later in 2013, there was talk of the Turchino Pass being missed out and even of postponement. However, bypassing the Turchino requires such a lengthy diversion that it is never likely to happen. In the end, the riders set off at six in the morning in a freezing downpour. Almost 15 hours later, only seven had finished, and three of those brave souls would be disqualified for what in the circumstances might be argued was legitimate bending of the rules.

The victor was Frenchman Eugène Christophe, who would gain greater fame as the rider whose front fork broke on the descent of the Tourmalet in the 1913 Tour de France. Forced to carry his bike for two hours down the pass until he reached a smithy's forge, he fixed the fork only to be penalised for receiving outside assistance during the course of the repair. A pernickety race judge had noticed that a seven-year-old boy had pumped the bellows while Christophe worked in the flames. Six years later, Christophe was the first rider to wear the Tour's yellow jersey. On the penultimate day of that 1919 Tour, his forks broke when he was still leading the race. He finished second and never wore the jersey again.

Christophe's account of what emerged as an unlikely but heroic Sanremo success appeared some days after in French magazine *Miroir des Sports*. Progress was swift as far as the Turchino, which had been dubbed 'the pass of death'. As the riders climbed it, the rain turned to snow, whipped into their faces by a glacial wind. Even as he overtook other riders on the hairpins leading to the summit, Christophe was battling the numbing effect of the cold.

'Not far from the summit I had to get off my bike because I started feeling bad. My fingers were rigid, my feet numb, my legs stiff and I was shaking continuously. I began walking and running to get my circulation back,' said the Frenchman, who recalled the wind moaning frighteningly. As he continued on, he described seeing some riders swigging brandy straight from the bottle, others swallowing eggs and a few chewing on grass, all of which were thought to stave off fatigue. Told he was six minutes down on leader Cyrille Van Hauwaert, Christophe trudged on to the tunnel at the summit of the Turchino, where he got a brief respite from the elements. He found he wasn't the only one taking advantage of this shelter.

'I came across Van Hauwaert with his bike in his hand and a cloak on his back. He told me he was packing it in. I was beyond feeling happy about that and I just got on with going down through the snow that lay on the road on that side of the mountain. The view was totally different now. The snow made the countryside beautiful. The sky was clear. But now it was my turn to have trouble. It was hard to keep going. In places there were 20cm of snow. Each time I was obliged to get off and push. Then I had to stop with stomach cramps. I collapsed on to a rock at the side of the road. I was freezing.'

Christophe noticed a house a few hundred metres away. He later admitted he was torn between carrying on (victory would see his wage doubled) or making for the house. In the end, a man emerged from nowhere and made the decision for him. 'He led me to what was a tiny inn. The landlord undressed me and wrapped me in a blanket. I murmured 'acqua calda' and pointed at the bottles of rum. I did some physical exercises and started to get some feeling back in my body. I wanted to go on but the *patron* wouldn't hear of it and pointed to the snow still falling outside. Not long after, first Van Hauwaert and then Ernest Paul came in. They were so frozen they put their hands in the flames. Ernest Paul had lost a shoe without noticing.'

Looking out of the window, Christophe saw 'at least four piles of mud' weaving past. Knowing others were still racing, he decided to press on despite protests from Paul and the innkeeper. 'Ernest Paul said,

"You're crazy," and I had to trick the innkeeper by saying I was going to meet someone who would get me to Sanremo by train,' said the Frenchman, who took up the innkeeper's offer of dry clothes and a new pair of trousers, which he soon had cut down to shorts to relieve himself of the mud weighing them down. Back on the road, he steadily caught and passed the four Italians ahead of him, including defending champion Ganna.

'At the control point at Savona everyone was astonished to see me alone. The crowd didn't know me. I didn't stop long and took Trousselier's spare bike because I knew he and Garrigou had abandoned before Ovada. I was sure of my victory and with only 100km to go I felt a new strength. The idea of crossing the line brought back all my energy,' Christophe recalled. He finally completed the course in 12 hours and 24 minutes. Ganna came in second, but was later disqualified for putting his bike in a car and walking up the Turchino. A second Italian was disqualified for taking the train between Pavia and Novi Ligure, while a third, Sante Goi, finished seventh but after the Sanremo control point had closed.

Writing under the byline Magno in *La Gazzetta*, Costamagna declared, 'The fourth edition of Milan–Sanremo was not a race as such, but a demonstration of resistance of the human fibres that reveal the specialist qualities needed to fight against the fury of the elements.' Of Christophe's heroic triumph, he said: 'Just one man, blessed undoubtedly with a certain amount of extra substance, withstood all the pitfalls, every brutal expression of nature at its most violent. He is a Frenchman, a son of the great Latin race, a strongman whom lovers of sport must recall with admiration. His performance exemplifies the battle between man and furious nature on this appalling day.'

As well as in Italy, Christophe's epic ride made headlines in France and Belgium, helping to cement Sanremo's reputation. His employers at Alcyon did indeed double his salary, but this came at a considerable price. Transported from the finish to hospital, the Frenchman spent a

251

month recovering from frostbite to his hands and other cold-related injuries. It took him two more years to regain full health. 'Two years without success, miserably trailing along at the back of the peloton,' he later grumbled.

The French reign in Sanremo continued for the next two seasons as Gustave Garrigou and Henri Pélissier claimed victory on the Corso Cavallotti. Pélissier's success came after he had won the Tour of Lombardy and Milan–Turin the previous season. 'Even a mediocre French rider can beat the Italians,' one French paper crowed, although future Tour de France winner Pélissier was by no means average. Blessed with almost perfect pedalling technique, his riding style was almost effortless, while he had a finishing burst that few could match. The race was the first to be run in good weather – making dust rather than mud the main difficulty – and the first to be decided in a sprint, which pitched Italy's Ezio Corlaita against four of Alcyon's aces. Easily outmanoeuvred, Corlaita didn't even manage a podium finish.

Milan–Sanremo's status as one of the sport's Classic one-day races was confirmed in 1913 when Belgium's Odile Defraye signed up to race. Although the event had welcomed most of the sport's leading names, Defraye was the defending Tour de France champion, and the first such to enter. The Belgian sensation had been talent-spotted by one of Alcyon's agents in Belgium and won the Tour at his second attempt. He claimed that he could repeat the feat in Sanremo, saying he would come out on top in a sprint if required but was equally sure he could make a winning break if the Italians sat back and waited for him to make the race.

The Italians weren't impressed. They felt the papers were talking the Belgian up to boost sales. They were probably right, but they underestimated Defraye, who duly beat compatriot Louis Mottiat in a two-up sprint, with Corlaita third, but more than four minutes behind. Just 24 and apparently set for a glorious career, Defraye never won a major event again and disappeared as quickly as he had emerged, blaming odd pains in his legs, which, he complained, felt like his nerve endings were being cut.

The 1913 race also saw young Italian Costante Girardengo making his debut in the race, which passed right through his home town of Novi Ligure. Newly professional with the Maino team, the diminutive Girardengo, commonly referred to as 'the little guy from Novi' or, rather more disparagingly, 'the Novi runt', had turned 20 two weeks before Sanremo, but failed to make it to the finish after getting caught up in a big crash near Ovada. He fared better the following year, finishing seventeenth. By then he was the Italian champion, but was upstaged by Bianchi's Ugo Agostoni, who won the sprint disputed by ten riders, becoming only the second Italian Sanremo winner and the first since Luigi Ganna in 1909. The headline in Monday morning's *Gazzetta dello Sport* exclaimed, 'We Have Won!'

The race report by Emilio Colombo focused on Agostoni's triumph, but also picked up on the race's main curiosity – the appearance of a trio of Australian riders, the first English-speakers to feature in the event. Don Kirkham, Ivor Munro and Charles Piercey had sailed to Europe with the aim of riding the Tour de France after gaining experience in the Classics, starting with Milan–Sanremo. According to Colombo, the Australians were the revelation of the race. 'With enormous gears, curious positions, they looked more like [track] stayers than road riders, they responded to every attempt by their rivals to break clear and even went on the offensive many times themselves.'

Kirkham made it into the group that contested the final sprint, but his chance went when a car in the race convoy that was zigzagging through the group caused him to skid and lose ground coming into the finish. He came home a remarkable ninth, with Munro twenty-sixth and Piercey twenty-eighth.

The increasing internationalisation of Milan–Sanremo ended with the outbreak of the Great War. Although the race only missed one edition, in 1916, during the hostilities because the fighting in Italy was confined to its northern border, it wasn't until 1919 that foreigners returned to challenge the home riders. By then, one of Italy's all-time greats was well on his way to becoming the *campionissimo* – the champion of champions.

14

'A CRAZY, PASSION-FILLED RACE'

Although the Tour de France has long been the race that has made and cemented the reputation of cycling's great champions, the rider first anointed '*Il Campionissimo*' only ever appeared in the race once and didn't even finish. The fifth of nine children born to a farmer in a village on the edge of the very unremarkable Piedmontese farming town of Novi Ligure, Costante Girardengo was perhaps the first rider to build up a fortune from bike racing and was undoubtedly the first great star of Italian cycling.

Girardengo was a tiny figure, often seeming to be on the verge of disappearing beneath the fans engulfing him after another victory. He dominated Italian cycling for a decade up to the late 1920s, winning nine Italian road titles, two editions of the Giro d'Italia and no fewer than 30 stages, as well as six Milan–Sanremo titles in ten appearances. Although Eddy Merckx would go one better than him 50 years later, Girardengo could have won a couple more times in Sanremo. In fact, he was adamant to the end of his life, in 1978, that he had been the victim of a huge injustice after being disqualified from first position in 1915.

Having judged his effort well through the first two-thirds of the race, Girardengo began to reel in the pacesetters after crossing the three *capi*, the Mele, Cervo and Berta, headlands so huge the designers of the coastal road opted to go over them rather than cutting a route out of the rock around them. He had spent more than a month beforehand training on and checking over the course, and knew it in both directions.

Unfortunately for him, on the day of the race the route had been altered as it went through the small resort of Porto Maurizio, the diversion adding 200m or so to the 289km course. Not noticing a barrier that half closed the road he had ridden on so many times over the previous weeks, Girardengo went straight on. At the finish, he was the best part of a kilometre clear of runner-up Ezio Corlaita, who was declared the winner the following day.

'I only gained 250 metres. This saving did almost nothing in terms of winning me the race,' the indignant Girardengo raged. 'How could I guess that the organisation had decided to send the race on a road that bypassed the town centre when no one had said anything to me about it? It's scandalous.' He missed out again in 1917 when Sanremo reappeared after a year's war-enforced absence. On that occasion, Gaetano Belloni beat him comprehensively. Yet Belloni would soon be dubbed 'the eternal runner-up', such was the rule that Girardengo was about to impose. From his second-place finish in 1917 up to his victory in 1926, he was never outside the top three in Sanremo.

In 1918, Girardengo won with the kind of solo break that would later become the trademark of Fausto Coppi, who, coincidentally, hailed from a small village not far from Novi. Physically, the two men had little in common, Girardengo being small and wiry, while Coppi was much taller, rather stooped, with a cavernous chest. Neither man looked capable of producing astounding individual feats of endurance, but both came alive on the bike and were guided by Biagio Cavanna, who, from his home in the centre of Novi Ligure, oversaw every aspect of their training regime and life from first thing in the morning to last thing at night.

An ex-rider who had competed against Girardengo, Cavanna became a team manager, masseur and much else besides. He is most often remembered for being Coppi's masseur and closest adviser, and this despite losing his sight in the mid-1930s. But it was his relationship with Girardengo that led to him being dubbed 'The Wizard of Novi'.

He established what was effectively cycling's first training camp. Unlike those of the modern era that tend to last a fortnight at most, Cavanna's was a permanent set-up in Novi Ligure. Girardengo (and later Coppi) was very much the main focus, with *gregari*, fiercely loyal teammates brought in to do what was needed to ensure the little genius stayed on top of the pile. An imposing figure, Cavanna didn't need to rely on his size to ensure his word was law. Everyone knew him in Novi, and all of the riders under his charge knew if they stepped even slightly out of line he would be informed very quickly. Consequently, they all did what they were told or were swiftly shipped out.

Girardengo was an innovator, too. He made a point of moving his training base from Novi Ligure to the Ligurian coast in the weeks leading up to Sanremo in order to memorise the most crucial sections of the route. He already knew the first half of it by heart, having ridden on those roads since he was a boy. In 1918, he called on all of that knowledge. He was riding with the leaders, including defending champion and his now Bianchi teammate Belloni, heading into Tortona, where he had worked in a car factory during the war. Perhaps spurred by thoughts of his past career and his former workmates looking on, Girardengo first conferred with Belloni, then accelerated away from the pack.

Four minutes clear at Ovada and more than seven ahead of second-placed Belloni crossing the Turchino, Girardengo kept pressing and widening his advantage on typically sticky roads. As his advantage grew, demoralised riders on rival teams dropped out at the checkpoints along the coast. Only six riders eventually trailed in behind Girardengo. Belloni was the first of them, finishing 13 minutes behind his team-mate; 1914 champion Ugo Agostoni was an hour behind, his successor Corlaita more than an hour and a half down. It was a rout. 'The best man has won ... and he has written the most beautiful page in his cycling career,' Emilio Colombo wrote in *La Gazzetta*, describing him as '*Il Campionissimo*'.

Late on in 1918, as the Great War ended, a 'Spanish' flu pandemic infected millions of people across the world. The virus struck Girardengo hard, to the point where there were fears he might die. By the end of the year, however, he was back in training on the roads around Novi and talking up his prospects to the press. Bianchi, though, were not at all convinced by his recovery. Such was the impact the virus had had on their little leader they decided to release him from his contract. Picked up by the far less prestigious and powerful Stucchi team, the fiery Girardengo was even more determined to return to his best.

Milan–Sanremo offered him an early opportunity to demonstrate his authority. However, after hearing what one journalist described as 'that hiss that to riders has the same effect as a stab in the back', he came home two minutes behind winner Angelo Gremo, who rode for his Stucchi team. Held up by punctures, he spent most of the race pursuing the pacesetters on his own. He finally caught lone leader Gremo on the Capo Berta when he heard that hiss for the fourth time. The question of why Gremo continued riding when his team leader halted has never been clearly answered. By that point, the two Stucchi riders were well clear of the chasers and both men could have paused. One version has it that Girardengo urged his teammate on. More likely, though, is that Gremo carried on regardless.

Girardengo headed to the Giro d'Italia feeling he still had something to prove to Bianchi. He made his point extremely clearly, winning seven of the ten stages and relegating his former team's leaders, Belloni and Marcel Buysse, to very distant second and third place finishes. He went on to add the Italian title and the Tour of Lombardy crown to his palmarès in what was his career-best season.

Although known for his quick temper, Girardengo doesn't appear to have held a grudge against Bianchi for long, or at least not when it came to his long-time adversary Belloni. Although their rivalry had none of the bitterness that would later mark the relationship between Fausto Coppi and Gino Bartali, it did split Italian fans into opposing camps.

Yet the two men were such good friends that Girardengo would stay at Belloni's home whenever a race began in Milan. Belloni's mother, Luigia Cavenaghi, regarded Girardengo almost as another son, instructing them both as they left on race day mornings, 'Don't behave badly, and make sure you finish first and second.'

In 1920, only Bianchi ringer Henri Pélissier managed to prevent them achieving that by finishing between them. Belloni won for a second time and, after being mobbed by ecstatic fans, battled his way through to Girardengo, telling everyone, 'I want to shake his hand.' He later told *La Gazzetta* that he had 'followed Girardengo's wheel for 125km', the pair of them having punctured at the same time and then joined forces to chase down the leaders.

Photographs from the time reveal how much of an impact the rivalry between the two men had on Milan–Sanremo. Crowds would not only pack the start and finish, but stood several deep at every town and village. In one image from the summit of the Turchino in 1921, every possible vantage point is taken by flat cap-wearing men craning their necks to get a view of the two champions. Girardengo is leading the way, as he did on four other occasions at what was then one of the key points of the race. First place there was often a good indicator of the winner in Sanremo, as proved to be the case that year when 'Gira' had too much zip in his sprinting legs for Giovanni Brunero.

A year on, he led over the Turchino again and, as before, he ended up duelling with Brunero. On this occasion, though, the younger man, who had also emerged from Piedmont, learned his lesson. He led out the sprint from the front and, as he sensed Girardengo coming up to challenge him, he edged closer and closer to the crowd. The defending champion kept accelerating but got so close to the crowd that a red flag being waved by one fan became entangled in his wheel, sending him crashing to the road. By the time he had remounted, Brunero had crossed the line victorious. Girardengo didn't let that setback stay with him for long. A third Sanremo title came in 1923, when he narrowly beat Belloni in the sprint.

Like many of his peers, Girardengo turned to track racing during the winter, taking on specialists such as 1924 Sanremo champion Pietro Linari, who achieved huge fame for his successes in six-day races at Madison Square Garden in New York. In 1928 he won a $2,000 prize offered by Rudolph Valentino's former lover, Pola Negri, and found a new fan in Ernest Hemingway, who described him as 'statuesque, a marvellous specimen who moves with the agility of a cat'. Girardengo also boosted his wealth and fame on the tracks of Europe and North America, where the spot prizes offered during races ensured he kept an edge to his sprinting, a talent he came to rely on increasingly as the depth of his competition grew.

A new challenger to Girardengo

Prior to 1925, Sanremo's date moved considerably from year to year. In some seasons it took place a few days before the end of March, in others as late as mid-April. Gradually, though, the racing calendar was taking on a more formal structure, requiring organisers to stick to pre-agreed dates. Consequently, *La Gazzetta* opted for a mid-March slot to coincide with the feast day of San Giuseppe, a public holiday, which ensured their event maintained its place among the first races of the season and guaranteed fans would turn out in droves.

The riders, however, weren't happy with the move. The weather for Sanremo tended to be bad even when it took place well into April. Many racers suggested a move to mid-March could lead to an event more befitting the winter cyclo-cross calendar given the likely appalling state of the roads. They showed their discontent by refusing to race aggressively in the 1925 edition, resulting in two dozen riders contesting the finish, the biggest group ever to do so. The organisers weren't happy with this unattractive truce, but *La Gazzetta* noted the elements favoured the race for once.

Subsequently, the Italian press began to refer to Milan–Sanremo as *La Primavera*, the Spring Classic. By the end of the 1920s, as Alfredo

Binda, Learco Guerra and an increasingly large and potent contingent of foreign riders emerged to take on established stars such as Girardengo, Sanremo had also been dubbed *La Classicissima* – the Classic of Classics – a rather immodest term apparently coined by the organising newspaper's Emilio Colombo, which clearly suggested Sanremo was the biggest one-day race of the season, perhaps to the detriment of the Tour of Lombardy, the other major Classic in their stable.

In that 1925 race of the go-slow, the foreign competition included the French Automoto team led by Italy's Tour de France champion Ottavio Bottecchia, who was seen as a huge threat by the Italian teams. After two seasons with Maino, Girardengo was riding for Wolsit, whose owner, Emilio Bozzi, also had the Legnano brand in his portfolio. Their stars included Linari and Brunero. Speaking to the riders on both teams prior to the start of Milan–Sanremo, Bozzi made it quite clear what was to happen, telling them: 'Automoto must not profit from the rivalry between Girardengo and Brunero or Girardengo and Linari. Whether Legnano or Wolsit win is all the same to me. Is that clear?' With that, Bozzi jumped into his car and drove off to watch the action unfold.

Not surprisingly, given the truce that had been called between some of the main protagonists, there wasn't a great deal of action to see, although this was to a large extent due to Bottecchia's withdrawal when the race reached the coast. By that point, Girardengo and Brunero were away on their own, with Linari vainly chasing after being halted for some minutes by a broken wheel. It was all going exactly as Bozzi had ordered, but events took a bizarre turn when Girardengo punctured at Oneglia with little more than 30km to the finish. Rather than take advantage, Brunero eased up, allowing his erstwhile rival to catch up. Given Brunero's odd decision to wait rather than attack, it was little surprise when Girardengo cruised to a fourth title in the deciding sprint.

Had Bozzi given the pair an additional instruction? No one has ever lifted the lid. All Brunero would say about his lack of performance was that he had stomach problems, an excuse Linari refused to believe. He was so incensed he wouldn't speak to his teammate at the finish. It is interesting to note that, like Girardengo, Brunero was also a Piedmontese and Linari must have known the two men were close. When Brunero died in 1934, Girardengo was, according to one report, the only rider who attended his funeral.

Writing in *La Gazzetta*, Emilio Colombo glossed over the differences within the Legnano team, as he explained: 'It's not certain that all of the men on the Legnano team have been in perfect accord.' On Girardengo, though, Colombo was far more expansive, describing him as 'a miraculous athlete who always seems to come back renewed every year', and adding that all of the other Italian riders were unfortunate to be competing in the same era as 'the phenomenon Girardengo'.

'The little guy from Novi' was just as sensational in 1926, when, three days on from his thirty-third birthday, he set a pace along the coast that no one could stay with, eventually finishing more than six minutes ahead of runner-up Nello Ciaccheri. But his final, and arguably his best, Sanremo success was still to come in 1928, by which time he was 35 and very much the target for Italy's new generation, led by Alfredo Binda.

The rivalry between old campaigner Girardengo and new sensation Binda, who had won the Giro d'Italia in 1925 and would do so again on four more occasions, had been built up leading into Milan–Sanremo in 1927, but 'Gira' was forced out of the race by injury. In his absence, the general feeling was that all Binda had to do was turn up and take the title. However, cycle sport is never quite that straightforward.

In Tortona, just north of Girardengo's home patch in Novi Ligure, three riders broke clear, among them a Tuscan called Pietro Chesi, a part-time coalman who had a reputation for exactly this kind of kamikaze raid. At Novi they led by seven minutes, and at Ovada by 17. On the Turchino, Chesi's two companions fell back, but he descended down to the coast and continued on, encouraged at key points by comrades from his bike club in Carpi, just to the north of Modena. Behind, the big names, including Binda, took up the chase, but were still not fully committed, believing Chesi would run out of gas. But he didn't – not quite. He crossed the line with both legs rigid with cramp and had to be helped off his bike and on to the victory podium. Binda led in the pursuers nine minutes later. The next day in *La Gazzetta*, Colombo chided 'the illustrious champions' for their approach, telling them, 'You can't play around like that in sport.'

The contest everyone had been waiting for took place the following year, in 1928, pitting five-time champion Girardengo against Binda, described by *La Gazzetta*'s Bruno Roghi as 'the young hope he couldn't contain any longer'. The rain turned the roads south to the coast into a sea of mud. Passing through Novi Ligure, Girardengo heard his children cry out 'Win, Papa!' He later admitted: 'I did so partly so as not to disappoint them.'

This was by far the most hard-fought of Girardengo's six successes. He went over the Turchino just a few seconds behind Binda. Two more riders joined the pair on the descent, Angelo Oliveri and Girardengo's Maino teammate Antonio Negrini. Oliveri soon fell back, leaving just three in contention. On the Capo Berta, Binda accelerated. The two Maino riders chased frantically, so much so that Negrini lost contact before Girardengo succeeded in closing the gap. It is said that the two rivals then rode side by side into Sanremo, neither wanting to give the slightest appearance of weakness. The sprint finally separated them, Girardengo finishing two bike lengths clear.

La Gazzetta's lead reporter Colombo called it his 'greatest triumph', citing the appalling weather, the road conditions and the need to respond to an attack by a rival at the top of his form. He described how the now six-time champion had been untypically defensive, but had needed to be. Of the runner-up, he said, 'I think he committed a very serious mistake: he didn't believe Girardengo would be so dangerous.' Over the months that followed, Binda made it clear he would not make the same mistake again. He announced, 'If I need to drop Girardengo to win Sanremo, then I will indeed drop him.'

The defending champion responded by training harder than ever with teammate Negrini, undertaking shorter but faster rides to deal with the challenge. He was, said those who knew him well in Novi, better than ever, and certainly good enough to defeat Binda. In fact, they said, Negrini was good enough to beat him as well. The two Maino men appeared to be living up to these claims when they went clear in a small group early on in the 1929 race, but Binda bided his time and reeled them back in on the Turchino, where Girardengo fell back.

On the coast road, Binda and Negrini went clear together, but Girardengo's ally crashed at Varazze, with 115km still to cover. Knowing from his own training that he could ride at 35km/h all day if necessary, Binda steamed on, increasing his advantage all the way into the finish, where he set a new record for the course, bettering the pre-war mark of Odile Defraye by more than eight minutes, which was also his margin over runner-up Leonida Frascarelli.

Days later, Binda declared that, having won Sanremo with a solo break, he would retain the title by beating Girardengo in a sprint in order to avenge his 1928 loss, but the rematch never happened. Binda crashed out in 1930 as his teammate Michele Mara retained the title for Bianchi, with Girardengo fifth in the bunch finish. When Binda did win in a sprint in 1931, becoming the first man to take the title wearing the rainbow jersey of world champion, the Maino leader he beat was Learco Guerra rather than Girardengo.

By then Guerra, 'The Human Locomotive' who had only turned pro in his mid-twenties, having failed to make the grade as a professional footballer, had taken up Girardengo's mantle at Maino and had wasted no time in ramping up his own rivalry with Binda. The pair marked each other out of contention the following year, when Swiss-born Italian Alfredo Bovet knocked almost an hour off Binda's previous best time for the course thanks to a brisk following wind. Just as notable, though, was the farewell appearance of Giovanni Gerbi, whose grip on Gustave Garrigou's collar had ensured Lucien Petit-Breton had been unopposed in the sprint that decided the first Sanremo a quarter of a century earlier. Gerbi was nearing his forty-seventh birthday, making him seven years older than 1917 champion Gaetano Belloni, who also bowed out. In 1933, the 40-year-old Girardengo followed them, going on to a successful acting and writing career.

The foreign challenge wanes

Italy's political landscape had changed radically in the aftermath of the First World War. By the mid-1920s, Mussolini's Fascist Party had established total control over every aspect of life in Italy, including sport, which was regarded as crucial to the party's popularity. In 1934, Sanremo was put back a day to avoid a clash with general elections, held in the form of a plebiscite on the single-party list of candidates put forward by the Fascist Party. Only 0.16 per cent of voters rejected the list of what was by that point Italy's only legal political party, with Mussolini as the dictator at its head. Racing on a Monday in front of smaller crowds than usual didn't appear to suit the big guns, Binda and Guerra, who were beaten by another rider known as 'The Locomotive', in this case Belgian Joseph Demuysere, who broke clear on Capo Berta to become his country's third winner.

After Demuysere's triumph, the title remained in Italian hands until well into the post-war period, partly thanks to Mussolini's political and military actions, which resulted in Italy becoming increasingly isolated. Although Italian riders still competed abroad, foreign riders were reluctant to challenge the Italians on their home ground. But it wasn't only politics that kept most foreign stars away. French teams received so much publicity at home that there was no need to campaign in Italy, especially as it was widely held that vehicles in the Sanremo race caravan went out of their way to hinder foreign riders and help their own.

In 1937, *L'Auto* reporter Jean Leulliot, who would go on to manage the French team at the Tour that same year and relaunch Paris–Nice after the war, made one of his paper's by now rare visits to Milan–Sanremo. He decried the number of vehicles on the course, describing how they kicked up so much dust that no one in them could possibly know what was happening in the race. He praised breakaway winner Cesare Del Gancia, calling him 'a beautiful athlete', but was highly critical of the Italian professional scene as a whole.

'Italian racing is perhaps based more around individuals than French racing, but there are a lot fewer riders with class. There are very few attacks and the ones that are made are almost always successful … We are convinced that a good French rider would find it easier to win Milan–Sanremo than the Critérium National or Paris–Roubaix,' wrote Leulliot. But he balanced his view by pointing out that riders based in Paris should do less complaining about Italians being unbeatable in their races. They should, he suggested, put themselves and the Italians to the test. 'Milan–Sanremo is undoubtedly a crazy race, but it's a passion-filled event that offers the best riders a hundred opportunities to escape,' he concluded.

Leulliot may have been less dismissive of Italian riders if he had witnessed the 1935 edition, when a 20-year-old from Tuscany made a staggering impact on his debut. Listed as Giuseppe Bartali in the official list of finishers, Gino Bartali was the most unexpected member of a small group of riders who engaged in a thrilling battle over the *capi* and all of the way into Sanremo. On Capo Mele, Learco Guerra neutralised an attack made by the unheralded Bartali, who tried his luck again on the Capo Cervo. Temporarily held up at one of the dozens of level crossings at points where the road and railway intersected on the tight passage below the rugged hills that overshadow the coastal passage, Guerra lost 100m.

To widespread surprise, the youngster extended his lead to almost two minutes. However, he would be denied a race-winning debut. With little more than 30km remaining, and having just tackled a small climb, Bartali found his derailleur would not budge from the low gear he was in. He resisted his pursuers for 15km, but Guerra, Mario Cipriani and local favourite Giuseppe Olmo eventually caught the stymied Tuscan. The quartet stayed together until just 200m from the line, when Cipriani opened the sprint. With the crowd baying for him, local favourite Olmo, from the port of Savona along the coast, responded quickest as the fast-finishing Guerra hesitated. Olmo flew past Cipriani, gaining enough of a gap to hold off Guerra by a wheel, provoking pandemonium as jubilant fans mobbed him.

Bartali's startling performance heralded the emergence of a new generation of champions. Like Girardengo before him, two time Sanremo champion and five-time Giro winner Binda was on the wane. His fabulous career came to an unfortunate end as the 1936 edition of *La Classicissima* was exiting Novi Ligure. In heavy rain, 30 riders fell. Binda was one of just two who were unable to continue. Taken to hospital in Novi, where Girardengo's wife was among the first to comfort him, Binda was diagnosed with a broken femur. He never raced again, although he would go on to play a very significant role in the careers of Bartali and Fausto Coppi when he became the Italian national team manager.

Signed by Legnano in 1936 to ride alongside Binda, Bartali quickly filled the shoes of the stricken champion, winning that year's Giro when still only 21. But Sanremo continued to evade him. In 1937, when it was decided to fix the race on 19 March, the feast day of San Giuseppe, or the Saturday before it if it fell on a Sunday, Cesare Del Cancia took the victory bouquet. There was also a special prize for the first foreign finisher, which went to little-remembered American Joseph Magnani, who was the first American to start *La Primavera* and finished twenty-fifth. Olmo picked up a second success in 1938. But the bigger news that year came from abroad, where Bartali became just the second Italian to win the Tour de France. Heading into 1939, the press was proclaiming, 'Bartali will enter the Olympus of cycling as soon as he manages to win Milan–Sanremo.'

Bartali made it clear he didn't intend to have that obvious gap on his palmarès for too long. Unlike most of his peers, he stayed fit during the off-season, which meant that he came into the first races in good form. Blessed with a strong constitution, he also claimed poor conditions didn't bother him. However, his doubters pointed out he was not quick in a sprint and that Sanremo was increasingly decided that way. Bartali had a reply for them, too: 'It's true that I am not very quick over 200 metres, but when it comes to a sprint after 300 kilometres, well, I don't fear anyone.'

In 1939, snow was falling as 145 riders set out at just after eight in the morning for the thirty-second running of Milan–Sanremo. Although the snow eased once the riders were over the Turchino, the cold never released its grip. Just as he had in 1935, Bartali made his move on the *capi*, first reeling in a group of four riders ahead of him, then shaking them off one by one until only Mario Vicini remained. Bartali kept attacking, but could not lose his dogged rival, and he paid for this starting and stopping when a trio of riders joined them. A sprint would once again decide the race, and Bartali opted to get it under way, accelerating from 200m out. In any other race, Aldo Bini would have caught and passed the Tuscan, but at the end of 281.5km on sapping roads and in crippling cold, he didn't even manage to get within two bike lengths of Bartali.

'In the end it was a San Remo stripped of every coefficient of certainty, a San Remo made for absolute champions … In a certain sense, Bartali has ridden a San Remo in his own image,' wrote Bruno Roghi in *La Gazzetta*. Note here Roghi's spelling of San Remo rather than the traditional Sanremo. Enforced by decree by Mussolini's Fascists in 1928, it is believed the change was made to honour the Catholic saint San Remo. However, locals insist the name derives from San Romolo, a bishop of Genoa in the ninth century, who was known as Sanremü in the local dialect. Consequently, they steadfastly refused to acknowledge the town's designation as San Remo. In 2002, the city council overturned the 1928 decree, returning Sanremo to its original spelling.

The hyperbole when the chain-smoking, wine-loving, God-fearing Bartali retained the title was rather less overblown, largely because his victory owed everything to Olimpio Bizzi's chain coming off just as he was passing the Legnano leader 50m from the line. Pictures show Bartali surging through in the middle of the road, while over on the right-hand side Bizzi has both feet out of the toe-clips as he battles to stay upright. Somewhere among the blurred figures behind the two of them is Sanremo debutant Fausto Coppi. Riding for Legnano, he fulfilled his task of setting Bartali up for the sprint and, like Bizzi and 19 others, was classified in joint tenth place.

With war engulfing Europe, Sanremo became even more of an Italian affair. In 1940, the foreign contingent comprised two Swiss riders. A year later, when Bartali and rising stars Coppi and Fiorenzo Magni were upstaged by solo winner Piero Favalli, the field was entirely Italian. By 1943, many of those Italian riders had been called into active service, including Coppi, who was sent to North Africa to fight but spent most of his active service as a British prisoner of war.

In the wake of the Allied invasion of September 1943, Italian soldiers found themselves fighting on both sides, some having followed orders to join the Allied forces while others refused to switch from the Axis powers. Only when the war in Europe ended in May 1945 did the thoughts of Italians turn to cycling once again. It would only take one towering performance for the sport to regain its place in Italian hearts.

15

FEAST AND FAMINE FOR ITALY

Unlike the First World War, when Italy had remained largely untouched by hostilities, the Second World War left much of the country in ruins. Intense fighting continued right up until the German surrender on 2 May 1945, two days after the liberation of Milan.

Having been released from captivity by the British and recovered from a bout of malaria, Fausto Coppi had been reacquainting himself with bike racing hundreds of kilometres to the south. Travelling around the southern regions in the company of the Leoni brothers, Ricci and Adolfo, he had been competing in small races that offered meagre prizes, but at least enabled the three of them to survive. When news of the Allied victory reached them, Coppi set out on the most perilous ride of his life, heading north through the devastated Italian countryside to rejoin his family in Castellania. En route, he signed a contract with Bianchi.

Once back in the north and newly married, he moved to a modest house at Sestri Ponente, near Genoa, and began to train furiously on the slopes on the Turchino Pass in the company of his brother, Serse. His objective was to win the 1946 edition of Milan–Sanremo, the first race in Italy in the post-war era. In the months leading up to the race, Coppi recorded 6,000km in training, an amount so huge at that time that he was repeatedly questioned about the wisdom of his relentless regime. 'If I don't train like this, I won't be sure of my chances when the day comes,' he would reply.

Under the tutelage of Biagio Cavanna, Costante Girardengo's former team manager whose fading eyesight had gone completely in 1937, the Coppi brothers weren't the only ones working hard to be ready for Sanremo. Cavanna looked after a whole stable of riders, who lived, ate and trained together. He claimed to know exactly how many kilometres they had covered and what their level of form was simply by feeling their legs. An imposing figure, prone to fits of rage, Cavanna insisted on a strict hierarchy being maintained. Fausto Coppi was at the top. Most of the rest were *gregari*, who set the pace for Coppi, chased down breaks, and brought him food and drink.

In a biography of Cavanna by *La Gazzetta*'s Marco Pastonesi, 'The Wizard of Novi' is quoted as saying: 'My whole life with Fausto Coppi was accompanied by his voice, his breathing, the sounds of his wheels turning, the smell of sweat and the sharpness of his spiky bones, which were both fragile and formidable at the same time, which I felt pulsing in my blind man's hands ... massaging his legs was like playing a guitar.' Cavanna's wizardry also extended to him providing his riders with substances designed to fortify them. Coppi himself admitted regularly using 'La Bomba', as amphetamines had been dubbed.

Coppi went into Sanremo unsure of his tactics. Cavanna advised him: 'If you want to win Milan–Sanremo, you must make your move when no one is expecting it.' However, until the day before the race, Coppi was still mulling over where to make that move. Having registered to race, he looked through the prizes on offer along the route and the list of entrants for the race. Noticing several track specialists were down to start, Coppi's plan began to come together. He knew very well the track riders would go all out from the start to win as many of the intermediate *primes* as possible and then pull out of the race once the course started to climb. Feeling he could benefit from this, Coppi, wearing number 13, lined up in the front row of the peloton in Milan.

The attacks began almost right from the start. At Binasco, on the outskirts of Milan, Luigi Mutti sprinted clear of a group of 11 riders to claim the spot prize of 3,000 lire. Sensing an opportunity, Frenchman Lucien Teisseire, winner of the Paris–Tours Classic two years earlier, continued the momentum created by Mutti, and three more riders – Giovanni Bardelli, Secondo Barisone and Coppi – sped across the gap to join them.

To those in the bunch behind, the offensive must have seemed ridiculous. Only Coppi and Teisseire had the endurance and experience to survive all the way to the finish, while the breeze was almost head-on, making the chances of them doing so vitually nil. Consequently, the peloton was happy to let them go clear, no doubt believing two of the principal favourites had committed a gross error of judgement.

With Teisseire and Coppi doing almost all of the pace-making, the five leaders quickly gained an advantage of five minutes. At Ovada, with little more than a third of the course covered, Teisseire pushed the pace higher and only Coppi was able to follow. Starting up the Turchino, the pair led the peloton by more than six minutes, but Coppi was worried. Teisseire looked strong, to the point where Coppi felt he might not be able to follow the Frenchman if he made an attack on the flat. In order to test out his rival, the Bianchi leader attacked hard on the lower slopes of the Turchino, gained 100m, then eased off, allowing Teisseire to catch him.

In most instances, such an attack would result in co-operation between the breakaway riders ending. But in this case, Teisseire had been outwitted by his companion for the morning. He kept driving hard, thinking Coppi was struggling. Yet Coppi could sense Teisseire's pedal cadence was dropping.

'About three kilometres below the tunnel, I made a furious attack, going right to my very limits,' Coppi explained. 'My compatriots, who were weary and embittered by the war, were counting on me to bring them some satisfaction. I was lifted by their shouts. Climbing through the mist, I could see them jumping with delight and urging me on as I passed. With 150 kilometres to the finish, this escape was pure folly.'

It may have well have been madness, but Coppi knew winning Sanremo would secure his financial future. Bianchi boss Aldo Zambrini had promised him a new lorry. 'If you win you will be able to set up a trucking company,' Zambrini had joked. Coppi had also asked for the 36,000 lire Bianchi had held for him from before the war, plus the interest due on that amount.

When he reached the coast road, his advantage on Teisseire had ballooned to more than seven minutes. While Italian reports from the time focus on Coppi's brilliance and almost inevitably suggest Teisseire was a broken man, that wasn't entirely the case. Just 150m behind the Italian as he came out of the Turchino tunnel, the Frenchman, who didn't know the road at all, found himself riding through a dust cloud kicked up by all of the vehicles descending in Coppi's wake. Given that he was struggling to see the way ahead, it would have been suicidal for Teisseire to try to match the leader's pace.

Coppi continued to increase his advantage once on the coast road. Motorcyclists told him his great rival Bartali was furious with rage in the peloton, which was now more than quarter of an hour behind, encouraging Coppi to keep pressing. 'I chose to do the impossible, or rather the impossible chose me. I belted along like a beast being pursued by the pack,' he said. His final advantage was 14 minutes on the plucky Teisseire and more than 18 on what remained of the peloton. *La Gazzetta*'s headline the next morning shouted, 'We're proud of you'. They eulogised Coppi's feat, but also the event itself. 'You're just a bicycle race but ... you tell us there is a reason to live,' said one report. In a symbolic way if nothing else, normal life had returned to Italy.

In *Pedalare! Pedalare!*, John Foot says of Coppi's victory in 1946: 'At that moment, Coppi and Italy became one. They were fused together. A myth of endurance, or a superman in peasant's clothing, had come into being and for many it wiped out, if only briefly, bad memories of the war ... His unforgettable solo raid chimed with Italy in the immediate post-war months, with the desire for reconstruction, for new heroes to inspire and unite a fractured population. Coppi's emergence out of the darkness of the Turchino and into the light symbolised Italy's rebirth.'

The impact of Coppi's success was not only felt in Italy. Writing in *L'Équipe*, the post-war relaunched version of *L'Auto*, Pierre Chany noted the significance of the moment, saying of the Turchino: 'The tunnel was of modest dimensions, just 50 metres long, but on 19 March 1946 it assumed exceptional proportions in the eyes of the world. That day it was six years in length and lost in the gloom of the war ... A rumbling was heard from the depths of those six years and suddenly there appeared in the light of day an olive-greenish car stirring up a cloud of dust. 'Arriva Coppi' the messenger announced, a revelation only the initiated had foreseen.'

Coppi's victory also changed the perception of Sanremo. While it had long been revered, riders feared its terrible roads and appalling weather. Coppi's success under clear skies and in front of ecstatic crowds cemented Sanremo's status as *La Classicissima di Primavera*, the race that signalled the end of winter and the start of a new season. It also confirmed the rivalry between Coppi and Bartali, which some have argued was the most divisive in the history of sport given the status of the two men in that era. It certainly split Italy over the years that followed.

Asked in the aftermath of his victory whether he felt Bartali would be disheartened by the thrashing he had received, Coppi said: 'That guy will only ever give in on the day when he doesn't have a bike within his grasp!' Those words were prophetic as Bartali bounced back in 1947 with an epic performance of his own in appalling conditions.

With snow lying at the roadside, the riders endured close to freezing temperatures and driving rain. Coppi was among the 98 of the 135 starters who quit the race, complaining his eyes were burning. Lone breakaway Ezio Cecchi had the race of his life, building a lead of ten minutes. However, once Bartali had accelerated away from the chasing pack on the Capo Berta, Cecchi's chances all but disappeared. Bartali caught him 22km from the finish and powered past.

The 1948 edition heralded some significant developments. The race was the first event in the newly introduced Desgrange-Colombo Trophy and also saw the debut of a new *La Gazzetta* director, Vincenzo Torriani, who shared the role of race director for this one edition with Armando Cougnet. Although not as notable, Henry C. Blomfield became the first British rider to line up in *La Primavera*. He lost his shoes and kit in transit and raced on a borrowed bike. Once under way, he was the first rider to quit before an hour's racing was done.

The winner needed no introduction, though. After tracking his rivals all day, Coppi produced one scintillating acceleration on Capo Mele and went on to triumph by more than five minutes. Twelve months later, he produced a similar burst on Capo Berta. Only 100m clear passing over the top of it, he finished four minutes clear despite the group of strong riders chasing behind him averaging almost 40km/h for the final 29km. It was quite a way to mark the race's new finish on the Via Roma in the heart of Sanremo. Coppi's success tied him with Bartali at three wins each.

The 1950 edition was billed as a showdown between Italy's two greats, and lived up to the pre-race hype, although the dénouement was rather surprising. A group of more than 60 riders approached Capo Berta, all of them expecting Coppi to attack on the slopes of the toughest of the three *capi*. But as they waited for the attack to come, Coppi punctured. Bartali didn't hesitate, bounding clear with just three French riders able to follow, among them future radio journalist Robert Chapatte.

Chapatte said he glanced back and saw the bunch had been ripped to pieces behind them. 'The nearest rider to us was 100 metres back. Another kilometre further up and they had all lost sight of us. And Gino was still accelerating.' Chapatte described the relief that he, Édouard Fachleitner and Pierre Molinéris felt when Bartali moved across to let them take over the pace-making, and then the disbelief that struck all four of them. 'An astonishing event had occurred. A bullet came flying towards us, forcing the crowd to one side as it passed by. Fausto Coppi was there. It was stupefying. His mouth was agape, his eyes bulging due to the phenomenal effort he had made by climbing that terrible hill at 40km/h.'

Bartali instantly refused to co-operate, knowing that to do so would almost certainly hand the title to Coppi. As the front group eased, most of the dropped riders rejoined it. Coming into Sanremo the group was more than 50-strong. Coppi had one card left to play. From a kilometre out, he went to the front and wound up the pace for his Bianchi team-mate and sprinter, Oreste Conte, who made his surge from 400m, only to see first Nedo Logli and then Bartali come past him. Bartali was two bike lengths clear at the line.

With the Sanremo tally between Bartali and Coppi standing at four to three in favour of 'Gino the Pious', the whole of Italy awaited the rematch. However, it never materialised. Indeed, following back-to-back wins by Loretto Petrucci in 1952 and 1953, Italy experienced what would be its longest drought in *La Classicissima*. Seventeen years would pass before another Italian savoured victory on the Via Roma.

Louison Bobet, an aloof and sometimes moody man who was no great stylist on the bike but more than made up for that with an astonishing ability to get every ounce of effort out of his body, had given a sign of the foreign domination to come in 1951, when he became the first French winner since Henri Pélissier in 1912. Bobet came to the race with just a single teammate, Pierre Barbotin. The only riders from 'the hexagon' in the starting line-up, the two Frenchmen had agreed a deal to compete in Bottecchia's colours.

The lead group numbered 17 at the foot of Capo Mele, but was only four-strong approaching Capo Berta, where the two Frenchmen were still together along with Belgium's Raymond Impanis and sole Italian Petrucci. As the French duo maintained a high pace on the steep ascent of the rugged headland, first Petrucci and then Impanis fell back.

Once clear, Bobet and Barbotin were never in danger of being reeled in. On the closing kilometres, the two friends and teammates agreed to split the prize money for first and second between them, then went head to head, with Bobet the clear victor in the sprint.

Change for cycling and Sanremo

In 1954, cycling was on the verge of a fundamental change. After the war, sales of scooters and motorbikes had taken off, resulting in a rapid drop in bicycle sales. Up to that point, the UCI's rules prevented so-called *extrasportif* sponsors that came from outside the sport backing teams. However, bike manufacturers were finding it increasingly difficult to fund resource-needy teams when their revenue was falling. The Ganna team led by Fiorenzo Magni was among those initially hit. When the manufacturer pulled out of the sport, Magni, who had a sharp business mind and would go on to run a chain of car showrooms around Milan, realised he needed to challenge the regulations in place.

He agreed a deal with the Cosmochimici company that produced Nivea suncream. Italian race organisers and the Italian federation tried to thwart Magni's scheme, but he managed to avoid a boycott of his team by agreeing to bring a bike manufacturer on board as a co-sponsor. In early 1954, the Nivea-Fuchs team was born. Although resistance in some countries, particularly France, to *extrasportives* would continue for some years, Magni's vision of cycling's future would eventually become accepted throughout the sport.

When the focus returned to racing, Rik Van Steenbergen's devastatingly impressive 1954 bunch sprint win on the Via Roma signalled a change in the balance of power. The Belgians were coming, led by Van Steenbergen. He had contested the bunch sprint clinched by Bartali in 1950 after doing reconnaissance of all but two of Sanremo's 288km. Surprisingly for a sprinter, those two were the final ones, which he assumed were straight. However, leading into the finish there was a sharp turn around a fountain running into the finish on the Via Roma. The Belgian was badly placed coming into it, lost momentum and his chance of victory. He made no mistake this time, crossing the line several lengths clear and falling into the arms of his team boss, Costante Girardengo.

Two more Belgian victories followed. In 1955, the British Hercules team lined up alongside the sport's biggest names, Fred Krebs finishing a respectable seventeenth and Brian Robinson sixtieth as Germain Derycke took the title. Alfred De Bruyne extended Belgium's run in 1956, becoming the first rider to win Paris–Nice and Sanremo in the same season.

By that point, the equipment riders used, their training methods and levels of fitness, and the state of the roads had improved to the extent that the Turchino was no longer the crucial test it had long been. It was now too far out from the finish to have a significant impact on the outcome. The best sprinters could pass it with relative ease and were dominating. That didn't suit the Italians, who couldn't boast a rider with the finishing speed of Van Steenbergen or Miguel Poblet, who became the first Spaniard to win *La Classicissima* in 1957, the year third-placed Brian Robinson was the first Briton to finish on the podium.

Change looked even more likely when Rik Van Looy led in a 69-rider bunch in 1958 at a record average speed of 42.179km/h. After Poblet took a second victory at the head of another substantial bunch of riders in 1959, Vincenzo Torriani and his organising team made the first notable change to the route since its inception in 1907.

In itself, the Poggio ('little hill') climb doesn't amount to much. The name derives from the village that sits three kilometres up the Via Duca d'Aosta and overlooks Sanremo. The road branches off to the right from the main coastal route, the Via Aurelia, ensuring the riders hit it at speed. It climbs via seven hairpins and 23 bends past plush houses, the occasional olive grove and vineyard, and dozens of large greenhouses, topping out at 162m. Apart from one brief section of eight per cent, its gradient remains at around three to four per cent. Certainly, Jacques Anquetil wasn't impressed by it when he undertook his pre-race reconnaissance in 1960, describing it to *L'Équipe* as 'insufficient to provoke a rigorous selection'.

Torriani, though, was insistent that, after 280km of racing, it would have a significant impact and prevent the sprinters dominating. 'This final difficulty will enable the best riders on Capo Berta to maintain their advantage and even to extend it. Those riders who are fatigued when the race moves beyond the *capi* will definitely fall away on the Poggio, from where the descent runs to a point just 1,100 metres from the line,' he affirmed before the race got under way.

It started in a sombre atmosphere. *La Gazzetta* director Giuseppe Ambrosini asked for a minute's silence to remember race founder Armando Cougnet, who had passed away the previous September, three-time Sanremo champion Fausto Coppi, whose death from malaria at the start of the year had stunned the cycling world, and French rider Gérard Saint, who had died after crashing in a race at Le Mans just three days beforehand.

The first key moment arrived on the Turchino, where Britain's Tom Simpson went on the attack, resulting in a sizeable breakaway group forming. The pace up Capo Berta trimmed that group back to just seven riders, including René Privat, who had been narrowly thwarted just three kilometres from the finish after an epic escape two years earlier. On the Poggio, Privat accelerated clear and held what appeared a winning advantage at the top. But he was no great shakes on descents.

As he tentatively negotiated the twisting drop down through the vineyards, compatriot Jean Graczyk was hurtling down the Poggio behind him. Blessed with far superior finishing speed, Graczyk would almost certainly have beaten Privat in the sprint. However, he misjudged a corner and hit the deck, giving his compatriot the breathing space he needed. He won by 11 seconds, with Graczyk cursing his luck. 'In the fall I lost the time that ended up costing me victory,' he complained.

So Torriani had been proved right, although only to an extent. Privat's average speed was the fastest up to that point at almost 43km/h, while hopes that the home riders would be more competitive were dashed. Although Gastone Nencini had led on to the Poggio, not a single Italian finished in the top ten.

In 1961, an Italian did finish on the podium, Rino Benedetti coming in behind Rik Van Looy as the peloton sprinted for second place. Victory had been clinched three seconds earlier by another Frenchman, riding for the same Mercier team as Privat, and even with the same initials. Even more remarkable, though, was that Raymond Poulidor, 'The Eternal Second' who finished on the Tour de France podium eight times but never won it, had decided to quit the race when he punctured in Varazze 125km from the finish and had to wait two minutes before Mercier team manager Antonin Magne appeared on the scene in his trademark white shirt and Basque beret. When Magne saw Poulidor starting to unlace his shoes, he asked:

'What are you doing?'

'As you can see, I'm abandoning. Continuing on is pointless as the leaders are too far ahead,' Sanremo debutant Poulidor replied.

'Raymond, I am forbidding you from abandoning. You have no right to do so. A race is not lost in advance,' Magne insisted once and then again when his team leader questioned him. Seeing Frenchmen Albert Bouvet and Louison Bobet pass by, he ordered Poulidor to chase after them, telling him the pace at the front would drop. Magne, a two-time Tour de France winner who was one of the most astute team managers around, drove on ahead and soon noticed that the bunch had slowed as riders ate their final supplies. He dropped back to tell his leader: 'They are only one minute thirty ahead ... You are going to get back up to them easily, like flies landing on a big cheese.'

Once back in the peloton, Poulidor recalled the plan Magne had laid out for him when they had driven the course in the opposite direction to get to Milan a couple of days before. In 1956 Magne had advised

Fred De Bruyne to attack at the foot of Capo Berta, and told Poulidor to employ the same strategy. When he did, just two riders jumped across to join him, Dutchman Albertus 'Ab' Geldermans and his own Mercier teammate Jean-Claude Annaert, who helped drive the pace along to the foot of the Poggio, where Magne had told Poulidor to make a second attack. Poulidor accelerated and quickly opened a substantial gap.

Magne played another card, too. Rather than drive up behind his leader, he slyly followed Geldermans and Annaert, giving the peloton closing in behind the impression the three leaders were still together. However, Poulidor was by now 300m ahead. The ruse was enough to make the difference. 'Poupou' held on to win by 60m despite being sent off course by a policeman on the final bend.

'I so often lost races I should have won, but on that day I won a race that I almost lost twice,' said Poulidor, who not only missed out on the Tour title, but never even managed to spend a day in the Tour's fabled yellow jersey. Mercier doubled his salary that evening, enabling him to marry his fiancée Gisèle a month later.

Italy's drought continues

In 1962, Italian desperation for a first win in a decade had reached the point where Sanremo's organisers invited the home nation's last victor, Loretto Petrucci, to wave the start flag. Would this lift the curse that had bedevilled Italy's stars since 1953? Not quite …

Although Belgium's Émile Daems took the title ahead of three of his compatriots, Italian Antonio Bailetti received immense praise for his performance. Away on his own for 112km, Bailetti was caught by Daems just a dozen kilometres from home. When the Belgian kicked hard on the Poggio, Bailetti was too spent to respond and rolled in tenth.

The situation wasn't about to improve for the Italians either. In 1963, Frenchman Joseph Groussard and Germany's world cyclo-cross champion Rolf Wolfshohl proved the strongest members of a small breakaway group that reached the Poggio together. Coming into the finish, Wolfshohl led out the sprint and seemed, to those close to the line, to have just held off the Frenchman's final surge. Word reached both riders that Wolfshohl had won and as the German went on to the podium to receive the victory bouquet, the disconsolate Groussard told a friend, 'I thought I had beaten him, but it was a tight finish.'

It was so tight the photo-finish judge took some minutes to deliver his verdict. To those watching it may well have seemed that Wolfshohl had done just enough as he had 'thrown' his bike at the line in textbook fashion, pushing it forwards with his whole body tucked in below and behind his arms. To his right, Groussard had crossed the line with his head thrown back and his torso pushed forward, as if trying to break an invisible chest-high tape. In effect, he had done exactly that, as Wolfshohl was hurried off the podium and informed he had lost out by two centimetres.

La Gazzetta pointed out that the first three finishers had all ridden the French stage race Paris–Nice as part of their build-up to Sanremo and asked of the Italian riders: 'How much more time will they need to understand this?' The answer was at least another year. In 1964, two riders contested the title again. Both had ridden Paris–Nice. Neither was Italian. Instead victory went to a British rider for the first time.

Tom Simpson attacked aggressively on the steep ramps of Capo Berta. Cresting the headland, he looked back to find there were just three riders on his wheel: Belgium's Willy Bocklant, Italy's Vincenzo Meco and 1961 winner Poulidor. When the Frenchman made his move on the Poggio, Simpson was the only one of the trio able to stay with him. Their duel continued down the dangerously fast switchbacks into Sanremo, where the Briton won at a canter. While the *Daily Express* crowed, 'Simpson has annihilated the stars of world cycling', the Italians continued to wonder where their next champion was going to come from.

It should have been one of Vittorio Adorni or Franco Balmanion, who looked destined to decide the title between them in 1965. However, a few kilometres before the Poggio, blond Dutchman Arie den Hartog came across the gap from the peloton to join them. After the trio passed the Poggio, the two Italians seemed to have reached an agreement: Balmanion would lead out the sprint for Adorni. However, Den Hartog sneaked in between them, got up to speed on Balmanion's wheel then shot out from behind him as Balmanion flagged, unwittingly – so it was said – blocking Adorni's route to the line as he did so.

A few weeks later, Eddy Merckx turned pro and quickly lived up to the reputation he'd gained as the sport's best amateur rider. *La Gazzetta's* Bruno Raschi described the Belgian as a sprinter with a good range of skills, but limited in some key ways. He was, wrote Raschi, a modern version of Rik Van Steenbergen, a rider set to 'dominate the Classics but not the grand tours'. Raschi was quickly proved half right. Merckx went into his first Sanremo on the back of a fourth-place finish at Paris–Nice. Although tipped for a glittering career, at 21 he was not yet among the favourites for a race as long as *La Primavera*.

He tracked the favourites as far as Capo Berta, where Poulidor produced an acceleration that split the lead group. On the Poggio, knowing he had little chance in a sprint, the Frenchman accelerated again. Merckx clung on, apparently at his limit. Close to the front at the top of the final ascent, Merckx pressed hard on the subsequent drop into Sanremo, determined to keep the front group as small as possible.

It contained 11 riders and no fewer than five Italians, including national champion Michele Dancelli and the very nippy Adriano Durante. On the opening stage of Paris–Nice less than a fortnight before, Merckx had contested victory with both men and had ended up third as Durante came out on top. Rather than start his sprint from a long way out as he had done that day in Auxerre, Merckx waited as long as possible, tracking compatriot Herman Van Springel down the left-hand side of the Via Roma while the Italians stayed in the shadows on the right. In the final metres, Merckx surged past Van Springel, his chin jutting forwards, elbows splayed and teeth gritted. Durante tried to respond, but came too late. Merckx had claimed the first of what would eventually be an astounding 19 successes in the Monuments.

His second came a year later and was even harder for the Italians to take. Winner of two stages at Paris–Nice, Merckx was presented as the Sanremo favourite, but initially found himself stranded in the bunch as his Peugeot teammate Tom Simpson seized the initiative – apparently to prevent Merckx doing so – by joining a break after just eight kilometres. Fortunately for Merckx, the leading Italians missed the move as well, and they reeled Simpson's group in with 59km remaining.

Merckx didn't hesitate, attacking as he had previously said he would do on Capo Berta, and then again before the Poggio, when only Gianni Motta was able to stay on his wheel. The pair worked together going up and over the Poggio, but began to toy with each other approaching the finish, enabling two more Italians to join them. Along with Motta, Franco Bitossi and Felice Gimondi were Italy's three biggest stars. Once again, however, thoughts of a rival Italian winning ensured the trio were more concerned with each other than the foreigner in their midst. With his hands on the drops and his elbows flung wide, Merckx produced what was almost a carbon copy of his victory 12 months earlier, the Italians trailing in his wake.

In the inquest that followed, Motta and Bitossi confessed they had both tried to get on Merckx's wheel at the same time, hindering each other in the process. 'Crazy Heart' Bitossi explained: 'I had no problem with my heart racing. It was just that when we caught Merckx and Motta I didn't have the time to gather breath or think. I swerved and I may have got in Motta's way a bit.'

In 1968, Merckx had become such a strong favourite for the Sanremo title that all his rivals tracked him everywhere he went, effectively marking the Belgian and themselves out of contention. When a group of seven went clear 20km from the finish, the chase behind them started too late, allowing the strapping figure of Rudi Altig the opportunity to become the first German to add his name to Sanremo's roll of honour.

By the spring of 1969, Merckx had been anointed 'The Cannibal'. As well as adding Paris–Roubaix to his list of Classics wins, he had also shown Raschi and the rest of the cycling world he was just as strong in the grand tours by winning the Giro d'Italia in 1968. He arrived in Milan fresh from a crushing victory in Paris–Nice, where he had picked up three stage wins. No matter what the race or terrain, he now looked close to invincible.

The race saw one of Rik Van Looy's final flourishes as he joined the break that clipped away after a frantic first hour of racing. Michele Dancelli was one of five Italians alongside the Belgian, and one of the last to be picked up by the peloton as it approached the Poggio 200km later. Once on the 'little hill', Merckx unleashed the attack everyone was expecting. Vittorio Adorni and Raymond Poulidor got in each other's way as they frantically tried to stay with him, leaving a gap that no one could close. For the first time, Merckx didn't need to call on his wits and finishing speed on the Via Roma. He coasted across the line, telling journalists soon after, 'I feel like a boxer who has won by a knockout with his first punch.'

Fiorenzo Magni encapsulated the wonder that many felt watching Merckx crush his rivals time after time. 'I rode with Coppi and Bartali, I remember the original greats. None of them did what Merckx has done – with such style and ease. When he decides to be so, he is unbeatable. He will win everything,' said the three-time Giro champion.

Writing about the Belgian in his pomp, *L'Équipe*'s Philippe Brunel described Merckx as being 'better than Van Steenbergen, better than Van Looy. Merckx was Van Looy plus Anquetil. He was a global champion, orchestral, respectful of tradition, a rider the Italians would have to learn how to relate to.' The problem for the Italians was that they were still finding this task beyond them. Their race once again ended in recriminations. Dancelli complained of Gimondi and Bitossi, 'They were focused on chasing me. What did they achieve? They just helped Merckx.'

Dancelli and his sporting director at Molteni, Giorgio Albani, knew all too well it would take something special to deny both Merckx and the increasingly dominant band of sprinters from the nations to the north. In the early weeks of 1970, they drew up a detailed plan designed to ensure one of their riders was in contention at all stages. However, the plan quickly became obsolete, largely because it failed to accommodate Dancelli's approach to racing.

Nicknamed 'The Owl' thanks to his captivatingly dark eyes, Dancelli was not regarded as being at the same level as Bitossi, Gimondi and Motta, primarily because, according to Italian-based writer Herbie Sykes, 'He acted on a bike precisely as he did in the clubs and bars around Brescia – on pure instinct. They said he didn't think things through, he did just whatever his body told him, and this was why he didn't win more often.' His style, says Sykes, was 'anachronistic, almost delusional . . . The tragedy was that he was physically among his country's very best.'

Merckx was, of course, heavily backed to win a fourth title in five years, but the Belgian was not feeling his best in the days leading up to the race and made it clear he would be riding for teammate Italo Zilioli. This buoyed everyone else's hopes, and perhaps induced Dancelli to follow his own teammate Carlo Chiappano into a break at Novi Ligure, with less than 100km covered. Zilioli, Bitossi, the De Vlaeminck brothers and Van Looy were also among the 18 who went clear. A crash in the bunch soon after meant the title would probably go to one of them, with sprinters Gerben Karstens and Walter Godefroot the favourites. None of the eight Italians was likely to win if the group came into Sanremo together.

With 70km left, Chiappano jumped clear to win an intermediate sprint prize and Dancelli went after him. As his leader went by, Chiappano sensed an opportunity and eased up. Dancelli pressed on in typically bullish, and apparently unthinking, fashion. However, in the absence of Merckx and his Faema henchmen, no one took responsibility for organising the chase. Roared on over the Poggio with the Italians in the break refusing to aid the pursuit behind him, Dancelli claimed the title and burst into tears as he fell into the arms of a policeman beyond the line. 'Please don't ask me to talk. I don't understand anything any more,' he said. The Italians finally had a San Giuseppe feast day to relish. Thanks to Michele Dancelli, spring had arrived after 17 years.

16

'IT BUILDS UP LIKE A THRILLER'

Michele Dancelli may have ended the home nation's Sanremo drought, but his success didn't presage a flood of Italian victories. In fact, it spurred Eddy Merckx on to even greater feats. Although even the Belgian admitted he was never as strong following his crash on the velodrome at Blois in late 1969, victories continued to come at a staggering rate, and never more so than in 1971.

He arrived in Milan with a third consecutive Paris–Nice title and a new, lightweight and extremely rigid bike courtesy of his Italian framebuilder, Ernesto Colnago. 'The Cannibal' made clear his intentions at the start, telling journalists: 'Last year we allowed the morning breakaways too much autonomy and I never managed to get back on terms with Dancelli. This time, we will have to neutralise all attacks before the Turchino and then take the initiative ourselves.'

Merckx and his team stuck precisely to that plan, helped to an extent by driving rain and cold, which resulted in just 47 of the 172 starters reaching the finish. Having kept a lid on the action as far as the coast, the troops in his new Molteni team detonated the race. At Varazze, the three-time Sanremo champion ordered them to push up the pace to slim down the large peloton before the *capi*.

The Belgian was particularly aware of the threat presented by the Italians now Dancelli had lifted the hoodoo on them. Merckx's old adversary Felice Gimondi was the most prominent of them, 'riding like a locomotive pulling along three wagons', as *La Gazzetta* put it.

Unfortunately for Gimondi, two of those wagons were Molteni riders, Jos Bruyere and Jos Spruyt. They weren't about to do any work to assist Gimondi, especially as Merckx was bridging across to join them with Gianni Motta and Swede Gosta Pettersson.

At the foot of the Poggio, Spruyt and Bruyere accelerated hard, only to see Gimondi shoot by them. Merckx, though, was ready for the attack and quickly latched on to the Italian's wheel. On the false flat near the summit, Merckx skipped past Gimondi, gaining a crucial ten seconds by the top of the Poggio. On the descent back down on to the Via Aurelia, the speed with which he accelerated out of each of the corners extended his advantage to 30 seconds at the finish on the Via Roma. His victory was a poignant one. The next day, Merckx laid his victor's bouquet on the grave of Belgium's world champion Jean-Pierre Monséré, who had died just four days before Sanremo.

With Merckx close to unbeatable in *La Primavera* – in six appearances he had won four times – it was suggested only half jokingly that Sanremo's organisers should follow the example set in the 1930s when Alfredo Binda had been paid not to ride the Giro d'Italia in order to make it less predictable as a contest. As it turned out, Merckx's chances of defending his title looked remote after he suffered a heavy crash in a sprint finish at St-Etienne during Paris–Nice. Suffering from pain in the kidneys and all manner of cuts and grazes, Merckx had been advised by Molteni's doctor not to ride, but insisted, as world champion, on doing so.

His chances looked less likely when he was one of 40 riders caught up in a crash well before the Turchino. But, having got a new bike and been escorted back to the bunch by his teammates, Merckx continued. Approaching the Poggio, a first bunch-sprint finish since the introduction of the 'little hill' looked likely. Yet again, though, Merckx imposed himself over the concluding 7,900m of the course up and over the Poggio.

Where it had been Gimondi leading the assault on the Poggio in 1971, now it was Gianni Motta, the blond Lombard whose career had been kickstarted by unofficial races he had entered as a teenager with fellow workers commuting to a Milan cake factory. He split the bunch to pieces, but, like Gimondi, could not respond when Merckx darted past him on the false flat, gaining 50m by the summit. It wasn't much but it was enough, as Merckx came home alone flourishing all five digits on his right hand. 'I didn't want it to finish in a sprint because that's always more difficult for me. Also, after the crash in St-Etienne, I'm scared of crazy sprints,' he said as he moved to within one victory of Costante Girardengo's all-time record.

Where his rivals had foundered, the common cold succeeded in getting the better of Merckx in both 1973 and 1974. The first of those races was lit up by an attack two kilometres into the race by Ti-Raleigh duo Dave Lloyd and Phil 'The Engine' Bayton. 'I didn't plan to do it. I didn't say to anyone, "I'm going to attack in Milan–Sanremo." It just came into my head and off I went,' Lloyd later recalled. 'It was the crowds I remember. They were standing ten deep through every village we went through, shouting "Allez Raleigh!" and things like that ... In the end Luis Ocaña came up with another bloke, and then we were caught and the bunch came by. I was shattered. I could have gone on to the Poggio and tottered on to the finish but I packed it in. I'd done my job and got some publicity and that was enough.'

After that, the script followed a familiar pattern. A large bunch of riders approached the Poggio, an Italian rider – Wilmo Francioni – blew the group apart, and a Belgian rider crossed the line with his arms aloft. Seeing Felice Gimondi was coming across to join him and Francioni, Roger De Vlaeminck made a Merckx-like move near the top of the Poggio, which resulted in a fine solo win and a flashy car. The car came courtesy of Giorgio Perfetti, vice-president of the Brooklyn clothing company, whose striped team jersey is one of the most iconic in cycling history. 'I've won, I hope he's got the keys in the ignition,' quipped De Vlaeminck.

Merckx was far from being the only rider affected by the poor weather during the early part of the 1974 season. World champion

Gimondi, the son of a cycling-obsessed truck driver who delivered gravel and a postwoman whose bike offered young Felice his first experience of cycling, had been struggling with pharyngitis at Paris–Nice, as he often did in poor weather. He insisted he wouldn't last 100km. However, he joined the group that gradually reeled in the day's two escapees on the Ligurian coast. Gimondi later confessed that when afflicted by this respiratory ailment, it took him time to get up to full speed on the climbs but he wasn't affected in the same way on the flat. Consequently, he attacked persistently in between the *capi* and the Poggio. With 14km left, he had ridden everyone off his wheel.

Gimondi increased his advantage all of the way into the finish, where a mob of ecstatic Italians engulfed him. Naturally, one of the first questions put to him related to the absence of Merckx. 'Do you know I prefer to finish first in his absence to being second behind him,' said the rider from Bergamo. In one notable way, however, his victory 'out-Merckxed' the Belgian. His winning margin of 1′53″ over Eric Leman was the biggest since Fausto Coppi's victory by 4′17″ in 1949.

When Merckx returned to Milan–Sanremo as world champion in 1975, he left no doubt about his intentions. 'I will win today,' he told *Corriere della Sera*. He had looked some way short of his best in finishing a distant second to Joop Zoetemelk at Paris–Nice, but a number of brief attacks before the Turchino had his rivals in a quandary. Was he bluffing? Riding for a teammate? All they could do was respond to his thrusts, which led to a 20-rider group forming before the pass.

As the wind blew in savagely off the sea, sending three-metre waves crashing on to the coast and spray billowing across the riders, no one risked instigating an escapade away from the security of the peloton until the Poggio, where seven riders powered away. Merckx was among them, but was not then one of the trio who edged away on the descent into Sanremo, although his Molteni lieutenant Bruyere was. However, when rising Italian star Francesco Moser bridged across to the leaders, Bruyere's chances of prevailing looked slim.

As the finish neared, Moser glanced back to assess the lead the quartet had, only to see Merckx bearing down on them. The Italian didn't wait for Merckx to close the gap. He accelerated hard, but Bruyere, transformed from potential winner to loyal teammate, was glued to his wheel and ready to lead out Merckx in the sprint. The junction made with the two leaders, this time it was Merckx who didn't hesitate, launching the sprint from 250m out and easily holding off Moser to tie Girardengo's record of six victories.

Merckx's final Monument

With a seventh title now in his sights, Merckx opted to prepare for the 1976 edition of Sanremo at Italian stage race Tirreno–Adriatico, which, after a decade in the shadow of Paris–Nice, had been toughened up. 'The Cannibal' won a stage, but was outclassed in the overall standings by De Vlaeminck, leading to growing questions about Merckx's chances of adding a record seventh Sanremo title. 'Others didn't win a stage at all,' he responded to queries about his form. 'I don't think I'm in that bad a shape at the moment.'

As if to prove that he shouldn't be written off at the age of 30, Merckx remained close to the action up to the *capi*, where he began to test out the other members of a select lead group that featured De Vlaeminck and Moser. Coming to the Poggio, the launchpad for his previous triumphs, Merckx went hard again, opening up a gap that only new 20-year-old Belgian pro Jean-Luc Vandenbroucke managed to bridge. In the final sprint, Merckx was too canny and quick for the neophyte, who was later stripped of second place following a positive dope test.

Although it was clear Merckx's powers were on the wane, no one suspected that this seventh Sanremo success in just nine appearances would be the final major victory of his career. Winner of 445 races in total, he had a palmarès that compared favourably with those of Coppi and Anquetil combined. He had announced himself on the Via Roma in 1966, so it was entirely fitting that he bowed out in the same illustrious location with a quite uncharacteristic punch of his fist as he crossed the line.

In *La Gazzetta*, Bruno Raschi apologised in advance for his hyperbole, then heaped praise on Merckx, describing him as 'a guy blessed with unbelievable power and who seems to have been given the gift of immortality when it comes to the bike'. Merckx, said Raschi, had for the first time been like just another one of 200 riders at the start in Milan. 'But cycling has been returned to its former state. Eddy Merckx is once again the king of the bunch.'

He returned to defend his throne the following year, but, hampered by a chill, worked instead for teammate Patrick Sercu and trailed in ninety-sixth after Dutchman Jan Raas had put on a Merckx-like performance on the Poggio to finish just ahead of De Vlaeminck. Of more significance, though, was an appalling performance by the home favourites, some of whom were jeered at the finish.

The race, too, was under critical scrutiny. Sanremo's high profile ensured that, in addition to the major foreign teams, every professional team in Italy wanted to ride it. Worryingly, in terms of safety, the organisers let them. In 1977, 260 riders registered to start and 231 of them had taken to the line in Milan, 40 more than the previous year and only seven short of the all-time high, set in 1970. 'There are little riders in the field who have no right to be there,' complained Wladimiro Panizza, who holds the record for starts at the Giro d'Italia with 18 appearances. 'We spend all of our time trying to avoid crashing, without always managing to do so, gripping the brakes with fear in our hearts,' railed Felice Gimondi.

De Vlaeminck wasn't happy either, although his concern was with the route rather than the size of the field. 'When [Vincenzo] Torriani included the Poggio for the first time, Milan–Sanremo once again became the great Classic that it must always be. Nowadays, however, the Poggio isn't enough to split the best riders. The riders are getting used to what is now almost the only difficulty, as Capo Berta no longer presents a problem, and the race is becoming insipid,' said the 1973 champion. De Vlaeminck suggested a new route that ran inland from the coast over the Testico, near Alassio.

While the race's organisers mulled over these gripes, De Vlaeminck added two more Sanremo victories, outwitting young Italian sensation Giuseppe Saronni in 1978 and 1979. *La Gazzetta*'s Rino Negri described the Belgian's three victories on the Via Roma as 'a lot for a rider who isn't Merckx and isn't Italian'. He pointed out that, unlike many Italian riders, De Vlaeminck only tended to commit himself when he needed to and had worked incredibly hard to become a Classics star. He recalled how, as a young man, De Vlaeminck had done nightshifts in a factory so that he could train and race during the day, and thought nothing of riding home behind a motorbike having taken part in the Gent–Wevelgem Classic.

The introduction of the Cipressa

Complaints about the number of starters didn't result in any attempt by the organisers to rein in the size of the peloton – an astounding 271 riders started in 1981 and two more than that would line up in 1987. However, 1982 saw the first change to the route since the introduction of the Poggio in 1960. The addition of the Cipressa was designed to toughen up the finale, ensuring only the best Classics riders were in contention. Rising to 240m above San Lorenzo al Mare, the Cipressa is significantly higher than the Poggio, and comes 14km before it.

It begins with a tightish right-hand turn, the road then switching back and forth rather more gently than the Poggio. Cutting through olive groves, its slopes are hardly challenging, unless, of course, tackled in the big ring after 270km of racing. A narrow gateway next to the church at the top leads into the picturesque village of Cipressa, from where the road descends in similar fashion back to the coast. Its inclusion boosted the race distance to 294km, which was not a significant increase, but was enough to please the likely contenders for the title. However, by the time the race reached the Cipressa for the first time, all of those big names were out of contention.

Thirteen riders regarded mostly as no-hopers in a field 260-strong broke away after eight kilometres. Two teammates of race favourite Beppe Saronni instigated the move. Among those quick to join them was the world professional pursuit champion, Frenchman Alain Bondue, and his compatriot Marc Gomez, a pro for less than two months with Wolber. 'I was in a small team and we didn't have a leader, so the important thing was to show myself and the sponsors of the team,' said 27-year-old Gomez.

The group's lead stretched rapidly, reaching a quarter of an hour on the early slopes of the Turchino, where steady rain turned to hail as the temperature dropped. A series of crashes hampered the chase behind the escapees and led to a number of the favourites quitting due to the cold. Saronni was among them, explaining later that he had waited too long before getting a rain jacket, by which point his hands and arms were so cold he couldn't grip his bars. 'It was an unforgivable error,' he acknowledged.

Up ahead, the group of 13, blown along by a tailwind, had steadily shed riders until only Bondue, Gomez and Saronni's teammate Claudio Bortolotto remained at the front heading on to the Cipressa. The whole route was new to Gomez, who only knew at that point that there were 30km remaining. The rain had finally stopped, making racing a good deal easier for the bespectacled Frenchman, who attacked, gaining 200m as he dropped back down to the coast.

Sensing Bortolotto was flagging, track pursuiting ace Bondue jumped away from the Italian and ate up the ground to Gomez. 'I thought I'd beat him in a sprint, so for him to win, he'd have to drop me, so that was that – I'd do no more work. I let him lead up the Poggio,' Bondue told *Cycle Sport*. He knew the importance of the descent into Sanremo, and sprinted past Gomez to set the pace down it. But going around the first corner, with the roads still slippery, he skidded and lost momentum, allowing Gomez an opening. At the next corner, Bondue skidded again. Tentative when he needed to be bold, Bondue lost his chance.

Gomez rode down the Via Roma with the packed crowds wondering who he was. 'They must have been waiting for one of their heroes – Moser or Saronni. Instead they got an unknown. There was probably more noise than I realised but my memory is that it was very quiet. This was one of the most beautiful races in the world – how could I have won it?'

There was no chance of the big guns making such a mess the following year. Indeed, the likes of Moser, Saronni and Sean Kelly were so determined to keep a lid on the action that the race was rather lifeless for the opening 200km. Irishman Kelly increased pulses with an attack on Capo Berta, but it was Moser who brought it to life on the Cipressa, impressing with his speed up the climb, then astounding everyone with his risk-taking on the descent.

'The Sheriff's' acrobatics split the bunch, leaving most of the favourites at the front. The elastic between them stretched considerably on the big ring ascent of the Poggio, but it was not until they reached the false flat just short of the summit that it snapped, when world champion Saronni produced a bullet-like acceleration of the kind that had won him the rainbow jersey in 1982. 'His attack was so violent that he removed all hope of anyone else getting on his wheel,' said Italian sprinter Guido Bontempi, with even Saronni's arch-rival Moser admitting: 'He rode a race worthy of a true world champion.'

In 1984, two months on from setting a new mark for the world hour record in Mexico City, albeit aided by blood transfusions courtesy of Professor Francesco Conconi, Moser won *La Primavera* at the eleventh attempt. His victory mirrored Saronni's. France's Marc Madiot, Ireland's Stephen Roche and Scotland's Robert Millar opened a gap on the Poggio, only to see the rampant Moser bridge across to them and lead into the descent, where his daredevil acrobatics gave him the gap he needed.

By the mid-1980s, it was clear the riders' attitude towards *La Primavera* had changed. Better levels of fitness, equipment and roads meant the Turchino was no longer anywhere near as crucial to the final verdict as it had long been. The race assumed a standard pattern. A kamikaze break would form in the opening kilometres, gaining an advantage that could reach as much as 20 minutes or more. Once the peloton reached the coast, its speed would rise and the break would gradually yield, often quite quickly if there was a cross- or tailwind. The favourites would test each other out on the *capi*, go harder on the Cipressa, then all out on the Poggio, where a small group or solitary rider would slip away. The victories taken by Hennie Kuiper in 1985, Sean Kelly in 1986, Erich Maechler in 1987 and Laurent Fignon in both 1988 and 1989 all followed this template more or less.

Fignon's consecutive wins both came thanks to the irresistible power he demonstrated on the Poggio. On the first occasion the ponytailed Frenchman, who was rediscovering the form that had won him the Tour de France title in 1983 and 1984, broke clear near the top of the hill, where only second-year Italian pro Maurizio Fondriest was able to match him, but yielded in the two-up sprint.

Writing in his autobiography, *We Were Young and Carefree*, Fignon confesses he was surprised by Fondriest's performance, but knew he would still prevail. 'On the descent I used a cunning old man's trick; I swung wide out on the bends, pretending to be a poor descender. The idea was to let him come past so that he would make the pace on the straights. He fell for it like an amateur. On the television, the commentators didn't have any idea what was going on: I was totally in charge and deliberately saving my strength and they said I was "struggling". Idiots.' A year on, no one could match Fignon. 'On the Poggio he pedalled with a gear [53x15] that most would only use on the flat and for the rest of them the race was over,' Bruno Raschi wrote in *La Gazzetta*.

It was only when some unforeseen event occurred that the action varied from this gripping script, in which the tension gradually built up to the point where the best riders in the field had to decide where to make the one move that could win them the race. In 1990, a strong crosswind upset the calculations of the favourites, but provided two Italians with an opportunity before the Cipressa. Heading through Imperia, Angelo Canzonieri attacked and Gianni Bugno, then emerging as a grand tour contender, ignored established Sanremo logic by going with him. 'I realised straightaway that it was the key moment when Canzonieri attacked in Imperia. It's the kind of thing you sense when you're on the bike. He attacked just as the teams were taking a breather and the peloton was spreading out. Then, on the Cipressa, I noticed Canzonieri was struggling so I played my card,' Bugno explained as he became the first home winner since Moser in 1984.

The weather disrupted the favourites' plans the following year, too. All the talk leading into the 1991 race focused on the UCI's desire to make the use of helmets compulsory. The riders and teams were against the move on the grounds that helmets were still too bulky and uncomfortable, but they agreed to use them in Sanremo until a final decision was reached. The Saturday that followed the San Giuseppe feast day was perishingly cold and very wet, resulting in a string of crashes in the peloton, where many were no doubt grateful for their unwanted headgear.

Heading up the Turchino, the bulky form of Guido Bontempi accelerated off the front of the bunch with Carrera teammate Claudio Chiappucci tucked in on his wheel, followed by Dane Rolf Sørensen, Frenchman Charly Mottet, Spaniard Marino Lejarreta and Dutchman Adri van der Poel. It was a strong group, but Sanremo logic suggested it had formed too far out from the finish to threaten the expected contenders. However, Chiappucci, whose ever-present smile and second place in the Tour de France the previous season had made him a favourite among Italian fans, knew the Ligurian coastal roads well and had a plan with a sole objective: victory in Sanremo.

When the peloton upped its pace, the lead group responded. 'Then I put my plan into action,' Chiappucci explained. The Italian attacked hard on Capo Berta, riding everyone except for Sørensen off his wheel. 'He suffered on the Cipressa, but I didn't want to ride the last 20km alone, so I was happy to give everything I had on the Poggio, to respect my plan to the letter. Doing that makes me especially proud,' said Chiappucci, whose acceleration halfway up the Poggio killed off the Dane's hopes.

Some of the gloss was subsequently taken off this and Chiappucci's other successes when he admitted to an Italian prosecutor he had used the blood-boosting hormone EPO, although he later retracted his statement. Like Moser a few years earlier, Chiappucci had worked with Professor Conconi, who was accused of supplying riders with EPO. Although the charge was never proven and the case against Conconi was dropped in 2004, the judge overseeing the case said Conconi and two colleagues were 'morally guilty' of promoting doping among the riders they worked with, who included Sanremo winners Bugno and Chiappucci.

Although not a single Sanremo winner has ever tested positive in the obligatory post-victory test, the influence of EPO and other performance-enhancing products could be seen in the way that an increasing number of riders were able to cope with the extreme demands of the great Classics, such as Milan–Sanremo. From 1982, the year of the Cipressa's introduction, only the strongest riders tended to be in contention on this climb and the Poggio. However, from the mid-1990s onwards, the peloton was still a substantial size when the race reached the Poggio. Could better training methods and equipment have resulted in so noticeable a difference in such a short period of time?

Although there is no doubt of the impact doping had on professional cycling from the early 1990s onwards, experience, guts and fearlessness still made the difference on occasions. The 1992 edition of Sanremo was built up as the coronation of Moreno Argentin, a regular winner of

Classics in Belgium's Ardennes, but never better than fourth at Sanremo to that point.

Argentin's Ariostea team shackled all of his rivals as far as the Poggio, where, according to *La Gazzetta*, Argentin 'with five attacks from the anthology of cycling shredded the group ... He seemed to be moving as easily as the motorbikes in front of him, such was the rage that he was putting through the pedals.' Cresting the Poggio, Argentin had seven seconds on Maurizio Fondriest and Rolf Sørensen, and a handful more on 35-year-old Sean Kelly, whose Classic-winning days appeared to be over. This should have been enough.

Cycling's annals feature endless tales of brilliance on climbs, but on very few occasions does a rider's astounding ability going downhill rate a reference. Kelly's performance on the descent of the Poggio that afternoon is one that does. Watching the footage shot from the helicopter above, it is difficult to judge his speed and degree of risk. Having barrelled past Fondriest and Sørensen, Kelly devours the ground between himself and Argentin, who can't imagine anyone is going to catch him following his show of force moments earlier. Just inside the final kilometre, Kelly does exactly that. Although Argentin is no mug in a sprint, he is no match for a specialist like Kelly. As the Irishman celebrates what will be the final big win of his career, Argentin appears paralysed by shock. He will never win *La Primavera*.

The sprinters take over

After Pierino Gavazzi's bunch sprint success in 1980, the bunch's *puncheurs* had held sway, but the sprinters were inexorably closing in on them, led by charismatic Italian Mario Cipollini. With his long, gelled locks that led to him being dubbed 'The Lion King' and even 'Moussolini', Cipollini looked the most likely sprinter to end their drought after finishing second in 1994. However, and rather unexpectedly, when a 39-strong group charged into the finish in 1997, it was his long-term

German rival Erik Zabel who led them in. Just as surprisingly, the easygoing 26-year-old who had started his career in the Communist cycling academy in his native East Berlin, took almost as strong a grip on the race as he did on the Tour de France's points title, which he won a record six years in succession.

Zabel's victories were timely both in terms of his judgement of the sprint and also for his Telekom team, which had been in real danger of losing its very generous backer before the East Berliner claimed the first of his Tour green jerseys. He retained his title in 1998, an achievement legendary Belgian rider Rik Van Steenbergen said was worth three times his first success because of the pressure that was on him as favourite. Perhaps that pressure got to him a year later, when veteran Andrei Tchmil pipped him. Born in Siberia and resident on the shores of Lake Garda, Tchmil had represented Russia, Ukraine and Moldova before taking up Belgian citizenship. At 36 years and 57 days, Tchmil became Sanremo's oldest champion, 16 days older than 1985 winner Hennie Kuiper.

Zabel bounced back to become the only rider apart from Eddy Merckx to win consecutive Sanremo titles on two occasions – the incomparable Merckx achieved that feat three times. Asked to analyse his victories in the wake of his fourth success, Zabel said: 'The first was the most difficult because I didn't have the determination and confidence I have now; the second was the most surprising, I wasn't expecting it; the third was the simplest because it all went to plan; and this one … the most beautiful.'

Zabel went on to become a highly rated sprint coach following his retirement in 2008, working first for the American HTC-Columbia team and then for the Russian Katusha squad. In July 2013, his name appeared on a list of riders whose samples from the 1998 Tour de France had shown evidence of EPO use during retesting in 2004. The German subsequently admitted to doping between 1996 and 2004, the period covering both his Sanremo and Tour de France points title wins.

Zabel's fourth and final Sanremo victory in 2001, which moved him alongside Gino Bartali and behind only Merckx and Costante Girardengo in the all-time list, was unique as it was the first Sanremo that didn't cross the Turchino Pass, which had closed following a landslide. The alternative route took the riders over the much loftier Bric Berton (773m as against 532m), down to Sassello, then over the Colle del Giovo to meet the long-established route at Albisola Marina.

On paper, the significant increase in climbing should have worked against the sprinters. However, when the race followed the same route a year later the most renowned and flamboyant of them all finally took the title. Mario Cipollini had ridden *La Primavera* 13 times, finishing second twice, and had made no secret of the fact it was the race he wanted to win more than any other. When Zabel was held up by a crash just before the Cipressa, Cipollini wasn't to be denied. Set up perfectly by his Acqua & Sapone team, their tiger stripes reminiscent of the fake animal skins thrown down in front of 1970s fireplaces, Cipollini powered through, finishing with both arms flung high, a huge smile and the crowd chanting 'Mario! Mario!' By the end of the year he would be world champion, too.

After Paolo Bettini had provided a one-year hiatus from bunch sprint victories in 2003, the fastmen reasserted themselves a year later, although two of them came up short in embarrassing fashion. Alessandro Petacchi, who had delivered Cipollini with the lead-out that launched him to the world title in 2002, had subsequently emerged as the fastest and most consistent sprinter in the sport. In the early weeks of 2004, Petacchi swept all of his rivals before him and went into *La Classicissima* as the hottest of favourites at the head of a very powerful Fassa Bortolo team.

The race ran exactly to the plan drawn out by veteran Fassa Bortolo director Giancarlo Ferretti. Going into the final 1,500m, five white and blue jerseys were perfectly placed to set up their sprinter. Fabio Sacchi got them up to speed, Frank Vandenbroucke kept that momentum going until the kilometre banner, where Filippo Pozzato took over. He moved aside to let Marco Velo through, before Guido Trenti provided the final boost for Petacchi, who went to the front and realised, at the most crucial moment, that he had nothing left in his legs.

As the Italian faded to fourth, Zabel emerged and threw his arms high. But even as he was celebrating a fifth success, he glanced down to see that Oscar Freire's front wheel was edging past. Thanks to his track-style 'throw' for the line, the Spaniard beat the German by 11 thousandths of a second – or about 17cm.

Slated for his performance, Petacchi nonetheless took heart from it. 'Although I was disappointed to come fourth last year and other people interpreted it as a failure, it proved to me that I am capable of winning it … The course makes it appear simple, but it's a very stressful race because as a sprinter you have 290km of waiting and hoping that you have judged the breaks correctly, that there are no accidents or complications. And then when you get to Via Roma and the sprint, it's all over in an instant. These are considerations in every race, but the importance of Milan–Sanremo magnifies them. When you don't win Sanremo, your first thoughts are about how long you will have to wait until your next opportunity and how many opportunities you have left in your career.'

As it turned out, the Ligurian tropical bird fancier made amends 12 months later when he was the convincing winner on the Via Roma, his wife Chiara giving him a bright blue parrot as a reward. Another bunch sprint prompted more talk about Sanremo's route needing to be toughened up. Race organisers RCS intimated that a new and much tougher climb, the Pompeiana, would replace the Cipressa for the 2006 edition. Opinion on it was split, local rider Mirko Celestino saying: 'The sprinters aren't going to be happy, but I think the new route will make Sanremo tougher and more spectacular.'

Giancarlo Ferretti of Fassa Bortolo was among those unconvinced by the need for change: 'It seems absurd to me to make a race that is already 290km long even harder … I don't believe that seeing one or two riders get clear on this climb is going to make it more spectacular.

The beauty of Sanremo is that it's a straight battle between aggressive riders and sprinters.' Although change did finally come in 2008 with the introduction of the Le Manie climb, much to the relief of the peloton's top sprinters the traditional finish remained unaltered until Pompeiana replaced Le Manie on the 2014 route.

Among the best of those sprinters was 2004 winner Freire. As two-time Sanremo winner Miguel Poblet discovered back in the 1950s when he raced mostly for Italian teams, the Spanish focus is very much on stage racing. Consequently, Freire's exploits in one-day races were largely ignored in his homeland. Three times the world champion, Freire, who had a reputation for being clumsy and lacking in focus off the bike but transformed completely when on it, also notched three bunch sprint victories in Sanremo, all of them coming in the orange, blue and white colours of Dutch team Rabobank.

His Sanremo wins in 2007 and 2010 bookended two remarkable finishes. The first came at a new seafront finish on the Piazzale Carlo Dapporto. Fifteen riders went clear on the Poggio, including pre-race favourite Fabian Cancellara, who attacked two kilometres from the line. As the riders in the group all waited for each other to respond, the multiple world time trial champion churned his biggest gear around and never looked like being caught.

Cancellara, arguably the pre-eminent Classics rider of his generation, believes Sanremo is by far the most complicated of the Monuments in terms of strategy, explaining: 'Winning alone in a big race is always special but winning alone in Sanremo is like getting checkmate in a really long, hard game of chess. They always say it is the hardest to win but the easiest to finish and I agree. It's the toughest because there are so many key points – from the Poggio to the Cipressa, the downhill, the flat and the final run-in. And then meshing across that you have a whole number of different outcomes, from an individual rider winning to a bunch sprint to a small group. It's very hard to predict and there's very often never a second chance. All too often you have to play it all on one card.'

In 2008, the year Cancellara played his card at precisely the right moment, RCS finally responded to growing calls for a change to the route, introducing the climb of Le Manie at the 200km mark. It starts on the coast at Noli, although it is easy to miss the narrow archway on to it. The right-hand turn is so sharp that riders not in the peloton's vanguard are sure to lose almost all of their momentum, so positioning is crucial, particularly as the road doesn't get any wider as it corkscrews up the hillside behind Noli. The switchbacks are so tight the road passes by front doors one moment and the second-floor windows on the rear side of the same houses the next. It remains relentlessly steep until reaching a plateau four kilometres into the hills, where those who have been tailed off have a chance to recoup lost ground, before the road plunges down an equally narrow and precipitous lane to the coast.

For the 100th edition of *La Classicissima* in 2009, Britain had a realistic contender for the title for the first time since the 1960s. Cocky Manx sprinter Mark Cavendish had started the season well but had appeared to be struggling on the climbs during Tirreno–Adriatico, which led many to question his chances of staying the pace, particularly on Le Manie. Yet Cavendish had been cannily bluffing his way through Tirreno, winning sprints when he was expected to and falling back on the climbs when everyone expected him to, even though he and his Columbia-HTC team knew he was in the form of his life.

Many expressed astonishment when Cavendish not only took Le Manie in his stride, but was also in contention after the Cipressa and, more importantly, the Poggio. However, as his teammates attempted to set up the sprint for the Briton, Heinrich Haussler, an Australian whose father is German, caught the peloton unawares when he accelerated away on the left-hand side of the final straight. Haussler's intention was to lead out his Cervélo team leader Thor Hushovd for the sprint, but having opened a gap on the bunch, he just kept going.

With 200m left, Cavendish unleashed the kick that had made him the sport's most devastating finisher. Even as he exploded clear of the rest of the peloton, his deficit on Haussler looked too big to retrieve. But as the Australian started to tie up, Cavendish closed him down and 'threw' his bike at the line to win by half a wheel. 'I take a lot of desire to win from the fact that a lot of people write me off. A lot of people do not believe I can do what I can do,' Cavendish later said of his success.

Freire, Cancellara and Cavendish's victories supported the long-standing belief that Tirreno–Adriatico provides the best preparation for *La Primavera*. That position was long held by Paris–Nice, which attracted a strong field right from its foundation in 1933. However, in 1976, Tirreno's organisers toughened up the route of what was then a five-day stage race and which now extends to a full week. Eddy Merckx was among the big names immediately attracted to 'the race of the two seas', and when the Belgian went on to win his seventh Sanremo that year, Tirreno's standing rocketed.

Tirreno's advantage over Paris–Nice is primarily one of timing. While the final day of the French race falls a full week before Sanremo, the Italian event finishes five days before it. In addition, the weather for Tirreno is usually not as harsh as it can be for Paris–Nice, which not only begins in northern Europe but often features stages in the Massif Central, where winter can still have a firm grip in early March. Added together, these factors tend to result in the racing at Tirreno being a touch more competitive than it is in 'the race to the sun'.

Yet in the wake of Freire's third Sanremo victory, Paris–Nice struck back, thanks to two Australians who had made their home that race's finishing city. In 2011, Matt Goss not only became his country's first victor in *La Primavera*, but also ended a ten-year winning sequence for riders who had sharpened their form at Tirreno. His victory underlined that the descent off the Poggio is as crucial as the climb up it, when he tucked in behind Fabian Cancellara as the Swiss stormed down the hill and wiped out the advantage of lone breakaway Greg Van Avermaet. Sprinter Goss remained cool as the nine-man lead group sped into Sanremo, sitting on wheels as his rivals tried and failed to escape, then made a textbook move with 200m left, leaving

Cancellara and Philippe Gilbert in his wake. A year on, compatriot Simon Gerrans emulated him, and also got the better of Cancellara, who had instigated the winning break but was once again too tightly marked to escape and repeat his 2008 success.

Like those two victories for Australia, the 2013 edition of Milan–Sanremo proved that even after more than 100 years *La Classicissima* can still surprise. The long, hard winter of 2012/13 had not relented when the race got under way. Although it was cold and drizzly at the start in Milan, there were few indications of what was to come. There was talk of snow and possible diversions, but, as many pointed out, where can you divert a race that has to cross a mountain ridge to reach the sea?

The snow started to fall well before the Turchino Pass. By Ovada, it was so thick that race director Michele Acquarone had to call a halt. The team buses were called back to pick up the riders, many of whom assumed the race would be abandoned. But almost three hours later, and with the riders now on the coast at Cogoleto, the race restarted. Although Le Manie was, like the Turchino, removed from the route, that concession did not make racing much easier for riders who had been chilled to the point where many could barely grip the bars. The long spell on the buses had enabled them to thaw out, but driving rain and stubbornly low temperatures had quickly ensured most were as cold as they had been before halting.

The dropout rate was high, which scuppered everyone's tactical plans. To an extent the race resembled the epic edition of 1910, when it was every man for himself against the elements. After a short flurry of attacks on the Cipressa and Poggio, Britain's Ian Stannard and France's Sylvain Chavanel led the race into Sanremo. But a group headed by race favourites Fabian Cancellara and Peter Sagan closed them down. Swinging into the final straight on the Lungomare Italo Calvino, young Slovak sensation Sagan seemed to have the race won, but at the very last moment German sprinter Gerald Ciolek came off his wheel and flashed by to take the biggest win of his career. The most unpredictable of days had produced the most unexpected of winners. So far had the precocious Ciolek's star fallen that he was leading the South African MTN-Qhubeka team, which viewed selection for its first Monument as a success in itself. Team manager Doug Ryder, talking a mile a minute in his excitement at the start, could barely get a word out after the finish, such was his shock.

There was little sign of spring in 2014 either, although the temperature didn't drop quite far enough to turn persistent rain to snow. The organisers dropped Le Manie from the course and planned to replace it with a new climb in between the Cipressa and the Poggio, up to the village of Pompeiana. However, this attempt to toughen up the finale had to be shelved following a landslide in the weeks before the race, which subsequently took place on the traditional route. Vincenzo Nibali attempted to make up for the absence of these difficulties by applying pressure on the sprinters and their teams with a daring attack on the Cipressa, and a thrilling descent off it, that enabled him to attack the Poggio on his own. But the future Tour de France winner's margin was only a dozen seconds on a group that contained past winners Ciolek, Cancellara and Cavendish, and the Italian was soon swallowed up as 30-odd riders swept into Sanremo. Reigning world champion Cavendish opened up first, but couldn't respond as Alexander Kristoff burst from the middle of the pack. The Norwegian sprinter was still going clear as he hit the line, two bike lengths ahead of Cancellara, who was thumping his bars with anger at finishing second for the third time in four years, and Britain's Ben Swift.

Kristoff had the tables turned on him 12 months later when he led out the sprint from a distance, only to see John Degenkolb flash past him in the last few metres. The sprinters fought it out again in 2016, when the finish switched back to the Via Roma. Victory went to Arnaud Démare, who recovered from a crash at the foot of the Cipressa to get back up to the lead group coming into the finish and then powered past rivals, disrupted by race favourite Fernando Gaviria crashing 500m from the line. Démare was the first French winner of a Monument since Laurent Jalabert clinched the Tour of Lombardy in 1997 and the first to win Sanremo since Jalabert's 1995 success.

Yet, just when it seemed that the decision to drop Le Manie and to push any thoughts about the climb to Pompeinana into a siding had ensured that the peloton's sprinters would always have an edge on this most finely balanced of finales, the momentum tipped away from them in 2017 and towards a new generation of *puncheurs*. Peter Sagan, the punchiest of sprinters, triggered the winning move with a blistering attack on the Poggio. Michał Kwiatkowski set off in pursuit, but the Pole needed a further injection of pace from Julian Alaphilippe to bridge up to Sagan before the crest of this key climb. The trio flew down on to the Via Roma, where Sagan led out the sprint from the front. Maybe the Slovak had burned too many matches with his attack on the Poggio, or perhaps he had simply forgotten from their many duels during their junior days how fast Kwiatkowski can be in a sprint, but he was pipped by the Pole. The trio were so close to each other as they crossed the line you could have thrown a sheet over them, Kwiatkowski's final 'throw' of his bike giving him the narrowest of victories.

After years of trying to break the peloton's shackles on both the Cipressa and the Poggio, Vincenzo Nibali finally escaped on the final climb in 2018. 'The Shark of Messina' reached the summit with a dozen seconds in hand, which was enough for a supreme descender like him to maintain his advantage into Sanremo and all the way up the Via Roma to the line, where he gave the home nation its first success in *La Classicissma* for a dozen years. Nibali was in the mix again the following season, when an acceleration by Julian Alaphilippe caused a split near the front of a very stretched-out line of riders on the Poggio, a group of 10 coming together in Sanremo, where Matej Mohorič led out. He erroneously thought his Bahrain teammate Sonny Colbrelli was among them, but instead set Alaphilippe up perfectly for the final dash, the Frenchman finishing a bike length clear of Oliver Naesen and Kwiatkowski.

Sanremo retained its place as the year's first Monument in the Covid-affected 2020 season, taking place on the second weekend of August, a week after Strade Bianche, which had been won by Wout van Aert. Sixth the previous year in what was only his third appearance in Jumbo-Visma yellow colours, the Belgian began as favourite for what was, at 305 kilometres, the longest edition in history, thanks to roadworks on the Turchino pass that forced the introduction of a new, more inland route to the sea via the Colle di Nava, which missed out much of the coastal road, including the three *capi*. This alteration and the blazing heat of summer didn't cool the fervour of the *puncheurs*, though, and most obviously of Alaphilippe. The Frenchman was untouchable on the ascent of the Poggio, but the effort he'd made to distance van Aert took its toll on the descent where, he later confessed, he lost his lucidity. His raggedness on the tight, technical descent allowed the Belgian to make up the ground he'd lost and they approached the finish together, where van Aert just had the edge in the sprint.

Sanremo has been decried by some as a race where little happens all day and then develops into a predictable duel between sprinters and *puncheurs*, yet those racing it describe it as the hardest Monument to win, because the margins between the best riders are so small that any misjudgement can prove fatal, especially going up and down the Poggio. In short, there are opportunities for other types of rider if they've got the form to be in the mix at the crest of this little hill and the nous to make the best of being in this position, which explains the successes of Jasper Stuyven and Matej Mohorič in 2021 and 2022, respectively.

On the first occasion, the Belgian, a decent bunch sprinter who's also quite punchy, appeared one of the riders least likely to win when a dozen-strong group that included Alaphilippe, van Aert and Mathieu van der Poel, three of the most dynamic riders from a new generation of riders who thrive on instinct and flair, zig-zagged down towards Sanremo. As their pace eased a touch almost at the foot of the Poggio, Stuyven sensed his chance. He accelerated away, Søren Kragh Andersen the only one able to bridge up to him. Approaching the line, Stuyven finessed his Danish rival, sitting tight on Kragh's wheel, looking back to see the group closing, before accelerating again, his final burst just enough to hold off Australian sprinter Caleb Ewan.

While that was crafty, Mohorič took his most renowned attribute to another level. The Slovenian was a former junior and under-23 world road champion who was renowned for his invention of the 'Mohorič supertuck' position on descents, whereby he shifted forwards off his saddle and crouched over his top tube in order to be as aerodynamic as possible. It became commonly used within the peloton until banned by the UCI from April 2021. However, the Slovenian had another trick up his sleeve. He'd seen how mountain bikers use a dropper post, a seatpost that could be moved up for optimal pedalling when climbing or down to allow a more comfortable and aero position when descending. Having finished close to Sanremo's frontrunners in the three previous seasons, he believed this would give him a decisive edge.

The Slovenian champion's first task, though, was to be near the front at the top of the Poggio. He managed that, going over in fifth place, right behind Tadej Pogačar, van Aert, van der Poel and Kragh Andersen. He quickly cut past them to get to the front, dropped his saddle, almost coming a cropper in the gutter as he did so, then flew clear. While not as smooth and controlled as Nibali's descent off the Civiglio in the 2015 Tour of Lombardy, his on-the-limit style was equally effective. Once in Sanremo, Mohorič engaged a huge gear, his comparatively slow cadence belying the speed he was travelling at. No one could catch him. Mohorič and his dropper post had won *La Classicissima*.

Stuyven's and Mohorič's victories underlined what makes Milan–Sanremo such a remarkable event. No one would ever consider launching a race of such a huge length nowadays, but Sanremo remains both special and vital to the sport. 'That's because of the history, because of the tradition, because of the mystery,' says Marco Pastonesi, formerly of *La Gazzetta dello Sport*. 'It seems the same old race, but every time there's something different. It depends on the road, on the weather, on the riders. I think it gives the riders a special feeling. They start in Milan, in the city, which is still cloaked in winter, and in the middle of the race they pass into a different dimension. They pass through the very narrow tunnel at the top of the Turchino and they find themselves at the seaside, where the air is different, the colours are different, the whole atmosphere is different. And that's when the race really starts. All of the difficulties are in that final section and it builds up like a thriller.'

PART V

THE TOUR OF FLANDERS –
VLAANDERENS MOOISTE

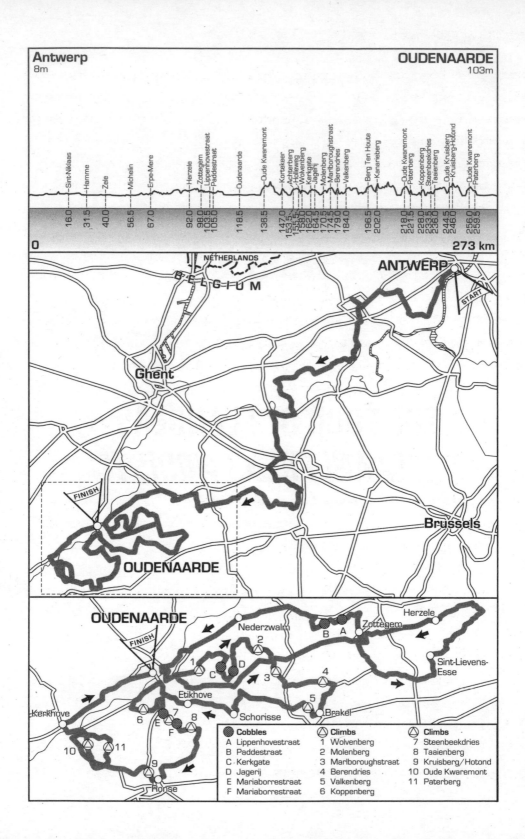

17

EMANCIPATION FOR FLANDERS

Football may be the world's sport, but in Flanders cycling rules, if only for five weeks between the end of February and early April. According to modern-day king of the Classics Fabian Cancellara, 'When you go to Flanders, you go into another world, a world where people have such passion for this one-day race', that race being the Ronde van Vlaanderen – the Tour of Flanders, the last of the Monuments to be established.

Once described as 'the Cup Final and the Grand National rolled into one', the Ronde is indelibly entwined with the Flemish psyche. Founded in 1913, when everyone who wanted to be anyone in Belgium spoke French, and Dutch was a language reserved for the dinner table or for work in the fields, over the past century it has played an extremely significant role in re-establishing both the language and the identity of the Flemish people.

On the fourteenth Sunday of the year, up to 800,000 Flemings line muddy lanes and tight, cobbled climbs for *Vlaanderens Mooiste*, Flanders' Finest, a celebration not only of the region's passion for cycling, but of all things Flemish. Mussels, chips and beer may be the most obvious passions, but on a more fundamental level it evokes 'national' pride.

As for the Ronde itself, Cancellara says: 'You have left, you have right, you have down, you have up, you have climbs with cobbles, climbs without cobbles, you have everything. It is a mix of everything. You have to be aware of everything. For me, it's the biggest challenge you can get in a one-day race during the entire season.'

As with many of the other great events on the cycling calendar, the Ronde emerged from a desire to promote a newspaper, in this case *Sportwereld*. The race's official history describes how the key moment in the race's foundation came in the summer of 1912, just a few days after Odile Defraye had become the first Belgian rider to win the Tour de France. In early August, print company owner August De Maeght met with young sports journalist Karel Van Wijnendaele, then working for a publication called *Sportvriend*, to gauge his interest in working for *Sportwereld*, which was about to be launched.

Van Wijnendaele, a passionate cycling fan who had started off as a racer but turned to writing when he realised he didn't have the talent to amount to anything in the saddle, hesitated initially, but soon signed up and enlisted several of his colleagues to work on the new title. Perhaps not auspiciously, *Sportwereld*'s yellow-papered first edition appeared on Friday 13 September, 1912, the day before the Championship of Flanders race.

As well as the race's official history, almost every account of the Ronde's early years relates the story of this meeting and, subsequently, goes on to outline the predominant role Van Wijnendaele played in establishing and widening the appeal of the race. However, in May 2013, little more than a month after the Ronde's centenary edition, historian Stijn Knuts and Pascal Deleye, a professor of sports history at the University of Leuven, revealed that there was a third man at that meeting in August 1912, and he played a much more fundamental role in establishing the race.

Leon – or, according to his birth certificate, Leo – Van den Haute was the son of a notary born in Hemiksem, just south of Antwerp, in October 1887. Sent to a Jesuit college in Etterbeek for the best French education, he became friends with Marcel Dupuis and Paul Beving. All three would end up writing about cycling in *Sportwereld*. Van den Haute's first job was as a wax and varnish salesman, but he also began to contribute to cycling magazines. In 1909, he became the Brussels correspondent of weekly magazine *Sportvriend*, where he came into contact with Van Wijnendaele.

When he was considering investing in a new sports title, August De Maeght's first approach was to Van den Haute, who would provide it with business and financial acumen, as well as a huge amount of passion. Both men then went to Van Wijnendaele with the aim of persuading him to oversee *Sportwereld*'s editorial output. Once they had lured him on board, Van Wijnendaele was soon appointed editor of the fledgling title, taking up that role on 1 January 1913.

By that point, Van den Haute was already considering establishing a Tour of Flanders, with Paris–Roubaix as his inspiration. It is likely that he also had some experience of working on the Circuit of Flanders, which was organised by the Cyclists' Association of East Flanders between 1908 and 1910. In the latter two years, the race was backed by *Sportvriend*. According to Knuts and Deleye, writing in cycling history magazine *Etappe* in May 2013, 'As a director with experience of organising competitions and having a nose for business, Van den Haute also realised that a Flemish sports newspaper and a Tour of Flanders could promote each other.'

On 17 February 1913, *Sportwereld* unveiled the Tour of Flanders, announcing the race would take place on 25 May 1913. Van den Haute's commitment to the project in the three months between the announcement and race day was total. As well as organising the finances, he sorted out the route, a task that was not without complications as the towns of Lokeren and Oudenaarde refused the race passage, or at least demanded the race was neutralised when it passed through. Oudenaarde's reluctance to welcome the Ronde is particularly notable as it is now the proud home of the event's finish and of the Tour of Flanders museum.

In the days immediately before the race, Van den Haute put out the signs marking the route, decided on the position of control points and checked the condition of the roads, all of which makes it harder to understand why someone with such a fundamental role has been all but erased from the Ronde's history. Knuts and Deleye proposed two theories. 'One hypothesis is that an error in the first biography of Van Wijnendaele was invariably taken up by other media. A second hypothesis is that Van Wijnendaele did not want his own glory taken away,' they suggest. Yet they went on to point out that Van Wijnendaele did give full credit to Van den Haute in the pages of *Sportwereld* for the essential role he had played.

In 1921, shortly before the fifth edition of the Ronde, Van Wijnendaele wrote: 'Leon Van den Haute, you have every right to be proud of your work as organiser and leader of the Tour of Flanders!' In 1932, the year after Van den Haute's death, Van Wijnendaele penned a tribute to his 'best of best friends … the never forgotten creator of the Tour of Flanders: Leon van den Haute'. Ultimately, Knuts and Deleye came to the conclusion that, 'Leon Van den Haute was the man behind the scenes. Karel Van Wijnendaele was the marketing man.'

Born Carolus Ludovicus Stayaert in Torhout, near Bruges, Van den Haute's sidekick was the fifth of 15 children. His father died when he was 18 months old and his mother married a farmer who lived near the castle at Wijnendaele, just a few kilometres from Torhout. A bright boy, he remained at school until the age of 14 thanks to the support of his mother and a local priest. He then worked with his stepfather on the farm, but eventually reaped the benefit of his extended education by becoming a notary's clerk in Torhout. By now in his early twenties and very committed to a passion for cycling, he began to write for sports titles across Flanders under the pen-name Karel Van Wijnendaele.

Once appointed to the editorship of *Sportwereld*, Van Wijnendaele, who favoured a racy looking waxed moustache that turned up at the ends, was determined not only to promote cycling in whatever way he could, but also the Dutch language, which had only been recognised as Belgium's official tongue alongside French in 1898. 'We thought there was a lot we could do in the area. We wanted to publish a paper to speak to our own Flemish people in their own language and give them confidence as Flandrians,' he later explained. His objective was no less than the emancipation of the Flemish people, whose language and culture had been suppressed by Belgium's French-speaking elite since the country's establishment in 1830.

The desire to popularise both the written and spoken use of the Dutch language gained pace in the nineteenth century. In 1860, Roman Catholic priest and poet Guido Gezelle penned a verse of defiance, that began: "You say Flemish will fade away: It shan't! That Walloon twaddle will have its way: It shan't!" while Van Wijnendaele drew heavily on the literary works of Hendrik Conscience, who had scandalised his family and society in general when he wrote a book in Flemish in the late 1830s. His French-born father considered the action so vulgar, he cast him out of their home. In 1838, Conscience penned his most famous work, *De Leeuw van Vlaanderen* (The Lion of Flanders), a historical novel that took significant liberties with established facts – the Dutch-speaking hero of the book, Robert of Béthune, was not actually a Dutch-speaker – but also laid out the qualities of the Flemish people, who were presented as hard-working, tough, blessed with incredible willpower and proud of their land and heritage.

Inspired by Conscience's works, Van Wijnendaele decided he needed to provide the Flemish people with their own sporting heroes, which meant raising the profile of events from which those heroes could emerge, and particularly the Ronde. In the early weeks of 1913, Van Wijnendaele sat down with Van den Haute and their editorial team, spread out a map of Flanders and sketched out a route that circled the provinces of East and West Flanders. Starting in Gent, it headed east to Sint-Niklaas, then south to Aalst, Zottegem and Oudenaarde, then on to Kortrijk and Ieper, then turned north to the coast and Ostend, went south from there to Roeselare, then back north to Bruges, before finishing with four laps of a track around a pond in Mariakerke, a suburb on the northern edge of Gent where British rider Tom Simpson would live 50 years later. It covered 324km on roads that were mostly cobbled, but often had a cinder track running alongside them.

The choice of Gent for the start and finish was deliberate and even provocative. The French-speaking elite held sway in the historic city deep in Flanders, but *Sportwereld*'s directors hoped to subvert this control by attracting ordinary Flemish men and women to the start in the Korenmarkt. The route subsequently ran through all the major cities of East and West Flanders because, wrote Van Wijnendaele, 'All Flemish cities had to contribute to the emancipation of the Flemish people.'

Although *Sportwereld* promoted the event hard up to race day on Sunday, 25 May 1913, just 37 riders, all of them Belgian, lined up at the start in the Korenmarkt square that morning. At quarter past six, Van den Haute signalled them to the start line, and Van Wijnendaele shouted: 'Gentlemen, you may start.'

Twelve hours and three minutes later, seven riders came on to the track at Mariakerke. Two promptly collided with each other and crashed to the ground – some reports suggest at least one of the stricken riders ended up in the mid-track pond – leaving five to contest the sprint. Paul Deman led them over the finish line having covered the 324km course at an average speed of slightly less than 27km/h. His prize was 500 Belgian francs, the equivalent of about six months' salary for a teacher in pre-war Belgium.

In a number of ways the race was a success. For a start, Van den Haute and Van Wijnendaele had got it off the ground and showcased some of the best of the young Flemish talent, headed by Deman, who would go on to win Bordeaux–Paris the following season and Paris–Roubaix in 1920. Spectators also turned out in respectable numbers, but the takings at the finish in Mariakerke were only half what had been expected, leaving *Sportwereld* to fill the gap when it came to paying out the prizes.

Crucially, though, the French manufacturers such as Alcyon and La Française that dominated the sport in that era refused to release any of their riders to compete, including Tour champion Defraye and the rest of Belgium's best-known names. Winning a new race in Flanders didn't offer these French teams much in terms of publicity, while at the same time the roughness of the course with its uneven cobbles and treacherous tram tracks made it a dangerous test.

It was mainly thanks to Van den Haute's determination to continue backing the event that the second edition took place in 1914. In the hope of attracting a stronger field by moving the race to an earlier start date, it took place on 22 March over a course that was significantly shorter at 280km. Once again, though, the French manufacturers refused to release their riders to compete, including defending champion Deman, who had been signed up by Alcyon. However, Deman's teammate Marcel Buysse refused to be cowed by his French employers. He knew that having won six stages and finished third overall at the Tour de France the previous year, he was in a strong position. 'Paris is a long way off. They won't be there to stop me from riding ... and from winning,' he declared. Buysse was right on both counts. A proven sprinter at the very highest level, he claimed the title at the new finish on the track at Evergem, just north of Gent.

Van Wijnendaele was delighted the race had a champion of the stature of Buysse, but was concerned his paper was still struggling to make it pay. He later reflected: '*Sportwereld* was so young and so small for the big Ronde we wanted. We had bitten off more than we could chew. It was hard seeing a band of second-class riders riding round Flanders, scraping up a handful of centimes to help cover the costs. The same happened in 1914. No Van Hauwaert, no Masselis, no Defraye, no Mosson, no Mottiat, no Van den Berghe – all forbidden to take part by their French bike companies.'

The post-war Ronde

The outbreak of war meant it was five years before the third edition of the Ronde took place, partly as a result of a controversial decision by the

Belgian Cycling Federation to ban all racing. Dozens of cycling's leading names died during the conflict, and Paul Deman, the Ronde's first champion, went close to becoming another casualty.

He continued to train during the hostilities, but at the same time was spying for the Allies behind enemy lines, carrying messages back and forth to Belgium's neutral neighbour, the Netherlands. On his fifteenth mission, Deman was arrested by the Germans and held in prison at Leuven. Condemned to death by firing squad, he was saved by the Armistice and was later decorated by the Belgians, French and British for his wartime service.

During the war, *Sportwereld* was replaced by *De Telegraaf*, a general information sheet that focused on the war rather than sport. However, Van den Haute and Van Wijnendaele did manage to stage a 'surrogate' edition of the Ronde on the track at Evergem. On 22 August 1915, 26 riders took part in a 150km race around the track. Leon Buysse, who was no relation to reigning Flanders champion Marcel, won the event. Staging an event in the years following that was next to impossible, as the Germans requisitioned the rubber needed to make bike tyres, while wooden tracks were ripped up for fuel.

Like Paris–Roubaix, much of the Ronde's route was located in areas most affected by the war, particularly around Ieper (Ypres) in Western Flanders, which had been one of the principal battlegrounds throughout the four-year conflict. According to Van Wijnendaele, the Ronde could easily have disappeared from the post-war racing calendar, but Van den Haute once again pushed hard to make it happen, 'despite almost insurmountable and difficult circumstances'.

The third edition took place on a much-shortened and war-damaged course in March 1919. Victory went to 1914 runner-up Henri Van Leerberghe, who came to the race with a point to prove. An erratic performer, the ex-soldier had been the butt of his rivals' jokes during an afternoon's training at the new Palais des Sports in Brussels. Van Wijnendaele, who managed many of the best Flemish riders, was on hand too and bluntly advised him to give up and do something else. Instead, Van Leerberghe, nicknamed 'The Death Rider of Lichtervelde' because he used to tell his rivals he would ride them into an early grave during races or would die trying, arrived at the start of the Ronde on a one-speed bike that was hardly suitable for a course that now included two cobbled climbs, the Tiegemberg and Kwaremont.

On the second of the two climbs, Van Leerberghe set a pace that none of his three companions in the lead group could follow. Unfortunately, having broken clear, he came upon a train that had stopped on a level crossing. As would be the case just four weeks later when the leading trio at Paris–Roubaix faced the same obstacle, he calmly shouldered his bike, walked through the train and carried on. He finished almost a quarter of an hour ahead of the pack on the track at Gentbrugge, which he circled slowly, accepting the acclaim of the crowd and, Flemish cycling legend has it, a beer or two courtesy of the track director. He eventually swayed across the line shouting, 'I'm half a day ahead. You can all go home now!' Van Leerberghe's prize was three kilos of beef and two bottles of wine, which it appears he would have relished.

Although Van Wijnendaele may not have approved of Van Leerberghe's rather eccentric behaviour, the 1919 winner of the Ronde encapsulated the race director's idealised image of a 'Flandrien'. These riders, who in Van Wijnendaele's opinion could only come from the provinces of West and East Flanders because those from Antwerp, Limburg and Flemish Brabant were simply not tough enough, were brutally strong, uncomplaining and, to an extent, rode in an uncomplicated way, depending more than anything on exceptional power. Van Leerberghe's tactic, if it could be called that, was to ride as hard as he could for as long as he could. Generally, it got him nowhere, but two podium finishes in the Ronde demonstrated his approach could be effective if the race was tough enough to match his bone-headedly simple tactic. On the devastated roads of post-war Flanders, the Ronde undoubtedly was.

Van Wijnendaele's ideal of the 'Flandriens' had been formed in the immediate pre-war years. He had raced on the track under the name of Mac Bolle in order to hide his competitive career from his wife, but he quickly moved into rider management. In 1912, he led a team of rugged Flemish track riders on a tour of Europe's major six-day races. After the war, he broadened his scope, travelling for a number of years to the United States with his track riders on the Red Star Line ships that sailed from Antwerp.

The 'Flandriens' were a sensation on the American tracks, their never-say-die approach ensuring they not only managed to cope with the extreme mental and physical demands of six days of almost constant competition, but finished them triumphant more often that not. As track racing's importance faded, from the mid-1920s, Van Wijnendaele focused his attention more on the road, where the mythical status of the 'Flandriens' continued to grow, and was still much debated in the 1960s, when Walter Godefroot was one of several anointed with that status. 'A true Flandrien,' said Godefroot, 'is a man who knows how to fight because he has always been dominated by someone: the Walloons, who owned the industries and had all the culture, or the Dutch and Germans, who wanted the land itself.'

Before the Great War, foreign riders and teams, particularly the most illustrious of all in France, didn't hide their dislike for the Ronde. When Buysse had won the title in 1914, *L'Auto* devoted just a single line to his success, declaring simply, 'Marcel Buysse won the Tour of Flanders for Alcyon.' Following the war, though, their attitude had to change simply because in those straitened times bike manufacturers needed to sell as many units as possible and Belgium was becoming a big market. French company J. B. Louvet were the first to take the plunge, sending Jean Brunier and brothers Henri and Francis Pélissier to Gent for the start of the 1922 edition. Aware that they needed some local talent to back up their French stars, they signed up 1919 Liège–Bastogne–Liège champion Léon Devos.

As the lead group headed up the 2.5km cobbled climb of the Kwaremont, Henri Pélissier noted the ease with which the strapping Devos coped with the climb. Riding up alongside him, he is reported to have whispered, 'Today, Léon, you are the best! You attack and I will keep a rein on the peloton!' Pélissier was as good as his word. Devos finished seven minutes clear with the three Frenchmen filling the next three places.

While Van Wijnendaele must have been pleased to see his race attracting riders from beyond Belgium's borders, his reaction to the first foreign victory in the Ronde underlined the limit of his benevolence towards foreign riders. When Swiss Heiri Suter outsprinted Flemish riders Charles De Ruyter and Albert Dejonghe at Gentbrugge in 1923, Van Wijnendaele lambasted the local riders for their parochial approach, telling them they needed to gain experience abroad. He also criticised their training methods, even though the 'get the kilometres in' approach they tended towards chimed very much with his own views on training. In the wake of Suter's victory, he changed tack, insisting Flemish riders needed to train more on the track in order to gain the 'intrinsic speed' of the Swiss.

Van Wijnendaele's attitude did a huge disservice to Suter, who was rightly regarded as the Fabian Cancellara of his day. Victory at Paris–Roubaix a fortnight later made him the first man to complete that famous double, which Cancellara emulated in 2010 and again in 2013. The two Swiss are the only non-Belgians to have achieved this feat. The youngest of six cycling brothers, Suter was one of the outstanding Classics riders of the inter-war period. Incredibly, his career extended across all of those years, beginning in 1918 and finishing in 1941, when he was 42 years old. He had plenty of track experience and honed his training based on that – he rode short distances at a very high intensity, which boosted his finishing speed.

Van Wijnendaele's criticism had the desired effect on the Flemish riders. More than quarter of a century would pass before another foreign rider celebrated victory in the Ronde. However, bizarre scheduling also helped local riders to maintain their grip on the Ronde's crown. Up until 1931, the Flemish Classic tended to take place either on the same day or within a day or two of Milan–Sanremo. This didn't help either event, as the Belgians stuck with Flanders and the Italians with Sanremo. French interest flitted between the two, although most French manufacturers and riders were indifferent to both events, such was the extent of their national calendar.

The stay-at-home attitude of the French was also underpinned by the horror stories related by those French riders who did venture across the border. They told of racing packs of powerfully built Belgians who could ride all day on the flat and were blessed with a rapid turn of speed in a sprint. These were the qualities that counted in a region where the two-kilometre ascent of the Kwaremont was one of the longest climbs.

When Frenchman André Leducq got permission to take part in the 1926 edition of the Ronde during his military service, he decided to test the reputation of the local riders and cooked up a strategy with his friend Henri Sausin. 'We planned to stay in the wheels for a while, to get used to the speed, then, when we had warmed up, we would go to the front and show the Flemish riders what we were capable of,' he told journalist Raymond Huttier. Only when the pair registered for the race in Gent did they fully realise what they were up against. 'What funny looking guys they were. They were all the size of wardrobes and we looked like little boys next to them. It wasn't reassuring.'

Leducq, who would go on to the win the Tour de France on two occasions, struggled to follow the pace set from the start. 'I could never advance beyond twenty-fifth position and, in the end, having reached my limit, I was really happy, with Sausin, to accompany Gerard Debaets, who had decided to abandon the race in front of his café in Kortrijk,' he said. The French duo were at least in very good company. Debaets had taken the title in 1924 and would do so again in 1927, before going on to enjoy a long career as a six-day rider in North America, where he won 17 events, seven of those successes coming in New York's prestigious Madison Square Garden.

Hills and cobbles

Nowadays, the Ronde is renowned for its *hellingen*, the 16 steep and mostly cobbled climbs that decide the race. But the early editions of the Ronde had a very different profile. No more than four of the now famous *bergs*, or hills, appeared in any one edition before the Second World War. In 1928, the Kruisberg at Ronse was added to the course, with the finish moved to Wetteren. Two years later, the Edelareberg at Oudenaarde was also included. From 1932 through to 1949, these two hills and the Kwaremont were the only climbs on a route that remained substantially cobbled until the post-Second World War years.

The nature of those cobbles had changed, though. Roundish, beach-sourced cobbles were used widely for road building throughout Europe and North America up to the nineteenth century. During the later decades of that century, many were replaced by quarried granite setts, often called 'Belgian blocks' because most had been quarried there. Unlike cobbles taken from beaches and waterways, which were smooth but often resulted in an uneven and gappy surface, the granite stones were cut – often roughly – and could be placed fairly snugly together so there was little space between them, providing an easier passage for vehicles of all types. Evidence of the long-lasting qualities of these igneous blocks can be found on the quays of New York and other American ports, which are still covered with 'cobbles' quarried in Belgium.

The Dutch word for these granite blocks is *kassei*, which is believed to come from the Latin 'via calciata' – a road covered with stone. Although they offer a smoother ride than beach-sourced cobbles, *kassei*-surfaced roads still provide a jarring experience on a bike. The sport's top riders use speed to alleviate this discomfort to an extent, which would explain why Leducq and Sausin were so surprised by the rate at which Belgian riders started the Ronde. Riding this way undoubtedly made racing harder from the perspective of endurance, but is also a fundamental reason why Flemish riders became and remain so adept on this kind of surface, dominating on Roubaix's cobbles as well as at the Ronde.

The unforgiving nature of these roads made anything more than a few cobbled *hellingen* unnecessary. But when the Ronde's riders came to them, these hills offered a very different test. Steep ramps on climbs like the Kwaremont shatter momentum, especially for those riders who aren't at the very front of a group and don't have a clear road ahead of them. A slip by one rider can cause a domino effect behind, particularly when it is wet and difficult to maintain traction on the uneven surface. Long before crowd control barriers were introduced, riders usually attempted to avoid the cobbles on the hills, sticking instead to the cinder or gravel tracks at the edges of the road that were normally used by pedestrians, scattering the fans packed along them.

During the inter-war years, sales of *Sportwereld* soared. It was not unusual for the paper to sell 200,000 copies in the wake of a big race or football match. At the same time, coverage of sport and news in Dutch expanded, with a host of other titles and press agencies appearing. On the back of this, Van Wijnendaele's profile rose substantially, too, to the point where he became more renowned and popular in Flanders than any of the riders he wrote about. Reports from the 1930s talk of the crowds along the route of the Ronde chanting 'Koarle! Koarle!', as Van Wijnendaele was familiarly known, when his car passed by.

His control over Belgian cycling as a whole also increased. In 1930, when the Tour de France switched to national rather than trade teams, he became the selector and team manager for Belgium. Given Van Wijnendaele's leaning towards all things Flemish, it was no surprise that French-speaking riders didn't feature regularly in the Belgian line-up, and those that did were under instructions to do whatever the team's Flemish leaders asked of them. Van Wijnendaele wasn't subtle about his favouritism, but his team's results made it difficult to criticise him. They claimed the overall title in 1935 and 1936 thanks to Romain Maes and

Sylvère Maes, respectively. The latter also claimed the last pre-war edition of the Tour in 1939.

During the 1930s, many other Belgians who emerged initially at the Ronde went on to achieve great things at the Tour and other international races, helped by the fact that calendar clashes were more infrequent. This meant riders could tackle Milan–Sanremo, the Ronde and Paris–Roubaix in successive weeks, although most generally opted to take on two of the three. Sanremo and Roubaix were the most prestigious and attracted the best fields, but the Ronde was increasingly seen as the best way to prepare for Roubaix thanks to its cobbles and unpredictable weather. That didn't mean, however, that any foreigner was capable of breaking the tight Flemish grip on the Ronde's crown. Flanders had a legion of sprinters who were also hard-nosed *rouleurs*.

The 1930 Ronde champion Frans Bonduel was exactly this type of rider, as was Jean Aerts, who won 11 stages at the 1935 Tour and that year's World Championship. Aerts always started Flanders as one of the favourites, but never finished better than third, which he achieved in 1931. He and Dutchman Cesar Bogaert were outwitted by Romain Gijssels, another of those Flemish *routiers-sprinteurs*, as the French labelled riders who were all-round talents. Gijssels went on to become the first rider to defend the title successfully.

His triumph was owed partly to a serious error committed by Bogaert. Coming into the finish at Wetteren, the Dutchman started to sprint from a very long way out, only to realise the banner he thought marked the finish line was a cigarette advertisement. As Bogaert's legs gave up on him, Gijsssels steamed past to claim victory. A year later, there was no such controversy. Gijssels broke clear of his rivals in the rolling hills of the Flemish Ardennes and was three minutes clear at the line. He could have completed a hat-trick in 1933 but got his sprint all wrong, waiting too long before delivering his final kick, by which time Alfons Schepers was already victory-bound.

During this period, one rider was talked up more than the rest. Described by Pierre Chany as 'the prototype Flemish cyclist: hard, dogged and skilful', Gaston Rebry won Paris–Roubaix in 1931 and should probably have claimed the Ronde earlier than he eventually did. One year he crashed as the lead group headed into the velodrome at Gentbrugge. In 1933, an ill-timed puncture left him in sixth.

Rebry's peculiarity in the Ronde was that he always attacked in the same place: on the hill at Torhout. In 1934, his rivals must have known what to expect, but only three riders were capable of following him. Heading up the cinder track at the side of the Kwaremont, he attacked again, dropping these three, only to puncture on the Edelaere, where Félicien Vervaecke caught and passed him. 'The Bulldog' would not be denied, though. His puncture fixed, he caught and left Vervaecke, cruising away to a clear win. The following week he won the second edition of Paris–Nice, and from there went on to claim the second of what would be three Roubaix victories. His career lasted until 1939. After retiring he moved to Wevelgem, opened a bar called 'Paris–Roubaix' and liked nothing more than to smoke a fine cigar and nurse a beer. For Van Wijnendaele, Rebry fitted the template of a true 'Flandrien'.

Although Flanders continued to get the winners Van Wijnendaele wanted, the race director was still not happy. He regularly tinkered with the Ronde's route, but made a very different change in 1937, allowing derailleur gears for the first time, although they had already been used in other races. His objective was to prevent the race becoming formulaic by giving riders a broader range of gears to work with. Previously, when riders had used a single fixed gear, Rebry and some of the other strongmen would start off fast with the aim of splitting the field before the race reached the coast, where they would inevitably increase their advantage in the wind gusting in off the North Sea. Anyone dropped in that initial section of the race had no chance of getting back into contention.

Van Wijnendaele's modification brought a surprise winner in Michel d'Hooghe, whose short career ended when he was killed in May 1940 during a German air raid on the city of Lokeren. The Ronde's race director quickly realised, though, that as well as evening out the level of the riders, the derailleur also evened out the course. The few hills on the route became less of a challenge, to the point where a rider who competed largely on the track won the final pre-war edition.

On the back of a winter track season, Karel Kaers was hoping he might be able to upset the established road stars at Paris–Roubaix in 1939. Kaers was no mug as a road rider. In 1934, he had won the world title in Leipzig aged just 20 and remains the youngest ever champion. But the success came too early for him: according to one history of the Ronde, he became the 'spoiled child' of Belgian cycling. He was also held back by his weight. At 85kg, he struggled in anything other than flat races. Consequently, he considered a variety of racing options as preparation for Roubaix before reluctantly settling on Flanders, partly because his manager, Jules Deckx, had said he wouldn't dare do it after failing to finish in 1937 and 1938.

Kaers drove his car to the top of the Kwaremont, at around the halfway mark, with a view to racing that far and then pulling out to save himself for Roubaix a week later. However, the canny Deckx got wind of his plan and warned Kaers' accomplices, who were in on the scheme and were also among his clients, 'If you do that, I won't speak to you ever again.'

Coming towards the Kwaremont, Kaers attacked, thinking he was only a handful of kilometres from his finishing point. But, finding his car and his accomplices were nowhere to be seen, he was forced to carry on. On the Kruisberg he attacked again in the company of his training partner, Roger Van den Driessche, former Tour champion Romain Maes and Edward Vissers. Kaers clung on doggedly. Maes looked the strongest, but his sprint was no match for the track ace Kaers, who breezed by to win by three bike lengths. 'I've got nothing left in me. Five kilometres more and I'd have crumbled,' he told Van Wijnendaele. His finish at Roubaix backed that up. He rolled in a quarter of an hour behind the winner, sixty-seventh of 68 riders classified.

18

THE LEGEND OF THE 'FLANDRIENS'

Unlike the other Monuments, and indeed most other major races, the Ronde continued to run right through the Second World War. Some suggested at the time, and the claim has been made more regularly since, that this stemmed from Karel Van Wijnendaele collaborating with the occupying Nazi forces. However, it is hard to square this allegation with the recognition Van Wijnendaele received in the wake of the conflict. Not only did the Ronde's boss receive a letter of thanks from Field Marshal Bernard Montgomery for sheltering Allied airmen shot down over Belgium, but he was also awarded his country's highest honour, the Order of Leopold, for his actions during the war.

Instead, it appears the Ronde benefited from the implementation of *Flamenpolitik*, the policy implemented by the Nazis with the express goal of exacerbating divisions between the Flemings and the Walloons. Initially, it resulted in the release from captivity of many Flemish-speaking officers from the Belgian army that had been overrun by the Germans. Subsequently, it promoted attempts to foster the use of the Dutch language. The objective of the policy was not to encourage the emergence of a separate Flemish state, but to add the region to those other parts of the Low Countries where the population had been classified as 'racially Germanic'. This move was completed in late 1944 when Flanders became an official part of the greater Reich.

Although Flemish political parties and associations were guilty of collaborating with the Nazis, some of them were only looking to gain rights they felt they had previously been prevented from enjoying, notably recognition of their language and culture. Other groups, however, took this collaboration to much more sinister lengths, which has led to the linking of Flemish nationalism with right-wing ideology. Without going too deeply into the minefield of Belgian politics in the post-war era, the issue of Flemish nationalism remains a contentious one and still impacts on Belgian cycling because of the sport's importance as a cultural and political symbol in Flanders.

In early 2013, Belgium's world champion Philippe Gilbert, a French-speaking Walloon, found himself in hot water when he criticised fans who brandish the Lion of Flanders flag at races. 'Extremists, they're everywhere, even in Wallonia. It's like the National Front in France. People don't believe in politics any more and give their votes to these parties. It's negative voting, the electorate don't know what policies they're voting for,' he told Belgian magazine *Humo*. Flemish politicians leapt on his comments, leading to Gilbert explaining that he only wanted to express his desire, as a proud Belgian, to see fans waving the Belgian flag.

If nothing else, Gilbert's remarks underlined how potent the symbol of the Lion of Flanders remains within Flemish cycling. As we saw in the last chapter, Van Wijnendaele drew on the work of that name written by Hendrik Conscience in the nineteenth century, while the Ronde's greatest champions have also been anointed with that title – although not all have been Flemish, or even Belgian. As for the flag, there are two versions of it: the official standard of Flanders, which was legally adopted in 1973, shows a rampant black lion with red claws and tongue on a field of gold. However, those who support Flemish nationalism – and they come from all parts of the political spectrum, not just the right – favour a flag where the lion does not have the red claws and tongue, and consequently does not share the colours of Belgium's national flag. Both versions are much in evidence at the Ronde and other races in Flanders, and each may or may not say something about the political affiliation of the fan waving it.

On the final day of March 1940, though, the riders who had registered for the first wartime Ronde had plenty of other things to focus on. Although the conflict hadn't yet spread to Western Europe, troops were being mobilised and many of those who would have been among the contenders for the race had been conscripted. Defending champion Karel Kaers was on the start line, as was the first British entrant, Joe Bridges, of whom there is no further mention in the race reports or results. Before the start, the riders paused to remember Marcel Buysse, the 1914 champion, who, until his death the previous October, had run a hotel opposite the station in Gent where many of the racers stayed.

Reduced to 230km the year before in order to allow riders to vote in a general election, the route was cut again as the country prepared for war. The riders faced a much less severe challenge of 211km, on a course that no longer touched the coast, where sea defences were being fortified. Consequently, the key action took place on the three *hellingen*. On the Edelareberg, half a dozen riders went clear, including talented 20-year-old Briek Schotte, race favourite Marcel Kint and Achiel Buysse, no relation to the late Marcel or any of his clan, who produced no fewer than 11 professional riders.

By the finish, the six leaders had become three. Kint had crashed out, while Jean Staeren and Albert Hendrickx had been 'visited by the man with the hammer', as one report put it. Buysse had the advantage in terms of finishing speed, but didn't wait for the final straight to demonstrate that. He attacked a few kilometres out from Wetteren and rolled home 20 seconds clear of Georges Christiaens and Schotte.

Buysse became the second rider to retain the title when he proved fastest of a seven-man group in 1941. That edition of the Ronde, which took place in early May because of another clash with an election, was the only one in history of less than 200km, but war damage made the 198km course as tough as ever. The 112 starters clocked up a staggering 144 punctures in the first 100km of racing, with Kaers, Hendrickx and Schotte among those who never reached Wetteren.

Schotte's lore

Briek Schotte had been hailed as a future winner of the Ronde ever since he had been prevented from completing victory in the Tour de l'Ouest in September 1939 because of the outbreak of war. Born in September 1919 in the small village of Kanegem, almost on the border between West and East Flanders, Schotte would become the latest, and eventually the most renowned, of Van Wijnendaele's 'Flandriens'. He moved towards that status when he won the Ronde in 1942. The race demonstrated one of the characteristics that made Schotte and other 'Flandriens' stand apart. Heading towards the finish on the Kuipke track in Gent, he attacked again and again, eventually opening a gap of 50m that he maintained all the way to the line.

His racing philosophy was simple: '*Geen woorden, maar deden.*' No words, just deeds. Crouched down over his bike, his cloth hat pulled down tight on his head, the peak pointing in the same direction as his unwavering gaze, Schotte never knew when to yield. Although some claim he produced his best performance when finishing runner-up in the 1948 Tour de France even though he was by no means a climber, he is inextricably associated with the Tour of Flanders. He rode it 20 times, won it twice and finished on the podium eight times.

In the Tour of Flanders Museum in Oudenaarde, a substantial section on Schotte includes his ten commandments:

1   Be content with what you have.
2   With determination and patience you can go anywhere.
3   Tired? If you are tired, you have to sleep.
4   Never lose your freedom.
5   Remain who you are.
6   By looking, you learn a lot.
7   Those who let go are lost.
8   Never forget where you come from.

9 Do not believe in dreams that cannot be achieved.
10 Whoever speaks evil will reap evil.

It's uncomplicated and uncompromising stuff, which encapsulates both Schotte and the ideal 'Flandrien' almost perfectly. Add in the description of Schotte by *L'Équipe*'s Pierre Chany and the image is complete: 'He's a conscientious rider, fierce in battle, sometimes slow to get going, but terribly effective at the end of races. He can deal with heat and bad weather, taking advantage of an ascetic's life and his commitment to training. Finally, he knows how to suffer more than the rest. Very stretched out on the bike, his chiselled face flush with bars, his blue hat pulled down to his ears, he can be picked out from afar.'

When journalist Albert Baker d'Isy, considered by Chany to be the greatest writer on cycling of his generation, visited Schotte in Flanders in 1948 after he had taken his second victory in the Ronde and won the World Championship, he painted a picture of a man standing very much against the tide of change within the sport. Schotte was going out training with some of the old guard, including Gaston Rebry. Their objective was to ride out into the wind to the coast, then turn for home, crossing the Kwaremont and Kruisberg on the road back.

'Don't expect to see this happening for much longer. There aren't any true "Flandriens" any more,' one of the riders told Baker d'Isy. 'The youngsters are too spoiled. Fans, money that's easily won in kermesse races, the increasing number of races in Belgium, the devaluation of the French franc, the lack of restrictions on life that is the result of the occupation, they've all contributed. They don't train any more. They race. And if it's too hard, they abandon.' There was, wrote Baker d'Isy, one exception to that rule – Schotte. He described him as 'The Last of the Flandriens'.

If Schotte was the last of the line, Achiel Buysse was only a place or two ahead of him. In 1943, he became the first rider to win the Ronde on three occasions, a feat no one has ever surpassed. Oddly, considering the situation in the war, the field was one of the most international ever seen up to that point, featuring nine French riders, three Dutchmen and Jules Rossi, who had been the first Italian to win Roubaix in 1937. The roads were still atrocious and once again took a considerable toll on tyres, with Schotte one of those waylaid by punctures.

Only the narrowness of the geographical area Van Wijnendaele laid down for those who could aspire to 'Flandrien' status prevented Rik Van Steenbergen from being thus anointed. He came from Arendonk, on the far eastern side of the province of Antwerp, right on the Dutch border. During the war he worked as a cigar roller in the Karel I cigar factory, but was gaining a better reputation for his performances on two wheels. He won the Belgian title in 1943 at the age of 18, but almost didn't make it to the start line.

'When I turned pro in 1943, I couldn't ride the Tour of Flanders straight away. There were three categories of rider: road riders A, road riders B, and track riders. I was registered with the federation as a track rider. At first, they wouldn't let me ride the national championship. But Jean Van Buggenhout, the manager, got me reclassified on the Wednesday before the race. I won it and became an A rider. That meant I could start the Tour of Flanders the following year. I was 19 and I'll probably remain the youngest person ever to win,' Van Steenbergen told cycling historian Les Woodland.

It was some race as well. Van Steenbergen had already surprised many observers with his aggressive riding on the climbs. Coming into Gent, he was one of nine riders in the front group. Schotte and Marcel Kint were also there, but both men crashed in the narrow, winding streets that led into the Kuipke velodrome. They did manage to rejoin the lead group, but Kint crashed again entering the grounds of the stadium. Georges Claes and Frans Sterckx took advantage of that distraction, accelerating away, only to collide with each other going through the entrance into the velodrome, leaving young Van Steenbergen on his own at the front with Schotte desperately trying to get on terms with the teenager. It was too late, though. Van Steenbergen had enough of a gap and more than enough finishing speed to hang on.

A familiar photograph of the pair says much more than a race report ever could. Van Steenbergen, his hair thick and curly and not yet showing signs of what would be a distinctive widow's peak, appears overwhelmed, almost dazed, his left arm draped around Schotte's shoulders. The older man would clearly rather be anywhere else but there at that moment. Stony-faced, anger evident in his eyes, his lips pursed, he's staring into the distance, determined to avoid catching a glimpse of the victory bouquet Van Steenbergen has unwittingly dropped into his lap.

Although questions could be asked about the legitimacy of Van Steenbergen's victory that day, his superiority when he claimed a second success two years later was undeniable. Less than a month on from Fausto Coppi's astounding solo victory at Milan–Sanremo, Van Steenbergen produced a performance that was almost as impressive.

A record 218 riders set out on a route that had returned to a more testing 246km following the lifting of restrictions imposed during the war. The three key climbs whittled the front group down. After Schotte flew up the Kwaremont, only 20 riders joined him. He repeated his show of force on the Kruisberg, reducing the front group to just seven. On the Edelareberg, Louis Thiétard was the surprising aggressor. At the top, the Frenchman had just Schotte and Van Steenbergen for company.

Thiétard and Schotte knew they would have no chance of outgunning Van Steenbergen in a sprint, but didn't get the opportunity to find out. As they crossed the bridge over the Schelde at Kwatrecht with five kilometres remaining, Van Steenbergen sprinted away. Stretched out low over his bike in track fashion, he opened up a gap of more than a minute on his two rivals, showing he had far more in his armoury than a blisteringly quick finish. Indeed, many felt Van Steenbergen could have been a grand tour contender if he had focused more on specific goals and hadn't gone chasing every cash prize in the sport. Thiétard initially took up the chase, but when he signalled for Schotte to come through, the Fleming gestured as if to say, 'What's the point?' However it played out, Van Steenbergen was going to win.

The Italian 'Lion of Flanders'

Frequent calendar clashes with Milan–Sanremo ensured foreign participation in the Ronde was piecemeal until the introduction of the Desgrange-Colombo Challenge in 1948. The new format encouraged riders to compete in all nine events, including Flanders. In an immense peloton of 265 were 17 Italians, 18 Frenchmen, 33 Dutchmen, one Pole and one Briton, Harold Bloomfield, who didn't finish. He was in good company as only 83 made it back to Wetteren, where Schotte finally claimed a second Ronde triumph, which set him on the way to the inaugural Desgrange-Colombo crown.

The Italians were prominent in the first half of the race, when Fiorenzo Magni was among the animators. Ultimately, though, they lacked the experience to deal with the Flemish on their cobbles and bergs. Only Pino Cerami, who would take on Belgian citizenship in the mid-1950s and still has a pro race named after him in Wallonia, managed a top 20 finish, just 30 seconds behind Schotte. The rest of his compatriots were nowhere.

A month later, Magni, who was a decent but not great climber, won the Giro d'Italia by what is still the narrowest margin in history – 11 seconds. That success owed much to his daring on descents, his Schotte-like ability to push himself to his limit and his uncanny ability to read exactly the right time to commit himself, as well as to his fans pushing him up some of the biggest climbs. Many claimed the pushing had been pre-planned, and it led to Fausto Coppi quitting the race with his team in disgust. There was concerted booing when Magni won the final stage and wrapped up the title on the Vigorelli velodrome in Milan.

Unfortunately for Magni, who made a tearful exit from the Vigorelli with a police escort, he was a ready-made villain. Partly this was because he was neither Coppi nor Gino Bartali, the only two riders the Italian fans and media were interested in during the three weeks of their national tour. Mostly, though, it was the result of his questionable wartime activities. Magni joined the Fascist side in the war after being called up in 1943. In this he was no different from thousands of other Italians, but Magni's wartime activities were clouded by his alleged involvement in a massacre of anti-Fascist partisans at Valibona in January 1944.

In 1947, an Italian court investigating the incident said it was unable to decide whether Magni had taken part in the massacre and he was cleared under a general amnesty. But many in his home region remained unconvinced. In Belgium, though, Magni was on the threshold of greatness thanks to a series of performances that remain almost unparalleled in the Monuments.

When he had made his Flanders debut in 1948, Magni had just four teammates to support him in the Wilier-Triestina team until he abandoned when his forks broke. A year later, he returned with just two. By now Van Wijnendaele was convinced Heiri Suter's victory in 1923, the only occasion the title had evaded the home riders, was nothing more than a fluke. There was, he declared, no chance of a foreigner winning the Ronde. Racing over the three climbs in the Flemish Ardennes, a 100-strong group shattered, leaving just two riders in the lead: Magni and Frenchman Louis Caput. Realising they were too far from the finish to hold off the combined strength of the Belgians, they eased up, and 16 more riders joined them on the approach to Wetteren. In the sprint, Schotte and Valère Ollivier eyed each other, but paid little attention to Magni, who was regarded as a stage race specialist rather than a sprinter. Perhaps they had forgotten his final stage win on the Vigorelli in the 1948 Giro. Magni accelerated and kept going. Schotte got close to him, but the Italian hung on.

In the wake of this second foreign victory, the Ronde entered a new era, one of radical changes and not all of them appreciated by Van Wijnendaele and the Flemings. The race organiser's primary concern was the zeal with which local councils were applying themselves to the task of covering cobbled roads with tarmac. As would be the case at Paris–Roubaix a decade or so later, smoother surfaces drew the sting from the challenge the Ronde offered. Without dozens of kilometres of cobbles, it was in danger of becoming a much easier race, albeit still a long one. Van Wijnendaele asked friends and colleagues who knew the road network well to seek out alternative routes, while he pored over maps, hoping to stay a step ahead of the road gangs. Over the course of the 1950s, he increasingly noted that the cobbled sections that escaped resurfacing were those in the worst condition, often tracks that were only used by tractors.

Van Wijnendaele's solution was to add more climbs to the race, although it would be 1980 before the number of *hellingen* reached double figures. In 1950, he returned the Tiegemberg to the course and added the Muur de Grammont at Geraardsbergen, which would become the Ronde's signature climb. In the modern era, riders have tackled the Muur on the cobbled roads running straight up from the centre of the town, but initially they came at it from the west, skirting around the town centre.

As it turned out, Van Wijnendaele needn't have worried about the course being tough that first year the Muur featured. It was cold, snow lay on parts of the course, and an icy wind blew 90 per cent of the starters out of the race. Only 22 riders finished.

Magni was back to defend the title, once again with just two team-mates to assist him. Eight riders were clear going over the Tiegemberg and Kwaremont. On the Kruisberg, eight became 11. Magni, Dutchman Wim Van Est and Frenchman André Mahé joined them. Most riders would have paused for a while before pressing on, but not Magni. His pace didn't relent, and only Van Est and Mahé were strong enough to stay with him.

The effort the leading trio had made appeared wasted when Mahé punctured and, soon after, Van Est broke a pedal. With 70km to the finish, Magni was alone. By now the cold had become so severe that riders were abandoning in droves, but the Italian persisted, his bald dome still uncovered, the sleeves of his wool jersey pushed up to his elbows despite the chill. At the top of the Muur his lead had stretched to five and a half minutes. Briek Schotte set off after Magni, knocking lumps out of his lead, but it was no more than a consolation effort. Magni was still more than two minutes clear after eight and a quarter hours of racing.

Schotte described the Italian as being 'like a non-stopping express train. Once he had set off he only stopped at the finish line.' Louis Caput, who finished nine minutes back in third place, later offered a less laudatory but more insightful perspective: 'Magni is undoubtedly a rider of quality, an incredible fighter at the end of races, when he feels victory is within his reach, but he often lets others take on the role of policing the race, of provoking the selection. He's not a Coppi, a Bartali, a Bobet, a Van Steenbergen, a Kübler.' Caput's analysis may be slightly dismissive but it underlines how much Magni compensated for his relative lack of talent compared to the very best riders of his era by drawing on almost inexhaustible reserves of courage and sheer bloody-mindedness.

Although his reputation remained tarnished in his homeland, for the tens of thousands of Italians who had emigrated to Belgium to find work in the steel and coal industries he was a hero, one of their own who overcame every obstacle set in his way. Even the Flemish were won over by his extraordinary exploits, anointing him the 'Lion of Flanders' as one of the Ronde's most illustrious performers. Yet his best was still to come.

On 1 April 1951, a day when the wind and cold were even more biting than they had been 12 months earlier and rain showers and flurries of snow peppered the riders throughout, Magni won for the third year in a row. Once again, he made his move from a long way out, attacking on the Kwaremont and going clear with three others –

Belgium's Roger Decock and fellow Italians Loretto Petrucci and Attilio Redolfi. With 70km left, Magni accelerated away from his companions, sticking to the strategy that had served him so well the year before: get as far ahead as possible and try to hang on. With only four teammates, who had little experience of the Ronde's unique demands, he simply couldn't sit tight in the peloton and hope to keep all his Belgian rivals in check.

Caput's description of Magni may have been accurate, but over those final 70km he put on a performance worthy of Coppi, Van Steenbergen or any other of the greatest Classics riders. He finished five and a half minutes clear of runner-up Bernard Gauthier, with Redolfi and Petrucci taking third and fourth place respectively, more than ten minutes later. As he rolled up to the line, Magni was already loosening the toe straps on his pedals. He stepped off his bike and declared he would never ride the Ronde again; it was too brutal a test.

Magni never did return, but he changed the international perception of the Tour of Flanders with his three consecutive wins. Foreign riders not only turned up in greater numbers, but also went into battle on the cobbles and bergs believing they could beat Belgium's best Classics exponents. That year, there was no Belgian finisher in the top five, which did not happen again until 1997 and has occurred only once since.

The following season, Frenchman Louison Bobet adopted a strategy similar to Magni, attacking hard on the Muur, which Van Steenbergen and many others climbed on foot, and opening up what appeared to be a winning lead. However, eight kilometres from home, he punctured, allowing Roger Decock, Briek Schotte and Loretto Petrucci back into contention, with Decock victorious after the two Flemish riders had ganged up on the nippy Italian coming into the finish. A year later, the unthinkable happened. Not only was there just one Belgian finisher in the top seven, but the Netherlands celebrated its first Ronde success thanks to Wim Van Est. Schotte was still gamely plugging away, but he now looked very much like 'the last of the Flandriens'. The Flemish press and the fans railed more than ever about the new generation, complaining they weren't committed or tough enough, and wondering where the next Schotte or Van Steenbergen was going to come from.

19

THE REMAKING OF THE RONDE

Flanders appeared to have found a new icon when Raymond Impanis won the Ronde in 1954. Already a two-time runner-up in Liège–Bastogne–Liège, Impanis arrived at the Ronde fresh from victory at Paris–Nice and would go on to win Paris–Roubaix a week later.

His success in Flanders encapsulated his all-round ability. He could fly up the climbs, ride hard on the flat and boasted a rapid turn of finishing speed that always made him a favourite from a small group of riders. Delayed by a puncture in the hills in the Flemish Ardennes, which meant he missed out on the washing machine offered as a prize to the first man over the Edelareberg – Désiré Keteleer claimed it – he chased back up to the leaders together with François Mahé, who had crashed into a manure-filled ditch.

Almost as soon as they joined the leaders, with 27km remaining to the finish, Impanis attacked. Louison Bobet chased him down, followed by Mahé, who countered immediately, shaking off his compatriot Bobet but not the Belgian, who had come into the race as favourite on the back of that Paris–Nice success. The two-up sprint in Wetteren went to Impanis, with Mahé unable to match his burst on cobbles that Pierre Chany referred to as being like 'the headgear of priests'.

French riders seemed forever fated to miss out on the main prize in the Ronde. Mahé's second place was their fourth podium finish in five years. To those must be added Bobet's untimely puncture in 1952, which almost certainly prevented him taking the title. According to

Willem Van Wijnendaele, *Sportwereld* journalist and son of the race organiser, Bobet was so crushed by that defeat that he spent the evening in tears. 'It's so unfair. I was the strongest. I dropped everyone. I couldn't lose. And then I had that stupid puncture eight kilometres from Wetteren,' he sobbed to Van Wijnendaele when the journalist visited him in his room. The next morning, when the pair met again for a radio interview, Bobet's mood was still black. 'You and your damned race. Your Ronde! I will never take part in it again. Do you understand me? Never!'

He did come back in 1954, but three early punctures and the subsequent pursuit he had to undertake cost him in the finale. In 1955, he returned again as world champion. This time, he heeded the advice he'd been given by Rik Van Steenbergen to hold back for as long as possible, to commit himself only when he was sure he could make it count.

The race came to life when Bobet's Mercier teammate Bernard Gauthier attacked on the Muur. Bobet, Van Steenbergen and Switzerland's Hugo Koblet, three of the greats of that era, bridged across to Gauthier, and the quartet joined forces for the final 60km into the finish. Although they never had much more than a minute on the group chasing hard behind them, their only moment of concern came when they reached a level crossing with its barriers down with 15km left. They all ducked under them, sprinted across the tracks and continued on.

Gauthier kept pushing as hard as he could every time he went to the front of the group, with the aim of blunting Van Steenbergen's finishing speed. The tactic paid off perfectly, Bobet roaring with joy as he flashed through the line a bike length clear of Koblet and two clear of Van Steenbergen, who paid the penalty for being too active during the opening 100km of the race. If only he had heeded his own advice to Bobet.

Van Steenbergen, though, still had a card to play. As Willem Van Wijnendaele rushed up to him for his post-race comments, the Belgian pushed through the throng to find Karel Debaere, who had led in the sprint for fifth place. 'Karel, you must lodge a protest immediately,' Van Wijnendaele heard Van Steenbergen tell his compatriot, who also happened to be Bobet's teammate. 'At Wichelen we went through a level crossing that was closed. The rules in Belgium don't allow that. Consequently, the four riders who finished ahead of you must be disqualified. That means you will be the winner of the Tour of Flanders.'

While Debaere went off to lodge his protest, Van Wijnendaele told one of the race commissaires what he had heard. There is now no way of knowing whether Van Wijnendaele's intervention had an impact on the race jury's decision, but within a few minutes it was announced that Debaere's protest had been rejected. Van Wijnendaele pointed out that the level-crossing rule didn't apply in other countries and said the motorbike-borne race marshals should have prevented the four riders crossing the tracks. After a nervous wait, Bobet climbed on to the podium to receive the plaudits as France's first Tour of Flanders champion.

While Bobet was lauded, Van Steenbergen was very much the villain of the day. In the weeks after the Ronde, a rumour circulated suggesting he had sold the race to Bobet, which explained his poor sprint. But if this were the case, why would Van Steenbergen have encouraged Debaere to lodge a complaint? If Debaere's protest had been upheld, Van Steenbergen would not only have lost the Ronde, but also the money he had allegedly been promised for losing the Ronde.

Van Steenbergen came under fire the following year as well, together with a host of other Belgians, when Jean Forestier kept the title in French hands. A large group containing most of Belgium's fastest finishers came into Wetteren together. As the sprinters watched each other, Forestier jumped away from a kilometre out, guessing the Belgians would all wait for each other to chase. Forestier looked shocked as he crossed the line still 50m clear, the unsmiling fans wondering who on earth he was.

That year was Van Steenbergen's last as a likely contender for victory at the Ronde. Although he did win the world road title for a third time in 1957, he focused primarily on track racing after that, taking his win total on the boards to 1,313 before he retired in 1966 at the age of 42. The professional scene had been Van Steenbergen's life for a quarter of a century, and without it he looked for something to fill the void. He confessed he began to live out the youth he'd missed, due to both his racing commitments and the war. He started drinking, playing cards and got in with the wrong crowd. He frittered away his money to the point where, in 1968, he starred in a pornographic film, *Pandora*, playing a Greek fisherman who takes up with the bored wife of a Belgian industrialist.

He subsequently confessed that marriage saved him. As Gent-born Bradley Wiggins would do 40 years later, Van Steenbergen found love with a Lancashire woman. Doreen Hewitt had no idea of his racing exploits, but, as Van Steenbergen readily admitted, she got him back on track, enabling him to enjoy his later years as an elder statesman of the sport. He died in 2003 and was hailed as one of the four great riders in Belgian history alongside Eddy Merckx, Roger De Vlaeminck and Rik Van Looy. He was, said contemporary Raphaël Geminiani, 'the typical cold Fleming, not saying much, with a cloud of boredom on his forehead'.

While Van Steenbergen and several of his compatriots were put through the wringer in the wake of Forestier's 1956 success, Fred De Bruyne was one of the few Flemish stars who escaped criticism in the wake of that debacle, helped by the fact he had won Paris–Nice and Milan–Sanremo a few weeks beforehand. He would go on to claim Liège–Bastogne–Liège a few weeks later. That was some year for De Bruyne, but 1957 was even better. Very much Louison Bobet's lieutenant at Mercier, he had joined Carpano-Coppi that year at Fausto Coppi's insistence and was able to benefit from the expertise of the team's road captain, Désiré Keteleer.

The pair spent the weeks leading up to the Ronde training on the course. On race day, Keteleer marshalled Carpano's troops, ensuring De Bruyne was always well placed and well protected. On the Muur,

Keteleer performed this role himself. At the top, the two men were at the front in a 12-strong group that co-operated all the way into the finish. 'He led for the last five kilometres. Sitting behind him I felt like I was riding pillion on a motorbike. Nobody could get past. In the sprint I won by twenty metres,' De Bruyne explained.

After one Rik another

Following some fallow years in the early and mid-1950s, Belgian, and particularly Flemish, prospects rose towards the end of the decade. The mantle worn by established names such as Schotte and Van Steenbergen was moving on to a younger generation, even though this pair were still rather reluctant to hand it over. This was especially true of Van Steenbergen, who, it is said, racked up 1,000 training kilometres in a single week in the spring of 1958 in order to better an upcoming rival who had been described as 'the best in the world'. Van Steenbergen followed up on that training by winning Flèche Wallonne, but it hardly slowed the arrival of the young man, who, to the consternation of both, was quickly dubbed 'Rik II'.

Rik Van Looy had grown up idolising his fellow Antwerper, but any reverence he had for Van Steenbergen quickly disappeared when he joined Van Steenbergen's Girardengo team in 1955. It soon became apparent Van Looy wasn't prepared to work hard for others and wait for his opportunity to come. He wanted to lead from the off. Consequently, it was little surprise when he jumped ship to join Faema in 1956.

Over the next few seasons, Van Looy surrounded himself with his so-called 'Red Guard', riders signed by Faema to do whatever their team leader asked of them, which meant devoting themselves completely to him in the Classics. Van Looy, who much preferred his other nickname, 'The Emperor of Herentals', has always insisted his was a benevolent dictatorship. However, some former teammates don't see it that way. Britain's Vin Denson, who rode for Van Looy at the Solo team in the

1960s, told cycling historian Les Woodland: 'It was Solo by name and solo by nature. You rode for Van Looy and did whatever he wanted, including the fetching of beers, which he had a great fondness for mid-race. Domestiques were reduced to chasing long miles to bring the great man a bottle of Stella.'

Although Van Steenbergen attempted to establish a rapport with Van Looy, the younger man made it quite clear he was determined to follow his own path. He viewed himself as a born leader and, once installed at Faema, aimed to prove both to his teammates and everyone else beyond he was exactly that. This guaranteed a clash with each and every one of his rivals in the Classics. Van Steenbergen is the most renowned of them, but De Bruyne was another and Eddy Merckx would later join their number. In 1958, Van Looy and De Bruyne's rivalry was so arch that they marked each other out of contention in the Ronde as the title went to one of De Bruyne's Carpano teammates, Germain Derycke.

By 1959, Van Looy had started to build up a palmarès that would eventually include every major Classic on the calendar, a feat that no other rider has ever equalled, even the great Eddy Merckx, who never managed to win Paris–Tours. He had begun his run through the Monuments by winning Sanremo the previous year, and admitted he relished the prospect of a Flanders course that had been toughened up with the addition of the Valkenberg, a short but steep cobbled climb at Nederbrakel, some 11km before the Muur.

Once into the most critical section of the race, Faema's 'Red Guard' went to the front of the bunch and set a pace that blew several of Van Looy's rivals out of contention. The selection continued over the Valkenberg. On the Muur, Van Looy upped the pace himself. At the summit he only had a handful of riders for company. Naturally, De Bruyne was among them. When Van Looy attacked again 40km from the finish, De Bruyne was the only rider able to respond, but he paid for that effort. Van Looy drove through every time he went past his rival, forcing De Bruyne to push himself even harder to get back on his wheel. Once De Bruyne had fought his way back in behind his rival, Van Looy would ease off, move aside and drop in behind his compatriot, gathering himself for his next surge. The attritional tactic steadily sapped the vigour from De Bruyne's legs.

Although a group of 20-odd riders reeled the two favourites in, Van Looy had another card to play. On the final circuit in Wetteren, Faema's Gilbert Desmet clipped away, ensuring his leader Van Looy could follow any rider who chased behind without offering a stroke of assistance. Peugeot's Frans Schoubben took up the pursuit, but immediately had Van Looy on his wheel. Although Schoubben overhauled Desmet, he had nothing left to offer when 'Rik II' opened up his sprint in the final 200m. If Van Looy couldn't win one way, he could often find another route to success.

Van Looy should have retained his Flanders title in 1960. However, he seemed determined that he and the 'Red Guard' should take on and overpower Jacques Anquetil and the Frenchman's powerful Helyett-Leroux team. The French squad won that battle on points thanks to Irishman Shay Elliott's brave solo attack that ended just five kilometres from the line and Anquetil's late assault, which might have produced a winning finish if he had been in his mid-summer form. But Van Looy chased him down, then countered several attacks, only to end up third in the sprint behind unheralded Belgian Arthur De Cabooter and Helyett galloper Jean Graczyk.

The Ronde was now as popular as it had ever been, but as a result an old problem resurfaced. From almost its very first years of the Ronde, the race had been plagued by excessive traffic on the course. This first became a serious problem in the 1930s, when car ownership grew rapidly. Fans would trail behind the race convoy, often blocking the progress of riders who had crashed or been held up by punctures. Out on the course itself, cars would be parked two and three deep at key points in the race, creating bottlenecks for the riders.

Petrol rationing had made this less of an issue during and after the war, but the problem resurfaced in the 1950s. In 1959, the organisers attempted to deal with excess traffic by distributing official and press cars with accreditation plates, but handed out so many that this perennial headache remained until well into the present century, when the organisers opted for a more radical solution of holding the last half of the race on a closed circuit.

There were other organisational headaches, too. The 1961 Ronde began once again with Van Looy as most people's favourite. But when he crashed turning on to the climb of the Kruisberg, sustaining injuries that would soon force him to abandon, the race was thrown wide open. With 40km remaining, Italy's Nino Defilippis and Britain's Tom Simpson bridged across from the peloton to the four riders at the front. On the newly introduced climb of the Grotenberge at Zottegem, the pair kicked on again to dispute the finish between them.

Simpson's chances of taking the title looked extremely remote even with only one rider to beat. Defilippis was a track specialist with a very fast sprint finish, who had won a host of stages in all three grand tours. Although no mug in a sprint, Simpson was making his debut in the Ronde, a race that none of the previous British starters had ever finished. Simpson was on course to do that, but, the weather was about to give him some unexpected and extremely beneficial assistance.

At the finish in Wetteren, a gusting wind loosened the bindings on one side of the finishing banner, leaving it flapping in the breeze. Efforts to resecure it failed, so the finish line judges decided to take it down. The best alternative they could find at very short notice was a man waving a red flag to indicate the position of the line.

Also on Simpson's side was the fact that Defilippis was another Flanders novice. Despite furious waving of the red flag, the Italian started sprinting for the wrong line. He reached this first, but the jubilant Simpson, sporting what appeared to be a natty pair of Ray-Bans, surged by on his right to win by a wheel as they flew past the gent with the red flag. There was uproar, but what could be done? Simpson had done nothing wrong and won the race. Ultimately, Wetteren paid the price. The following year, the finish was moved to Gentbrugge, which had last had that honour in the 1920s.

The finish may have changed, but Van Looy was once again the overwhelming favourite in the rainbow jersey of the world champion in 1962. This was despite his lack of popularity among his peers, who didn't appreciate his imperious attitude and had dubbed him, with a clear sense of irony, 'Gentleman Rik'. Writing in *Sporting Cyclist*, French journalist René De Latour said of Van Looy: 'Apart from his teammates, Van Looy has no friends in the peloton. Indeed, he has many enemies. Everybody works against him.' Everybody, that is, apart from his 'Red Guard', who set a scorching pace out to the coast and then from the Kwaremont, where the race got more serious.

Defending champion Simpson managed to escape their grip, but when the Englishman moved Van Looy himself countered to follow. Four more riders joined them, including two of Van Looy's Faema teammates, who drew the sting out of their leader's rivals with fierce pace-setting and occasional short, but aggressive attacks. When Van Looy made an attack of his own on the finishing circuit at Gentbrugge, no one was able to respond. Victorious at Gent–Wevelgem just before the Ronde, Van Looy claimed the much bigger prize. A week later, he added Paris–Roubaix to his collection. Unpopular he may have been, but no one could question his brilliance.

Going into 1963, Van Looy's determination to do things his own way left him caught between two teams: Flandria-Faema, for whom he had long been the leader, and GBC, who were offering him a bigger contract. When Flandria took legal action against him for breach of contract, GBC stood back, not wanting to get involved in the dispute. Although the issue was settled before the Ronde and Van Looy led GBC into battle, his former lieutenants rose up against him, under the canny guidance of team director Lomme Driessens, who had worked with

Coppi and would go on to manage Eddy Merckx, Freddy Maertens and Sean Kelly.

Van Looy split the race with an attack on the Kruisberg, but then expended so much energy keeping his rivals in check that he couldn't respond when Simpson made a late break, taking three riders with him, including Flandria-Faema's Noël Foré, who held off Frans Melckenbeeck in the sprint, with Simpson third. Van Looy moved again the following season, taking over as leader of the Solo-Superia team. Yet the acrimony hanging over from his messy departure from Faema still created complications. The two teams marked each other closely, but let Germany's Rudi Altig slip away with 50km remaining. A track pursuit specialist, Altig breezed away to win by more than four minutes at a then record average speed of 40.990km/h. It was Germany's first success in the Ronde, but the way the Belgians marked each other out of contention showed little respect to Karel Van Wijnendaele, in whose memory a monument had been unveiled at the top of the Kwaremont following his death in December 1961.

Belgium retightens its grip

Just as Van Looy had ended the Classics supremacy of Rik Van Steenbergen, so Eddy Merckx would do for Van Looy. In 1965, the two Belgians had been brought under Solo Superia's banner in an uneasy partnership that ended after only eight months, when Merckx signed for Peugeot. Merckx later said of his compatriot: 'If Van Looy couldn't win, then he preferred a rival to win rather than a teammate.' However, this cutting analysis isn't backed by events at the Ronde in 1965, when Van Looy kept a chase group in check after his teammate Ward Sels had escaped with Jo De Roo. Sadly for Sels, a problem with his gears left him underpowered in the sprint and he committed one of the worst crimes for a Flemish rider of losing out to a Dutchman, although he did redeem himself by getting the sprint right the following year.

By early 1967, 21-year-old Merckx had already himself established as a favourite for every one-day race he lined up in. Having just successfully defended his Sanremo title, he returned to Belgium, won Gent–Wevelgem and set his focus on Flanders. His challenge, he admitted, was to eliminate the threat posed by the sprinters, notably Walter Godefroot, Gent-born and very much the local hero. Merckx's task was complicated by the make-up of his Peugeot team, which featured only two other Belgians, Ferdi Bracke and Theo Mertens, among its 11-man line-up.

The race was an odd one. Belgians Noël Foré and Willy Monty, and Britain's Barry Hoban, went clear early on. Such was the stalemate behind them, with everyone eyeing Merckx, the trio were still out in front just a handful of kilometres from the finish. Merckx had managed to split the group behind them by driving hard up the Muur in Geraardsbergen, but he had ended up isolated from his teammates, taking Italians Felice Gimondi and Dino Zandegù from the Salvarani team with him. In truth, 1965 Tour de France winner Gimondi wasn't in the very best of form, but Merckx feared the Italian's racing nous. When they got up to the three leaders, he was sure Gimondi was the main threat.

Merckx was both right and wrong about this. Gimondi knew his best chance of victory would come if he could get away on his own, but he needed to soften Merckx up before making his move. He instructed Zandegù to attack, expecting the Belgian to chase him down and expend vital reserves in doing so. Yet Merckx was hoping his compatriot Foré might become a temporary ally and agree to commit himself to an attack that would force Gimondi into an energy-sapping chase. As it was, when Zandegù shot away Foré went with him and no one else reacted. Because Foré had spent most of the race at the front, the result was a foregone conclusion. Zandegù won easily. Renowned for his baritone voice, with which he often entertained his peers during the quieter moments of races, Zandegù was urged by the expatriate Italians in the crowd to give them a song and had responded with 'O sole mio'! Unfortunately for the

Italian, his performance on the podium earned him more attention than his beautifully crafted victory over the raging Merckx.

In Daniel Friebe's *Eddy Merckx: The Cannibal*, the ebullient Zandegù recalled his victory and subsequent performance well, but admitted that, like the rest of the pro peloton, he had no idea what Merckx's arrival would mean for them. 'This kid just arrived, this big, handsome Belgian kid with high cheekbones – the face of an immense athlete – and pretty quickly we all realised that on the bike he was a brute. I say quickly, but it wasn't straightaway. It took a while, a couple of years. We, we didn't know, we didn't …'

That evening, still disconsolate, Merckx told his personal manager, Jean Van Buggenhout, to speak to Peugeot about signing more Belgian riders: just two or three. If they weren't prepared to consider this, Van Buggenhout was to sound out other interested parties, of whom there were sure to be plenty. As a French team focused primarily on French races, Peugeot weren't interested in bringing in a clutch of Belgians to suit a young rider who had been widely branded as a one-day specialist with no chance of contending for grand tour titles. When Van Buggenhout spoke to Peugeot manager Gaston Plaud about new signings for the following season, Plaud pointed out he had already had very marketable leaders in Roger Pingeon and Tom Simpson, and indicated 'Van Bug' should make enquiries elsewhere.

Although Plaud attempted to backtrack on his decision in the wake of Simpson's tragic death on the Ventoux during the 1967 Tour, Van Buggenhout had already brokered a deal with Vincenzo Giacotto, who wanted a leader for his new Faema team. When Merckx returned to the Ronde the following year, it was as world champion at the head of a ten-man team that contained no fewer than seven of his compatriots. But this would still not be enough to enable him to finish atop the podium on a revamped Flanders course.

Writing in organising newspaper, *Het Nieuwsblad-Sportwereld*, Willem Van Wijnendaele described the modifications as inevitable, 'because of the restrictions brought in with regard to the use of certain roads, but also due to … improvements in the road network'. He made a comparison with Paris–Roubaix, pointing out that 'the organisers are having more and more difficulty in guaranteeing its "hellish" physiognomy. The Tour of Flanders is in the same situation. Its cobbles are also becoming rarer.'

With this in mind, the Ronde returned to a more traditional route that included the Kwaremont, Kruisberg and Edelareberg, as well as the Muur. Yet this was not the Kwaremont of old, with a pitted cobbled surface and a gravel track up the side that almost every rider would quickly jump on to. The willow trees that had long loomed over the pavé, keeping the cobbles damp and treacherous, their roots rippling the road surface, had been cut down. The pavé had been relaid and the path alongside it had been incorporated as well. Now there was no escape from the cobbles.

In the end, though, the Muur proved decisive once again. Raymond Poulidor flew up it, reducing the front group to 17 members. Merckx was there with teammate Guido Reybroeck, but he had a shadow. Everywhere Merckx went, Rik Van Looy followed, glued to his rear wheel as if determined to unnerve him. Unlike Simpson, with whom the young Merckx had had a close relationship both on and off the bike at Peugeot – so much so that the Belgian was the only continental rider to attend the Englishman's funeral – Van Looy had never offered encouragement or advice when he and Merckx were teammates. They were rivals from the outset. Although Van Looy was now 35 and past his best, he still had very good days and this was one of them.

Only in a TV interview in 2010 did 'Gentleman Rik' finally admit he had deliberately sat on Merckx's wheel with the aim of unsettling him. He didn't hide his preference for fellow Fleming Godefroot, who steamed through to win the sprint, breezing away from Reybroeck, who had been led out by a rather rattled Merckx. The Faema leader later confessed he was developing something of a complex about Flanders, that it was becoming such an obsession his rivals were able to play on it, as Van Looy so clearly had.

He returned having steamrollered his rivals during the opening weeks of the 1969 season, winning three stages and the overall at both the Vuelta a Levante and Paris–Nice, before claiming a third Sanremo victory in four years. But he played down his chances for Flanders, insisting he was troubled by a knee injury.

His rivals weren't convinced. Informed by a journalist of Merckx's injury, Felice Gimondi smiled knowingly. 'Last year at the Giro d'Italia he was troubled by headaches, and he won – and you know the manner in which he did since you were there. At Paris–Nice he had cotton-wool in his left ear: he was coming down with an ear infection, he was saying. You know what happened next. The day before Milan–Sanremo I was told that he was having knee problems. Even then, I could guess what was going to happen next.' Tapping the side of his nose with his finger, Gimondi added: 'I respect Merckx for his qualities as a rider, but I don't give a damn for what he says before a race.'

Any injury worries Merckx might have had were forgotten when he read a preview of the Ronde in *Het Nieuwsblad*. It said he lacked the qualities required to win such a tough race, a ridiculous claim given his victories in Sanremo, Roubaix and the Giro. It was nothing more than pro-Flemish bias against a rider from cosmopolitan Brussels, and would rebound on those whom the story had been designed to laud. 'We'll see about that. As long as the weather is right ...' Merckx told his Faema soigneur, Guillaume Michiels. If Merckx had meant that he wanted it to be as viciously cold and brutal as possible, he got just what he asked for. Snow was blowing in on a cruel wind off the North Sea.

Figuring the Italians would be strong late on in the race, he instructed his team to make the pace as fierce as possible before reaching the Kwaremont after 143 of 259km. Merckx took the lead himself on the hills. On the Kwaremont and Kluisberg he whittled down the front group to just 11 riders, among them Barry Hoban. 'He went up the

Muur like a man possessed,' Hoban recalled. As the group pressed on towards the next climb of the Valkenberg, Merckx went to the front of the line to contribute to the pace-making and simply kept going. There were still 70km to the finish, mostly into the wind and incessant rain.

It seemed like madness, certainly to Faema *directeur sportif* Lomme Driessens, with whom Merckx had a prickly relationship. A master of motivation whose nickname 'Lomme the Liar' stemmed from his propensity to talk himself up even when he had no reason to do so, Driessens drove up alongside his team leader.

'*Verdomme*, Eddy! What are you doing? Have you gone completely mad? You've attacked from too far out. Ease off a bit,' he bluntly ordered Merckx.

'Go fuck yourself!' Merckx spat back at Driessens even more bluntly. 'I've dropped them and they won't be able to get back up to me without a huge effort. And the wind's not too bad really.'

Driessens needn't have worried. The group behind Merckx was being blown apart by the elements and the pluck of one or two determined to give chase, notably Gimondi, who engaged in a lone pursuit. By the finish, the Italian's advantage over the Hoban group behind had stretched to two and a half minutes. Even so, Gimondi came home five and a half minutes down on Merckx, who bettered Magni's 1951 record of 5'35" for the biggest winning margin in the post-war period by a second. While Merckx received plaudits on the podium, Driessens held court next to it, telling anyone who would listen that the whole strategy had been his idea. When Merckx read the newspapers the next day it's said he hit the roof.

He had proved there was no limit to the range of his ability in the Classics. Three months later, he went on to dominate the Tour de France in the same fashion. Although there were still races he hadn't won, there was seemingly nothing he couldn't win. At least, not until he suffered a terrifying crash on the track at Blois. He said later he had never suffered on the bike up to that point; he just turned the pedals and went. After Blois, however, he often suffered discomfort when he rode, although perhaps not as much as his rivals, as his rate of success barely dropped off.

At the Ronde, though, another Belgian would emerge as the king of the cobbles, a rider who was by no means as talented or as flamboyant as Merckx, but could, by Karel Van Wijnendaele's standards at least, qualify as a 'Flandrien'.

20

BRING ON THE BERGS

As Eddy Merckx recovered from his crash at Blois, the Belgian press obsessed about the impact the incident would have on him. By the early spring of 1970, they had the beginnings of an answer as Merckx won three stages and stomped all over the hopes of his rivals at Paris–Nice. Although he missed out at Sanremo, where Michele Dancelli ended Italy's long drought, Merckx went into Flanders heavily backed to retain his crown.

Leading the now renamed Faemino team, he wasn't disappointed to find the weather glacial and the wind gusty, just as it had been 12 months earlier. The course had been toughened up as well, with a record eight *hellingen* on the route, including the kilometre-long partly cobbled climb of the Bosberg, located close to the Muur. To guarantee he could take advantage of these difficulties, Merckx instructed his teammates to make the pace as relentless as possible. His main rivals at Mars-Flandria and Salvarani, meanwhile, did all they could to escape from Faemino's yoke, forcing Merckx himself to chase down attacks.

While the Belgians attempted to wear each other down, 1967 Tour de France champion Roger Pingeon opened up a useful lead as the wind pushed him up and over the Muur and Bosberg. However, when he turned into the teeth of it at Ninove, the Frenchman realised the folly of a solo effort. On the Valkenberg, Merckx and Walter Godefroot caught the wilting Pingeon and soon after there were 14 riders at the front. Merckx was the only Faemino representative in the group, and was up against a quartet from Mars-Flandria, plus Salvarani leaders Godefroot and Felice Gimondi.

Flandria's Eric Leman, a former butcher's assistant, who had won a stage of his own at Paris–Nice, attacked, Merckx and Godefroot chasing after him. With all of the strongest teams represented in the break, this trio eased away approaching the finish at Gentbrugge. The slowest of the three in a sprint, Merckx was further handicapped by the work he had done in chasing down earlier breaks and, crucially, by a slowly deflating rear tyre, which was certain to cost him a bit of speed on the cobbles at the finish.

When Leman accelerated from 250m out, Godefroot jumped on his wheel but made no impression as he tried to come by. 'Merckx also responded quickly but he had nothing left to give,' wrote Belgian journalist René Jacobs in *Les Sports*, who described the hostility evident between the many Belgian contenders. 'All of them had one objective: to have a fresh rider in contention at the finish in order to respond to the threat offered by Merckx and to beat him if possible. The reason Leman was the freshest of the riders up there was because he was a talented rider who was in perfect physical condition and possessed to a very high degree the ability to discern which were the most dangerous attacks and therefore be able to get into them without going too deeply into his reserves. It is sometimes said of Leman that he is a "profiteer". Let's say instead that he makes best use of the ability he has.'

When Leman returned to defend his title, he was a man in mourning. Earlier that year, his wife had died in a car crash. In mid-March his Mars-Flandria teammate Jean-Pierre 'Jempi' Monséré had been killed during a race in West Flanders. In the circumstances, Leman's twenty-fourth place was a courageous performance. Dutchman Evert Dolman's attack from a kilometre out won him the race and did at least keep the title within the Mars-Flandria camp.

Merckx had been so tightly marked during that race that he let his domestiques off the leash, and was sorely disappointed when victory evaded his three teammates in the winning break. Even though he was as tightly marked in 1972 and 1973, he didn't allow his teammates the same leeway again. In the first of those races, the rain was so heavy that only three riders managed to stay in the saddle all the way to the top of the mud-covered Muur, and 'The Cannibal' wasn't among them. Yet, once again, he was in the winning group, together with six of his compatriots.

Although as belligerent as ever during the race, Merckx was unusually tentative following a bunch sprint crash during Paris–Nice a couple of weeks earlier. As was the case that day in St-Etienne, Eric Leman burst from the pack to win, although he moved sharply to his right during the sprint to ensure Frans Verbeeck didn't find a way past him. 'I'm afraid of crashing,' Merckx confessed, before complaining: 'Sprint finishes are dangerous enough but they become kamikaze affairs with all the jersey-pullers who achieve with their hands what they should be doing with their legs.'

In 1973, he did all he could to scatter the sprinters on another blustery day, leading over the Kwaremont, the Kruisberg and the Muur, constantly pushing on the front of the lead group to prevent riders coming across from behind. However, the introduction of a finishing circuit at the new finish in Meerbeke, to the west of Brussels, didn't benefit him because the closing kilometres weren't as tough as they had been. Although only three riders survived Merckx's constant harrying, sprinters Leman and Freddy Maertens were two of them. Described by Flemish legend Briek Schotte as 'the perfect prototype of a Tour of Flanders rider', Leman outpaced Maertens, with Merckx a very distant third.

When Merckx finished in the group led in by Dutch sprinter Cees Bal in 1974, some observers wondered if he would ever win the Ronde again. But that elusive second Ronde success wasn't far away. A year later, wearing the world champion's rainbow jersey for the third time, Merckx felt he was on the verge of something special when he claimed a sixth victory in Sanremo. But he knew the Ronde would be tougher for him because of the number of very durable sprinters he was up against. Speaking before the race, 1963 champion Noël Foré, who had taken up a role as one of the Ronde's assistant directors, explained that Merckx had just one option if he were to prevail. 'He will have to make the race hard and try to distance his rivals a long way out from the finish.'

Merckx had failed to do exactly this in the three previous editions. Another failure, he said, could only be avoided if he could shed all the sprinters before the top of the final climb. He discussed his strategy with his Molteni team directors, Giorgio Albani and Bob Lelangue. Albani advised him to hold back as long as he could, but Merckx felt this would suit his rivals. He insisted he needed to attack from a long way out, and decided the Oude Kwaremont was the ideal place to make an initial move, even though it was 100km from the finish.

The weather was stereotypically Flemish – a cold front was gusting through, sending squalls of rain and even occasional flurries of snow hurrying across the peloton as it neared the shiny cobbles and muddy ruts of the Kwaremont. At the foot of the hill, Flandria's Marc Demeyer whistled a warning to his teammate and close friend Freddy Maertens, nodding in Merckx's direction. But before Maertens could manoeuvre across the pavé to get close to his rival's wheel, Merckx had accelerated, with just Frans Verbeeck in close attention. As the pair passed the memorial to Karel Van Wijnendaele at the top of the Kwaremont, they were 200m clear with just lone breakaway Dirk Baert still ahead of them. Merckx led Verbeeck past Baert minutes later on the Kruisberg.

The two leaders pressed on, Merckx doing almost all of the pace-making, Verbeeck, his face a picture of pain, grimly hanging on, able to provide only occasional relays. When they reached the top of the Taaienberg, Lelangue, who had been shuttling backwards and forwards between the two leaders and their pursuers, drove up alongside Merckx to inform him his advantage was more than a minute and growing. If anything, the world champion now pushed harder, crossing the Eikenberg, Volkegemberg and Varentberg, with Verbeeck looking older on each passing hill, more and more lines evident on his grimacing face. Somehow he stuck with Merckx on the Muur and the Bosberg, but could offer no response when 'The Cannibal' stomped hard on the pedals five kilometres from the finish, determined to prevent any chance of a sprint. The gap between them was 30 seconds at the line. Five minutes passed before Demeyer took third place.

'I've never ridden as well as that,' Merckx declared. After being helped off his bike by a spectator, Verbeeck murmured: 'Merckx rode five kilometres an hour too fast for us. I couldn't do anything against him. He's from another world. I don't think he's ever been as strong.'

'Moral Winner' Maertens

It was Merckx's final tilt at the Ronde title. Although he rode the next two years, he was undone by the Ronde's newest addition, a 682m-long climb rising at an average of ten per cent straight up on to the ridge of the Flemish Ardennes from Melden, south-west of Oudenaarde. In 1976, the Koppenberg was one of a record ten *hellingen* on the latest reconfiguration of the route, but at the finish it was the only climb anyone was talking about. A paltry five riders managed to ride it from bottom to top – Maertens, Demeyer, Roger De Vlaeminck, Walter Planckaert and young Italian Francesco Moser. One hundred and sixty-two others had to take to their feet, including Merckx, who famously complained: 'It's irresponsible to keep this hill in the race. You might as well make the cyclists climb ladders with bikes around their necks.'

The five conquerors of the Koppenberg were never caught, Planckaert winning the sprint. Despite many complaints, the climb remained on the route for more than a decade. In 1977, Merckx did manage to lead the race over it after attacking beforehand with this objective in mind. Soon after, he was joined by two of the riders who had coped with the

Koppenberg the year before, De Vlaeminck and Maertens, who had taken the world title in the meantime.

The barrel-chested and bullish Maertens had already won 15 races coming into the Ronde on the back of 54 the previous season and believed the race was his for the taking. At the foot of the Koppenberg he had hopped off his bike to pick up a more lightweight alternative from his soigneur, Jef D'hont. After Maertens and De Vlaeminck had finally caught and dropped Merckx, who abandoned on what would be his final appearance in the race, UCI commissaire Jos Fabri came alongside them, informing Maertens he had had an illegal bike change. 'No new bikes on the Koppenberg,' he yelled, telling the Belgian he was disqualified.

Unbeknown to Maertens, the UCI had told a meeting of team managers the day before the Ronde that bike changes were not allowed at the foot of the Koppenberg in order to prevent a bottleneck occurring. Maertens' manager, the self-aggrandising Lomme Driessens, hadn't bothered to turn up to the meeting, and thanks to that foolish oversight he had sanctioned the prohibited handover.

As Fabri gesticulated, Maertens insisted he would continue and appeal the decision. You'll be wasting your breath on both counts, Fabri told him. Athough he had messed up, Driessens still felt Maertens could gain from the situation. There were 60km to the finish and De Vlaeminck was unlikely to hold off the chasing pack on his own. Consequently, Driessens put an idea to Maertens, who rode back up to De Vlaeminck. 'Shall we say 300,000 Belgian francs, Roger?' he asked.

De Vlaeminck agreed, then determined to make Maertens earn every franc by sitting on his wheel for most of the way into the finish. This suited Maertens perfectly. His chance of victory may have gone, but he was going to end the race with a big payout having demonstrated he was the strongest man on the day. In the finishing straight, De Vlaeminck, who had branded Walter Planckaert 'a wheelsucker' the previous year, finally came to the front to claim the title as the crowd jeered, which hardly befitted his achievement of becoming just the third rider in history to win all five of the Monuments. The fall-out from the day's antics overshadowed De Vlaeminck's feat of completing a full set of victories in the Monuments, which set him alongside Rik Van Looy and Eddy Merckx.

As expected, Maertens' appeal was rejected, although the commissaires did not strip him of second place 'as a show of humanity for his efforts'. The Belgian federation was less generous, disqualifying him when it was confirmed the bike had been handed over by a member of Flandria-Velda's staff as part of what was clearly a pre-arranged strategy.

Some days later, it was revealed that two of the three podium finishers had tested positive for the amphetamine Stimul. Third-placed Walter Planckaert was disqualified, while De Vlaeminck remained the winner. No mention was made of Maertens, but he had effectively been disqualified twice from the same race, although even now he is regarded as the rightful victor, his 'success' even commemorated with an extra stone in the wall of winners constructed in the Tour of Flanders Museum in Oudenaarde. It bears the words 'Moral Winner' above the year and his name. It is perhaps no coincidence that Maertens works there as one of the guides.

Still hulkingly powerful, Maertens is very friendly and approachable, and happy to talk about his racing days, although mention of the deal he struck with De Vlaeminck is best avoided. Both admitted an agreement had been reached, but De Vlaeminck insisted he didn't buy the race. For his part, Maertens complained for more than three decades that De Vlaeminck had only paid half the money he owed. In 2010, Belgium's famous 'fixer' of all things professional cycling-related, Noël Demeulenaere, drew up a contract in which both men agreed not to mention the incident, but the dispute still simmers.

Maertens never did win the title he wanted more than any other. Indeed, Godefroot's surprising second success in 1978, a decade after his first, marked the end of Flemish superiority in the Ronde. In 34 subsequent editions, there have been as many foreign winners as Belgian, and some of the hardcore Flemish fans rank the 1987 success achieved by Walloon Claude Criquielion as the former rather than the latter.

Godefroot later suggested one reason for this evening out in the honours. Very much a 'Flandrien' in the mould of Schotte, although blessed with a much better turn of finishing speed, Godefroot said cycling offered him the chance to rise up the social scale, and not just financially, but required an absolute commitment no matter what hurdles you might have to cross. 'When I was sixteen I used to work fifty to sixty hours a week as a carpenter, and still used to fit in two four-hour rides on top of that. What father would let his son do that today?'

By the late 1970s and into the 1980s, there were many far easier options to make a good living in Flanders, which was replacing Wallonia as Belgium's financial and business centre. As new, more technologically based industries emerged in the Dutch-speaking north of the country, the heavy industries in the French-speaking south went into a steady decline.

The first indication of a change in the balance of power at the Ronde occurred in 1979, when bespectacled Dutchman Jan Raas soloed away to victory. Although his oversized specs gave the impression of a geek, Raas was one of the few riders from outside Flanders who would surely have found favour with Van Wijnendaele. The son of a farmer and one of ten children, Raas was brought up less than ten miles from Flanders in the Dutch province of Zeeland and was renowned as one of the hardest men in the bunch. A five-time winner of the Amstel Gold Classic, the biggest one-day race in the Netherlands, he was a supreme *rouleur* who struggled on most climbs but came to life on the short, steep ramps of Amstel and Flanders. His powerful surges on the Koppenberg split the lead group in 1979, 1980 and 1983, when he claimed a second Ronde crown.

His manager at Ti-Raleigh was the equally unyielding Peter Post, a Dutch former track star nicknamed 'The Emperor of the Six Days'. Post had taken over as manager at Ti-Raleigh in 1974. During his early years with the team, there were a number of British riders on the roster, including Liverpudlian Bill Nickson, who joined them in 1977 after winning the Milk Race, which was effectively the British national tour.

'I did a year with Peter Post – well, a year and a couple of months. The couple of months cracked me,' Nickson later recalled. 'I never had any upset with him to be honest, but he couldn't understand, though, why I had to come back to England for my sister's wedding, which coincided with Paris–Roubaix. He couldn't get it into his head why I would rather go to my sister's wedding than ride Paris–Roubaix. But that was the intensity of the man and the sport, I suppose.

'You didn't expect an awful lot from him and he didn't expect an awful lot from you either to be honest. The British riders were like cannon fodder, there's no doubt about that. Post had a team to run and a budget to run it on. He was a hard taskmaster and rightly so. You were told what to ride and just left to get on with it.' The opinion of another of Raleigh's Brits, Yorkshireman Sid Barras, on Post is unprintable. Needless to say, Post's word was law, a situation that would later lead to a titanic fallout with Raas that split Dutch cycling in two.

Post built up a team of mainly Dutch riders that became one of the dominant forces of the 1970s and 1980s. As well as the rock-hard Raas, Ti-Raleigh featured a host of strongmen, including Gerrie Knetemann, Henk Lubberding, Hennie Kuiper and Bert Oosterbosch. Although some, including 1981 Ronde winner Kuiper, enjoyed some of their best successes after leaving Ti-Raleigh, it was Post who set them on their way, instilling an unparalleled work and team ethic. There was a more sinister side, too, according to Nickson. 'There was a lot going on at the time, an awful lot going on, and I just refused point blank to get involved with it. At the time I just thought, "Well, they're strong lads", and just got on with it. And they were, they were super strong ...'

In Kuiper's 1981 Ronde, Dutch riders filled the podium as Frits Pirard held off Raas in the sprint for second. Although the Flemish struck back when René Martens claimed a fine solo win a year later, he was not a star by any means and didn't go on to achieve headlining status. In truth, Flemish cycling was in a rut. Godefroot had retired, De Vlaeminck was in decline and no obvious names were coming through to replace them. In 1983 and 1984, Post's team started as favourites and achieved solo wins on both occasions thanks to Raas and Johan Lammerts, respectively, after Raleigh's domestiques had ridden their rivals into submission.

That strategy proved successful again in 1985, when the elements, which were described by one paper as 'a meteorological apocalypse', made the cobbled hills almost impossible to climb and turned the flatter roads into mud-covered skidpans. It suited the grittiest and most resilient performers, a day when 'Flandriens' such as Schotte and Van Steenbergen would have thrived. Appropriately, one of their youthful successors did exactly that.

By now, the route featured a number of new additions, including the Molenberg and the Kapelmuur, the road that carries on beyond the Muur, winding up and around the knoll on which the Chapel of the Virgin Mary sits, before dropping back down to Geraardsbergen past Oudeberg castle and the Orangerie des Roses, now the headquarters of an accountancy firm. Initially, former Ti-Raleigh stalwart Hennie Kuiper made the running, forcing a split on the Oude Kwaremont, then going clear of a 12-strong group on the Varentberg. Kuiper was in great form having won Sanremo three weeks before. When his advantage began to stretch, Panasonic-Raleigh duo Phil Anderson and Eric Vanderaerden set off in pursuit.

The tenacious Aussie and the curly-haired Belgian, who had won the junior edition of the Ronde in 1979, caught Kuiper on the Muur. With thousands of fans roaring him on all the way up to the chapel on the top, Vanderaerden made his move, while Anderson sat on the wheel of the fast-fading Kuiper. Once Vanderaerden's advantage had reached the point where his victory was all but assured, Anderson accelerated away from Kuiper to secure second place.

Asked about the hellish conditions that resulted in only 24 of 173 starters reaching the finish, Vanderaerden responded: 'The most dangerous aspect is not the bad weather. It is the stress you're under on the climbs that makes you crazy. You have to be like a trapeze artist. One moment you're hanging in mid-air, then you're pushing, using your elbows, swearing and doing things that are not sensible. Everyone is ready to fight. You have to be a little crazy to do things like this.'

The demise of the Koppenberg

It appeared that even this mangling of the world's leading professionals wasn't enough for the Ronde's organisers. The following year they introduced a new cobbled climb, the Paterberg, which rises up above Berchem, giving a fine view of the power station near the town on the banks of the Schelde. Averaging almost 13 per cent, it remains the steepest climb to appear on the route.

For once, Post's Panasonics were out of the running. His dismay at that was no doubt heightened by the fact that Adri van der Poel took the title in the colours of the Kwantum team that had been established in 1984 by Jan Raas following his retirement. Raas had stocked his roster with former Ti-Raleigh riders, a move that ensured his squad were quickly competitive but also guaranteed Post's ongoing ire.

The two teams marked each other so tightly the following year that they hardly noticed Claude Criquielion slip away to become the first Walloon winner of Flanders. But 'Criq's' canny manoeuvring was not the main topic of discussion post-race. Instead attention focused on little-known Danish rider Jesper Skibby and the infamous Koppenberg. The deteriorating state of the pavé on that climb had been the cause of complaints in several previous seasons, notably 1984 when Raas and Anderson were the only two riders to complete the ascent on their bikes.

Three years on, Skibby was the sole survivor of the early break coming on to the Koppenberg, but the peloton was closing fast. As the Dane reached the mid-point of the Koppenberg, where the roadside banks rise up steeply to create a narrow valley, he began to lose momentum, weave across the road, and finally fell. Still strapped into his pedals, Skibby and his bike blocked most of the road, which left the driver of the race organisation car that was right behind him with a dilemma. Should he drive on and over Skibby or stop, blocking the whole peloton closing in behind? He chose option number one, driving over Skibby's front wheel but somehow managing to avoid the screaming Dane's feet. As the crowd booed, fans ran on to the cobbles to rescue the stricken rider.

It meant the end for the Koppenberg, which was removed from the route, seemingly never to return. Its surface, warped by willow-tree roots and tractors, was almost unrideable. The slightest incident would result in someone halting or toppling, producing a domino effect that left the world's top cyclists sliding around on their metal cleats in a slapstick and rather demeaning manner. Although there was some grumbling about the route becoming easier, the Koppenberg was quickly forgotten, helped by the emergence of a new generation of Flemish one-day stars.

Signed by Jan Raas in 1987 when Superconfex took over from Kwantum as the Dutchman's primary sponsor, Edwig Van Hooydonck stood out thanks to his height, red hair and ability as a *puncheur*. Winner of the under-23 edition of the Ronde in 1986, Van Hooydonck hardly made an impression on his first two pro appearances in the race, but became a Flemish hero on his third, in the process adding renown to one of the race's less celebrated climbs. In lashing rain, Van Hooydonck was among a small group of riders who overhauled lone breakaway Marco Lietti on the Muur. Approaching the chapel, Norway's Dag-Otto Lauritzen, an ex-paratrooper who always performed exceptionally well in bad weather despite admitting he didn't particularly like it, eased away. The towering Van Hooydonck was the only rider able to get across to him.

The pair didn't establish much of a lead and were about to be reeled in by their former companions on the final climb, the Bosberg, when Van Hooydonck hit the gas. No one could follow his acceleration and he powered away to win the title at the age of just 22.

A disastrous defence of the title in 1990 suggested Van Hooydonck might be a one-hit wonder, although he was by no means to the only Belgian to disappoint as Moreno Argentin became just the third Italian after Fiorenzo Magni and Dino Zandegù to win Flanders. It seemed the pressure had got to the humble and rather timid Van Hooydonck, or at least it did until he provided a second demonstration of his incredible power on the Bosberg in 1991. Having forced a selection at the front of the race with a surge on the climb of the Berendries, Van Hooydonck had just three riders for company heading to the Muur – Rolfs Golz and Sørensen from Argentin's Ariostea team and fellow Fleming Johan Museeuw of Lotto.

The quartet remained together crossing the Muur, after which only the Bosberg lay between them and the finish in Meerbeke. Van Hooydonck's rivals must have known what was likely to come next, but when he engaged his 42x15 gear and went with everything he had, none of them could follow and 'Eddy Bosberg' cruised to a second victory. 'I know that climb like the back of my hand,' he said. 'There's a tree on it that acts as a marker for me.'

The Belgian press wondered if his victory signalled the arrival of a second 'ogre', making fitting comparisons with Eddy Merckx given the way Van Hooydonck had ridden everyone off his wheel. The young Fleming played them down. 'Our country is always afflicted by the same problem. As soon as a Belgian rider shows his nose at the front of a race, everyone immediately starts making comparisons with Eddy. It's flattering, but do you think it's very reasonable?'

He would surely have been even more successful but for two drawbacks. The first was physical. The over-the-knee shorts that became his trademark were employed instead of bandages around his knees, which troubled him persistently. He also refused to join so many of his peers in taking advantage of a new generation of performance-enhancing drugs, notably the 'blood-boosting' EPO. Van Hooydonck retired in April 1996 at the age of 29 when he should have been in his prime.

He exchanged the suspect world of professional cycling in the 1990s for the duplicitous environment of politics, becoming an MP for the liberal VLD party. In 2007, he hit out at Museeuw, the rider who claimed what once seemed likely to be Van Hooydonck's status as 'the Lion of Flanders'. In an interview with the *Gazet van Antwerpen*, Van Hooydonck explained that his choice in 1996 was either to take EPO or end his career, recalling the Brabantse Pijl race of that spring when he was in the lead group with Museeuw.

'A few days before he had won the GP E3, a race I'd not taken part in, I said to myself, "I am the freshest and I've got a real chance of winning." And then you see that guy pushing a gear three teeth bigger than you on the Alsemberg and leaving you behind. Later, we heard Museeuw state that he only doped in his final year of racing. What a load of crap! That guy charged throughout his career, it's as simple as that.' Museeuw hit back, saying he regretted hearing 'a two-time winner of the Tour of Flanders making unfounded and false allegations'. Five years later, however, in an interview with the same paper, Museeuw confessed to doping throughout his career, admitting 'doping was part of daily life for almost everyone back then'.

Van Hooydonck should have added another win in Flanders in 1992. However, he and the rest of the contenders misjudged the pursuit of the quartet of riders in the kamikaze break of the race. Among them was Frenchman Jacky Durand, a rider who regarded the waving of a start flag in the same way a cocker spaniel views their owner brandishing a stick. Almost as soon as it had dropped, 'Dudu' would bound away, grinning like a loon, and riding like one, too.

Usually, Durand's breaks came to nothing, although his sponsors were always delighted with the publicity he earned them. On this occasion, though, he scooped the lot. With only Switzerland's Thomas Wegmuller for company coming on to the Bosberg, where their 23-minute advantage had been reduced to less than three, Durand attacked and scurried off to become the first French winner since Jean

Forestier in 1956. Van Hooydonck finished third and best of the favourites behind Wegmuller.

Museeuw vs Van Petegem

For the rest of the decade one man and one team dominated the Ronde. A sprinter when he first emerged on the pro scene, Johan Museeuw hails from Gistel, in the flatlands of Flanders close to the North Sea. Known as a sprinter initially, his career as a Classics contender took off when he joined the GB-MG team managed by Patrick Lefevere, a fellow West Flandrian who had worked his way up the managerial ranks after a short pro career during which the highlight was victory in the 1978 edition of Kuurne–Brussels–Kuurne, a 'semi-Classic' that is one of the preparatory races for Flanders. An amalgamation of the Belgian GB team and the Italian MG squad, Lefevere's outfit boasted several riders who would become one-day icons, including Andrey Tchmil, Franco Ballerini and Mario Cipollini, as well as Museeuw.

It was Museeuw who began Lefevere's run of success when he outsprinted Frans Maassen in 1993. The Dutchman had refused to collaborate with Museeuw when they went clear with 25km left, but still failed to get the better of his rival. Museeuw described the victory as the best of his career, saying there could be no greater highlight for a Fleming than victory in the Ronde. After that high, though, he experienced one of his career lows 12 months later when he got his strategy right by allowing Gianni Bugno to lead out the sprint, but misjudged the Italian's finishing speed. He failed to overhaul him by two centimetres. Surrounded by the press in the aftermath, Museeuw could barely manage a word, his face white with shock.

Unsurprisingly, Museeuw didn't contemplate a sprint when he found himself with another Italian for company in the final 25km another year on. It was a wise decision as Fabio Baldato had some decent history in bunch sprints and would have been no pushover in a head-to-head.

Museeuw attacked hard on the Muur and had the Flemish crowd in raptures on the Bosberg as he romped away to victory. But for that two-centimetre loss to Bugno, he might have been the first rider to emulate Fiorenzo Magni's three Rondes in a row.

He did complete a hat-trick of wins in 1998, when the start was moved from Sint-Niklaas to the centre of historic Bruges. His attack on the Tenbosse in Brakel, 26km from the finish, once again left him alone at the front, the crowd baying as Museeuw, wearing his trademark white 'hairnet' headgear that once kept his curls in place but now covered an expensive weave on his balding pate, rode alone over the Muur and Bosberg, joining Achiel Buysse, Magni and Eric Leman at the top of the list of winners.

It seemed likely he would surpass this illustrious trio, but he never quite managed it. He went close in 1999, when outsprinted by fellow Belgians Peter Van Petegem and Frank Vandenbroucke, and in 2002, when he finished a tearful second behind solo victor Andrea Tafi. Given his later admissions, though, it was perhaps just as well Museeuw's run ended when it did.

His mantle as the locals' favourite was taken up by Van Petegem, whose swarthy presence was rarely evident at the front of any race until it really mattered. Born in Brakel, close to the Tenbosse climb, Van Petegem had steadily edged towards the Ronde's podium. Tenth in 1996, ninth the year after and fifth another 12 months on, he had all the characteristics required to contend, above all local knowledge. Andreas Klier, a German rider so enamoured of Flanders that he moved to Dendermonde in the heart of the region, said of his close friend and training partner: 'Peter knew those roads better than anyone. I learned everything from him. You didn't see him for 220 kilometres, then all of a sudden he was there. He had a better eye than anyone else.'

Klier highlighted just how much Van Petegem's hard-wired knowledge of Flanders benefited the Belgian at the Ronde, when he explained: 'It's the sections in between the climbs that people don't know, and that can often be even more crucial. You have to know where the wind comes from on every road.'

After his victory in 1999, Van Petegem explained his approach to the Ronde. 'If you want to win it you have to be cool, relaxed and attentive. The last thing you should do is throw your powers away too fast, too soon. The days when Eddy Merckx would attack and ride on his own for more than a hundred kilometres are gone. Winning a Classic now is all about waiting and picking your moment,' he said. 'I was sure I would win. Museeuw was still suffering with a knee injury so I knew I could easily beat him, and Vandenbroucke had been showing himself at the front all day.'

If that first victory felt good, Van Petegem's second left him ecstatic. He attacked on the Tenbosse, a climb he'd ridden on since he was a small child. 'No one could beat me in 2003 – no one. That was my moment on the Tenbosse and I did it. Only Vandenbroucke could follow me, but I was certain I would win the sprint.'

A new Ronde takes shape

In between Van Petegem's two victories, the riders were reintroduced to an old foe – the Koppenberg. On 1 April 1997, *Het Nieuwsblad* had reported that its cobbles were about to be covered with tarmac and called on fans to protest against the move. More than a thousand people who failed to note the date of publication turned up, including the mayor of Melden. A collection was started and, unwittingly, the hoax led to the restoration of the rutted berg, which was resurfaced with stones imported from Poland. The climb returned to the race in 2002, but was dropped again four years later after a rider near the front of the pack ended up with his wheel stuck in the grooves between the cobbles, which forced all those behind him on to their feet. Further restoration included the use of mortar between the stones to set them in place. The climb returned to the race in 2008 and has remained an integral part of the route.

The formidable berg's return in 2002 coincided with the emergence of a new and largely untainted generation of cobbled Classics specialists. As had been the case when Museeuw emerged in the early 1990s, the man behind them was Patrick Lefevere, a director with the Midas touch when it comes to identifying and developing Classics contenders. At their head was Tom Boonen.

Although from Mol in the province of Antwerp, and therefore outside the strict boundaries laid by Ronde founder Karel Van Wijnendaele for 'Flandrien' status, 'Tornado Tom' would become the biggest star Belgian cycling has ever seen. He may not compare in ability or results with Eddy Merckx, but in the internet age when the top riders' every move is recorded and analysed, Boonen is very much Belgium's David Beckham.

Standing six foot four, easygoing and just as easy on the eye, Boonen is the son of ex-pro André, who rode for a series of small Belgian teams in the early 1980s. Spotted by Belgian *directeur sportif* Dirk Demol when he was a teenager, Boonen turned pro with Demol's US Postal team in 2002. That spring he produced a staggering debut performance at Paris–Roubaix, finishing third. Courted by Lefevere and his boyhood hero Museeuw, he joined their QuickStep team in 2003. Museeuw anointed Boonen his successor and the handover came in 2005.

One of six riders well clear cresting the Bosberg, Boonen had the sprinting prowess to beat all of them in a straight match, but after 16 climbs and 250km, sprints are anything but predictable, especially with two-time champion Van Petegem and six-time Tour de France points winner Erik Zabel among the 24-year-old Belgian's rivals. Boonen knew Zabel's T-Mobile teammate Andreas Klier would try to soften him up by attacking all the way into the finish, and he caught his rivals out by countering one of Klier's accelerations with nine kilometres left.

The Belgian returned the following year wearing the world champion's rainbow bands and was just as impressive in retaining his title. Supported by a super-strong QuickStep team, Boonen was the only rider able to follow Leif Hoste's attack on the Valkenberg with 30km remaining and easily dispatched his compatriot in the sprint at Meerbeke.

By now living in the very un-'Flandrien' setting of Monaco, Boonen continued to hoover up titles, but it soon became apparent that he had a similar appetite for cocaine. Between November 2007 and April 2009, he tested positive for the recreational drug on three occasions. Although the positives did not lead to bans because cocaine is not considered performance-enhancing to athletes, Boonen's status as the sport's outstanding force in the cobbled Classics came under threat from within his own team when Stijn Devolder won back-to-back editions of the Ronde in 2008 and 2009. To an extent, though, West Flandrian Devolder owed these successes to the close marking of Boonen by QuickStep's rivals.

After four wins in five years, QuickStep encountered a new challenger to their hegemony. Initially known for his prowess in time trials, which brought him four world titles and an Olympic gold medal, Fabian Cancellara had many similar traits to Boonen, although they differed in the way they tended to deliver the *coup de grâce*. Boonen was a better sprinter and often relied on this, while Cancellara's almost unparalleled ability as a time triallist meant he preferred to ride more aggressively with the aim of making a solo attack that no one could follow.

Although their off-the-bike relationship was friendly rather than fierce, their clashes were not to be missed. The pick of them was at Flanders in 2010. Hyped it may have been, but the contest fully lived up to expectations. Both were riding in national champion's colours, watching each other closely. On the Molenberg, 40km from the finish, Cancellara accelerated and Boonen went with him. What was going on behind them quickly became an irrelevance. The pair collaborated until they reached the Muur. Cancellara went to the front as they turned right, opposite the 'T Kapelleke bar, on to the steep ramps off Oudenbergstraat, passing Willie Verhegghe's three bronze statues of cap-wearing fans and towards the sharp right-hander on to the Kapelmuur.

At the point where the road starts to wind left around the knoll on which the hilltop chapel sits and the cobbles ramp up steeply, Cancellara pressed harder, edging away from Boonen, whose face was a picture of torment as victory began to slip away with every pedal stroke his rival made. At the summit, Cancellara's lead was a dozen seconds; by the finish he had added another minute. 'It was not planned. I looked back, saw there was a gap and pushed a bit more,' said 'Spartacus'. 'To win, to attack on the Muur and drop Tom Boonen, the king of Belgium – when I get old and tell people this ... It was the perfect scenario.'

Cancellara's victory produced the most ridiculous of stories, as some riders claimed they had heard a strange whirring come from the new bike he'd been given by his team car late in the race. Rumours circulated of 'mechanical doping'. French pro Anthony Roux told *Le Républicain Lorrain*: 'In the peloton it's being talked about. Everyone thought he was incredible but we wonder whether it is real or not, and whether he has a motor in his bike.' Italian TV channel RAI even analysed Cancellara's gestures, saying they were suspicious and alleging he was engaging the motor. The UCI said it would investigate and went as far as introducing bike scanners at the start of the Tour de France, where Cancellara quipped: 'You'd better scan me, because I am the motor.'

After Nick Nuyens regained the title for Belgium in 2011, the Ronde's organisers unveiled the biggest overhaul to the route in the race's history. There were two principal reasons for it, the first relating to spectator safety, the other to the event's finances. Ever since the inter-war years, the Ronde had been plagued by an excessive number of vehicles, both on the route and, more particularly, around it. In the twenty-first century, the fourteenth Sunday of the year had become nothing less than a gigantic edition of *Wacky Races*. The solution? The introduction of a finishing circuit on which fans could see the race three times.

At the same time, race director Wouter Vandenhaute admitted the race organisation would gain substantially from the sale of VIP packages on the circuit, notably in a 250m VIP tent erected on the Oude Kwaremont to wine and dine more than 5,000 people. If this was bad for the Ronde's diehards, worse was to follow when Vandenhaute unveiled a new route that featured three ascents of the Oude Kwaremont and Paterberg, but bypassed the iconic Muur completely.

Irate fans signed a petition demanding the Muur be kept in the race, while 500 protesters went further, staging a mock funeral for the Muur in Geraardsbergen. Six Lycra-clad men, wearing masks bearing Vandenhaute's face, carried a coffin. Trumpets played as it was borne up the climb before being laid to rest in the chapel at the top, where people queued to pay a final tribute and sign a book of condolence. Many dug cobbles out of the road surface as mementos.

Opinion among the pros was split. Two-time champion Devolder commented: 'I think it's a bad thing to change things in cycling that are successful – and the Muur and the Bosberg at the Tour of Flanders was an especially successful combination.' Devolder spoke for many when he added: 'One thing for sure is that it's going to be a hard race. The new route may be too tough and will prevent guys wanting to attack.'

Defending champion Nuyens was more accepting, saying: 'I think you can see a similarity between the Muur–Bosberg climbs and the Kwaremont Paterberg: long then steep … In reality, not much has changed. It's still sixteen climbs – you hit a climb, recover some, then you hit the next climb – they're just in a different order. For me, it's still the most beautiful race.'

By now retired from racing, Peter Van Petegem, who many still insist knows these roads better than anyone, offered what was perhaps the most reasoned insight. 'The day of the Tour of Flanders is just about the race – it doesn't matter so much where it goes. You have to do cobblestones and climbs and small roads – that's the character of the race. If you do the Muur, the Koppenberg or the Paterberg after 250 kilometres, they're all very hard. Every climb has its own characteristics, but they are all a little bit the same, too,' he said. 'If you had changed the route maybe thirty years ago it probably wouldn't have been big news but now the race is international – it's shown on television all over the world and everybody in cycling is talking about it.'

Ultimately, most were persuaded the right decision had been made. The *frietkraams* selling chips around the course still did a roaring trade, as did the impromptu bars that spring up in garages and on driveways on the climbs. More importantly, though, Tom Boonen emerged from two years of struggle to take his third title, beating two Italians in the sprint at the new finish in Oudenaarde, just metres from the Tour of Flanders Museum. 'I have to thank Tom Boonen for winning. If Alessandro Ballan or Filippo Pozzato had won, the feeling in Flanders might have been very different,' Vandenhaute gamely admitted.

A victory for Cancellara in 2013 backed up Vandenhaute's insistence that the best riders would thrive on this course, but didn't prevent him tinkering with it again in 2014. The VIPs on the Oude Kwaremont still got to see the race three times, but the Paterberg featured just twice and the Koppenberg only once. The result? A third victory for Cancellara, whose status as an adopted Flandrian wasn't dented by his defeat of three home riders in the four-up sprint. A year on, a crash at the GP E3, in which he sustained two broken vertebrae, prevented the Swiss from attempting to emulate Fiorenzo Magni by winning three consecutive editions of the Ronde. In his absence, the title went to Norway for the first time. Alexander Kristoff joined Niki Terpstra in an attack going over the Kruisberg, 28km from the finish, the pair cooperating until the final kilometre, where the Dutchman ended the collaboration. Terpstra sat on his rival's wheel until 200 metres out, but Kristoff still had far too much speed for him.

In 2016, the 100th edition of Flanders began with the peloton paying tribute to the recent loss of two of its members. Before the start, there was a minute's silence in memory of Belgian rider Antoine Demoitié, who had been killed in a collision with a race organisation motorbike at

Gent–Wevelgem just a week earlier. At Hooglede, 25km into the race, the peloton slowed its pace in tribute to local pro Daan Myngheer, who had died following a heart attack at the Critérium International the day after Demoitié's death.

The decisive race action began on the approach to the Kruisberg, with 30km remaining, where Michał Kwiatkowski and world champion Peter Sagan attacked from the group of favourites. Sep Vanmarcke bridged up to them, but Cancellara, riding his final Ronde, just missed the move and his chance of going for a fourth win. This trio caught the survivors from the breakaway going on to the Oude Kwaremont, where Sagan and Vanmarcke pushed on together, Cancellara frantically chasing, but still unable to catch them. Climbing the Paterberg, Sagan powered away from Vanmarcke, who soon found himself with Cancellara for company. Although the pair worked together to bring the Slovak back, their efforts were in vain, Sagan lapping up the applause of the huge crowd at the finish and celebrating with a trademark wheelie once he'd crossed the line.

After 19 years hosting the start, Bruges stepped aside after the 2016 edition to be replaced by Antwerp, a move that allowed the race organisers to rework the route again and restore the Muur and Tenbosse. 'The Muur van Geraardsbergen is monumental in the world of cycle racing and far beyond,' said race director Wim Van Herreweghe of organisers Flanders Classics. 'The return of this iconic climb is a win-win situation for both parties: the Ronde brings prestige to the city of Geraardsbergen; the Muur adds allure to *Vlaanderens Mooiste*.' The two climbs were slotted in almost two-thirds of the way into the course, the climb of Tenbosse leading into the Kapelmuur, before the riders entered the now widely accepted finishing circuit. Some complained that, coming 95km from the finish, the Muur was still an irrelevance, bearing in mind its former stature as the maker or breaker of Ronde dreams, but the action on race day proved otherwise in what turned out to be one of the most extraordinary editions of the race.

Coming on to the Muur's cobbles, Tom Boonen, making his farewell appearance in the Ronde, went to the front of the group of favourites and began to pound out a blistering tempo, which resulted in a small group going clear over the top of the emblematic climb. Boonen's QuickStep teammates Philippe Gilbert and Matteo Trentin were on hand, but contenders such as Sagan and Greg Van Avermaet were absent. The riders off the front maintained a narrow lead until the Oude Kwaremont, with 55km kilometres remaining, where Gilbert, clad in the Belgian champion's jersey, burst away on his own, roared on by the home fans. His attack seemed premature, especially when Sagan, Van Avermaet and others rejoined the group in his wake following the Paterberg.

Gilbert carried a lead of a minute on to the third and final ascent of the Oude Kwaremont, where Sagan struck out in pursuit, Van Avermaet and Oliver Naesen tracking him closely. As they raced up the left-hand gutter, right next to the barrier holding back the baying fans, Sagan's bars snagged on a spectator's jacket and he tumbled on to the cobbles, taking the two riders on his wheel down with him. As they stumbled back to their feet and got going again, Gilbert ploughed on, his lead now unassailable. He milked the tumultuous reception in the final straight, unclipped before the line and walked the last two steps to victory, brandishing his bike above his head. Third that year behind his QuickStep teammate, Niki Terpstra switched positions with Gilbert in 2018, becoming the Ronde's first Dutch winner since Adri van der Poel in 1986. After attacking on the Kruisberg, he finished a dozen seconds clear of Mads Pedersen, with Gilbert third.

The Ronde has not had a tradition of producing surprise winners, particularly in recent seasons, and few would have picked out Alberto Bettiol as a likely champion in 2019. The 25-year-old Italian had never finished in the top 10 at any Monument and didn't even have a pro victory to his credit. He'd shown good form that spring, when he was eleventh at the week-long Tirreno–Adriatico stage race, but regular Flanders challengers Sebastian Langeveld and Sep Vanmarcke were the most likely picks for success on Bettiol's EF Education First team.

Yet, as the favourites ascended the Oude Kwaremont for the final time, the Italian was on Van Avermaet's wheel. He said he was expecting the Belgian to accelerate, but when that didn't happen he followed the instructions of Andreas Klier, his highly experienced *directeur sportif*, who encouraged his rider to attack if his legs felt good. Bettiol jumped away just before the flatter section towards the top of the climb, maintained a slim advantage of little more than a dozen seconds to the top of the Paterberg, then had 14km left to the finish. He had three things in his favour: a tailwind; the presence of Vanmarcke and Langeveld in the group behind and the delaying tactics they employed; and his ability as a time triallist, which had been highlighted at Tirreno, where he'd been a close second in the 10km test on the final day. Despite a committed chase by another emerging spring Classics contender, young Dane Kasper Asgreen, Bettiol hung on.

In a post-race interview, his former teammate Van Avermaet suggested that the Italian was, 'A great talent, but also a bit lazy. Last year he was too fat.' Bettiol admitted that he hadn't really believed in himself before. It was also interesting to note his comments about the Ronde in a 2017 interview with *Cyclingtips*. 'The Tour of Flanders is a very, very hard race to win, but if you feel good, it's not such a hard race. It's the easiest race, because people that are not good on the cobbles are at the back and if you know where is the moment to go in the front, then you stay in the front for so many kilometres, because the roads are narrow. Once you are there, you stay there. Then the selection is made and it is all about your legs. You don't have to do anything, just stay in the front and move.' This was how to win Flanders and two years on he confirmed it.

That race also highlighted the thrilling potential of Mathieu van der Poel, the son of 1986 Flanders winner Adri and grandson of 1961 Milan–Sanremo victor Raymond Poulidor. Fourth in Oudenaarde, despite taking a spectacular tumble approaching the Oude Kwaremont the final time, he emerged as one of the principal actors in the 2020 edition that was postponed to mid-October as a result of the Covid pandemic and cut by 29km to 241km in order to reduce the physical demands on riders during what had become a very intense period of competition, the Muur a victim of that curtailment.

The trigger for what became the winning move was an attack by Flanders debutant Julian Alaphilippe on the Koppenberg, which split the group of favourites. When the Frenchman, wearing the rainbow bands of world champion, attacked again on the next climb, Steenbeekdries, only van der Poel was initially able to follow him, but Wout van Aert managed to bridge up to the pair soon after. A couple of kilometres later, as van Aert set the pace at the head of the trio, the Belgian had to change direction suddenly to avoid a slowing motorbike piloted by a race commissaire. This meant van der Poel, next in line, had to swerve more violently to miss it, but Alaphilippe, right at the back, had no time to react and clipped the bike. The collision sent him crashing to the ground, the impact leaving him with a broken hand. The two leaders, rivals since their mid-teenage years and both multiple winners of the world cyclo-cross championship, glanced back, then sped on, opening a lead of more than a minute on their pursuers. That gap fell dramatically as they played cat and mouse in the final kilometre. With 200 metres left, van Aert accelerated off van der Poel's wheel and got up alongside the Dutchman, but was still half a wheel short at the line.

The trio of main actors from that race were involved in the dénouement of the next edition little more than six months later, when victory eluded all three of them. Van der Poel's attack the second time up the Oude Kwaremont took him clear with Kasper Asgreen briefly. Alaphilippe reprised his 2020 attack on the Koppenberg, which led to a group of nine forming at the front. Soon after the Kruisberg, Asgreen went away again, followed only by van der Poel and van Aert, the latter dropping away when his perennial rival made a stinging attack the final time up the Oude Kwaremont. That ultimately left the Dutchman in the same position he'd been in in 2020, at the front with 200 metres remaining and one rider on his wheel. The final sprint was even until, with 50 metres to the line, van der Poel completely tied up. He had nothing left to give. Asgreen's roar of delight in a finish area empty of fans due to Covid restrictions announced Denmark's second success in the Ronde after Rolf Sørensen's win in 1997.

Flanders' lore has it that experience is essential if a rider is to have a sniff at success. Alaphilippe went some way to burying that trope with his spectacular debut ride in 2019. Three years on, Tadej Pogačar all but entombed it with a breathtaking first appearance where he did everything right – until victory was within his grasp, that is. His first demonstration of ease on the cobbled climbs came the second time up the Oude Kwaremont, where he led the favourites up to the break. A few kilometres later, after young Briton Fred Wright and Dutchman Dylan van Baarle had enjoyed some time off the front, he bridged up to this pair with Mathieu van der Poel and Frenchman Valentin Madouas.

Now Pogačar really got into his stride, dropping everyone bar van der Poel the final time up the Oude Kwaremont and very nearly cracking the 2020 champion on the Paterberg soon after. Surprisingly, the attacks finished there and the pair rode into the finish together, where they slowed and each waited for the other to commit. Their dallying allowed van Baarle and Madouas to regain contact and, as van der Poel finally opened up from the front, Pogačar's clear route towards the line suddenly disappeared. The Dutchman held on to win, his compatriot van Baarle was second, while the irate Pogačar was left gesturing at his rivals and complaining that he'd been blocked.

It's worth noting that the Muur didn't reappear on the route for either of those thrilling races that followed the Covid-shortened 2020 edition. Decried a decade earlier, its absence is now accepted, although regretfully by many. What's more, a good case can even be made for the revamped course, with its circuits and VIP areas, being just as good or even better than what was regarded as the traditional one. It's certainly far less chaotic now that fans on motorbikes and in cars can no longer access the course and even the race convoy as was often the case. The continuing and immense popularity of the Ronde is further evidence of its success. By attracting 800,000 fans to watch an event that remains not only Belgium's biggest sporting spectacle, but also an event of huge significance to the Flemish, it remains a unique race, woven into the local cultural fabric like no other on the calendar, still *Vlaanderens Mooiste.*

ENDPIECE:
TRULY MONUMENTAL

'These races are brutally hard, they are dirty, they are very long. Everyone knows the rider who wins these races is a really tough guy, a true hard man. Then you think about the history of these races, you look at the great names that have won them in the past, and you realise what it would mean to win one of them, that your name would go down alongside all of cycling's legends. I love riding them.'

Thor Hushovd's words encapsulate the regard most professional cyclists have for the Monuments. The Norwegian, winner of the world title in 2010, went on to confess he would gladly swap one of his eight Tour de France stage victories for success in a Monument.

While there is no question that the Monuments and, indeed, every other bike race of significance, will always be overshadowed by the Tour de France, such is the epic scale and reach of that extraordinary event, cycling's greatest one-day tests are essential pillars of the sport. To an extent, this status stems from their longevity and highly illustrious history. More importantly, though, they provide something that the Tour can't: a classic challenge that is within the reach of any of the riders lining up on their start lines.

At the Tour, might is always right and often no more than a handful of riders have any chance of winning the fabled yellow jersey. The Monuments, on the other hand, provide a more level playing field, offering every member of the 200-strong peloton a reason for hope, the belief that they may be able to emulate 1992 Tour of Flanders champion Jacky Durand, 2011 Lombardy victor Oliver Zaugg or 2016 Roubaix winner Mat Hayman by upsetting bike racing's established hierarchy and putting their name next to those of Merckx, De Vlaeminck, Van Looy, Coppi, Girardengo and Kelly. In short, unlike most editions of the Tour, they present that essential quality required for a gripping sporting contest: unpredictability.

This essence of randomness is also reflected in their evolution over the last century and more. Of the quintet, only Sanremo's has been linear. *La Classicissima*'s route, a total anomaly in the modern era but one of the factors that makes it so compelling, was established at its very first edition and has remained largely unchanged, bar the introduction of slight diversions designed to provide a level playing field for as many contenders as possible. What's more, it has always attracted a strong field. While Roubaix has boasted this same drawing power, the modernisation of the French road network in the two decades following the Second World War almost resulted in 'The Hell of the North' being wiped from the map, or at the very least undergoing a radical modification of the test it offered. Thankfully, that threat to its legitimacy was avoided and, the Tour de France apart, it is arguably the most eagerly awaited race in any season.

Flanders, Liège and Lombardy, meanwhile, have struggled to overcome a more fundamental vulnerability, that of recognition. The former was very much a domestic affair until Fiorenzo Magni unlocked its maze of straats and bergs for foreign riders with his hat-trick of wins at the turn of the 1950s. Subsequently, its standing has rocketed, to a large degree because it is bracketed alongside Roubaix as the most exalted of the cobbled Classics. Its significance as both a sporting event and a cultural landmark for the Flemish people has also ensured its vitality. While Liège is the oldest of the quintet, more than six decades passed until it began to be regarded as a title that could be compared with the other Monuments, and it too might have gone under if ASO hadn't stepped in as co-organisers in 1990 and, later on, as owners of *La Doyenne*.

Turning to Lombardy, its prestige was long affected by its isolation from its peers at the tail-end of the calendar, which, perversely, had been the reason for its popularity in the first place. Its travails have reflected those of a sport that is dominated so hugely by the Tour de France, a climactic sporting event that sits in the middle of the calendar. During the period when the UCI attempted to rebalance the racing calendar in the decades either side of the Millennium by introducing first the World Cup and then the ProTour in order to encourage the participation of as many of the highest-ranked riders as possible, Lombardy lost its way. To a degree, the race became the largely domestic affair it had been in the years following its establishment. This drift, partly the result of organisational issues, also highlighted a fundamental flaw inherent in the implementation of the F1-style ranking model within cycling. In F1, victory in the drivers' championship dwarfs success in individual Grand Prix. In bike racing, the opposite is true. No one would prize victory in the ProTour individual standings above a success in a Monument.

Lombardy's ebbing fortunes reversed, though, in the late noughties, just before the transformation of the ProTour into the WorldTour in 2011. One key reason for this was growing acceptance of the Monuments as a collective of the five most coveted one-day races. Up to that point, they'd been highly prized, but so too had others – the Amstel Gold Race, Paris–Tours, Paris–Brussels, Flèche Wallonne, the Championship of Zurich. Yet the label of 'Monuments' – introduced, it should be remembered, by the UCI – set them further above and apart from the other Classics. The term had resonance. At the same time, the leading teams became more international. Their sponsors had a global rather than a national focus, and their rosters and objectives began to reflect this more obviously. As a consequence, victories in these elite races were much more significant, especially as cycling's TV audience grew rapidly beyond its traditional heartlands and particularly in those nations where the market for televised sport is extremely competitive, including the UK, Australia, North America, the Middle East and the Far East.

The Monuments have been in the vanguard of the races benefiting from this demand. They not only attract some of the strongest fields of the cycling season, including many of the riders so familiar to everyone during the Tour de France in July, but they also offer a very different, but equally compelling, perspective on the sport. Who could resist the spectacle of watching racers battling each other, the cobbles and the elements at Roubaix? Or the contest between *puncheurs* and sprinters at Sanremo? Or the challenge offered by fearsome 'walls' such as the Koppenberg, Roche-aux-Faucons and the Sormano?

Looking ahead, the iconic status of these five great races seems assured and radiant, but questions still linger. Why, for instance, do the two Italian Monuments still not have a women's edition? If this oversight isn't rectified, should two other races be considered for inclusion to eliminate this disparity? Furthermore, should there be a sixth Monument? There has been plenty of lobbying by riders and fans for the addition of Strade Bianche to the elite list of five. Since its inception in 2007, this race over Tuscany's white gravel roads has enjoyed a stratospheric rise in popularity. Run over the March weekend before Milan–Sanremo, it attracts strong fields to both its men's and women's events, and undoubtedly has the anomalous and even anachronistic flavour of a Monument. The naysayers argue, though, that it lacks the distance and history to be worthy of this ranking. Whichever way the debate goes, it helps to feed the emblematic nature of these captivating races.

Like the twisting streets of F1's Monaco Grand Prix or the seaside links courses that play to golf's British Open, the unique nature of the Monuments is their attraction. Like those events, the Monuments are nothing less than anomalies in modern sport, yet they continue to provide cycling's purest tests of skill and ability. Unlike the grand tours, where mediocrity one day can be rectified by brilliance on another, one-day races punish anything less than superlative effort.

The Tour may offer fame and wealth, but the Monuments provide their own special glory and an indelible connection to the great champions of the past; to those riders whose deeds made landmarks like the Poggio, Oude Kwaremont, Arenberg, La Redoute and Ghisallo as renowned as any of the sport's legendary places.

APPENDIX

Liège–Bastogne–Liège
Founded: 1892
Organiser: ASO
Race distance (2022): 257.2km

Key climbs (2022):
76km: Côte de La Roche-en-Ardenne, 2.8km averaging 6.2%
123.5km: Côte de Saint Roch, 1km averaging 11%
164.5: Côte de Mont-le-Soie, 4km averaging 6.1%
172.5km: Côte de Wanne, 2.7km averaging 7.3%
179km: Côte de Stockeu, 1km averaging 12.2%
183.5km: Côte de la Haute Levée, 3.6km averaging 5.7%
197.5km: Col du Rosier, 4.4km averaging 5.9%
211km: Côte de Desnié, 1.6km averaging 8.1%
224km: Côte de La Redoute, 2km averaging 8.8%
241km: Côte de la Roche-aux-Faucons, 1.5km averaging 9.3%

Route of first edition: Liège, Angleur, Esneux, Aywaille, Barvaux, Hotton, Marche, Bande, Champlon and Bastogne, then return by the same route to Liège (250km)

Fastest average speed for winner: 41.397km/h by Remco Evenepoel in 2022

Slowest average speed for winner: 23.32km/h by Léon Houa in 1892

Winner of each edition:

1892 Léon Houa (Bel)

1893 Léon Houa (Bel)

1894 Léon Houa (Bel)

1895 Race not held

1896 Race not held

1897 Race not held

1898 Race not held

1899 Race not held

1900 Race not held

1901 Race not held

1902 Race not held

1903 Race not held

1904 Race not held

1905 Race not held

1906 Race not held

1907 Race not held

1908 André Trousselier (Fra)

1909 Victor Faste (Bel)

1910 Race not held

1911 Joseph Van Daele (Bel)

1912 Omer Verschoore (Bel)

1913 Maurits Moritz (Bel)

1914 Race not held

1915 Race not held

1916 Race not held

1917 Race not held

1918 Race not held

1919 Léon Devos (Bel)

1920 Léon Scieur (Bel)

1921 Louis Mottiat (Bel)

1922 Louis Mottiat (Bel)

1923 René Vermandel (Bel)

1924 René Vermandel (Bel)

1925 Georges Ronsse (Bel)

1926 Dieudonné Smets (Bel)

1927 Maurice Raes (Bel)

1928 Ernest Mottard (Bel)

1929 Alfons Schepers (Bel)

1930 Herman Buse (Bel)

1931 Alfons Schepers (Bel)

1932 Marcel Houyoux (Bel)

1933 François Gardier (Bel)

1934 Théo Herckenrath (Bel)

1935 Alfons Schepers (Bel)

1936 Albert Beckaert (Bel)

1937 Eloi Meulenberg (Bel)

1938 Alfons Deloor (Bel)

1939 Albert Ritserveldt (Bel)

1940 Race not held

1941 Race not held

1942 Race not held

1943 Richard Depoorter (Bel)

1944 Race not held

1945 Jean Engels (Bel)

1946 Prosper Depredomme (Bel)

1947 Richard Depoorter (Bel)

1948 Maurice Mollin (Bel)

1949 Camille Danguillaume (Fra)

1950 Prosper Depredomme (Bel)

1951 Ferdi Kübler (Swi)

1952 Ferdi Kübler (Swi)

1953 Aloïs Den Hertog (Bel)

1954 Marcel Ernzer (Lux)

1955 Stan Ockers (Bel)

1956 Fred De Bruyne (Bel)

1957 F. Schoubben (Bel) & G. Derijcke (Bel)

1958 Fred De Bruyne (Bel)

1959 Fred De Bruyne (Bel)

1960 Albertus Geldermans (Hol)

1961 Rik Van Looy (Bel)

1962 Jos Planckaert (Bel)

1963 Frans Melckenbeeck (Bel)

1964 Willy Bocklant (Bel)

1965 Carmine Preziosi (Ita)

1966 Jacques Anquetil (Fra)

1967 Walter Godefroot (Bel)

1968 Valere Van Sweevelt (Bel)

1969 Eddy Merckx (Bel)

1970 Roger De Vlaeminck (Bel)

1971 Eddy Merckx (Bel)

1972 Eddy Merckx (Bel)

1973 Eddy Merckx (Bel)

1974 Georges Pintens (Bel)

1975 Eddy Merckx (Bel)

1976 Joseph Bruyère (Bel)

1977 Bernard Hinault (Fra)

1978 Joseph Bruyère (Bel)

1979 Dietrich Thurau (Ger)

1980 Bernard Hinault (Fra)

1981 Jozef Fuchs (Swi)

1982 Silvano Contini (Ita)

1983 Steven Rooks (Ned)

1984 Sean Kelly (Irl)

1985 Moreno Argentin (Ita)

1986 Moreno Argentin (Ita)

1987 Moreno Argentin (Ita)

1988 Adrie van der Poel (Ned)

1989 Sean Kelly (Irl)

1990 Erik Van Lancker (Bel)

1991 Moreno Argentin (Ita)

1992 Dirk De Wolf (Bel)

1993 Rolf Sørensen (Den)

1994 Evgeni Berzin (Rus)

1995 Mauro Gianetti (Swi)

1996 Pascal Richard (Swi)

1997 Michele Bartoli (Ita)

1998 Michele Bartoli (Ita)

1999 Frank Vandenbroucke (Bel)

2000 Paolo Bettini (Ita)

2001 Oscar Camenzind (Swi)

2002 Paolo Bettini (Ita)

2003 Tyler Hamilton (USA)

2004 Davide Rebellin (Ita)

2005 Alexandre Vinokourov (Kaz)

2006 Alejandro Valverde (Spa)

2007 Danilo Di Luca (Ita)

2008 Alejandro Valverde (Spa)

2009 Andy Schleck (Lux)

2010 Alexandre Vinokourov (Kaz)

2011 Philippe Gilbert (Bel)

2012 Maxim Iglinsky (Kaz)

2013 Daniel Martin (Irl)

2014 Simon Gerrans (Aus)

2015 Alejandro Valverde (Spa)
2016 Wout Poels (Ned)
2017 Alejandro Valverde (Spa)
2018 Bob Jungels (Lux)
2019 Jakob Fuglsang (Den)
2020 Primož Roglič (Slo)
2021 Tadej Pogačar (Slo)
2022 Remco Evenepoel (Bel)

Victories by nation:
60 Belgium
12 Italy
6 Switzerland
5 France
4 Netherlands
4 Spain
3 Ireland
3 Kazakhstan
3 Luxembourg
2 Germany
2 Denmark
2 Slovenia
1 Russia
1 United States
1 Australia

Multiple victories:
5
Eddy Merckx (Bel) 1969, 1971–3, 1975

4
Moreno Argentin (Ita) 1985–7, 1991
Alejandro Valverde (Spa) 2006, 2008, 2015, 2017

3

Léon Houa (Bel) 1892–4
Alfons Schepers (Bel) 1929, 1931, 1935
Fred De Bruyne (Bel) 1956, 1958, 1959

2

Louis Mottiat (Bel) 1921, 1922
René Vermandel (Bel) 1923, 1924
Richard Depoorter (Bel) 1943, 1947
Prosper Depredomme (Bel) 1946, 1950
Ferdi Kübler (Swi) 1951, 1952
Joseph Bruyère (Bel) 1976, 1978
Bernard Hinault (Fra) 1977, 1980
Sean Kelly (Irl) 1984, 1989
Michele Bartoli (Ita) 1997, 1998
Paolo Bettini (Ita) 2000, 2002
Alexandre Vinokourov (Kaz) 2005, 2010

Paris–Roubaix
Founded: 1896
Organiser: ASO
Race distance (2022): 257.2km

Cobbled sectors (2022, with difficulty rating, five stars being the toughest):
Sector 30, 96.3km: Troisvilles to Inchy, 2.2km **
Sector 29, 102.8km: Viesly to Quiévy, 1.8km ***
Sector 28, 105.4km: Quiévy to St-Python, 3.7km ****
Sector 27, 110.1km: St-Python, 1.5km **
Sector 26, 117.9km: Vertain to Saint-Martin-sur-Écaillon, 2.3km ***
Sector 25, 123.7km: Haussy, 800m **
Sector 24, 130.6km: Saulzoir to Verchain-Maugré, 1.2km **
Sector 23, 134.9km: Verchain-Maugré to Quérénaing, 1.6km ***

Sector 22, 137.6km: Quérénaing to Maing, 2.5km ***

Sector 21, 140.7km: Maing to Monchaux-sur-Écaillon, 1.6km ***

Sector 20, 153.7km: Haveluy to Wallers, 2.5km ****

Sector 19, 161.9km: Arenberg Trench, 2.4km *****

Sector 18, 167.9km: Wallers to Hélesmes, 1.6km ***

Sector 17, 174.7km: Hornaing to Wandignies-Hamage, 3.7km ****

Sector 16, 182.2km: Warlaing to Brillon, 2.4km ***

Sector 15, 185.6km: Tilloy to Sars-et-Rosières, 2.4km ****

Sector 14, 192km: Beuvry-la-Forêt to Orchies, 1.4km ***

Sector 13, 197km: Orchies, 1.7km ***

Sector 12, 203.1km: Auchy-lez-Orchies to Bersée, 2.7km ****

Sector 11, 208.6km: Mons-en-Pévèle, 3km *****

Sector 10, 214.6km Mérignies to Avelin, 0.7km **

Sector 9, 218km: Pont-Thibaut to Ennevelin, 1.4km ***

Sector 8, 223.4km: Templeuve to L'Épinette, 0.2m * and 223.9km:
   Templeuve to Moulin-de-Vertain, 0.5km **

Sector 7, 230.3km: Cysoing to Bourghelles, 1.3km ***

Sector 6, 232.8km: Bourghelles to Wannehain, 1.1km ***

Sector 5, 237.3km: Camphin-en-Pévèle, 1.8km ****

Sector 4, 240km: Carrefour de l'Arbre, 2.1km *****

Sector 3, 242.3km: Gruson, 1.1km **

Sector 2, 249km: Willems to Hem, 1.4km **

Sector 1, 255.8km: Roubaix, 0.3km *

TOTAL 54.8km

Route of first edition: Paris, Rueil, St-Germain, Pontoise, Beauvais, Breteuil, Amiens, Doullens, Arras, Hénin-Liétard, Carvin, Seclin, Lesquin, Roubaix (280km)

Fastest average speed for winner: 45.792km/h by Dylan van Baarle in 2022

Slowest average speed for winner: 22.857km/h by Henri Pélissier in 1919

Winner of each edition:

1896 Josef Fischer (Ger)

1897 Maurice Garin (Fra)

1898 Maurice Garin (Fra)

1899 Albert Champion (Fra)

1900 Emile Bouhours (Fra)

1901 Lucien Lesna (Fra)

1902 Lucien Lesna (Fra)

1903 Hippolyte Aucouturier (Fra)

1904 Hippolyte Aucouturier (Fra)

1905 Louis Trousselier (Fra)

1906 Henri Cornet (Fra)

1907 Georges Passerieu (Fra)

1908 Cyrille Van Hauwaert (Bel)

1909 Octave Lapize (Fra)

1910 Octave Lapize (Fra)

1911 Octave Lapize (Fra)

1912 Charles Crupelandt (Fra)

1913 François Faber (Lux)

1914 Charles Crupelandt (Fra)

1915 Race not held

1916 Race not held

1917 Race not held

1918 Race not held

1919 Henri Pélissier (Fra)

1920 Paul Deman (Bel)

1921 Henri Pélissier (Fra)

1922 Albert Dejonghe (Bel)

1923 Heiri Suter (Swi)

1924 Jules Van Hevel (Bel)

1925 Félix Sellier (Bel)

1926 Julien Delbecque (Bel)

1927 Georges Ronsse (Bel)

1928 André Leducq (Fra)

1929 Charles Meunier (Bel)

1930 Julien Vervaecke (Bel)

1931 Gaston Rebry (Bel)

1932 Romain Gijssels (Bel)

1933 Sylvère Maes (Bel)

1934 Gaston Rebry (Bel)

1935 Gaston Rebry (Bel)

1936 Georges Speicher (Fra)

1937 Jules Rossi (Ita)

1938 Lucien Storme (Bel)

1939 Émile Masson Jr (Bel)

1940 Race not held

1941 Race not held

1942 Race not held

1943 Marcel Kint (Bel)

1944 Maurice Desimpelaere (Bel)

1945 Paul Maye (Fra)

1946 Georges Claes (Bel)

1947 Georges Claes (Bel)

1948 Rik Van Steenbergen (Bel)

1949 André Mahé (Fra) & Serse Coppi (Ita)

1950 Fausto Coppi (Ita)

1951 Antonio Bevilacqua (Ita)

1952 Rik Van Steenbergen (Bel)

1953 Germain Derycke (Bel)

1954 Raymond Impanis (Bel)

1955 Jean Forestier (Fra)

1956 Louison Bobet (Fra)

1957 Fred De Bruyne (Bel)

1958 Leon Vandaele (Bel)

1959 Noël Foré (Bel)

1960 Pino Cerami (Bel)

1961 Rik Van Looy (Bel)

1962 Rik Van Looy (Bel)

1963 Emile Daems (Bel)

1964 Peter Post (Ned)

1965 Rik Van Looy (Bel)

1966 Felice Gimondi (Ita)

1967 Jan Janssen (Ned)

1968 Eddy Merckx (Bel)

1969 Walter Godefroot (Bel)

1970 Eddy Merckx (Bel)

1971 Roger Rosiers (Bel)

1972 Roger De Vlaeminck (Bel)

1973 Eddy Merckx (Bel)

1974 Roger De Vlaeminck (Bel)

1975 Roger De Vlaeminck (Bel)

1976 Marc Demeyer (Bel)

1977 Roger De Vlaeminck (Bel)

1978 Francesco Moser (Ita)

1979 Francesco Moser (Ita)

1980 Francesco Moser (Ita)

1981 Bernard Hinault (Fra)

1982 Jan Raas (Ned)

1983 Hennie Kuiper (Ned)

1984 Sean Kelly (Irl)

1985 Marc Madiot (Fra)

1986 Sean Kelly (Irl)

1987 Eric Vanderaerden (Bel)

1988 Dirk Demol (Bel)

1989 Jean-Marie Wampers (Bel)

1990 Eddy Planckaert (Bel)

1991 Marc Madiot (Fra)

1992 Gilbert Duclos-Lassalle (Fra)

1993 Gilbert Duclos-Lassalle (Fra)

1994 Andrei Tchmil (Ukr)

1995 Franco Ballerini (Ita)

1996 Johan Museeuw (Bel)

1997 Frédéric Guesdon (Fra)

1998 Franco Ballerini (Ita)

1999 Andrea Tafi (Ita)

2000 Johan Museeuw (Bel)

2001 Servais Knaven (Ned)

2002 Johan Museeuw (Bel)

2003 Peter Van Petegem (Bel)

2004 Magnus Bäckstedt (Swe)

2005 Tom Boonen (Bel)

2006 Fabian Cancellara (Swi)

2007 Stuart O'Grady (Aus)

2008 Tom Boonen (Bel)

2009 Tom Boonen (Bel)

2010 Fabian Cancellara (Swi)

2011 Johan Vansummeren (Bel)

2012 Tom Boonen (Bel)

2013 Fabian Cancellara (Swi)

2014 Niki Terpstra (Ned)

2015 John Degenkolb (Ger)

2016 Mat Hayman (Aus)

2017 Greg Van Avermaet (Bel)

2018 Peter Sagan (Svk)

2019 Philippe Gilbert (Bel)

2020 Race not held

2021 Sonny Colbrelli (Ita)

2022 Dylan van Baarle (Ned)

Victories by nation:

Belgium 57

France 28

Italy 14

Netherlands 7

Switzerland 4

Ireland 2

Germany 2

Australia 2

Luxembourg 1

Sweden 1

Moldova 1

Slovakia 1

Multiple victories:

4

Roger De Vlaeminck (Bel) 1972, 1974, 1975, 1977

Tom Boonen (Bel) 2005, 2008, 2009, 2012

3

Octave Lapize (Fra) 1909–11

Gaston Rebry (Bel) 1931, 1934, 1935

Rik Van Looy (Bel) 1961, 1962, 1965

Eddy Merckx (Bel) 1968, 1970, 1973

Francesco Moser (Ita) 1978–80

Johan Museeuw (Bel) 1996, 2000, 2002

Fabian Cancellara (Swi) 2006, 2010, 2013

2

Maurice Garin (Fra) 1897, 1898

Lucien Lesna (Fra) 1901, 1902

Hippolyte Aucouturier (Fra) 1903, 1904

Charles Crupelandt (Fra) 1912, 1914
Henri Pélissier (Fra) 1919, 1921
Georges Claes (Bel) 1946, 1947
Rik Van Steenbergen (Bel) 1948, 1952
Sean Kelly (Bel) 1984, 1986
Marc Madiot (Fra) 1985, 1991
Gilbert Duclos-Lassalle (Fra) 1992, 1993
Franco Ballerini (Ita) 1995, 1998

Tour of Lombardy
Founded: 1905
Organiser: RCS Sport
Race distance (2022): 253km

Key climbs (2022):
29.7km, Forcellino di Bianzano: 6.3km averaging 5.0%
49.6km, Passo di Ganda: 9.2km averaging 7.3%
69.6km, Dossena: 5.5km averaging 4.9%
105.1km, Forcella di Bura: 7.1km averaging 3.3%
120.6km, Colle di Berbenno: 4.4km averaging 6.3%
192.2km, Madonna del Ghisallo: 8.6km averaging 6.2%
225.7km, San Fermo della Battaglia: 2.7km averaging 7.2%
236.3km, Civiglio: 4.2km averaging 9.7%
247.8km, San Fermo della Battaglia: 2.7km averaging 7.2%

Route of first edition: Milan, Rogoredo, Melegnano, Lodi, Crema, Bergamo, Lecco, Erba, Como, Varese, Gallarate, Legnano, Rho, Milan (230km)
Fastest average speed for winner: 43.32km/h by Gianni Faresin in 1995
Slowest average speed for winner: 24.970km/h by Giovanni Gerbi in 1905

Winner of each edition:

1905 Giovanni Gerbi (Ita)

1906 Giuseppe Brambilla (Ita)

1907 Gustave Garrigou (Fra)

1908 François Faber (Lux)

1909 Giovanni Cuniolo (Ita)

1910 Giovanni Michelotto (Ita)

1911 Henri Pélissier (Fra)

1912 Carlo Oriani (Ita)

1913 Henri Pélissier (Fra)

1914 Lauro Bordin (Ita)

1915 Gaetano Belloni (Ita)

1916 Leopoldo Torricelli (Ita)

1917 Philippe Thys (Bel)

1918 Gaetano Belloni (Ita)

1919 Costante Girardengo (Ita)

1920 Henri Pélissier (Fra)

1921 Costante Girardengo (Ita)

1922 Costante Girardengo (Ita)

1923 Giovanni Brunero (Ita)

1924 Giovanni Brunero (Ita)

1925 Alfredo Binda (Ita)

1926 Alfredo Binda (Ita)

1927 Alfredo Binda (Ita)

1928 Gaetano Belloni (Ita)

1929 Piero Fossati (Ita)

1930 Michele Mara (Ita)

1931 Alfredo Binda (Ita)

1932 Antonio Negrini (Ita)

1933 Domenico Piemontesi (Ita)

1934 Learco Guerra (Ita)

1935 Enrico Mollo (Ita)
1936 Gino Bartali (Ita)
1937 Aldo Bini (Ita)
1938 Cino Cinelli (Ita)
1939 Gino Bartali (Ita)
1940 Gino Bartali (Ita)
1941 Mario Ricci (Ita)
1942 Aldo Bini (Ita)
1943 Race not held
1944 Race not held
1945 Mario Ricci (Ita)
1946 Fausto Coppi (Ita)
1947 Fausto Coppi (Ita)
1948 Fausto Coppi (Ita)
1949 Fausto Coppi (Ita)
1950 Renzo Soldani (Ita)
1951 Louison Bobet (Fra)
1952 Giuseppe Minardi (Ita)
1953 Bruno Landi (Ita)
1954 Fausto Coppi (Ita)
1955 Cleto Maule (Ita)
1956 André Darrigade (Fra)
1957 Diego Ronchini (Ita)
1958 Nino Defilippis (Ita)
1959 Rik Van Looy (Bel)
1960 Emile Daems (Bel)
1961 Vito Taccone (Ita)
1962 Jo De Roo (Ned)
1963 Jo De Roo (Ned)
1964 Gianni Motta (Ita)
1965 Tom Simpson (GB)
1966 Felice Gimondi (Ita)

1967 Franco Bitossi (Ita)

1968 Herman Van Springel (Bel)

1969 Jean-Pierre Monseré (Bel)

1970 Franco Bitossi (Ita)

1971 Eddy Merckx (Bel)

1972 Eddy Merckx (Bel)

1973 Felice Gimondi (Ita)

1974 Roger De Vlaeminck (Bel)

1975 Francesco Moser (Ita)

1976 Roger De Vlaeminck (Bel)

1977 Gianbattista Baronchelli (Ita)

1978 Francesco Moser (Ita)

1979 Bernard Hinault (Fra)

1980 Fons De Wolf (Bel)

1981 Hennie Kuiper (Ned)

1982 Giuseppe Saronni (Ita)

1983 Sean Kelly (Irl)

1984 Bernard Hinault (Fra)

1985 Sean Kelly (Irl)

1986 Gianbattista Baronchelli (Ita)

1987 Moreno Argentin (Ita)

1988 Charly Mottet (Fra)

1989 Tony Rominger (Swi)

1990 Gilles Delion (Fra)

1991 Sean Kelly (Irl)

1992 Tony Rominger (Swi)

1993 Pascal Richard (Swi)

1994 Vladislav Bobrik (Rus)

1995 Gianni Faresin (Ita)

1996 Andrea Tafi (Ita)

1997 Laurent Jalabert (Fra)

1998 Oscar Camenzind (Swi)

1999 Mirko Celestino (Ita)
2000 Raimondas Rumsas (Lit)
2001 Danilo Di Luca (Ita)
2002 Michele Bartoli (Ita)
2003 Michele Bartoli (Ita)
2004 Damiano Cunego (Ita)
2005 Paolo Bettini (Ita)
2006 Paolo Bettini (Ita)
2007 Damiano Cunego (Ita)
2008 Damiano Cunego (Ita)
2009 Philippe Gilbert (Bel)
2010 Philippe Gilbert (Bel)
2011 Oliver Zaugg (Swi)
2012 Joaquim Rodríguez (Spa)
2013 Joaquim Rodríguez (Spa)
2014 Dan Martin (Irl)
2015 Vincenzo Nibali (Ita)
2016 Esteban Chaves (Col)
2017 Vincenzo Nibali (Ita)
2018 Thibaut Pinot (Fra)
2019 Bauke Mollema (Ned)
2020 Jakob Fuglsang (Den)
2021 Tadej Pogačar (Slo)
2022 Tadej Pogačar (Slo)

Victories by nation:
69 Italy
12 Belgium
12 France
5 Switzerland
4 Ireland
4 Netherlands
2 Spain

2 Slovenia
1 Lithuania
1 Luxembourg
1 Russia
1 Great Britain
1 Colombia
1 Denmark

Multiple victories:
5
Fausto Coppi (Ita) 1946–9, 1954

4
Alfredo Binda (Ita) 1925–7, 1931

3
Henri Pélissier (Fra) 1911, 1913, 1920
Gaetano Belloni (Ita) 1915, 1918, 1928
Costante Girardengo (Ita) 1919, 1921, 1922
Gino Bartali (Ita) 1936, 1939, 1940
Sean Kelly (Irl) 1983, 1985, 1991
Damiano Cunego (Ita) 2004, 2007, 2008

2
Giovanni Brunero (Ita) 1923, 1924
Aldo Bini (Ita) 1937, 1943
Mario Ricci (Ita) 1941, 1945
Jo De Roo (Ned) 1962, 1963
Franco Bitossi (Ita) 1967, 1970
Felice Gimondi (Ita) 1967, 1973
Eddy Merckx (Bel) 1971, 1972
Roger De Vlaeminck (Bel) 1974, 1976
Francesco Moser (Ita) 1975, 1978

Gianbattista Baronchelli (Ita) 1978, 1986
Bernard Hinault (Fra) 1979, 1984
Tony Rominger (Swi) 1989, 1992
Michele Bartoli (Ita) 2002, 2003
Paolo Bettini (Ita) 2005, 2006
Philippe Gilbert (Bel) 2009, 2010
Joaquim Rodríguez (Spa) 2012, 2013
Vincenzo Nibali (Ita) 2015, 2017
Tadej Pogačar (Slo) 2021, 2022

Milan–Sanremo
Founded: 1907
Organiser: RCS Sport
Race distance (2022): 293km

Key climbs (2022):
149.2km, Passo del Turchino: 25.8km averaging 1.4%
235.7km, Capo Mele: 2.5km averaging 5.2%
241.5km, Capo Cervo: 2.5km averaging 4.1%
254.2km, Capo Berta: 3km averaging 4.3%
271.4km, Cipressa: 5.7km averaging 4.1%
287.5km, Poggio di Sanremo: 3.7km averaging 3.7%

Route of first edition: Milan, Pavia, Novi Ligure, Ovada, Passo del Turchino, Voltri, Arenzano, Savona, Finale Ligure, Alassio, Capo Cervo, Capo Berta, Sanremo (288km)
Fastest average speed for winner: 45.806km/h by Gianni Bugno in 1990
Slowest average speed for winner: 22.496km/h by Gaetano Belloni in 1917

Winner of each edition:
1907 Lucien Petit-Breton (Fra)
1908 Cyrille Van Hauwaert (Bel)
1909 Luigi Ganna (Ita)

1910 Eugène Christophe (Fra)

1911 Gustave Garrigou (Fra)

1912 Henri Pelissier (Fra)

1913 Odile Defraye (Bel)

1914 Ugo Agostoni (Ita)

1915 Ezio Corlaita (Ita)

1916 Race not held

1917 Gaetano Belloni (Ita)

1918 Costante Girardengo (Ita)

1919 Angelo Cremo (Ita)

1920 Gaetano Belloni (Ita)

1921 Costante Girardengo (Ita)

1922 Giovanni Brunero (Ita)

1923 Costante Girardengo (Ita)

1924 Pietro Linari (Ita)

1925 Costante Girardengo (Ita)

1926 Costante Girardengo (Ita)

1927 Pietro Chesi (Ita)

1928 Costante Girardengo (Ita)

1929 Alfredo Binda (Ita)

1930 Michele Mara (Ita)

1931 Alfredo Binda (Ita)

1932 Alfredo Bovet (Ita)

1933 Learco Guerra (Ita)

1934 Joseph Demuysère (Bel)

1935 Giuseppe Olmo (Ita)

1936 Angelo Varetto (Ita)

1937 Cesare Del Cancia (Ita)

1938 Giuseppe Olmo (Ita)

1939 Gino Bartali (Ita)

1940 Gino Bartali (Ita)

1941 Pierino Favalli (Ita)

1942 Adolfo Leoni (Ita)

1943 Cino Cinelli (Ita)

1944 Race not held

1945 Race not held

1946 Fausto Coppi (Ita)

1947 Gino Bartali (Ita)

1948 Fausto Coppi (Ita)

1949 Fausto Coppi (Ita)

1950 Gino Bartali (Ita)

1951 Louison Bobet (Fra)

1952 Loretto Petrucci (Ita)

1953 Loretto Petrucci (Ita)

1954 Rik Van Steenbergen (Bel)

1955 Germain Derycke (Bel)

1956 Fred De Bruyne (Bel)

1957 Miguel Poblet (Spa)

1958 Rik Van Looy (Bel)

1959 Miguel Poblet (Spa)

1960 René Privat (Fra)

1961 Raymond Poulidor (Fra)

1962 Emile Daems (Bel)

1963 Joseph Groussard (Fra)

1964 Tom Simpson (GB)

1965 Arie Den Hartog (Ned)

1966 Eddy Merckx (Bel)

1967 Eddy Merckx (Bel)

1968 Rudi Altig (Ger)

1969 Eddy Merckx (Bel)

1970 Michele Dancelli (Ita)

1971 Eddy Merckx (Bel)

1972 Eddy Merckx (Bel)

1973 Roger De Vlaeminck (Bel)

1974 Felice Gimondi (Ita)

1975 Eddy Merckx (Bel)

1976 Eddy Merckx (Bel)

1977 Jan Raas (Ned)

1978 Roger De Vlaeminck (Bel)

1979 Roger De Vlaeminck (Bel)

1980 Pierino Gavazzi (Ita)

1981 Alfons De Wolf (Bel)

1982 Marc Gomez (Fra)

1983 Giuseppe Saronni (Ita)

1984 Francesco Moser (Ita)

1985 Hennie Kuiper (Ned)

1986 Sean Kelly (Irl)

1987 Erich Mächler (Swi)

1988 Laurent Fignon (Fra)

1989 Laurent Fignon (Fra)

1990 Gianni Bugno (Ita)

1991 Claudio Chiappucci (Ita)

1992 Sean Kelly (Irl)

1993 Maurizio Fondriest (Ita)

1994 Giorgio Furlan (Ita)

1995 Laurent Jalabert (Fra)

1996 Gabriele Colombo (Ita)

1997 Erik Zabel (Ger)

1998 Erik Zabel (Ger)

1999 Andrei Tchmil (Bel)

2000 Erik Zabel (Ger)

2001 Erik Zabel (Ger)

2002 Mario Cipollini (Ita)

2003 Paolo Bettini (Ita)

2004 Oscar Freire (Spa)

2005 Alessandro Petacchi (Ita)

2006 Filippo Pozzato (Ita)
2007 Oscar Freire (Spa)
2008 Fabian Cancellara (Swi)
2009 Mark Cavendish (GB)
2010 Oscar Freire (Spa)
2011 Matthew Goss (Aus)
2012 Simon Gerrans (Aus)
2013 Gerald Ciolek (Ger)
2014 Alexander Kristoff (Nor)
2015 John Degenkolb (Ger)
2016 Arnaud Démare (Fra)
2017 Michał Kwiatkowski (Pol)
2018 Vincenzo Nibali (Ita)
2019 Julian Alaphilippe (Fra)
2020 Wout van Aert (Bel)
2021 Jasper Stuyven (Bel)
2022 Matej Mohorič (Slo)

Victories by nation:
51 Italy
22 Belgium
14 France
7 Germany
5 Spain
3 Netherlands
2 Ireland
2 Switzerland
2 United Kingdom
2 Australia
1 Norway
1 Poland
1 Slovenia

Multiple victories:
7
Eddy Merckx (Bel) 1966, 1967, 1969, 1971, 1972, 1975, 1976

6
Costante Girardengo (Ita) 1918, 1921, 1923, 1925, 1926, 1928

4
Gino Bartali (Ita) 1939, 1940, 1947, 1950
Erik Zabel (Ger) 1997, 1998, 2000, 2001

3
Fausto Coppi (Ita) 1946, 1948, 1949
Roger De Vlaeminck (Bel) 1973, 1978, 1979
Oscar Freire (Spa) 2004, 2007, 2010

2
Gaetano Belloni (Ita) 1917, 1920
Alfredo Binda (Ita) 1929, 1931
Giuseppe Olmo (Ita) 1935, 1938
Lorenzo Petrucci (Ita) 1952, 1953
Miguel Poblet (Spa) 1957, 1959
Laurent Fignon (Fra) 1988, 1989
Sean Kelly (Irl) 1986, 1992

Tour of Flanders
Founded: 1913
Organiser: Flanders Classics
Race distance (2022): 272.5km

Key climbs (2022):

136km, Oude Kwaremont: 2,200m (1,500m cobbled) averaging 4%

147km, Kortekeer: 1,000m averaging 6.4%

153km, Achterberg: 1,300m averaging 5%

158km, Wolvenberg: 666m, averaging 6.8%

171km, Molenberg: 463m (300m cobbled) averaging 7%

175km, Marlboroughstraat: 2,040m averaging 4%

179km: Berendries: 940m averaging 7%

184km, Valkenberg: 540m averaging 8.1%

196km, Berg Ten Haute: 1,100m averaging 6%

202km, Kanarieberg: 1000m averaging 7.7%

218km, Oude Kwaremont: 2,200m (1,500m cobbled) averaging 4%

221km, Paterberg: 360m (all cobbled) averaging 12.9%

228km, Koppenberg: 600m (all cobbled) averaging 11.6%

233km, Steenbeekdries: 700m averaging 5.3%

236km, Taaienberg: 530m (500m cobbled) averaging 6.6%

246km, Kruisberg/Hotond: 2,500m averaging 5%

256km, Oude Kwaremont: 2,200m (1,500m cobbled) averaging 4%

259km, Paterberg: 360m (all cobbled) averaging 12.9%

Other notable climbs from previous editions:

Bosberg: 986m averaging 6%

Edelareberg: 1,425m averaging 5%

Eikenberg: 1,300m (1,200m cobbled) averaging 6.2%

Kaperij: 1,250m averaging 5%

Kluisberg: 926m averaging 7%

Leberg: 700m averaging 6.1%

Muur (via Kloosterstraat from 1950): 750m averaging 9%

Muur-Kapelmuur (via Kloosterstraat from 1981): 825m averaging 9%

Muur-Kapelmuur (via Geraardsbergen centre from 1998): 1,075m averaging 9.5%

Tenbosse: 454m averaging 7%

Varentberg: 809m averaging 8%

Volkegemberg: 1,007m averaging 5%

Route of first edition: Gent, Sint-Niklaas, Dendermonde, Aalst, Zottegem, Oudenaarde, Kortrijk, Ieper, Veurne, Ostend, Torhout, Roeselare, Bruges, Eeklo, Mariakerke (Gent) (324km)

Fastest average speed for winner: 43.576km/h by Gianluca Bortolami in 2001

Slowest average speed for winner: 25.167km/h by René Vermandel in 1921

Winner of each edition:

1913 Paul Deman (Bel)

1914 Marcel Buysse (Bel)

1915 Race not held

1916 Race not held

1917 Race not held

1918 Race not held

1919 Henri Van Leerberghe (Bel)

1920 Jules Van Hevel (Bel)

1921 René Vermandel (Bel)

1922 Léon De Vos (Bel)

1923 Heiri Suter (Swi)

1924 Gerard Debaets (Bel)

1925 Julien Delbecque (Bel)

1926 Denis Verschueren (Bel)

1927 Gerard Debaets (Bel)

1928 Jan Mertens (Bel)

1929 Jef Dervaes (Bel)

1930 Frans Bonduel (Bel)

1931 Romain Gijssels (Bel)

1932 Romain Gijssels (Bel)

1933 Alfons Schepers (Bel)

1934 Gaston Rebry (Bel)

1935 Louis Duerloo (Bel)

1936 Louis Hardiquest (Bel)

1937 Michel d'Hooghe (Bel)

1938 Edgard De Caluwé (Bel)

1939 Karel Kaers (Bel)

1940 Achiel Buysse (Bel)

1941 Achiel Buysse (Bel)

1942 Briek Schotte (Bel)

1943 Achiel Buysse (Bel)

1944 Rik Van Steenbergen (Bel)

1945 Sylvain Grysolle (Bel)

1946 Rik Van Steenbergen (Bel)

1947 Emiel Faignaert (Bel)

1948 Briek Schotte (Bel)

1949 Fiorenzo Magni (Ita)

1950 Fiorenzo Magni (Ita)

1951 Fiorenzo Magni (Ita)

1952 Roger Decock (Bel)

1953 Wim van Est (Ned)

1954 Raymond Impanis (Bel)

1955 Louison Bobet (Fra)

1956 Jean Forestier (Fra)

1957 Fred De Bruyne (Bel)

1958 Germain Derycke (Bel)

1959 Rik Van Looy (Bel)

1960 Arthur De Cabooter (Bel)

1961 Tom Simpson (GB)

1962 Rik Van Looy (Bel)

1963 Noël Foré (Bel)

1964 Rudi Altig (Ger)

1965 Jo De Roo (Ned)

1966 Edward Sels (Bel)

1967 Dino Zandegù (Ita)

1968 Walter Godefroot (Bel)

1969 Eddy Merckx (Bel)

1970 Eric Leman (Bel)

1971 Evert Dolman (Ned)

1972 Eric Leman (Bel)

1973 Eric Leman (Bel)

1974 Cees Bal (Ned)

1975 Eddy Merckx (Bel)

1976 Walter Planckaert (Bel)

1977 Roger De Vlaeminck (Bel)

1978 Walter Godefroot (Bel)

1979 Jan Raas (Ned)

1980 Michel Pollentier (Bel)

1981 Hennie Kuiper (Ned)

1982 René Martens (Bel)

1983 Jan Raas (Ned)

1984 Johan Lammerts (Ned)

1985 Eric Vanderaerden (Bel)

1986 Adri van der Poel (Ned)

1987 Claude Criquielion (Bel)

1988 Eddy Planckaert (Bel)

1989 Edwig Van Hooydonck (Bel)

1990 Moreno Argentin (Ita)

1991 Edwig Van Hooydonck (Bel)

1992 Jacky Durand (Fra)

1993 Johan Museeuw (Bel)

1994 Gianni Bugno (Ita)

1995 Johan Museeuw (Bel)

1996 Michele Bartoli (Ita)

1997 Rolf Sørensen (Den)
1998 Johan Museeuw (Bel)
1999 Peter Van Petegem (Bel)
2000 Andrei Tchmil (Bel)
2001 Gianluca Bortolami (Ita)
2002 Andrea Tafi (Ita)
2003 Peter Van Petegem (Bel)
2004 Steffen Wesemann (Ger)
2005 Tom Boonen (Bel)
2006 Tom Boonen (Bel)
2007 Alessandro Ballan (Ita)
2008 Stijn Devolder (Bel)
2009 Stijn Devolder (Bel)
2010 Fabian Cancellara (Swi)
2011 Nick Nuyens (Bel)
2012 Tom Boonen (Bel)
2013 Fabian Cancellara (Swi)
2014 Fabian Cancellara (Swi)
2015 Alexander Kristoff (Nor)
2016 Peter Sagan (Svk)
2017 Philippe Gilbert (Bel)
2018 Niki Terpstra (Ned)
2019 Alberto Bettiol (Ita)
2020 Mathieu van der Poel (Ned)
2021 Kasper Asgreen (Den)
2022 Mathieu van der Poel (Ned)

Victories by nation:
Belgium 69
Netherlands 12
Italy 11
Switzerland 4

France 3

Germany 2

Denmark 2

Great Britain 1

Norway 1

Slovakia 1

Multiple victories:

3

Achiel Buysse (Bel) 1940, 1941, 1943

Fiorenzo Magni (Ita) 1949–1951

Eric Leman (Bel) 1970, 1972, 1973

Johan Museeuw (Bel) 1993, 1995, 1998

Tom Boonen (Bel) 2005, 2006, 2012

Fabian Cancellara (Swi) 2010, 2013, 2014

2

Gerard Debaets (Bel) 1924, 1927

Romain Gijssels (Bel) 1931, 1932

Rik Van Steenbergen (Bel) 1944, 1946

Briek Schotte (Bel) 1942, 1948

Rik Van Looy (Bel) 1959, 1962

Eddy Merckx (Bel) 1969, 1975

Walter Godefroot (Bel) 1968, 1978

Jan Raas (Ned) 1979, 1983

Edwig Van Hooydonck (Bel) 1989, 1991

Peter Van Petegem (Bel) 1999, 2003

Stijn Devolder (Bel) 2008, 2009

Mathieu van der Poel (Ned) 2020, 2022

Riders who have won three or more Monuments

Rider	MSR	Flanders	Roubaix	Liège	Lombardy	Total
Eddy Merckx (Bel)	7	2	3	5	2	19
Roger De Vlaeminck (Bel)	3	1	4	1	2	11
Costante Girardengo (Ita)	6	–	–	–	3	9
Fausto Coppi (Ita)	3	–	1	–	5	9
Sean Kelly (Irl)	2	–	2	2	3	9
Rik Van Looy (Bel)	1	2	3	1	1	8
Gino Bartali (Ita)	4	–	–	–	3	7
Tom Boonen (Bel)	–	3	4	–	–	7
Fabian Cancellara (Swi)	1	3	3	–	–	7
Henri Pélissier (Fra)		1	–	2	3	6
Alfredo Binda (Ita)	2	–	–	–	4	6
Fred De Bruyne (Bel)	1	1	1	3	–	6
Francesco Moser (Ita)	1	–	3	–	2	6
Moreno Argentin (Ita)	–	1	–	4	1	6
Johan Museeuw (Bel)	–	3	3	–	–	6
Gaetano Belloni (Ita)	2	–	–	–	3	5
Rik Van Steenbergen (Bel)	1	2	2	–	–	5
Bernard Hinault (Fra)	–	–	1	2	2	5
Michele Bartoli (Ita)	–	1	–	2	2	5
Paolo Bettini (Ita)	1	–	–	2	2	5
Philippe Gilbert (Bel)	–	1	1	1	2	5
Gaston Rebry (Bel)	–	1	3	–	–	4

APPENDIX

Rider	MSR	Flanders	Roubaix	Liège	Lombardy	Total
Alfons Schepers (Bel)	–	1	–	3	–	4
Louison Bobet (Fra)	1	1	1	–	1	4
Germain Derycke (Bel)	–	1	1	1	1	4
Felice Gimondi (Ita)	1	–	1	–	2	4
Walter Godefroot (Bel)	–	2	1	1	–	4
Hennie Kuiper (Ned)	1	1	1	–	1	4
Jan Raas (Ned)	1	2	1	–	–	4
Erik Zabel (Ger)	4	–	–	–	–	4
Alejandro Valverde (Spa)	–	–	–	4	–	4
Octave Lapize (Fra)	–	–	3	–	–	3
Giovanni Brunero (Ita)	1	–	–	–	2	3
Romain Gijssels (Bel)	–	2	1	–	–	3
Achiel Buysse (Bel)	–	3	–	–	–	3
Fiorenzo Magni (Ita)	–	3	–	–	–	3
Jo De Roo (Ned)	–	1	–	–	2	3
Emile Daems (Bel)	1	–	1	–	1	3
Tom Simpson (GB)	1	1	–	–	1	3
Eric Leman (Bel)	–	3	–	–	–	3
Peter Van Petegem (Bel)	–	2	1	–	–	3
Andrea Tafi (Ita)	–	1	1	–	1	3
Andrei Tchmil (Bel)	1	1	1	–	–	3
Oscar Freire (Spa)	3	–	–	–	–	3
Damiano Cunego (Ita)	–	–	–	–	3	3
Vincenzo Nibali (Ita)	1	–	–	–	2	3

BIBLIOGRAPHY

I made eager use of the back catalogue of *Procycling*, a magazine with which I have had a long association and which remains the sport's best title. Among other publications and newspapers I drew on for my research and would highly recommend were *Coups de Pédales*, *La Stampa*, *Le Soir*, *La Dernière Heure*, *Het Nieuwsblad*, *L'Équipe* and *La Gazzetta dello Sport*. The pages of Cyclingnews.com and Memoire-du-Cyclisme.eu were also a vital and very reliable source of detail.

For further insight into these illustrious races, I would also recommend the following books:

Baroni, Enzo and Pesenti, Cesare, *Il Lombardia: Una Corsa, 100 Storie*, RCS Sport, Milan, 2006
— *Milano Sanremo: 100 Anni Leggendari*, RCS Sport, Milan, 2007
Chany, Pierre, *La Fabuleuse Histoire des Grandes Classiques et des Championnats du Monde*, Éditions ODIL, Paris, 1979
Dargenton, Michel and Degauquier, Claude, 'La Merveilleuse Histoire du Tour des Flandres', *Coup des Pédales*, No. 16, December 2004, Seraing
L'Équipe, *Belles d'un Jour: Histoires des Grandes Classiques*, Paris, 2007
— *Paris Roubaix: Une Journée en Enfer*, Paris, 2006
Fignon, Laurent, *We Were Young and Carefree*, Yellow Jersey Press, London, 2010

BIBLIOGRAPHY

Fleuriel, Sébastien (ed.), *100 Paris–Roubaix: Patrimoine d'un Siècle*, Septentrion, 2002

Foot, John, *Pedalare! Pedalare!* Bloomsbury, London, 2011

Fotheringham, William, *Put Me Back On My Bike: In Search of Tom Simpson*, Yellow Jersey Press, London, 2002

Friebe, Daniel, *Eddy Merckx: The Cannibal*, Ebury Press, London, 2012

Howard, Paul, *Sex, Lies and Handlebar Tape: The Remarkable Life of Jacques Anquetil*, Mainstream Publishing, London, 2011

Kelly, Sean, *Hunger*, Peloton Publishing, London, 2013

Leblanc, Jean-Marie, *Le Tour de Ma Vie*, Solar, 2007

Roche, Stephen, *Born to Ride*, Yellow Jersey Press, London, 2012

Sergent, Pascal, *Paris–Roubaix: Chronique d'une Légende*, tome I, Édition Véloclub de Roubaix, 1989

— *Paris–Roubaix: Chronique d'une Légende*, tome II, Édition Véloclub de Roubaix, 1991

Vanwalleghem, Rik, *100x De Ronde*, Pinguin Productions-CRVV, Belgium, 2013

Voet, Willy, *Breaking the Chain*, Yellow Jersey Press, London, 2002

Woodland, Les, *Cycling Heroes: The Golden Years*, McGann Publishing, Cherokee Village, Arkansas, 2011

— *Paris–Roubaix: The Inside Story*, McGann Publishing, Cherokee Village, Arkansas, 2013

ACKNOWLEDGEMENTS

Much like the races featured, writing this book has required a huge effort and couldn't have been completed without a great deal of support along the way. I owe particular thanks to Charlotte Atyeo, my editor at Bloomsbury, who recognised the appeal of these great events and kept me on the right road by providing much appreciated insight at all stages. I'm also grateful to Charlotte Croft, Sarah Skipper and Robert Sharman who guided me through the updating of the second edition. I would also like to express my gratitude to my literary agent, David Luxton, who played a key role in getting this book off the ground in the first place, gained me precious time when I needed it and was never short of words of encouragement. An Elland Road meat pie has your name on it, David.

Dozens of fellow journalists provided advice, contacts and expertise during my travels around Italy, France and Belgium. I would like to thank Daniel Benson, Barry Ryan, Stephen Farrand, Jane Aubrey, Lionel Birnie, Andy Hood, Marco Pastonesi, Gregor 'Burgundy' Brown, Sophie Smith, Kenny Pryde, Pierre Carrey, Cillian Kelly and Jan Pieter de Vlieger. My special thanks to Brecht De Caluwe, who laughed off my massacring of the Dutch language and provided crucial insight into Flanders, the Flemish people and De Ronde.

My thanks also go to the press officers who accommodated my requests for interviews at what were often extremely busy moments, including Philippe Maertens, Sean Weide, George Lüchinger, Chris Haynes, Bryan Nygaard, Xylon Van Eyck and Marya Pongrace.

ACKNOWLEDGEMENTS

My gratitude also to the riders and team staff who provided their time and expert analysis of the Monuments, including Thor Hushovd, Dirk Demol, Fabian Cancellara, Taylor Phinney, Philippe Gilbert, Luca Guercilena, Barry Hoban, Hendrik Redant, Gerald Ciolek, Jaco Venter and Dan Martin.

I owe a considerable debt to Phil Liggett, Andy Sutcliffe and Robert Garbutt for providing my initial opportunities in cycling journalism. In more recent years, I have relished working with Sven Thiele and Stephen Roche, as well as on *Procycling*, where I benefited hugely from the professionalism and friendship of Paul Godfrey, Pete Goding, Ellis Bacon and, particularly, Daniel Friebe, who provided much-valued assistance during my research for this book. I must also offer special thanks to Jeremy Whittle and James Poole, with whom I will one day ride up Mont Ventoux.

I would also like to thank my mum and dad, and my sisters Vicky and Evie for their support. Finally, my love and gratitude goes to my wife, Elaine, and children, Lewis and Eleanor, to whom this book is dedicated. You kept me going throughout the hectic months I devoted to this project, providing unwavering love and encouragement, plus strong coffee and Digestive biscuits. I can't thank you enough for that.

INDEX

430